John Bale, John Studley

The Pageant of Popes

contayninge the lyues of all the bishops of Rome

John Bale, John Studley

The Pageant of Popes
contayninge the lyues of all the bishops of Rome

ISBN/EAN: 9783337100810

Printed in Europe, USA, Canada, Australia, Japan

Cover: Foto ©Lupo / pixelio.de

More available books at **www.hansebooks.com**

THE PAGE=
ANT OF POPES,

Contayninge the lyues of all the Bishops of Rome, from the beginninge of them to the
yeare of Grace 1555. Deuided into iii. sortes bishops, Archbishops, and Popes, vvhereof the two first are
contayned in two bookes, and the third sort in fiue. In the
vvhich is manifestlye shevved the beginning of Antichriste and
increasing to his fulnesse, and also the vvayning of his
povver againe, accordinge to the Prophe-
cye of Iohn in the Apocalips.

Shewing manye straunge, notorious,
outragious and tragicall partes, played by them
the like vvhereof hath not els bin hearde: both pleasant and profitable for this age. Written in Latin by Maister Bale, and now Englished with
sondrye additions by I.S.

※※※※※※※※※※※※※※

✱Behold I come vpon thee sayth the Lorde of hostes, and vvill
discouer thy skirts vppon thy face, and vvill shevv to the Nations thy filthynes, and to the kingdomes thy shame. I vvill
cast filth vpon thee and make the loathsome, and vvill set thee
as a gazing stocke.   Nahum. 3.

ℭ Come away from her my people, that ye be not partakers of
her sinnes, and that ye receiue not of her plagues. &c. Reward her as she hath rewarded you, and giue her double according to her workes.   Apoca. 18.

Anno 1574.

TO THE RIGHT HO-
nourable Lorde Thomas Earle of
Suſſex, Uicount Fitzwalter, Lorde of Egre-
mont and of Burnel, one of the Queenes Maieſtyes
honourable priuye Counſaile, & Lord highe Chamberlaine of her houſe, Of the noble order of the
Garter knighte, Juſtice of Oyer, of the Fo-
reſts, Parkes, VVarraines and chaſes from
Trent Southward, and Captaine of the
Gentlemen Penſioners: Encreaſe
of honour and godlye wyſedome
in Chriſte Ieſus.

Monge many worthie ſayings of the moſt eloquent Lactan-tius (right Honourable) this one is eſpecially worthye to be noted, which is ſo oftē repea-ted by him: that No wiſedome is to be allowed without (true) Religion. And againe that where Religion is not there is no wyſedome. VVherby we are inſtructed that frō thoſe in whō wyſedome is requiſite, religiō muſt in no caſe be ſeperate. And againe that they in whō greater fruites of wiſedome ought to flou-riſhe (as it ſhould be in them whoſe handes G O D hath framed to guid y ſterne of the cōmon wealth) muſt alſo beare a more feruent zeale towards the true ſeruice and Honour of G O D. So that theſe twaine VVyſedome and Religion, are linked and

*a   ij   placed.

The Epistle

placed together in y̓ minde of mā, as the eyes thereof to giue light to his whole vnderstanding. And therefore to staye a while in this similitude, as the one eye of our bodye is so assisting to the other for the making perfite of our sight together, that hauing the vse of both we attaine thereunto: and otherwise the one being blinded, the light of the other is somwhat dimmed and shadowed, and perhaps in the ende fadeth away and leaueth vs altogether in darcknes: Euen so standeth the case betweene Religion and wisedome, the lightes of the minde. And therfore grosse hath bin the errour of manye great estates, who because they being lifted hie in the vew of all mēs eyes and therfore desirous to be accompted wyse, haue yet in their wisedome made no accompt of Religiō at all, but set it bie as a thinge nothing pertayning to ther estate. Who though for a time they haue seemed to groape out the channell well, and so by dilligence to sayle in safetye, and with one dim eye to see their waye perfectly, yet lacking y̓ light of Religion they haue euer bin blind on the one side and wāted the right and better eye: wherby in the ende the eye of their pollicye euer poaring downeward to things on the left hand, and not able stedfastly to loke vp to heauen nor to abide the glorye thereof, hath drawne them

Dedicatorie.

them into such deepe darcknes, that vnware they haue strayed farre from the drift of their deuices, and beinge not able to walke vprightlye in their owne wayes without slackering and stubling, haue in the ende fallen so desperatlye ỹ they neuer were able to ryse againe: wherby to late they finde true that There is no wisedome where Religion is not. And that whereas they thought themselues to be wyse without it, they neuer came to the first step thereof, it being as Salomō sayth: that The feare of the Lord (which such haue neglected) is ỹ beginning of wysedome. The commaundementes of ỹ Lord are pure and giue light to the eyes, Againe * Thy worde O Lord is a lanterne vnto my feete, Psalm. 8. and a light vnto my pathes. And therefore when soeuer we leaue this light, though the lampe of mās braine burne neuer so bright, we fall perforce in ỹ end: For neither the wyse head of Achitophell, nor the fayre and flattering face of Absolon that stale from Dauid the peoples hartes, coulde preuaile in their purposes, so pollitickly attempted against the rule of Religion, but ỹ it turned to their owne confusion: +For euerye plant that the Heauenlye father hath not planted shalbe rooted out. Yea most Matt. 15. miserable and desperat is their case and cursed of Gods owne mouth, that thincke the care of Religion be-

The Epistle

on belongeth not to them.

Another sort of mē there is which being of better iudgemente proccede a step farther then these, and yet not so farre as they oughte in deede. For some hauing an inward regard of Religion, do yet thincke it pollicye, that it should be hidden and secrete to themselues, and not apparent vnto other: and in this point especially they would be esteemed wyse. But greatly are these likewyse deceiued: for wysedome is no wysedome and not to be accompted of in anye, so longe as it is dissembled and not employed, that other men maye see good proofe thereof. And Religion is no Religion that sheweth not it selfe by his plētifull fruites. And what choyse so euer they y̌ seeme wysest or holiest make of religiō, doing it so as other men shal not be able to discerne it in them, nor to be witnesses therof, they are to be esteemed neither wyse nor Religious. For who wil not accōpt him rather blind or blincking thē other wyse, that shall say he hath his eyes sound, pure & perfit, and yet in the open daye will neuer shew vse of them in the presence of men, but continuallye be wimpled and weare a veale, so that no man cā perceaue whether he do see or no? Eyther such are blinde in deede whē as they say that they see, or els their meaning is very deceitfull.

Shevv me thy fayth by thy vvorkes. &c. Iacob.2.

Faith if it haue no vvorkes is deade in it selfe. Ia. 2.

And

Dedicatorie.

And so may we iudge of these wilye winkers in Religion, that either they be blindstockes in deede and lacke the light of that Heauenlye wysedome, which they pretende to haue, or els their wicked wysedome is but a cloake of wickednes, & then in deede they doate in their worldly pollicye, not knowinge that the wysest of all hath sayd: *Let your light so shine before men y̌ they may see your good workes & glorify your father which is in Heauē. And y̌ Euery tree that doth not beare good fruite shalbe cut downe & cast into euerlastig fier. And therfore these Nicodemites that will visit Christ onelye in y̌ darcke and by night and not openly before men, the Lord will not acknowledge him before his Heauenly father. Such is y̌ ende of fleshly pollicy.   So that (Right honourable) onely such ar to be held as wyse in deede which thincke that it lyeth vpō them & especially belōgeth vnto them, to make a constant and opē profession of true Religion. If then to be wyse be to professe Religion, it is worthy to be farther considered how a man may attaine to perfection herein.

 The heathen that euer measured wysedomē by ciuill pollicy, haue accompted best of those by whose good endeuour their commō wealth hath bin most vpheld and strengthned from forain inuasions:

Matt. 5.

Matt. 3.

and

The Epistle

and that haue employed themselues to breake the force of such as would assault it. And so (my very good Lord) they that haue bin the most worthye members of the Church of God, haue euer excelled in this point, to shew themselues forward in promoting Religion and suppressing to their power y̓ enemyes therof: and especially I say in suppressing the enemyes. For the houlding downe of them is the houlding vp of y̓ other.

2. Sam. 5. 8   So the godly Dauid did both fetch home y̓ arke of God, and scourged his ennemyes the Philistines and Iebusites. So the zealous king Iosias both restored the Law of the Lord, and put downe y̓ wic-

2. Reg. 23.   ked Chemerinus that sacrificed vnto Baal. So y̓ noble Cyrus deliuered Israell and held Babilō captiue. Finally so the worthy Cōstantine (the sonne

Euseb. li. 9 to Helen borne in this Island) brought peace to y̓
cap. 9. Ec- Church, set Christian Religiō at libertye, and also
cles. hist.   ouerthrew the cruell ennemy and tyraunt Maxētius. If these godly examples were euer to be followed in any place: If this zeale in Religion were euer to be shewed in any age, where more then in this our natiue countrye? If this perfit wysedome were euer to be wished in any gouernours, of whom rather then of the nobility of England? when rather then in this our time, against the tyrannye of

the

Dedicatorie.

the bishop of Rome? For what enemye hath made such greedy spoyle and wrought such broyle in any countrey, as he and his hath done continuallye in this little Isle, (as but for being tedious might be shewed) almost in euery kings time since ỹ cōquest, as William Rufus and Hēry the first, both were sore combred w̃ Pope Vrban ỹ second and Paschal the second, through Anselmus bishop of Cāterbury. Henry the second much more with Thomas Becket and Pope Alexander the 3. Richard the first complayned greuously of the Popes shamefull polling his Realme and yet could not redresse it. K. Iohn suffered a thousand stormes and ỹ Realme was myserablye spoyled and made tributarye to ỹ Pope for euer, by the treachery of Stephē Langtō bishop of Canterbury. In the time of Hēry the 3. the Pope ransackt all the Churches in Englande, and so hath he continued with the rest, vexing by exactiōs, excommunications, or some such meanes euerye one. But because his staffe hath here bin brokē & he throwē out of ỹ dores in this our time, what meanes doth he dailye leaue vnproued to worke our confusion, as sturring rebelliōs, mouing treasons, seditions and conspiracies within ỹ land, cursing and excōmunicating both Prince and people, nobilitye and commons, and yelding vs a praye

* b   vnto

The Epistle

vnto him whõ he hath assigned by his bulls to enioye their lyuings and dignities abroad, who hourelye wait whẽ eyther by nature it selfe or their violent hand, the thred shoulde faile whereon dependeth the staye of our estate. Such is the purpose of Antichrist against vs, and yet practised with colour of holines. So that if euer the bloud of Christ his Church ought euer to be precious in the eyes of men, the time is now. Now lyeth it vpon euery one to shew himselfe a freind to his countrey, by withstanding to his power the common enemye therof: and especially those that stande in the hyest place, both for their owne sakes because their fall shalbe the greater, and for charge of Gods people cõmitted vnto them, whose bloud he wil require at their hands if they leaue them to the wolfe.

For the which cause (Right honourable) I as a member of that bodye which is so assaulted by this Dragon both for the safetye of my selfe and other, employed my selfe a litle to discouer ỹ secret traynes of this deceitful enemye: and because this my enterprise of it selfe lyeth open to ỹ perill of the malicious mouthes of many his partakers, so ỹ it shold not be able to beare out it selfe agaĩst their force. Therfore necessitye driueth me to seeke for ỹ succour of such a Patrone in whom I might assure my

selfe

Dedicatorie.

selfe of that perfite wysedome which Lactancius alloweth, and find that rescue which this cause requireth: that is one who by power should be able, by wysedome skilfull, and in zeale and affection willing and forward to encounter this aduersarye with anye of his faction: whereof because it is not vnknowen to mee by many priuate occasions, that your honour hath made proofe that this perfite wysedome is planted in you as it was in Dauid, Iosius, Cyrus and Constantine, bearing on your lefte arme a target of defence for Religion, and hauing your right hand armed with a sword to wound the ennemye Antichrist: And againe seing it hath not bin so priuate but that this zeale hath shewed it selfe openlye in biddinge battell to the members of Antichrist, marchinge against them in fielde and pursuing them out of the countrye: I thought your Lorship most meete and I assured my selfe ẏ your honour would be most willing to suffer this my little volume to fight vnder your baner in that quarrell against the Pope, wherein your honour hath heretofore personallye proceeded. If therefore the worthines of the matter herein contayned & written by maister Bale, maye so excuse the vnworthines of my simple Stile in translating it, that your honour vouchsafe to accepte the one with the

*b ij.   other

The Epistle Dedicatorie.

other and beare with the one for the other, your curtesye shall the rather confirme all the professours of ye Gospel in that vndoubted opinion which they haue iustlye conceyued of you, and giue them cause still to glorifye God for such nobility, wishing the good encrease and longe prosperitye of such: and I hauing my trauaile most happely bestowed, shall acknowledge my dutye alwayes bounde vnto your honour for it. And thus crauinge pardon of this tedious volume wherewith I haue troubled your Honour ouer longe, I leaue you to the Almightye.

Your honours
most humble
Iohn Studley.

* Put your selues in araye against Babilon round about, all ye that bende the bovve shoote at her, spare no arrovves, for she hath sinned against the Lord. Iere. 50:

The translatour to the Reader.

It maye be (gentle Reader) that when thou shalt in this booke reade many monstrous & horrible histories rather to be suppressed then put in print, thou wilt not thincke well of my trauaile. I graūt that here are manye thinges vttered odious to be heard: but yet if any thing offend thy chaste eares, blame not me gentle Reader but ye importunitye of ye Papistes, who hath forced me thus to displaye their treacherye. For wher as their doctrine is so on all sides wounded and foyled by the force of ye Gospell, that they haue no shift to vphold their treacherye as men euidentlye conuinced and condemned by lawe and iustice, now are they compelled to practise some pollicy, seing they are spoyled both of the word and the sword. And for want of better practise their onelye shifte is by spreading open other mens infirmities to couer their owne, by lifting vp the leude liues of the Protestants to the vewe of all men, to shadow the horrours of their Church, in somuch that their outcryes are growne so great, that these spitefull speaches are often and dayly heard vpon euerye occasion: Lo these are oure Protestants: Such are oure Gospellers: to such miserye and wickednes is the worlde growne since this new doctrine came among vs: ye maye see by their fruite what their Religion is. So outragious are the outcryes ye they make against vs to discredite not vs but our Gospel, as though the defacing of vs by our sinnefull liues, were a confutacion of oure doctrine, and an approuing of their innocencye, and a confirmation of theyr vnclenlye dregs to be pure and good. So vehement are their spraches, and ye with such confidence on their partes, as if both theyr doctrine were on all sides true, and that the spirit of God had cleane forsakē this age, as if the like wickednes had neuer tainted any kind of men so harmously as it doth the professours of the Gospell, and as though sinne were but newe borne among mē and latelye sprong vp wyth the Gospell: and as thoughe that the tree whereon their doctrine is grafted (the Church of Rome I meane) had neuer yelded any rotten fruite, had neuer any catterpillers breeding in it, neuer any cankar corrupting it, but had euer bin greene, fresh and flourishing, pure and perfite in euerye leafe, braunche and twig. Therefore concerning vs and concerning them I will speake of both.

And first as concerning our selues (God be merciful vnto vs inscrable

To the Reader.

serable sinners) we haue al runne astray, If we say we haue no sinne we deceyue our selues and the truth is not in vs: There is not one $ doth good no not one. And if any Papist, Turke or infidel charge vs to be sinnefull men although we professe a pure Gospell, we will acknowledge it, and neuer like the worse of them for so sayinge, nor the better of our owne infirmityes. Nowe concerning the Papistes, if they speake of our sinnes for that they hate sinne in vs, they do vs no wronge, we accept it and thancke them for it: But if they laye the rebuke of our sinnes vpon $ the glorious Gospel of Christ which we professe, as if they meant by defacing vs to discredite it (as I haue sayde before) then do they offer great iniurye to the Maiesty of God, when as th:y say that by our deedes it appeareth, as by the fruite $ the tree is not good, that the Gospell which we professe is not perfite. Wee cannot and may not suffer it that the perfitnes of the Lawe should be tryed and condemned by the offence of the giltye: that the truth of Christe should depend vpon the workes of sinners, that eternall heauen should be valued by fading earth, that the most perfite iustice and equitye of the most glorious God, should be measured & esteemed by the frailtye of corruptible flesh & bloud. And therfore as we do not and dare not presume to confirme the certainty of our doctrine by our good deedes be they neuer so perfite, but rather confirme oure good deedes to be good by our doctrine: so should oure aduersaryes deale vprightly with vs, not to condemne our doctrine by our euil deedes, but rather condemne our euill deedes by our doctrine, which beinge pure and perfite shal condemne both our wickednes and theyrs, together with theyr wicked and detestable doctrine.

God forbid that the tryall of true religion should lye eyther vpon oure vpzighte conuersation or theirs, least if it laye in mans perfection both the Iewe and the Turke mighte eyther of them soner boast of it thē eyther of vs. The wysedome of God hath not so builded his Church vpon sande. If it were founded vpon the workes of man, then should his Church neuer stand neyther by them nor by vs. We are but feeble and windshaken pillers vnable to vnderprop and beare such a waight, & therfore how so euer they build theyr Church, we build not ours on our selues, but we build both it and our selues vpon that vnmoueable rocke Iesus Christe, and therefore how soeuer the winde and weather do shake vs and ouerthrowe vs throughe our owne weakenes, yet our foundation abydeth sure, and doth neyther fall nor slyp awaye but abydeth so for euer, $ we may be still raysed and set vp on the same againe. Deceitfull therefore is theyr dealing,

To the Reader.

ting, who to withdraw men from our Church, do vniustlye saye that when we fall, our foundation falleth also: but most iustlye maye wee assure men that theyr Babilonicall building must needes come to decaye, being founded on the sande of Tiber banckes, which is daylye washed and eaten awaye. How can that foundation stand which is made of earth and claye, dust and ashes, of fleshe, bloud and bones: of Popes miters, Cardinals hats, Monkes hoodes, Fryers cooles, Nonnes veales, shauen crownes, paxes, beades, tapers and crosses, annoyntings and greazings, blessings, kissings, images of mettall, woode, glasse and stone, holye oyle, holye creame, albes, vestments, palls, coapes, rothets, surplices, tippets, copes, chrismes, mantel & the ringe, sensinges, pilgrimages, offrings, creeping to crosses, Wenefreds nedle, the bloud of Hayles, fasting dayes, holye dayes, imber dayes, crogiers, polaxes, dirges, exorsims, coniurings, masses, trentals, holye water, Purgatorye saints relicks, S. Francis breeches, Limbo patrũ, s. John shorns bootes, the roode of Chester, our Lady of Walsingam, rotten boones, shrines, and a thousande such apishe toyes, which daylye (as they themselues perceiue) do putrifye rotte and consume to nothing. Seeing therefore this foundation wyll not last to vphold their Babilonicall buildinges against the assaultes of the Gospell, therefore now they will haue the tryall of doctrine to lye vpon the honesty of men, and herein they make the worlde beleeue that they haue a great abuauntage ouer vs.

Seeing they will needes dryue vs to this plouge and seeke hereby to foyle vs and vtterlye to ouerthrow our foundation, we wil be contente herein also to ioyne issue with them, not as hauinge affiaunce in oure owne iustice (the Lorde amende that which is amisse in vs, and blessed be his name for those sparkes of his mercye that haue preserued vs from beinge worse then we are) but because we haue such experience of their treacherye, and that we know none shalbe comparable to Antichriste in iniquitye. To set aside therefore all excusing of our selues in such matters as they do slaunder vs, and grast that we be as euill as they make vs, yet I dare bouldlye auouche that there hath not hetherto nor euer shall (I trust) proceede from vs such vnmeasurable aboundance of corrupt fruite, as hath done from those þ are the best, the most pure and perfits on theyr syde, euen in those who they saye cannot erre, that are the most holye vicars of Christe vpon earth, namelye the holye fathers Popes & bishops of Rome. Whose notorious villanyes from time to time swelled to the full and perfite measure of iniquitye, and so farre runne beyond our hainous sinnes,

that

To the Reader.

that supposing they dyed as they liued, I may bouldly warrant them this preferment, that if an hundreth of the rankest hellhoundes that euer raigned vpon the earth might be mustred out of hell, fourescore and nineteene of them should be Popes, perhaps for the last a hundred place, eyther VVolsey or some other Cardinall would scuffle in among them.

Whereof that thou mayest the better iudge (gentle Reader) I do here giue thee in this booke a little taste of theyr vnsauory liues, I haue set them all forth here in one Pageante in such order as they played theyr Papall partes both Tragicall and Comicall for these Thousand yeares vpon this worldly stage: wherein I haue chosen rather to translate them as they were gathered in Latin by maister Bale most faithfullye, then to follow the parciall and flattering storye of Platina. In some places also I haue added diuers thinges out of sondrye authors, not as thoughe I desired to make perfite in all pointes that which maister Bale omitted: but because in conferringe his alleaging of storyes, I found manye thinges that without anye combraunce might be added and were worth the mentioning, especially in ỹ sixt booke of this historye out of one Theodoricus of Nyem Secretarye to Pope Vrban the sixt, and wrote that which he sawe of that inserable and longe sciesme that set all the world together by ỹ eares the space of xxxix. yeares, betweene Vrban the sixte, Clement the seuenth, Boniface the ix, Benedict the xiii. otherwyse called Iohn Moone, and other: which booke I am sure maister Bale neuer saw, for he would neuer haue omitted such notable and straunge matters as are contayned in it, and are here partlye touched by mee.

Also for so much as these prelates do falsely colour al their prancks vnder the authoritye of S. Peters name, therfore I haue somwhat at large in the beginning shewed, how that thoughe they would haue him to play the first part in this Pageant, yet he is none of theyr company. But because of the sodaine finishing of this worke in ỹ printers hande, I am forced in this Preface to leaue out many matters which I thought to haue vttered, which I could neuer finde conuenient leasure to be setled in one certaine place, in suche wyse as I might apply my selfe to write that which I purposed since this was finished and came to the hande of the Printer. At this time therefore this onelye I haue to request of thee (gentle Reader) till God shal giue me better oportunitye to finishe that order which I purposed in publishing this booke, to marke as thou readest how the manner of these Prelates do agree to the description of Antichrist in the

Reuela-

To the Reader.

Reuelation, as I once purposed to haue noted vnto thee. Marke whether we that at this daye do professe the Gospel, and are so much noted of their freinds to transgresse hayuoustye in our conuersation, are to be compared with these holy Popes in anye kinde of enormitye. For what villanye is it whereof thou shalt not finde such monstrous examples among them, as the earth neuer els bread the like. It were tedious for mee here to drawe into tables the examples of their vnsaciable couetousnes, their bribery, polling & pilfringe, robbing and rysling, vntollerable pride, equal with the ambition of Lucifer, their baine and vnspeakable pompe, theyr whoredome and rauishinge of diuers, their incest with their owne sisters & doughters, their Sodomityes, treasōs practised against all Princes on ye earth, the rebellions, seditions, bloudshed, warres, conspiracyes, murtherings, factions, sciesmes, braules, contentions amonge them selues, poysoninge Princes, & themselues one another, euen in ministring the Sacramentes, theyr sorcerye, charmes, coniurings, familiaritye with deuils, and honouring of euill spirites: their abusing of Princes most slauishlye, theyr geuing, transporting, selling, setting vp and deposinge of all estates Empyres and kingdomes, theyr licensing of all villanye, as murthering, incest, Sodomitrye, periurye, blasphemye, and an hundred such like moste detestable enormityes, whereof thou shalt haue plenty euē to the loathing of thy stomacke. Which when thou seest, then iudge betweene oure fruites and theirs, then learne to discerne who is that whore of Babilon, the woman arayed in Purple and rose colour, and decked wyth gould, precious stones and pearles, hauing the cup of gould in her hand full of abhomination and filthines. Note what Citye is like to be that Babilō built on seuen hilles, & bearing rule ouer the Nations of the earth, What Citye is like to be that Babilon that is become the habitacion of deuils, the hole of all foule spirites, and a cage of all vncleane and hatefull byrdes. Note wyth whom the kinges of the earth haue cōmitted fornication, and with the aboundance of whose pleasures the marchauntes of the earth are become riche. Note who it is that hath bin dronken wyth the bloude of saintes, if by these thou finde ye these tokens of Antichrist be in these bishops of Rome, then surelye saye, thoughe wee wretched sinners be as euill as they make vs in deede (which they speake so much of) yet their holy fathers are farre worse, which the Papist wyll not confesse. Then saye that surelye Rome is Babilon, and the Pope Antichriste, and blame not mee for

Apoc. 17.

* C   detecting

Bales Epistle

Apoc. 18. detectinge anye his loathsome villanyes, but obeye the voyce of the Lorde agaynst this Babilon saying: Come avvaye from her my people that yee be not partakers of her sinnes, and that ye receiue not of her plagues.&c. but revvard her as she hath revvarded you, And giue her double according to her vvorkes.

Apoc. 19. Finallye let vs all saye Alleluya: Saluation, Glorye, Honour and povver be ascribed vnto the Lorde oure G O D, for true and righteous are his Iudgements, for he hath iudged the great vvhore vvhich did corrupt the earth vvith her fornication.&c. Alleluya.

Farewell.

TO THE

TO THE MOST WOR-
thie and learned men maister Simond Sulcer, Henry Bullenger, John Caluin, Philip Melancthon, most faithful ministers of Christe, John Bale wisheth grace and euerlastinge peace in Christe
IESVS.

Althoughe I sawe that my former edition of the liues of the Romaine bishops ioyned to my booke called þ Regester of Englishe writers, were safely planted vnder the protection of the most noble Electour Lorde Henry Otho Countie Palatine: Yet notwithstandinge I perceiued that this Edition being taken and seperated frõ the greater, being drawne into an abridgemente and enriched wyth such additions as are not to be misliked, seing it is not able sufficientlye to beare oute it selfe, neither by his owne force nor the credite of the wryter, it should neede be succoured and maintayned by some other. And therfore I thoughte it good in no wyse to turne it out rashlye, naked, vnarmed and vnprouided of rescue neither into the handes of freinde nor foe. For such a meete Patrone was to be sought for, who by his wit, doctrine and learning, should be able to maintaine a desperate cause, and receiue into his tuition as it were an Orphane counted giltye and condemned by the preiudicate opinion of all men, least it being desolate and berefte of all good mens ayde hauing no tutour left vnto it, should together with his father haue his dying daye. After I had longe debated this with ~~with~~ my selfe and had vewed all men rounde about with an especial and diligent care: you iiii. most excellent prelates of þ Church came first to my remẽbrance in whose ayde I might safely

repose

Bales Epistle

pose my selfe that haue oftētimes traueiled in this matter, by longe experience haue found out and beaten downe the assaultes and strokes of oure aduersaryes. So that the former booke ioyned with our historye sufficiētly fortifyed by the might of the most valiaunt Prince, & this booke beinge perused with my latter diligence trustinge vppon the learning and iudgemente of such men, maye freelye wyth cheerefull countenaunce not be afrayde to shewe it selfe amonge the middest of his ennempes. Verelye I am not ignoraunt that anye one of you is man good enoughe to encounter any in this deuine combate. And I freelye confesse that this my litle worke is vnworthy to be dedicated euen vnto anye one of you: yet notwithstanding I do not consider what you are able to do, but what I ought to do: Nether do I esteeme the price of the gift, but I regard ye most feruent zeale towardes you all. And though I imbrace you one after another, yet I desire to pleasure you all w this onelye gift becausè I haue no other, and to declare ye good will that I beare vnto you by this onely worke. Last of all whom one Religion, one Fayth, one Lord, one Baptisme do ioyne, what hindreth vs that one Epistle maye not couple vs together: wherefore I trust that you wil accept (as you oughte and as you were accustomed) my boldnes and presumption if there be anye, which is sprong through an opinion of your curtesye, & not rysen of any euill will.

But that you maye vnderstande the matter which I request & desire to be defended and cherished, if you seperate your mindes for a certaine season, frō your graue studyes & sacred busines, and giue diligēt care to heare that which I haue here purposed to declare, the gift which I bestow vpon you is Papall and Pontificall: And I haue declared ye historye from the beginning to the endinge, & shewed their beginnings, the race and the whole Tragedye of their gouernment deuiding ye state of ther liues into three bookes.

The first contayneth the auncient and holy fathers, not

decked

Dedicatorie.

decked w a crogier or a tripled Miter, but such as were diligent workers in adorninge the Lords Vyneyarde, euen vnto Siluester from the holye Apostles, which w the great daunger of their life did faithfully labour in planting and setting forth the worde of God. These maye worthelye be called the starres remayning on the right hand of Christe Apocal. 1.

The second contayneth the Mitred Archbishops & Patriarckes from Siluester the first vnto Boniface the third, who although they were not the wickedst and corruptest, yet with their traditions and humaine constitutions haue made a plaine waye to Antichriste. These be the starres y fell to the earth Apocal. 6.

The third mentioneth the whole rablement of y Popes from Boniface the third to Paule the fourth, the which being the Vicar of Sathā is said to haue auctoritye as yet at Rome. These were Antichristes not departinge from the steps of their fathers in all kinde of pryde, tyrannye, lying and filthines, these are the starres trulye, as it is described in the 9. Chapter of the Apocalips which fell to the earth. This thirde part is deuided into fiue, neither haue we applyed them vnaptlye to the Renelation of S. John.

Boniface before mentioned shal possesse the first place as he deserued to Ioane the eight an harlot, in the which part there are cōtayned 40. Popes, & called them y kingdome of the great beast sometime named Sodoma sometime Aegiptus, Apo. 11. From Ioane vnto Siluester the deuilish Magician y bowed & gaue himselfe vnto Sathan that hee might obtaine the Popedome: the kingdome of the greate harlot which sitteth on the beast doth comprehend 40. Popes Apocal. 17. From Siluester which is in the 3. place vnto Innocentius the fourth, the most wicked ennemye of our Sauiour Christe, who did establishe & fasten the foure orders of the begging monkes which were newlye made, to the intent that they might stoutlye and manfullye fight

for

Bales Epistle

for the maintayning of the kingdome of Antichrist: signifyeth the kingdome of the Dragon which is the diuill and Sathā Apocal. 20. And in this part were 40. Popes placed. From this Innocentius the second y dreadfull warriour and the moste cruell destroyer of Christian men, are nombred 40 Popes. And this is the kingdome of the Locustes which were vnder the gouernmente of Abadon the which signifyeth a destroyer Apocal. 9. Then Iulius in the ende of his raigne throwinge the keyes of S. Peter into y riuer of Tiber, being girded with a rusty sworde of Paule did fight against the French kinge and other Christians.

And the fift parte contayneth from this Iulius vnto the ende of the raigne of Paule the fourth 8. Popes, and al the times of their successours vnto the iudgement of Christe. And the fall of the kingdome of the Pope shalbe withoute power or handes, with the onely word of God and breath of the deuine spirite 2. Thessal. 2.

To conclude I haue disposed the whole historye in such sort that I haue compared all the Romaine bishops to the 4. horses in the Reuelation of S. John. The godlye and aunciente fathers to the white horse: The archbishops and the Patriarckes to the red: The Popes & the Antichristes vnto Siluester the seconde to the blacke, and from him to Iulius the seconde and all his companye of monkes, fryers and massemongers y which with al their power & strength did defend the Popes kingdome, I haue cōpared to y pale horse. I haue proposed this marke and methode in my booke, in the which I haue chalenged nothing to my selfe, but my labour in gathering, describing & destributig. For I knowe y a great part of this worke hath bin set forth by others, as by Damasus, Carsulanus, Platina Stella, Vuicelius and others, but oftētimes dissemblingly and obscurelye, somtimes falsly to please mens eares. To conclude, verye man ye most dilligent & faithfull wryters of our time: whom when I had perused with continuall reading I gathered

Dedicatorie.

thereto togither the dispersed and disagreeing members to one body, that those thinges which were scattered abroade in many places, and were therefore the harder to be founde out of the Readers, might the easier be searched out being gathered together into one booke, and layde out before all mens eyes, the which I rather were performed of any man then of me, and I had rather taken in hand my contry matters then foraine busines, bicause I haue spent my time in vayne. But I would not haue stirred vp this hudge puddel of the Romaine historie, the which twoe Hercules were not able to clime.

But hearken what occasion inforced me therto, chiefly the exhortatiō of my frends did draw me into this matter, otherwise I refused it, bicause my other worke in the Englishe tongue, being proper only to English men, & knowē to very fewe, did seeme to do small profite to straungers. But this being ioyned to it, might be a publike commoditie, and profitable to the vse of all men, and more prouided for in other matters. After this I went to it with a good courage, and although I did desire that other men whiche were more fit for this matter, and more garnished with eloquence, should take this matter in hād. Yet I thought that an accompt should be made of my talent, and that I had rather to stumble a little then that so great wickednes of Antichriste, so great crueltie and inordinate pleasure more and more breaking out, and filling all thinges with the stinke therof, being omitted of all men, should seeme to be detected to fewe or none.

And if I should seeme to any mā to speake to frely, let him thinke þ it doth not proceed of þ heat of affectiō but through the knowledge of my cōsciēce, which do not declare things heard or redde only, but things knowen by experience, who liued. 24. yeares in that secte, and was present among thē being no small souldiour of the Pope: where what is it that I haue not seene, what that I haue not heard, whiche

is vn-

Bales Epistle

is vnworthy of Christ, Christians, monkes, and also of mē, from whose superstitions at that time I was not free, but I vtterly abhorred their filthines and mischiefe. Wherefore seing ꝑ I perceiued many thinges whiche did offend, therefore I am nowe compelled to be more diligent in seeking them out, and more sharpe in reprouing them, seeing they do not repent. But sithe these thinges be done & haue biene done of this flocke in Italy, Sicil, Spayne, Frāce, and Englande, who doubteth that sheepe will not followe the shepehearde, or rather hogges their swyneheard, shall we not knowe the father by the childe, or the Lion by his talentes? when pryfons be full of mischiefe, shall we thinke that the Romaine court hath none? many thinges haue bene hidden in darkenesse & priuie places, the which the Sunne hath not seene, but tyme the mother of truthe. The monasteries being put down in England, hath learned to speake and to bewraye them. As for example, the registers of the kinges visitatiō, or as they call it, the abbrigemēt of things knowen by experience in the very congregation & colleges of the Papistes, the which things I sawe them to my great feare and terrour, but nowe I possesse them, and kepe them to their great ignominie and shame, and haue opened a few of them hereafter, in the Epistle to the Reader. If Ezechiel now should pearce through the wall, and should be brought into their entries, halles, and darke chambers, he shoulde not see the Israelites bewayle Thamnum, but gelded mē vnmaried, worthy to be wounzred at, for the godly profession, offring their sacrifice to Baalpeor, Bacchus, & Venus. And sithe I knowe these thinges to be certayne and true, should I not ouerthrowe them, should I not make them manifest and openly knowen to all the worlde? Truly they will saye that an Englishe man, whiche is separated from all other nations, dothe certainly knowe what is done at Rome in the secret chambers of the Pope and his Cardinall. Shall not I openlye declare for a truth those thin-

ges

Dedicatorie.

ges whiche are declared in Bookes, and seene wyth the eyes of the wryter, the whiche thinges not the secrete chambers, but the princely court, not the priuie corners, but the open streetes, do euidently shew, but they deny it not, and yet defende it wyth moste wicked Bookes set foorth in their owne tongue, the which Christian shamefastnes forbiddeth me to declare. The truth therfore ought to be expressed, and not couered with visard and disguising, but set foorth in his owne kinde, not darkened with cloke or sayle cloth, but decked finely in his owne collours: for they be grosse thinges and may be groped at with handes. But so great is the blindnesse of man, that at noone daye he can not see, and in the clearest Sunne his eyes be darkened.

This our miserable Realme of Englande may be vnto vs a familiar example, for whose sake more willinglye I toke in hande to write this booke, that oure Englishe men may see now at the last what a terrible beast they haue receyued into their common wealth, what a viper they cherishe in their bosome, whose hissinge before they could not wel abide, do now suffer themselues to be stong with their tributes, to be bitten with their leuying and takinge vp of money, & to be entoxicated with their idolatrous poyson. Vnto whom so many kinges, so manye noble men, did not once obeye: whom VVickliffe the moste godliest of hys time did openlye shewe in writing to be Antichrist. Whom K. Henry the eyght banished, whom Edward the vi. ye most godlye king cast forth, together with all the reliques and dregs of their religiō. Him Queene Mary receyued being thrust in by Cardinall Poole many men litle regarding it, manye winking at it as though they saw it not: euery man almost allowinge it, or at the least with diuers affections filthily reioysing in it. It greeueth mee for my countrey sake, because they offend God so greatly in forsaking him, and in violatinge the oath which they made before to theyr kinges: so that now they are compelled to obey at ye becke

*ij to the

Bales Epistle

to the newe monstrous & cruell gouernment of most wicked Antichriste, vnder whom they haue deserued to be oppressed with an idolatrous yoke, to be blinded wyth superstition and deuilish Poperye, and with a final assault of the ennemyes to be shamefullye ouercome. The which notwithstanding while Gods Religion flourished, and Poperye wythered and was wasted away, was neyther aflicted with the hand of God, neither assaulted with any external power, but if it were assaulted, yet at no time coulde they conquere it. I speake these things (most reuerent fathers) to my greate griefe, and so much the more, because I iudge the contempte of the word of God, and y gulfe of Romaine filthines to be the cause of the plagues, and that Christ beinge troden downe, we had rather that the Pope (y witch and Circes of the whole worlde, not the seruaunt of all seruauntes but the Lorde of all Lords, not y Uicar of Christe but the minister of the deuill) should treade and skip vpon our shoulders and neckes, then we would embrace & kisse the sweete yoke, the lighte burden and most pleasant crosse of oure Sauiour Jesus Christe. And I require this at your handes (most godlye fathers) that you will thincke this present calamity to be no small cause which stirred me vp to this matter, and I desire for the great mercye of our Sauiour Christe, that you go forwarde in that worke that you haue in hand, and that you will make your prayers for England, (that cãnot pray for it selfe) that this Pope may be exempted out of the mindes of all Christians, Italians, Spaniardes, Frenchmen and Englishmen, thruste out of all kingdomes and Churches, broken in two and vtterlye destroyed. Praye that the blind maye see, the deafe heare, and that those which be in darcknes and in the shadowe of death, maye come to the light and knowledge of the truth. For your prayers shal be of more effect with God, than all the blessinges and cursinges of the detestable Pope.

By these thinges I trust that you vnderstande what I haue

Dedicatorie.

haue taken in hande, and for what cause. First the desire of my freindes compelled mee thereunto. Secondly my conscience pricked mee forward hasting hereunto, ỹ I mighte communicate these thinges which I haue both heard and seene in the whole course of my life. Last of all, the lamentable state of Englande called mee hereunto, that for the loue which I beare to my brethren I would ayde it, and ỹ the begining of ỹ Romaine tyrānye being read & knowne, and the offspring of all the Popes, they might seeke a newe way and amende their liues. Also to restore the dignitye of the common wealth which was lost, and to the reforminge of the Church, and to the glorye of Iesus Christe the onely gouernour of the earth.

But not ẁout great cause do I dedicate this my booke vnto you which are in this our age ỹ greatest defendours of the Christian fayth, which also do beare this greuous & odious burden, and for that cause do burne with the same fire of enuye which I do. For truly I speake as I thincke & as I beleiue, & because I beleiue it I cānot hold my peace: If at VViteberg Luther ỹ vpholder of ỹ Christian fayth, at Tigur Zuinglius the inuincible defendour of the pure veritye, and a professour therof vnto the death, at Basil Oecolampadius a lighte and lampe in ỹ house of God had not opened the liuelye springes of the Scripture, and being opened had not defeded them against the boldnes of the Philistines, if others in those dayes in your places had not sustayned this oure Religion, if you would not haue put to your ayde and helping hands, if God had not left the seede of the truth in those Churches wherin you are Presidēts, there had bin no place for Christe on the earth where hee might put his head, ther should haue bin no refuge for exiles to flye vnto, Christian pietye shoulde finde no place in which it might be confirmed & safelye established. And all those things that I haue shewed here, were taught me of your pastours and writers. Therefore it is meete that I should

Bales Epistle

should render some part thereof with gaine from whence I had it, neyther do I honour & worship onely your Churches as the sprynges of pure Religion, the which with priuye passages doth flow vnto all the corners of the earth, & euen to vs beyonde the Ocean, but all Englishe peregrins are bounde of dutye vnto you, for your great benefites bestowed vppon them. The which thing I would haue shewed at large in the name of all my freindes, if I had not written vnto you to whom we are of dutye bound: yet trulye to passe all thinges in silence and declare none of them I cannot. Therefore I praye you pardō mee, and let your modestye and gentlenes giue place and pardon mine affections, while ꝑ of so many I declare a fewe, to the intent that other men may vnderstand if I had not a iust cause to dedicate this my booke to you before al other. The which thinge while I shewe briefelye as time and order doth require, so I will name euery one of you not respecting your dignitye, but doing after the imbecillitye of memorye, and the perspicuitye of the matter.

Therefore that I maye declare from the beginninge, & ascende from the farthest vnto the nighest, whereto much duty owe we to VVitenberg that most fayre marchandize of all artes, they euidently declare which go thither either to beholde the coūtrey, or to giue themselues to studye, with whose notable prayses many being styrred vppe would go thither in great companies, if riches would abouū as their good will both to go so longe a iourneye. For when they prayse other learned, not withoute gratefull testifyinge of many benefites towardes them. Than (O Philip) they do declare thy singuler curtesye, maruclous facilitye, and thy good wil alwayes ready to deserue wel of al men. Neither without a cause. For thou prosecutest al mē at home with all kinde of humanitye, and at home with thy preaching & louing letters doest ease the sorrowful & wauering minds. For it is not vnknowen what thou hast done at the councel of VVc-

Dedicatorie.

of VVesalia in the Englishe mens behalfe, who when thou sawest to take paynes for Religion sake, and to be greatly moued wyth the vniust outcryes of men þ helde opinion agaist thẽ, thou thoughtest good þ the cause should be heard wythout debate or strife, and not to be put oute with crye & clapping of hands: thou sayost that the men were to be retayned and relieued, and not to be vexed and afflicted with any sharpe iudgement. To this ende thou didst write to the maiestrates of Franckford, so that by thy letters which I chaunced to see, I am certified where thou didst thincke it meete that our men purelye thinkinge of the articles of our Christian fayth, and in diuers cõtrouersyes defending their opinion with feruour of zeale accordinge to their nature, to be taughte and not to be oppressed, to be warned tõ talke not troubled with force, sich that doubtfull matters ought to be handled of the aduersaryes parte wyth obscure wordes. Neither do I doubte but that the countryes bordring there about Strasburge, Basil, Arouia, Tigurũ Geneua, Emdona, being moued with such a notable testimonye, will receiue vs more into their fauour.

But leuing VVittenberge, I come to Basile, where I will be more parciall, not bicause I can not prayse him sufficiently inough, but bicause I am one ofthem which haue felt and do daily feele the great beneuolence of the Senate, ministers, and the whole people, leaft I should not seeme to be so gratefull a prayser as a deceitfull flatterer. Therfore I will saye nothing of thee at this tyme, moste wyse & learned Sulcer, nothinge of M. VVoulfangus VVisenburge, that moste excellent diuine, and worthy gouernour of the vniuersitie, nothing of Martin Borrham, the notable professor of dininitie, nothing of learned M. Iohn Iunius, my faithfull companion: nothing of Marcus Bersius, Iames Turkenbrot, Conradus Lycosthenes, his deare friende, Huldricus Coccius, Thomas Gyrenfalck, Iohn Ibelhard, Sebastian Lepusculus, Seuerinus Erimontanus, Iohn Mæder,

der, Iohn Brandmiller, and other ministers of Gods word, whose beneuolēce is daily seene. I omitte the griefes which you moste willingly suffered, not without great paines and trauaple. But this onely I will saye, that although the good will of the people and magistrate was sufficiently inflamed, of them selues toward, yet it did seeme to arise and spring for the moste part through your sermons, so that whatsoeuer beneuolence happened vnto vs at that tyme, was through your request and impulsion. But here (as I sayde before) I desire breuitie, bicause I am one of them which haue experience of you. I will speake more of Tigur and Geneua.

For Tigur alwayes being a safegard to such as flye frō their countreyes, and a moste excellent vniuersitie of learned diuines, and a moste renoumed schole, doth open vnto me a large fielde, in which this my oration may walke and haue his full course.

Whether I haue respect vnto, the common practise of al nations, or that, that is onely proper to Englãd, for what a notable oracle there is as it were for all Christendome, what a notable quire of moste learned men. For ÿ I may say nothing of thee D. Bullinger, who so many notable bookes compiled with such singular pietie and manifold learning, with suche varietie of all thinges, and sentences of aunciēt writers decked as it were with starres, doth prayse enough to the Catholike church, although I holde my peace. But that I may omitte al the other which were borne and bread at Tygur, As Bibliander and Hippius, whiche knewe all thinges, Radulph Gualther, the eloquent preacher and politik writer Cōradus Gesnerus, a notable library as it were of all disciplines, and my singuler friend, Iosias Simler, and Iohn Vuolphius, most learned men also, & my very friends with many other notable professors of other artes: Good Lorde, what notable olde men were those learned Straungers, M. Peter Martyr, and Barnardine Ochinus, whiche

yo

Dedicatorie.

you receiued into your citie? One of the whiche if some other congregatiõ should haue, they should seeme to be blessed, and enriched with a great treasure and ornamẽt. Happy was Englande when she possessed them, miserable whẽ she lost them: of this congregation sithe thou art president most learned Bullinger, I haue iustly chosen thee to be my patrone, with whose authoritie the Romaine court may be weakened, and my discription be established. Who if thou wouldest call into the fielde, these noble captaines, stoute souldious with their furnished bandes, with a reasonable power thou shalt ouercome, at the first one onset the whole troupes and bondes of the Papistes. But I will omitte these thinges, as common and knowen to all men, what he hath done to our Englishe men at Tigur, seeing that is proper to my purpose, and not the other, I will here leue that, and touch this but briefly. For when I was with you and had tasted thy hospitalitie O Bulliger, & the humanitie of others, I vnderstode the great good will you did beare to our coũtremen which were with you. That worthy man Iohñ Parckhurst, and worthy of a better fortune, did declare to me howe much bounde he was to thee, to M. Gualter, and to the whole citie. It was tolde me also of thẽ which were at Basill with me, of thy care and fatherly affection toward them, whyle they liued with you together in one house, euen vnder the shadowe of your citie, being defended from all persecution, with the great cõsent and loue of your citizẽs. Also the incredible liberalitie of your magistrates, the which frely gaue vnto them corne and wine sufficient to susteine.xiii.or.xiiii.men, and when they refused to take it, they were sory that they hadde not oportunitie to pleasure them.

But nowe I haste to Geneua, of which if I should make any long oratiõ, when I had saide all, I should seeme scarce to haue declared halfe that whiche might be saide. In the which I greatly marueile at the notable prouidence of our

God,

Bales Epistle

God, which so stirred vp the mindes of the citizens and magistrates, that they were not afrayde to receiue so many thousand straungers into the suburbes of one citie. Againe, did so turne the heartes of the straungers, that although they were moe in nūber, & the superiours, yet woulde submitte them selues vnder their power, as though they were the inferiours, in so muche that they did not acknowledge them selues to be Lordes and citizens, but priuate men and straungers. Let other men sayne other miracles, but Geneua seemeth to me to be the wonderfull miracle of the whole worlde: so many from all countries come thether, as it were vnto a sanctuary, not to gather riches but to liue in pouertie: not to be satisfied, but to be hungry, not to liue pleasauntly, but to liue miserably, not to saue their goodes, but to leese them. Many marchantes do rushe thether for gaynes, souldiours for spoyles, all for their owne profitte. But it seemeth to be a monsterous and a wonderfull miracle, that men should flye to scarcenes from plenteousnes, to trauaile frō ease; from plenteousnes of ryches, to miserable pouertie; Lutetia, London, Franckfort, are newe markets for marchandize, vnto the which men come, not for gaine, not for marchandise, not for tauerning, to chaūge heauenly thinges w earthly things, y in stede of humane treasures, they may gather heauenly treasures in heauen. We haue read that consuls haue bin taken from the plough to beare rule, but from florishinge fortune, from great riches and dignities to the plough, to great labours and trauayle, frō an horse to an asse weeting and knowing it, is it not a great maruelle? Is it not wonderfull that Spanyardes, Italians, Scottes, Englishemen, Frenchmen, Germaines, disagreeing in manners, speache and apparell, sheepe and wolues, bulles and beares, being coupled with the onely yoke of Christe, should liue so louingly and friendly, and that Monkes, Laymen, and Nunnes, disagreeing both in life and secte should dwell together, like a spirituall and
Christian

Dedicatorie.

Christian congregation, vsing one order, one cloyster, and like ceremonies. Is it not wonderfull that so many stoute enemies hanging ouer them, and looking still to deuoure them, as Sathan and the Pope their moste bitter enemies, they should not onely be safe, but also liue so long time in quietnes? Thankes be therfore vnto God, because he hath appointed the pastour of his scattered and dispersed flocke, the captaine of ye banished, to be ye chiefe of ye miserable people, with whose counsell gouernment & wisdome, so great a congregation of people, being not only diuerse, but contrary one to another, hath bene nourished together vnder one bande of loue, so that nowe nothing is more louing then those enemies, nothing more like, then their vnlikenes, no body more happy, then these miserable men. I thanke thee in this my writing in the name of them all, because when they would purely honoure God in their owne countrey, & cannot, it may be lawfull for them to come to the churche and celebrate the congregation, in the which they may frely call vpon their God, sincerely administer the Sacramentes, and may fulfill other rites as they were citizens, with the priuiledge, and highe fauour of the magistrates. Happy is that people who enioyeth these thinges, and haue so worthy a bishop, which gathereth together ye dispersed, comforteth the broken in heart, fauoureth exiles, and confirmeth the weake with example and doctrine.

But perchaunce I may seeme, to haue sayde to much to you and to you all, most gentle fathers, who are troubled with grauer matters, and haue no leysure to reade your prayses. And indued with suche modestie, that you will scarse attende vnto it. But beare with me while I doe but my dutie, for I prayse not you but the giftes of God that are of you, and commende the happy state of your churches vnto the faythful, yt they may learne to giue thankes and to imitate you. I would haue shewen the causes why I inscribed to your name the Papall historie of new Rome, partly

*8   to haue

Bales Epistle Dedicatorie.

to haue declared my loue towardes you, for your benefites bestowed vpon England & other countreis. Partly that the learning which you haue spread abroade in these dayes, may be defended with your ayde. Our Lorde Iesus Christe, the prince of sheepeheardes, the maister of al truthe, the enemy of Antechriste, strengthen and confirme you, and all your fellowe ministers, with the power of the holy ghoste, and preserue you in long health, to the comfort and ioye of the Christian flocke, to the o-
uerthrowing of Antichriste, and
the amplifying of his name.
Amen.

Iohn Bale

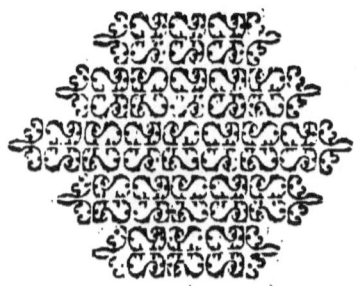

Iohn Bale to the Reader.

Desire thee (Christian Reader) whosoeuer thou art that delightest in ye glory of Christ against the malyce of Antichriste, and I beseech thee in the Lord to conster all thinges to the beste, euen those matters which seeme to be spoken more bitterly against that mostrous beast and not to depraue them with slaunderings, as I vnderstand some of late haue taken occasion to do by my late booke published of the writers of Englande. Among whom some are not ashamed vntrulye to saye that I deale vniustlye with some Princes that gouerne the estates of Christēdome. Othersome saye that I speake malepertlye and that against all Christiā modestye, that I speake vnreuerentlye of Queene Mary of England, because in one place I haue written that Iesabell raigneth in Englāde, and glutteth her selfe with the bloude of Martyrs: where as by that name I did not meane Queene Mary, but the tyrannie of Rome that miserablye ouerrunneth all Englande. For the places in Nicolas Grimohld, Traherne, Turner the Phisition, Hooper, Ridley, Rogers, Bradford, Filpot, and other, do sufficientlye interprete themselues to be spoken of the greate Antichriste and his mitred and scraped tormentours. For as the holye ghoste hath taughte mee I haue called that Romaine Sinagogge the murtherer of Godlye men, wicked Iesabell, the horned beast, the impe of the Dragō, the doughter of the deuill, the spouse of Sathan, speaking blasphemies, the purple beast, the misticall Babilon, the great strumpet with whom the kinges of the earth haue cōmitted fornication, which haue dronke of the wyne of her fornication, the womā cloathed in purple, scarlet, gould, pearles and precious stones, hauing a goulden cuppe full of all filthines & lustes of the world, the mother of fornication, and droncke with the bloud of the saintes of IESVS CHRIST, the habitatiō of deuils, and the cage of all euill spirites and hatefull birdes.

The occasiō which first moued mee herevnto was this, Anno domini 1554. our Realme of Englande after the xx. yeare of her deliueraunce throughe the mercye of God, most shamefullye forsooke the holye Gospel of Christe, which is the power and vertue of God to the health of all beleuers, & made a newe professiō vnto the great ennemye of God the Romaine deuil and wicked Antichrist. Of the which execrable deede thou shalt read more in ye end of this booke. Partlye also the horrible vices which follow this monster, whereof

*e ij the

Bales Epistle

the most prudent K. Henry the eight had good proofe, vvhen he caused the houses of the hooded hypocrites, & the colleges of the massemongers in his kingdome, before their vtter destruction vvhich vvas in the yeare of our Lord God 1538. to be visited, by the vvorshipfull doctours of the lavve, Thomas Lee, Richard Laiton, Thomas Bedill, Thomas Barthlet the publicke notarie, & such others. In the vvhich there vvere such svvarmes of vvhoremōgers, ruffians, filthie parsons, giltye of sinne against nature, Ganimedes, and yet votaries and vnmaryed all, so that thou vvouldest thincke that there vvere a nevve Gomorrha amonge them. The booke of them is called the breuiary of thinges founde out in abbeyes, assemblies, colleges, &c. Out of the vvhich booke I vvill shevv but one or other example, to an vnsauery tast thereof. In the monasterye called Battel abbey in the Diocesse of Chichester, these many gilty of sinne agaīst nature vvere foūd in the visitation, Iohn the Abbot, Richard Salchurst, Thomas Cuthberth, VVilliam March, Iohn Hasting, Gregorie Champiō, Clemēt VVestfild, Iohn Crosse, Thomas Crambroke, Thomas Basill, Iohn Hamfild, Iohn Hierome, Clemens Grigge, Richard Touye, and Iohn Austine. These vvere incontinente liuers, Thomas Lyuet vvyth one maryed vvife & one harlot, Thomas Cranbroke vvith the same, and other beside. Lo this is the chast Religion of the Pope.

At Canterbury amonge the Benedictine monkes these vvere gilty of sinne against nature, Richard Godmersham, VVilliam Lichfild, Christopher Iames, Iohn Goldmistone, Nicolas Clement, VVilliam Causton, Iohn Ambrose, Thomas Farlegh, and Thomas Morton. VVhoremongers, Christopher Iames aforesaide vvith three maried vvomen, and Nicolas Clement yvith one harlot. In the Abbey of S. Augustine these vvere found vnchast, Iohn the Abbot vvith one vvoman, Iohn Langdan vvith tvvo, Iohn Langport vvith one, Richarde Compton vvith one, VVilliam Reynsforth vvith one, VVilliā Godmerstone vvith tvvo, Dauid Franckes vvith tvvo, Robart saltvvood one, Laurence Goldstone one, VVilliam Holingborne one, VVilliā Milton one, Iohn Shrevvsbery one, and Thomas Barhā gilty of sinne against nature. In the abbey of Bath amonge many other Richard Lincombe had vii. harlots, iij. maryed vvomen, and iiii. singlevve men and he vvas giltye of sinne against nature also, VVilliam Benushon had xi. harlots, beside diuers gilty of sinne against nature. In the abbey of Monkenferlege in Salisbury diocesse, Levvis the Prior had 9. harlots, Richard the Prior of Mayden Bradley had v. harlots and sixe bastardes, VVilliam the Abbot of Bristovve had iiij. harlots, iij. vnmaried

To the Reader.

maried & one maryed. Thomas Abbot of Abingtō beſide his owne naturall ſiſter of whom he begat two children, had three other harlots, and this mā was the father of many that was gilty of ſin againſt nature. In the abbey of Sulbred in the diocéſſe of Ciceſter George Walden Prior had vij. harlots, Iohn Standney vij. Nicolas duke v. Henry Selwood two, with many others. Iohn Blanke Prior of Bermondſey had xi harlots.

At the caſtel of Wyndſor Henry Woodward had very many harlots, Nicolas Whyden had iiij. George Whitthorne v. Nicolas Spoke v. Simon Tod one, Nicolas Walker ij. William Vauſe one; Robart Dauiſon vj. Peter Boughe had many, and ſo other had others. In the Cathedrall Church at Chicheſter, Iohn Champion Prebendary of Waltam had ij. harlots, Williā Croſſe had one wyfe, Thomas Parker ij. harlots, Richard Buſteld one of whō he begat a child, Barthelmew Cokiſley i. Robart hunt had diuers, Tho. Goffe had ij. being other mens wyues, Iohn Hill xiij. harlots, Robart Moore had many, Roger Barham many, Iohn Bedfild many, with others, amōg þ which the forſaid Roger Barham and Iohn Champion were gilty of ſinne againſt nature. Theſe were taken out of the foreſaid booke. Behold what monſters Popery hath nouriſhed throughout England in abbeyes and colleges. Are not theſe foule birdes moſt iuſtlye baniſhed with their moſt filthye Pope, the Romiſhe Idoll? In all other places as well in congregations as colleges the like thinges are committed and done, the which were to longe or rather to ſhameful throughly to declare, for they gate vnto them in moſt places through this Popiſhe Religion, either the French pockes or the Spaniſhe deceaſe. And there were in Englande more then xl. Abbeyes of diuers kindes of mōkes, beſide the moſt wicked neſts of the begging fryers, of the which there were almoſt two hundreth. Vnto whom theſe verſes do aptlye agree.

𝔍𝔱 𝔦𝔰 𝔫𝔬𝔱 ſ𝔲𝔯𝔢 𝔞 𝔪𝔦ſſ𝔢 𝔱𝔥𝔞𝔱 𝔪𝔬𝔫𝔨𝔢𝔰 ſ𝔥𝔬𝔲𝔩𝔡 𝔣𝔞𝔱𝔥𝔢𝔯𝔰 𝔱𝔢𝔯𝔪𝔢𝔡 𝔟𝔢𝔢,
𝔖𝔦𝔱𝔥 ſ𝔲𝔠𝔥 ſ𝔴𝔞𝔯𝔪𝔢𝔰 𝔬𝔣 𝔱𝔥𝔢𝔦𝔯 𝔟𝔞ſ𝔱𝔞𝔯𝔡 𝔟𝔯𝔞𝔱𝔰 𝔦𝔫 𝔢𝔲𝔢𝔯𝔶 𝔭𝔩𝔞𝔠𝔢 𝔱𝔥𝔢𝔶 ſ𝔢𝔢.

There is yet a thirde matter which forced mee herevnto, and hauing ſeene and heard theſe thinges vehemently moued me to write. This is the precepte of Chriſte in the xviij. Chapter of the Reuelation of S. Iohn: For a voyce came from heauen from the right hand of the father and the euerlaſting throne of Chriſte, with a great voyce ſounded in our eares ſaying. Go from her my people leſt ye be made partakers of her wickednes, and ye receiue part of her puniſhment. For her ſinnes are gone vp to heauen, and God hath remembred her wickednes,

Bales Epistle

kednes. And then commaundemēt follovveth vvhich vvas giuen against the beast vvith seuen heades. Revvard her euen as she hath revvarded you, and giue her double according to her vvorks, and poure in double to her in the same cup vvhich she filled vnto you. And forasmuch as she glorified her selfe and liued vvantonly, so much poure you into her of punishment and sorrovve. This is the vvorde of the Lorde declared vnto vs as vvell here as in the fiftye Chap. of Ieremy. That this serpent might perish & all his doinges brought to nought. Yet for al this I do vvel remēber the sayings of S. Paule, that al Princes ought to be honoured although they be vvicked and vnprofitable for a common vvealth, becaufe they be placed there of God, neither to speake euill of them beinge but vvormes, dust and ashes, Neither dare I murmur against the prouidence of God, vvhich is contrary to his holy vvorde. Therefore from the bottome of my hart I beseech our Lorde and Redeemer Iesus Christe, that he vvould haue mercye vppon all Kinges, Princes and Nations, and so prouide that all nations maye be so gouerned as is most tending to his glory: For vvhose reueng he hath most stoutly fortifyed mee vp in this my old age. Not studying to derogate or take avvaye the honour from anye Christian Kinge, but onely to inuey against the Romishe beast, the Synagog of Sathan, and most vvicked Antichrist, vvith the vvritings and testimonye of most learned men.

If I shal haue said any thing sharper then thou didst loke for (most gentle Reader) cōsider I pray you the hudge tirāny of this most vvicked Viper of the vvorld, vvhose destruction accordinge to Gods promises is at hande. Great Babilon shall fall vvhich hath seduced many Nations, and shall be destroyed the vvhole vvorlde marueylinge thereat. If the vehemencye of my stile shall offende thee, beholde the maruelous force of the holye ghoste in the Prophete Dauid and most holy king, vvho in the Lordes cause most stoutlye saide: I haue hated the congregation of the vvicked, Psal. 25. He promiseth also aftervvarde by his Prophetes, that he vvoulde destroye the brothell houses and vvicked places. Ezechi. 16. I vvill shevve sayth the Lord vnto all Nations thy nakednes, and to al kingdomes thy shame Nahum. 3. Thy dishonour and filthines shall be opened, and thy reproche shall be seene, I vvill be reuenged, and none shall resiste mee, Esay 47. VVoe be vnto those Kinges as manye as haue vvorshipped the beast or haue ayded her, or haue receiued helpe of her, or haue committed fornication vvith her, as many as haue serued her, and haue ioyned handes against the Lambe, and vvaged battell for

hes

To the Reader.

her cause, because their names are not vvritten in the booke of lyfe from the beginninge of the vvorlde. And the Lambe shal ouercome them at the last like a Lorde of Lordes, and kinge of kinges, and they shall go together vvith the beast to destruction and vtter dampnation, Apocalips 17. GOD therefore giue in the hartes of Christians vvhom the x. hornes do shadovve, that they maye faithfully execute this his vvill and iudgement, that they maye make her desolate and leaue her naked, that they maye eate her flefhe and burne her in fire, that is, let her abide her last punishment for the sheding of the innocent bloud, of so manye faithfull Christians. Be it done, Be it done. Amen.

To the

To the Reader: T. R.
GENTLEMAN.

The worthy wittes of elder yeares haue trauelo sea and land,
To seeke and search the wondrous workes of natures skilful hand:
And mens delight hath euer bin most vgly things to vewe,
To looke on creatures out of kinde, as monsters olde and newe.
If therefore thou as other men my friend affected bee,
And dost desire vgly things, and monsters strange to see:
Then take the payne to seeke and searche within this little booke,
And here thou shalt vpon so strang a mongrell monster looke:
As neuer nature bread on earth, whose shape is in this wyse,
As I shall partly portrature the same before thine eyes.
It is a little beast that hath ten hornes, seuen heads, a crownets seuē,
Who w̄ his taile frō cloudes to cloudes swepes down ȳ stars of heauē.
Vpon whose backe in princely pompe, and glistring gold arape,
And proudly prackt in precious pearles, and clad in purple gape,
The stately strompet sittes, that is the whore of Babilon,
And in her hand a golden cuppe of fornication.
Wherwith the world she poysond hath, which dronken with her wine,
Hath falne downe flat vnto the beast, as to a god deuine:
Which forced kings to leaue their crownes, & Keiser stoupe for awe,
Whyle on his royall necke the beast hath layd his filthy pawe.
Who hath the mighty monarkes made to holde his stirrope low:
And caused them on humble knees to come to kisse his toe:
Who forced great estates to stand barefooted in the streate,
And proudly put the crowne on head of princes with his feete.
And made the sonne and subiect both against their king and syre,
Oft to rebell whose burning breath set all the world on fyre:
Who hath blasphemd our glorious God, w̄ thousand mischiefs more
Loe to be briefe, such is the beast of whom I spake before.
Which earst discouered was by Bale among the rockes of Rome,
And by the painfull penne of S. is into England come.
That euery man may know the same, and learne to shone the beast,
Who whyle she lorked close did spye mankinde by East and West.
Accept therfore my friendes good will, that thus his trauell spent,
Prayse God for it, and him for payne that this vnto thee sent.

FINIS.

THE FIRST BOOKE
of the Pageant of
Popes.

S. Peter not bishop of Rome.

FOR so muche as the Bishops of Rome haue claimed, and doo still clayme their vsurped supremacy by right of inheritāce and succession from Peter, because he (as they pretend) was bishop of Rome at the least. xxv. yeares, and so tied all this dignitie and prerogatiue (whiche they fight for) to his chayre for euer: It shalbe therfore nedeful to consider, how likely it is to be true, that Peter continued bishop in Rome according to their boasting. This matter shalbe the better displayed if these three pointes be layde open to the readers eye: that is the yeare that Peter came to Rome, the yeres that Peter sat at Rome, and the death of Peter.

¶ Of S. Peters comming to Rome.

Touching the time of his comming to Rome, their own histories doe wryte so vncertainly that it semeth more certaine that he neuer came there.

First their legendary of saintes liues called Passionale, counteth that he came not there till the viii. yeare of Claudius, and that should be the 55. yeare of the incarnacion of Christe, and 22. yeare after his death. *Passionale.*

Platina saith, that in the second yere of Claudius, being the xi. yeare after the death of Christe, Peter cam to Rome being the head of the worlde, partly because he perceiued *Platina in vita Petri.*

A i   that this

The first Booke of the

that this was a seate pontificali dignitati conuenientem, fit for pōtifical dignitie, partly becaufe of Simon Magus. Thus he maketh that partly ambicion and dignitie drewe Peter to Rome, there to take his eafe contrary to the duty and doing of the poore paynfull and godly Apoftle, who as he had in charge by Iefus Chrifte, trauailed ftil from place to place, not for the dignitie of a bifhop at Rome, but to plant the Gofpell throughout the worlde.

Orofius fayth he came foner, euen in the beginning of the raigne of Claudius: lib. 7. cap. 6.

Fafciculus temporum faith, he came not till the fourth yeare of Claudius.

Eufeb.lib.2. cap.13.

Eufebius faithe, that by Gods efpeciall prouidence he came to Rome, Eueftigio fub ipfo Claudij imperio. Out of hande vnder Claudius his raigne Peter came to Rome becaufe of Simon Magus.

In Claudio.

Vfpergenfis faith, fome reporte that he came in the beginning of the raigne of Claudius: fome fay, not till the feconde yeare: Other faye, that he came not till the fourth yeare of his regiment: Againe, fome thinke that he came in the beginning thereof, but toke not vpon him to be byfhop till the fourth yeare of Claudius: Other thinke that he was bifhop forthwith as fone as he came.

Ennead.7.li.2.

Sabellicus faith, that he came to Rome altero anno regiminis eius (Claudij): in the fecond peare of Claudius his regiment.

Naucler faith, that he came to Rome in the fourth yere of Claudius, and began his bifhoprike the fame yeare in Rome: in fecunda generatione vol: 2.

It were to long to recite all the opinions of Peters cōming to Rome and his enftalling: but by thefe it may appeare howe the Romaine Jury can giue no certain verdit vpon fuche vnconftant euidence.

¶ The continuance of Peter in his
Bifhoprike.

S. Ierome

Pageant of Popes.   Fol. 2.

S Ierome sayth, he raigned xxvii. yeares.
Beda sayth, he sat at Rome xxix. yeares.
 Fasciculus Temporum, hitteth it iump and misseth not one daye, saying: he was martyred by Nero after he had bene bishop of Rome xxv. yeres vii. monethes & viii. days.
 The moste do agree to this accompt as Vspergensis, Platina, and other, that he raigned not aboue xxv. yeares.

¶ Peters death.

Nicephorus sayth, he was buried in the xxxvii. yeare after the death of Christe.
 Of these premisses this is to be gathered that Peter came to Rome at the furthest in the fourth peare of Claudius, and that is, the xiii. yeare after the death of Christe, and raigned there xxv. yeares at the least: and was put to death there in the last yeare of Nero, being the 38. yeare after the death of Christe. This semeth to be moste probable, and in taking this tyme we shall seme to deale most fauourably with the papiste, who would so fayne deriue this bastard brauche of Romain prelates from the holy Apostle: so that if it can be proued, y Peter sat not bishop of Rome these xxv. yeares, then must the Pope seke out a new petagrewe for his succession falsely fathered vpon Peter: his auncient continuance of hundred peres, being disproued by the scripture being more auncient, can proue nothing for lawfull regiment, but rather improue him of vnlawefull vsurping for so long time. And therfore for the more euidēt vnderstanding hereof it shalbe moste cōuenient to conferre the yeares of the Emperours with the yeares of Christ his incarnation and death, whiche for the more ease I haue set foorth in this table folowing: wherein appeareth that our sauiour Christe suffered death in the 33. yeare of his age, in the 18. yeare of Tiberius, who raigned in all 23. yeares, therof v. peres after Christes death. The next is Caligula raigning three yeares x. monethes viii. dayes. Then suc-

A ii   ceded

The first Booke of the

ceded Claudius for 13. yeares 8. monethes and 28. dayes. Last was Nero, continuing 13. yeares 10. monethes and 18. dayes, all whiche time being added together doth make almoste 37. yeares, which is the time that Peter lyued after the death of our sauiour: as Nicephorus testifieth.

Nicepho. li.2. cap. 34

The yeares of Christes incarnatiō.	The yeares after Christes death.	The yeares of the Emperours.	The yeares after Paul. conuersion.
33	Christ died	Tiberius. 18	
34	1	19	
35	2	20	Paule con.
36	3	21	1
37	4	22	2
38	5	23	3
39	6	Caligula.	4
40	7	2	5
41	8	3	6
42	9	4	7
43	10	Claudius.	8
44	11	2	9
45	12	3	10
46	13	4	11
47	14	5	12
48	15	6	13
49	16	7	14

Pageant of Popes. Fol. 3.

50	17	8	15
51	18	9	16
52	19	10	17
53	20	11	18
54	21	12	19
55	22	13	20
56	23	14	21
57	24	Nero.	22
58	25	2	23
59	26	3	24
60	27	4	25
61	28	5	26
62	29	6	27
63	30	7	28
64	31	8	29
65	32	9	30
66	33	10	31
67	34	11	22
68	35	12	33
69	36	13	34
70	37	14	35
		Galba.	

The first Booke of the

Whether Peter were bishop of Rome before the death of Christe, seing there is no question to be made, it needeth not to be spoken of: for the time after his death it followeth that for the first yeare after our redemptiō Peter went not to Rome, but cōtinued about Hierusalē (sauing once that hee went to Samaria for a season) till the conuersion of Paule, as appeareth by all the discours of the Actes of the Apostles, till ye come to the ninth chapter thereof: whiche because it is easie there to finde, tedious to be set downe at large, and nothing doubted of, I leaue it to the diligence of the reader, who shall plainely perceaue, that Peter was still in Iudea to the conuersion of Paule, which was in the seconde yeare after the death of Christe, the yeare of thincarnatiō 35. for Niceph. saith, that he preached 35. yeares, lib. 2. cap. 34. and he died in the last yeare of Nero, being the 70. yeare of thincarnacion: from whiche take 35. and the remayne is as muche: so that in the 35. yeare of Christe Paule was conuerted.

Act. 8.

¶ Peter not at Rome from the yeare of the incarnation 35. to the yeare 38.

Anno Domini 37. Pilate (as Eusebius lib. 2. cap. 2. and Vspergensis testifie) wrote his letter to Tiberius, concerning Christe, his doctrine, diuine miracles, death, & resurrection; whereupon the Emperour commaunded that Christe should be placed among the Gods of Rome: If Peter nowe had bene bishop at Rome or a yeare before, this had not bene so straunge newes to the Emperour: Neither had Pilates letter preuayled so muche with the Emperour touching Christ, as the doctrine and miracles, whiche Peter would (for confirming of the faithe) haue done in the name of Iesus.

The yeare folowing being the 38. was the thirde yeare from the conuersion of Paule, in whiche yeare Paule retyrned to Hierusalē & founde Peter there, as is testified in

the first

the first to the Galathians: which comming of Paule is specified in the ninth of the Actes.

¶ From the yeare 38. to the yeare 46.

After Paule had bene a whyle in Hierusalem, he was
sent awaye to Tarsus. And at that time S. Luke sayth, Act.9.
that the churche had peace throughout all Iudea, Galilye,
and Samaria. And that Peter did walke ouer all those coūtreies, where they proceded in the feare of God, the bele-
uing multiplied. Howe many yeares Peter spent in these
countreies, it is not euident: but immediatly from thence
he did ascende to Lydda, and ther healed Aeneas, who had
bene lame eight yeares: the fame of whiche miracle drew
thether all the inhabitours of Lydda and Sarona, who by
Peters preaching were all conuerted to the lorde: These
thinges do argue that Peter made some aboue in Lydda
also: Immediatly from thence he went to Ioppa, where
he reuiued Tabitha, and taried at Ioppa with Simon the
Tanner a long season: From thence he went forthwith to
Cornelius the Centurion at Cesarea, where he preached, Act.10.
and baptized those that were conuerted: and there also he
was entreated to tary for a time. From thence he came to
Hierusalem, where he continued, till he being imprisoned Act.11
by Herode, was deliuered by Gods Angell, and being set
at libertie, shewed him selfe secretly to the congregacion Act.12.
at the house of Mary, and then conueyed hym selfe awaye.
And thys was done as appeareth by Luke, the same
peare that Herode or Agrippa hauing raigned 7. yeares, Ieseph.anti.
died afterwarde at Cesarea, stricken by Gods Angell: who lib.19.cap.7
being as Iosephus saith, released out of pryson, and made
king there by Caligula raigned, in all seuen yeares:
Caligula would haue restored this Agrippa to his li- Ioseph.Anti.
bertie, as sone as he him selfe came to the Empier, euen the lib.18.cap.8.
same daye that the solemnitie was kept for the buriall of
his predecessour Tiberius. But (saith Iosephus) Antonia
A iiii   the wife

The first Booke of the

the wyfe of Caligula, gaue him counsell that he should not do so, but pause a while longer, not because she was loth that Agrippa should be at libertie, but because the Emperour by deliuering of him so spedely, should be thought that he did it in despite of Tiberius, who had committed him to pryson, and therefore it was deferred for a season, & at length he was deliuered: then the next yeare Agrippa craued leaue of Caligula to go into Iudæa to his kingdom, whiche was graunted him. So that by this computation it may easely appeare, that whereas Agrippa (as Ioseph sayth) died in the seuenth yeare of his raigne, this seuenth yeare doth arise to the fourth yeare of Claudius, who did next succede Caligula. Thus it is apparent that Herode or Agrippa as Ioseph calleth him, died in the 46. yeare of the incarnation, and that the same yeare Peter was prisoner at Hierusalem as is saide before, and not byshop at Rome.

Another reason to proue that it should be this yere, may be this: S. Luke in the xii. chapter of the Actes sayth, that this Herode had conceiued displeasure againſt the Tirians and Sidonians, whiche was the cause, that after the same Easter that Peter was imprisoned, he went downe from Hierusalem to Cæsarea, whether the Tirians and Sidonians came vnto him, and by the intercession of Blastus the kinges chamberlaine they sued for peace at his haude, because (saith Luke) in the 20. verse of the 12. chapter of the Actes, their contrey was nourished by the kinges contrey: signifying that the prouision of king Agrippa ayded their necessitie in the time of the famine being then. This dearth & famin is that, wherof Agabus the prophet did prophecy at Antioch, which saith Luke Actes the xi. came to passe in the raigne of Claudius, and as other authours haue noted it was in the fourth yere of Claudius, so saith Vspergenſis: Thus we se that yet to this fourth yere of Claudius by whiche time at the vttermost Peter should not only be at Rome, but begin his regiment ouer the churche, he is
yet at

yet at Hierusalem, which is 1600. miles from Rome: But because that Luke saith, after that he was deliuered by the Angell out of pryson, and after that he had signified his deliuery to Mary, he conuayed him selfe away from thence. I will procede to examine, whether he went not now from Hierusalem to Rome, and therfore go to the twoo yeares that ensued next.

¶ Anno 48: and 49.

ANno domini 49. Peter was at Hierusalem: for this yeare the counsell was held at Hierusalem: mencioned in the xv. of the Actes. At whiche synode Peter was present, and made an oration as is shewed in the vii. verse of the said chapter. But nowe it remaineth to be proued, that this Synode was at this tyme: for proofe hereof Saint Paule speaking of his comming to this counsell in the seconde chapiter to the Galathians, saythe : Then after 14. yeares I came agayne vp to Hierusalem, and Barnabas with me &c. by the reste that foloweth it is euident that Paule signified his comming to this counsell, and not any other time of his repairing to Hierusalem: and so also doth S. Hierome vnderstande it, which being xiiii. yeares after the conuersion of Paule, falleth out to be in the yeare of our Lord 49. & the seuenth yere of the raigne of Claudius, as may appeare by the former table: And yet is Peter stil in his Apostelship at Hierusalem: and not in his pontificall dignitie at Rome.

But here it may be sayde, that S. Hierome and diuers other whiche followe him, do recken that this synode was helde Anno domini 51. and do grounde it vpō the foresaid wordes of Paule: for where as Paule speaking of his conuersion at Damasco, sayth: that after three yeares he came to Hierusalem, and then after fourtene yeres he retourned agayne to Hierusalem: this is to be vnderstoode, not xiiii. yeares from his conuersion, but from his former being at

Hierusalem

The first booke of the

Hierusalem, and so consequently in the xvii. yere of his conuersion, whiche should be also the ix. yeare of the raigne of Claudius: This is the computation of Hierome: but this is easely disproued: for in the * ninth yeare of Claudius, the Iewes were all banished from Rome, because saith Suetonius, they made tumultes, Impulsore Christo, by meanes of Christe: And at this time Paule was at Athens, as Vspergensis writeth, and it appeareth likewyse by the history of the Actes: for Paule departing from Athens, went to Corinth, where he met with Aquila and Priscilla, who (saith the text) were lately come from Italy, because Claudius had commaunded that all Iewes should depart from Rome: This being euident that Paule was at this time at Athens, it is further to be considered whether he might not be at Hierusalem the same yeare at the counsell or no. Moste certaine it is that Paule was at the counsell, and that it was held before his comming to Athens, and that so long time that the onely consideration thereof might be sufficient to proue, that the same synode was not helde the same yeare: For those questiōs being discussed about which they were assembled, Paule and Barnaba with certaine other returned with letters from Hierusalem to Antioche, where they stayed, and taried preaching and teaching for a tyme, till at the length Paule agreed with Barnabas to go visite the brethren, in those cities wher they had taught the gospell. So that Paule passed from Antioche to Syria, & Cilicia, confirming the churches: Afterwarde he came to Derba and Lystra, where he founde Timothie, and hauing circumcized him he toke him with him, and as they passed forth (saith Luke) from citie to citie they gaue vnto them the institutions of the Apostles and Elders of Hierusalem, that they should obserue them, so that the churches were confirmed in faith and encreased daily: Also they walked throughout Phrygia and Galacia, and being forbidde by the spirite to preache in Asia, they went to Nysia,

from

Marginal notes:
Orosius. li.7. cap.6.

In Claud. cap.24.

Act.18.

Act.15.

Act.16.

from thence to Troada, from thence to Samothracia, then to Neaples, and so to Philippis, and stayed there certayne daies, from thence to Thessalonica, where Paule preached three wekes, from thence he went to Beræa, and there preached with great fruite, till the Iewes came thether from Thessalonica to disquiet him, and from this Berea Paule was conueied to Athens: Nowe let the diligent reader consider all these iourneies with other circumstances, as continuance of time, and distance of place, and Paules abiding in euery place to preache diligently, and then iudge whether the forsayde synode could be held this same yeare that Paule came to Athens: Waying also that many moe notable cities are in these coūtreies Galacia, Mysia, Phrigia, and the rest, visited by Paule but not spokē of in the Actes: Againe considering that the Apostle traueled by lande all moste altogether & that by leasurable iourneyes on foote, he could not finishe thousandes of miles in short time, but ý it were very harde for him to come to Athens the same yere. Besyde al this if it were to be vnderstode as Hierome maketh it, then if ye accompt it in the table, ye shall finde it to be one yeare further, ý is the yeare 52. and it is plaine to be more vntrue, for then by this time Paule had continued a yeare in Corinthe, and so had not bene in Hierusalē in two yeares before:

The conclusion therefore is, that the said counsell could not be holdē according to the accompte made by Hierome, and therfore S. Paules wordes must be vnderstoode as I sayde before, namely of fourtene yeares after his conuersion: and then it is euident that Peter was yet in Hierusalem in the yeare 49.

But to proceede: it may be demaūded, where Peter was from the time of his deliuery out of pryson at Hierusalem to the time of this synode: that is from the fourth yeare of Claudius to the seueuth yere of his raigne. Perhaps Peter went to Rome at some time betwene those yeares. Nicephorus

The first booke of the

Nicepho. li. 1. cap. 21.

phorus sayth, that in the fifth yere of Claudius Peter was at Hierusalem, at the death of the virgin Mary. But if we weigh diligently the history of the scripture, conferring one place with an other, it shall appeare that although it be not specified in the actes, yet Peter was at Antioche in this time. For Paule in the secōd to the Gallathians saith, that Peter came to Antioche, whiche could not be at any time before this time of his deliuery out of pryson as may appeare by the former part of this discourse. Againe diuerse reasons there are, whiche moue me to thinke that it was before the tyme of this counsell: for first Peter being at Antioche Paule sayth of him self, that he reproued Peter euen to his face, because that he did eate with the Gentils, till certaine came from Iames from Hierusalem, and then Peter being afrayde to offende those circumcised, did shrinke away from the Gentils. And the rest of the Iewes yea and Barnabas also fell into the same dissimulation with them. This dissembling of Peter is one reason to proue that it was before the counsell, for it semed to Peter a doubtfull matter, whether he might be conuersaunt with the Gentils, whiche if it had bene as it was afterwarde by the counsell determined, that circumcision was not necessary, then had Peter bene out of doubt what to do therein, and would haue delt plainely according to the truth which he had knowen manifestly: Agayne if it had bene after the counsell, the matter being discussed and agreed vpon, Peter should not haue had any cause to dissemble for feare of offending them in that point, that came from Iames: neyther neded he to haue mistrusted that they would mistike of that, whiche should haue bene allowed by the churche: neither would Peter haue regarded more their vniust offēce, then the decre of the counsell. Last of all in the beginning of the 15. of the Actes Luke maketh mencion of suche that came from Hierusalem and troubled the churche at Antioche about circumcision, and howe Paule and Barnabas stoode against them, and hereupon ensued the said counsell. And thus it appeareth that Peter was at Antioch at this time, and hetherto therfore to the yeare of the incarnacion 49 he came not within a thousand miles of Rome.

¶ Anno Domini 50. and 51.

IN the latter yeare of these twayne being the ninth yeare of Claudius, al the Iewes (as is proued before) were banished from Rome: whiche ouerthroweth the establishing of Peters bishopricke for that yeare.

Orof. lib. 7 cap. 6.

And as for the former yeare by their owne stories it semeth not to be the time of his comming, for at his first cōming Simon Magus as Platina reportes, was in suche honour at Rome through the admiration of his sorcery, that he was honoured as a God: for a piller was set vp betwene two bridges, whereupon it was written, Simoni sancto Deo, To Simon the holy God: so that Peter had a great cōflict ere he could roote out the credit of Simon Magus, and plant the Gospell and Iesus Christe in the hartes of the Romaines, whiche by the testimony of Platina he did so effectually ere he left, that in the ende Simon Magus being brought to contempt, Simon Peter was reuerēced and honoured almoste like a God. All this asketh more time & leasure to be brought to passe, then Peter could hetherto obtayne in Rome.

Concerning these former two yeares this may be sayde briefely. Platina and the rest of the Romaine registers doe auoutche that Peter after he left Hierusalem, went to Antioche and continued there byshop seuen yeares, or as some other thinke fiue yeares at the least, or he came to Rome. This being allowed of them for a manifest truthe on the one side, and it being euident by the scripture by the premisses, that this bishoprike at Antioche could not be established at the vttermoste tyll the yeares 49. it foloweth by their accompt, that it is sure, that for these yeares 52. & 53.

being

The first booke of the

being within the compasse of the forenamed fyue yeares, Peter was not at Rome but at Antioche, nothing nearer to Rome then is Hierusalem.

¶ Anno 52, 53, and 54.

Touching the last yeare of these that is the yeare 54. and the twelth yeare of Claudius, it is euident that Peter was not bishop at Rome, for then Paule wrote his epistle thether to the Romains, in the sixtenth chapter wherof he endeth his epistle with particular salutacions to xviii. persones by name, beside priuate housholdes: and amõg those xviii. eight or nine were women, and yet there is no mention made of Peter, surely if Peter had gone thether before the wryting of this epistle, so that Paule might haue then thought that he had bene there, Paule would not so haue neglected the worthy Apostle among the rest, onlesse he should seeme to make lesse accompt of him in the churche then of women: if therfore the epistle were nowe written it is probable, Peter was not nowe at Rome. But it is apparent inough that the epistle was written at this time. Paule in the xv. chapter and the 24 verse to the Romains promiseth that he would come to Rome, but excuseth him selfe that hee came not presently, for nowe (saieth he) I am going to Hierusalẽ, so that hereby it semeth to be written in his iourney at some time going to Hierusalem. But it is nedefull to consider at what time especially this was because he went thether fiue seueral times as it appeareth, first in the ninth, secondly in the twelfth, thirdly in the xv. fourthly in the xviii. fiftly and last that is mencioned in scripture in the xxi. chapter of the Actes. And touching the first three times, it could not be at any of those voiages, because Paule had not yet met with Timothe, for he founde him not as it is shewed in the sixtenth of the actes, til after his thirde comming from Hierusalem, from the synode: but at the writing of this epistle Timothie was in his cõ-

company

panie, for in the ende of his epistle he sendeth commendations in the name of Timothie. Then of those two ascen- Roman. 16.
dings after his acquaintaunce with Timothie, it is plaine
that it could not be that he wrote it at the first time mentioned in the 18 of the Actes, for in the 18. verse of the same
chapter, ere Paule returned to Hierusalem it is saide that
he departed from Corinthe to Syria, and Priscilla and A-
quila, went with him to Ephesus, where he left them and
would not stay being thereto requested, because he hasted
to Hierusalem, whether he went immediatly: At this ascen-
ding to Hierusalem, this epistle semeth not to be written,
because in the 16. chapiter thereof he sendeth cōmendaciōs
to Aquila and Priscilla, who were with him in the moste   Act. 18.
part of this iourney, and almoste two yeares before continually at Corinthe, who parting from Paule went not to
Rome as he knewe, but stayed at Ephesus, where he lefte
them promising to retourne thether to them. But if any
make this obiection, that because of these salutacions to
Aquila and Priscilla this epistle might be written before
they came from Rome, at some time of Paules going to
Hierusalem, this is aunswered with that whiche I haue
noted before, that it could not be so, because Paule was
not then acquainted with Timothie, with whome he met
but euen lately before he came to Corinthe, and went not
to Hierusalem, from the time that he founde Timothie till
nowe, that he left Aquila and Priscilla at Ephesus: the cō-
clusion therefore is, that this epistle was written to Rome
at the last time that Paule went vp to Hierusalem, and by
that time might Aquila and Priscilla be retourned to Rome: Beside all this, in the 19. of the Actes & the 20. verse,
Luke sayth that Paule purposed through the spirite after
he had walked through Macedonia and Achaia to go to
Hierusalem, saying: after I haue bene there I must go to
sē Rome. here he semeth to be first (that is mēcioned) mindfull of Rome, and this was at his last going to Hierusalē:
But

The first booke of the

But conferre this place with his owne wordes in the xv. chapter and 23. verse of his epistle, and it will plaine appeare that the same epistle was written at this time aboue named, his wordes be these:

I haue longed many yeares to se you, when soeuer I go into Spayne I wil come to you &c. But nowe I go to Hierusalem to minister to the saintes: for it hath pleased Macedonia and Achaia, to imparte somewhat to the poore saintes at Hierusalem, &c. As soone as I haue dispatched this &c. I wil go from hence into Spayne.

Finally Paule mistrusting the crueltie of the Iewes againſt him at this time more then heretofore, and that truly as it fell out, Actes the 21. desireth the Romaines earnestly to praye for him, that God would deliuer him from those rebelles whiche were in Iudea. All the whiche I alleadge to testifie against the iudgemēt of diuers other that this epistle by moste presumpciōs was writtē the last time of Paules going to Hierusalem, whiche was in the twelft yeare of Claudius, the 54. yeare of the incarnatiō: for Luke testifieth that Paule was two yeare there prysoner before that Fœlix the president of Iudea departed, & Festus came in his steade: who was sent thether by Nero in the beginning of his raigne immediatly vpon the death of Claudius, who departed in the 14. yeare of his Empier, as Iosephus testifieth Antiquit. lib. 20. cap. 5. Again in the same place Iosephus sheweth that in the xi. peare of Claudius, Fœlix was made Liuetenaunt of Iudea, who as it appeareth by Tertullus oracion against Paule, Acts the 24. had bene in Iudea at the least a yeare ere Paule came thether, so that considering he came thether in the xi. yeare, and taried but to the xiiii. yeare of Claudius, and Paule was prysoner two yeares before his departure, it falleth out that Paule came to Hierusalem about the xii. yeare of Claudius, and that the epistle was written to Rome the same yeare, and finally that this yeare Peter had not his prerogatiue

gatiue papall at Rome. And of this iudgement is Caluine saiyng, þ this epistle to the Romaines semeth to be written foure yeares before that Paule came to Rome. Institutі. cap. 8. sectione. 101.

Furthermore S. Ambrose vpon the Epistle to the Romaines saith, that he hath red in certaine olde bookes that at the sending of this Epistle Narcissus whom with his familp Paule saluteth, was then the Seniour of the congregacion at Rome: Ergo not Peter.

Anno. 55. 56. 57. 58.

IN the seconde yeare of Nero, being the 58. yeare of the incarnacion, Paule came to Rome by the testimonie of Vspergensis: In Nerone: & Eusebius li. 2. cap. 21. At which time it is euident that Peter was not byshop according to the Romaine bragge: for whē Paule came to Rome, Luke being then with him saith, that the brethren hearing of vs came forth to mete vs &c. but there is no mention made of Peter, neither comming nor sending to Paule. The thirde daye after Paule sent for the chiefe of the Iewes, reasoning with them about the faith, who aunswered him thus. We will heare what thou doest thinke: for we knowe that this sect is spoken against euery where: When Paule had ended his sermon, the Iewes fell at variaunce about it, for some beleued, and some beleued not. This aunswere and doing of the Iewes sheweth, that they had heard but litle of Chriſte, till thr comming of Paule: nothing so muche as they should haue heard and knowen, if Peter beinge (by faith and promise their peculier Apostle) had bene bishop in Rome these twelue yeares since the fourth of Claudius, or but at any time within these foure yeares since the epistle of Paule was sent to Rome. Neither can it be excused to saye, that he might be bishop, and yet not medle with preaching to the Iewes, but exercise him selfe in conuerting the Gentiles, this excuse cannot take place, for if Peter had

Act. 28.

B bene

The first Booke of the

bene in Rome, he ought chiefly to haue conferred with the Iewes: for as Paule saith in the ninth verse of the seconde to the Galathians, that by promise Paule was appointed Apostle to the Gentiles, and Peter to the Iewes, & therefore as we se that Paule discharged his dutie in that point to the Gentiles, so is it to be thought, that Peter did likewyse to the circumsized, as partly appeareth by his firste epistle written namely to the dispersed Iewes in Pontus, Galatia, Capadocia, Asia, and Bithynia, vnto the whiche thing Eusebius lib. 3 cap. 4. thinketh he did wholly addict him selfe: And therfore it is not likely that Peter hetherto had any suche prerogatiue in Rome as the Pope dreameth of.

Anno. 59. and 60.

Act. 28.

IT appeareth that for these twoo yeares Peter came not yet to his dignitie, for Paule cōming prisoner to Rome, did continue there as Luke testifieth, twoo yeares, all the whiche time saieth Nicephorus, he liued by the labour of his handes, lib. 2. cap. 3. If Peter had bene at Rome as Platina would haue him in Pontificall dign●●● woulde haue prouided so, that Paule should not haue ●●● in suche distresse: But it is manifest, that he was not there all this time: by those epistles that were nowe written by Paule from Rome: For in those epistles there is no mencio made of Peters being with him. In the epistle to the Galathians Paule being compelled to confirme the authoritie of his doctrine and Apostleship, whiche some sought to deface, speaketh muche of former acquaintance betwene him and Peter, howe he came to Hierusalem, Act. 9. to se Peter: And howe he reproued him at Antioche &c. And yet he maketh no mencion of his being with him at this time, especially when Peters testimony by subscription or otherwyse might moste haue confirmed Paules cause, and haue testified his doctrine to be as autenticall, as that whiche the other Apostles taught. Whiche oportunitie if Paule

Galat. 1

should

should haue omitted, when it might both haue stoode hym in steede, and might best haue bene obtained, it should haue geuen greater occasion, to encrease the discredit & mistrust of Paules function & preaching: And this would the wise and carefull Apostle haue considered, who omitted no opportunitie to the furtheraunce of the Gospell. &c.

Againe by the latter Epistle to Timothie, wrytten at Paules latter impryfonnement in Rome, as Eusebius. li. 2 cap. 21. testifieth, it appeareth that Peter was not with hym at the time of his former captiuitie by these woordes: In my first defence (meaning when he aunswered for hym selfe first before Nero) no man assisted me. If Peter had bene there, surely Paule should not haue had cause thus to complayne, onles Peters charitie had waxen so colde that he would forsake his fellowe Apostle. Which if it had bene so (as I dare not imagine it) then woulde Paule haue noted him by name to Timothie as he did Demas, Hymeneus, and Philetus. If he had succoured him, he woulde haue bene so defull to make thankefull report thereof, as he did of Onesimus and diuers other, Aquila and Priscilla: Furthermore, ẏ Epistle to the Colossians was also written at this tyme as it appeareth by mencion made of Demas, who nowe was with Paule, but afterwarde forsoke hym, as appeareth in the seconde to Timothie. Beside that by Onesimus, (who was with Paule onele in his first captiuitie, and caried these letters to Colossa) it is playne that it was written at this time, and yet among all other that are there named Peter is put vp in silence.

Timoth. 2. cap. 4.

Tim. 2. 4. Rom. 18.

The Epistle beginneth, Paule and Timothie, if Peter had bene there he had bene added also.

Finally, S. Luke being all this time of imprisonment with Paule, and continuing his story till the end of Paules imprisonment. for so he concludeth the history of the Actes, saying that Paule continued two whole yeres in a place whiche he had hyred in Rome, receiuing all that came in

B ij
vnto

The firſt Booke of the

vnto him preaching with all libertie, and teaching thoſe things that were in Chriſt Jeſus, and no man forbad him. Thus doth Luke teſtifie of Paule, and yet he ſpeaketh not one woordes that Peter ſhould thē be there, or ỹ he had bene there at any time, neither that he ſhould come thether at any time after. Thus are foure yeares of Neroes raigne paſſed, and yet is Peter not raigning to this time in his dioceſſe whereof he toke poſſeſſion (by the Romiſhe regiſters) fourtene yeares ſince.

¶ From the yeare 60. to the yeare 67.

IN the yeare of thincarnation 60. Paule as is ſayde, was priſoner at Rome, who for the tyme of his aboue there, ſo planted the Goſpell, that at his departing from thence he left great fruite therof, and ſuche in deede as if Peter had ſucceded Paule within two, three, or foure yeres, and there ſupplied the roume of a byſhop, Cornelius Tacitus ſpeaking of the eſtate of the Chriſtians in Rome about the yeare 67. being but ſeuen yeares after Paules departure, ſhould not haue had cauſe ſo ſoone to ſaye as he doth, ỹ by that tyme the Chriſtian Religion was repreſſed: For Vſpergenſis ſaith, that in the 67. yere, Nero did ſet Rome on fier, of the whiche Cornelius Tacitus writing, lib. 15. Auguſtæ hiſtoriæ, ſayth: Ergo abolédo rumori Nero ſubdidit reos. &c. Therfore Nero (to ſtop the rumour of his ſetting the citie on fier) ſuborned giltie perſons, and executed with ſtrange puniſhment, thoſe whome the vulgar people deteſting for their wickednes, doth call Chriſtiãs. That miſcheuous ſuperſtition being repreſſed till nowe, brake out againe, &c. Therfore firſt they were taken that confeſſed it, afterward by their accuſatiõ an houge multitude, not ſo much for that they were gilty of fyreing the citie as for hatred, are condemned, and were put to death with great deſpite, ſome encaſed in the ſkinnes of wylde beaſtes, that they might bee torne in peces with

dogges,

dogges, some crucified, some were burned to giue light in the night time. &c. These are the woordes of Tacitus, notwithstanding, as it appeareth he was a blasphemer of the name of Christe. By these woordes of his it appeareth that nowe Christianitie began to reuiue, and that nowe it was quenched: which argueth plaine that from the former time of Paules departure til this time, Peter had not supplied in Rome the place of a preaching pastour and diligent bishop. And seing this broyle against the Christians, began now to be so hotte not in al places, but especially in Rome, howe could Peter sit quietly in this citie as bishop thereof and not be fyred out with his flocke: but they saye all that he lyued after this tyme about three yeares, for this was done in the eleuenth yeare of Nero, who raigned almoste fiiii. yeares, and Peter was martyred in the last yeare of Nero, as they saye all. If this reuiuing of the Gospel was by Peters meanes, why would Nero spare him being the head: if Peter escaped by flying, then he shewed him selfe to be an hierling and no true shepeherde that forsaketh his flocke when he seeth the wolfe come.

¶ From the yeare 67. to the 70. of thincarnation.

Nowe are we come to the latter tyme of Nero, in which yeres if Peter were not bishop of Rome, then is it certaine that he was not bishop there at all. But to come to the purpose, Naucler. Volu. 2. generat. 2. and the moste writers as Eusebius. lib. 2 cap. 25 Nicephorus li. 2. cap. 34. Sabellicus Ennead. 7. li. 2. agree that Paule died in the yeare of our Lord 70. the 37. yeare after the death of Christe: But it may sone appeare p Peter was not then byshop at Paules last comming to Rome, for after Paule was come thether he sent for Timothie to come vnto hym, shewing that he had nede of him to come to hym, because he was nowe desolate and had none with hym, Demas had forsaken hym nowe and embraced the worlde, &c. so that if this Epistle were not written at the firste imprisonment of Paule, but

B iii   at this

The first Booke of the

at this latter time, then was not Peter yet estalled in his Diocese, for if he had bene in Rome in his pontificall dignitie, I thinke Paule should not haue bene dryuen to sende to Ephesus 1000. miles frō Rome for Timothie to bryng Marke to come to minister to him. In the ende of this secōd Epistle to Timothie, Paule sendeth commendations from diuers, but none from Peter.

There are xiiii. Epistles whereof Paule and Seneca beare the name, the one wryting to the other at this later impryfonnement, and yet among them all nothing is saide of Peter, and yet by occasion he might easely haue bene mencioned in them, if he had bene then in Rome. But if by this time Peter were not yet Pope of Rome, there is no tyme left for him to come to enioye it during the raigne of Nero, till whose death this present persecutiō of the church endured with all crueltie.

¶ The death of Peter.

TOuching the death of Peter all wryters do not agree as it is sufficiently declared in the Actes and monumentes fol. 56. in these wordes. They that folow the common opinion and the Popes decrees saye that bothe Peter and Paule suffred both in one daye and one yeare, whiche opinion semeth to be taken out of Dionisius byshop of Corinthe. Hierome in his booke De viris illustr. affirmeth that they suffered both in one daye, but hee expresseth not the yeare, so doth Isiodorus and Eusebius. Prudentius in his Peristephano, noteth that they both were put to death vpon the same daye but not in the same yeare, & saythe that Paule folowed Peter a yeare after. Abdias recordeth that Paule suffered twoo yeares after Peter. Moreouer if it be true whiche Abdias sayth, that after the crucifying of Peter, Paule remayned in his free custody at Rome, mencioned in the 28. of the Actes of the Apostles, whiche was as S. Hierome witnesseth, in the thirde or fourth yeare of Nero, then must it be tenne yeares betwixt the martyrdome

of Peter

of Peter and of Paule, for as muche as it is by all wryters confessed that Paule suffered in the riiii. yeare, which was the last yeare of Nero. Vspergensis saithe that they were both executed in one yeare, but he noteth not that they died in one daye. Sabellicus sayth, both in one yeare & one daye. Some say as Ambrose, that they died together both in one place. But Dionysius saythe otherwyse, that the one bad thother farewel when they were parted asonder goyng to death. Againe, the moste wryters saye that Nero was the cause therof: But Linus saith, Agrippa cōmaunded that Peter should be slayne, because that by his persuasiō foure of the concubines of Agrippa refused to liue any longer in suche vnchast life with the king, therefore for anger he cōmaunded that Peter should be crucified. Finally S. Hierome and Lyra, wryting vpon the 34. verse of the 22. chap. of Mathewe: say that Peter was put to death at Hierusalē by the Iewes, and that Christe prophecied thereof sayinge: Lo I sende you prophetes &c. and some of them ye shall kyll.

Many thinges might be added to disproue this dotage of Peters being bishop at Rome, but because I thinke this to be sufficient, I let passe diuers necessary thinges least I should be ouer tedious. But if any be desirous to se this matter more sufficiently handled, let him reade Vlrichus Velenus, wryting purposely of this in a litle booke called Demonstrationes contra Romani Papæ primatus figmētum. Beside there hath bene of late set forth in Englishe a discours very learnedly and fully entreating hereof, wherin as wel the allegacions of the Papistes for Peters being at Rome substantially confuted, as reasons brought to improue the same. And therefore had it not bene so necessarely appertinent to the argument of this booke, I would rather haue referred the reader to their doyages, then haue spoken any thing thereof. Nowe it remayneth to leaue Peter, and to come to the bishops of Rome.

B iiii

The order

The first Booke of the

The order of this history requireth that everye byshop should be here placed as eche succeded other: But there is suche confusion amonge them that wryte of them, that no man can certainly tell whome to place first, second, thirde, nor fourth. And least it be thought to be spoken rather of affection then otherwyse, I thought good to shewe out of Vspergensis their owne authour, what wrangling and disagreement there is, for those that succeded Peter, which though it be somwhat long, yet is it necessary to be shewed, that it may appeare what certaintie they haue of Peter, & those to whome he committed this vniuersall Popedome. The wordes of Vspergēsis in the life of Claudius be these.

,, Touching the succession of the Romaine byshops, their
,, order, and the tymes, wherein they raigned from the be-
,, ginning, diuerse men thinke diuersly: whose opinions I wil
,, here briefly set downe, &c. Some wryte whereunto the ecclesiasticall history agreeth, that after the death of Peter sitting at Rome chiefe of the Churche xxv. peares. Linus did next take the gouernement vpon him. And when he had ruled xii. peares, in the second yeare of Titus, he lefte it to Anacletus, who also after other xii. peares gaue it to Clement, whiche semeth to be in the xiii. yeare of Domician. Clement after nine yeares suffered vnder Traian. After him in the fourth place, came Euaristus, the nexte was Alexander, and then Sixtus, and so forth. But other wryte that Linus and Cletus, were both vnder Peter (as his vicars or curates) and that Peter as soone as he had taken the Papacy vpon him, did appointe Linus in his steade to gouerne the churche, whereby he him selfe might the better folowe his function of preaching: and that he departing after twelue yeres, Peter did substitute Cletus in his place, who also dying after twelue yeres, euen the same yere that Peter suffered vnder Nero. Then Peter committed his seate to Clemēt, giuing to him and his successours power to bynde and loose, whome Anacletus succeded in the tyme of Do-

of Domician, then folowed Euaristus, &c. But because
these accomptes do not agree, let vs consider wherein they
differ, and so trie whiche semeth more credible. Therefore
if Linus left Anacletus, and he Clemens, then is Clement
thrust out of the beadroll of Popes, whose reuerence is so
great among all Churches, that he is not only mentioned
among martyrs, but also in the Canon of the masse, and in
the Letany or procession, is placed betwene Linus and Clemens. But if after Linus, Cletus be placed, and then Clemens, then Euaristus, then Alexander, &c there is no place
for Anacletus to get in. And Beda in his Martyrtologie,
that Anacletus was the fourthe after Peter, and suffered
vnder Domician, making Linus first, Cletus second, Clemens thirde, and Anacletus fourth. But if Anacletus be
placed after Clement, and as Beda sayeth, died vnder Domician, then cannot it holde that his predecessour Clemens
should suffer vnder Traian, because it may euidently be proued that he suffered vnder Domician, if his successour A-
nacletus bee not denied to suffer vnder the same Emperoure. Furthermore, if Linus and Anacletus, as some
saye, or Linus and Cletus, as other saye: did bothe rule
twelue yeares a peece after the death of Peter, dyinge
the xiiii. yeare of Nero, then it aryſing to 24. yeares, it falleth out that the latter of them should suffer in the xii. of
Domician, & so Clemens could not receaue power to binde
and loose, neither the seate of Peter. Whiche opinion also
is cōfirmed of diuerse: and to this is added that Dionyſius
Areopagita hasting from Athens to Rome againste the
martyrdome of the Apostles Peter and Paule, but comming a little to late, and sone after their deathes, did there
finde Clemens his scholefellowe bishop of Rome. &c. Who
sent the same Dionyſius into Fraunce to preache: But it is
saide that this Dionyſius was martyred Anno domini. 96
whiche is the xiiii. peare of Domician, and before his death
he had continued long, & had done very muche in Fraūce,
and yet

The first booke of the

and yet it is sayde that Clemens who sent him thether, was made byshop but the twelfth yeare of Domician. Againe, the booke of the passion of Pope Alexander saith, that Clemens was ye first after Peter, for so it is there written. In the fift place after Peter came Alexander. But if it were the second from Peter, then it followeth that Cletus being before Clement, and Anacletus after him be pushed out, because Alexander must be the fifte: Namely Peter first, Linus seconde, Clement thirde, Euariste the fourth, and Alexander the fifte: For otherwyse Alexander cannot be the fift from Peter, because if Linus be the seconde fro Peter, and Cletus after Anacletus, be placed before Clement, Alexander shalbe the sixt: But if Cletus be before Clement, and Anacletus after him, then shall Alexander be the seuenth, vnlesse Clement be the second after Peter.

Thus farre doth Vspergensis wander in this maze: and thus it appeareth what certaintie the Churche of Rome hath of her beginning, of Peters being there, & of bequeathing his supremacy, to whome neither they, nor any other for them can tell. But yese, howe many bishops here wrastle for the first place, and howe they are tossed from the first to the seconde, and an other whyle hoisted to the third and fourth place, yea and some time shoued cleane out of place. So harde a thing it is, to finde a sure man, that for the beginning of this history a man may wel doubt with whome to beginne, but we must be content in this hurly burly, either to cast lottes to finde out the ring leader, or els to take and set an order among them, though perhap not the same wherein they liued, yet as if it were the same. And if any of the good byshops lese his place of senioritie, we must desire him to take it paciently, and to blame the negligence of their parishioners and successours of Rome, who (because nature vseth not to ascende but to discend) so muche regarded them selues, and their children, with the tyme present, that they forgat their forefathers (if these were they)

they) and the tyme past.

¶ The first face of the Romaine churche vnder Heathen Emperours.

For the first sorte of Romayne byshops, that is from Linus to Syluester, they liued continually vnder persecutions. For as Eusebius sheweth, from the yeare of our lord 67. till the time of Constantine, being about thre hundred yeares, were tenne persecutions. The first by Nero, with al rigour and crueltie that might be, wherof Hierome in his epistle to Cramatius and Heliadorus, saith: that there wer fiue thousand Christians martyred euery daye in the yeare sauing the first daye of Ianuary: For they were persecuted by Nero his commaundement in all places with diuerse & straunge kinde of tormentes, and reprochefull villanies not to be mencioned.

The seconde persecution was moued by the Emperoure Domician, Anno. 96. who was a man so much delighted in killing & murthering, that as the prouerbe went of him, he would not haue a flye aliue with him, for being as he coueted moste, solitary by him selfe in his pallaice, he vsed to catche and kill all the flies that came in his waye. Againe he was so hawty aboue measure, that he woulde nedes be counted a God, and therefore it may easely be iudged, what rest the Christians had in his time.

The thirde persecution was raysed by Traianus Anno 100. so bloudely that euen the Heathen Pliny moued with pitie, bewayled it vnto the Emperoure.

The fourth persecution was styrred Anno. 167. by the Emperour Marcus Antonius, lasting long vnder sondrie Emperours vnmercifully.

The fift persecution was caused by Seuerus the Emperour with all seueritie, forbidding that any more should be baptized, purposing so to roote out the name of Christias, Anno. 205.

The sixth persecutiō was enkindled by Maximin⁹. 237.

The

The first booke of the

The seuenth was enflamed by Decius the Emperour, Anno. 250. as terrible as the rest.

The eight was broched by diuerse parsones in diuerse places. As by Galerius Maximus and Paternus, proconsuls in Aphrica, by Emilianus Liuetenaunt in Egypt, beside diuers other great magistrates in Rome & els where, Anno. 259.

The ninth by the Emperour Aurelianus, Anno. 278.

The tenth and last, as the last acte of a tragedy, was brought vpon the churche with all kinde of saueige crueltie without pity or compassion by the bloudy tyrant Dioclesian, and continued by other till the comming of the noble Constantine. And this was the state of the churche vnder the Emperours of Rome for these yeares. Nowe let the reader iudge of what maiestie and countenaunce the prelates in this time were like to be, of what wealth & abilitie to maintaine a pompous estate. Or what it was, that might moue them to make any suche ambicious decrees as haue bene falsely forged on them. And hereby discerne the after age in the Romaine churche to this daye, howe farre they differ from this, as shall appeare.

(.·.)

THE FIRST COM-
PANIE OF ROMAINE BISHOPS
being in nomber to Syluester the first, xxxij. all whiche were godly and faithfull pastours, farre from all worldly pompe and glory, either in pride of attier, as miter and pall, or of hawty and ambicious title of Christes generall vicar, but paynfull preachers of the Gospell, with all humilitie and constant martyrs in the ende.

1. Linus the first bishop of Rome as some thinke.

He first bishop was one Linus, a Thuscane borne, a man of pure and godly life, according to the example of the Apostles, who for preaching the Gospell, suffered martyrdome vnder Saturninus the Consull, while Vespasian raigned. Diuerse fansies are fathered vpon this man, as that he decreed by the commaundement of Peter being dead, that no woman should enter into the temple bareheaded: whiche cannot be, for there were no temples in Rome til the time of Constantine the Emperour, for Christian Congregations. And Mantuan Pastor. 1. testifieth that they were fayne for feare of the tyrantes, to forsake towne and City, and to lyue in these dayes in desertes, woodes, and mountaynes, whiche maye bewraye the dotage of Platina and other who charge these first godly martyrs with diuerse supersticions diuised by other long after.

2 Ana-

The first booke of the

2. Anacletus the first.

A Nacletus borne at Athens, by Irenæus is placed next after Linus. He was of an excellent and feruent spirite, and of great learning, planted the churche of God with daily labour. He was put to death by Domitia. Anno. 94. Certaine epistles and decrees stuffed full of falsehoode and vntruethes, ioyned with ambicion, touching the ordering & primacie of bishops, are counterfaited in his name. But Flaccus Illyricus, in the first Centurie, doth so rip the seames of them that euery man may perceiue what botched stuffe it is. Beside Mantuan saith, that he liued long not in any suche estate, to haue occasion to wryte of suche matters, but in caues and dennes, among woodes.

3. Clement the first.

The next was Clement a Romaine, who aduaunced the Gospell by continuall preaching and good deedes. They forge of him that he did deuide Rome into parishe churches who had scant a lodging in it: Againe, they slaunder him that he made orders in Rome for confirmation of children, for masses, apparell, vestures, and popishe ceremonies: and yet he sylly man, was of so smale power and authoritie to establishe these thinges in Rome, that he was a long tyme banished by the Emperour, to hewe marble stones, and at the length with an anchour about his necke, was cast into the sea, Anno. 102. so writeth Mantuan Fasto. 11.

4. Euaristus the first.

EVaristus a Grecian, was especially endewed with the grace of God, whereby in the time of persecutiō he ceased not to encrease the churche of Christe by his diligent preaching, till he was martyred vnder Traian. An. 110.

5. Alex-

5. Alexander the first.

ALexander a Romaine, did trauaile painfully, both to preache and baptize: He suffered great tormentes till he died thereof vnder one Aurelianus president to the Emperoure. Anno. 121.

6. Sixtus the first.

SIxtus a Romaine, did both preache diligently, and did many good workes. He beautified the churche with godly deedes, being euer vigilant and carefull for his flocke, and died for it Anno. 129.

These three good byshops are slaundered with certaine popishe decrees, as touching consecrating of the Clergy, holy water, and holy vessels, but olde verses made of these times, do testifie that they were not at suche leasure to furnishe, or rather disguise the churche with these superstitious ceremonies. Thus do some wryte of these tymes,

Vrbibus antiqui patres fugiere relictis.&c.
The tyrantes did our auncetours compell,
To flye to woodes and not in townes to dwell.

7. Telesphorus the first.

TElesphorus a Grecian, was a worthy man for learning and godly life: He bare witnesse of Christe moste faythfully, both by his wordes and death vnder the Emperoure Antoninus, who executed him. Anno. 140.

He is slaundered to haue decreed that thre masses should be sayde on Chrisimas daye: And yet at this time the masse was vnhatched, yea the dame thereof (except Sathan the bell sier) was (as a man maye saye) not yet an egge in the neaste of that vncleane byrde. Neyther was the superstitiō of making difference of dayes yet crepte into the churche
being

The first booke of the

being contrary to the doctrine of Paule, Galath. 4. But suche superstitious fasting as afterward choked the churches, was not diuised by this bishop, but rather by Montanus the heretike, who beside this made it lawfull to breake wedlocke, and to dissolue the band of matrimony.

8. Higinus the first.

Higinus borne in Athens, being of a Christian philosopher made a byshop, discharged the dutie of a good pastour and painfull labourer in the Lordes haruest, and at length was put to death cruelly, Anno. 144. It is reported that he wrote out of a caue, where he hid him selfe, an Epistle, touching God, and the incarnation of the sonne of God.

9. Pius of Aquilia.

Pius borne in Aquilia, is reported to haue done many godly dedes in the church vnder Antonius Verus: And in the end watered the churche of Christe with his bloud in martyrdome, Anno. 159.

10. Anicetus.

Anicetus a Sirian, was a diligent pastour of the church of Rome till he was martyred, Anno. 169.

11. Sother.

Sother borne in Campania, as the valiaunt souldiour of Christe Iesus, serued vnder his spirituall banner in the time of Antonius Cōmodus, He employed him self moste diligently to bring the soules of the baptized to saluation in Christe, both by doctrine and example of life. And in the ende confirmed the Gospell, whiche he had faithfully preached,

Pageant of Popes.   Fol. 17

ched with his bloud in martyrdome, Anno. 177.

12. Eleutherius.

ELeutherius a Grecian, was also a carefull and vigilant
pastour: in his time the persecution of the tyrants did
somewhat decrease, & many godly writers bestowed great
paynes to wryte sondry learned bookes against diuerse heresies and heretikes whiche then enfected the churche. And
among other this Eleutherius did also defende against Ti-
tianus, that no vsuall trade of life is to be reiected. But not
withstanding that the stormes of persecution were somewhat calmed in his time, because many of the Romayne
nobilitie beleued on Christe, yet Masseus saythe, he was
beheaded, Anno. 191.

13. Victor.

VIctor borne in Aphrica, did succeade Eleutherius. This
man was the first that when the storme of persecution
was calmed, vsurping authoritie vpon straungers, sought
to haue an oar in an other mans boate. In the former byshops (saith Vincelius) the spirite abounded, but in these y
folowe the temptacion of fleshe and bloud preuayled. Poli-
crates bishop of Ephesus, and Iræneus bishop of Lions, did
bouldly reproue this Victor, for exempting his bretheren
in Asia from the communiō, because in keping Easter day,
they folowed not the vse of the churche of Rome: So that
the churche was then rent in twayne, by meanes of his obstinacy, he died Anno. 203.

14. Zepherinus.

ZEpherinus was a Romaine borne, a man as wryters do
testifie, more addicted with all endeuour to the seruice
of God, then to the cure of any worldly affayres.   Where
C   as before

The first Booke of the

as before his time the wine in the celebrating the cōmuniō was ministred in a cup of woode, he first did alter that, and in steade thereof brought in cuppes or chalices of glasse: And yet he did not this vpon any supersticion, as thinking woode to be vnlawefull, or glasse to be more holy for that vse, but because the one is more comly and semely, as by experience it appeareth then the other. And yet some wooden doultes do dreame, that the wooden cuppes were chaunged by him, because that part of ye wine, or as they thought, the royall bloud of Christe, did soake into the woode, and so it can not be in glasse. Surely soner may wine soake into any woode then any witte into those winie heads, that thus both deceiue them selues, and slaunder this Godly martyr. Who in the yeare of our lorde 220. suffered martyrdome vnder Aurelius. In the time of this Zepherinus the Artemonites, were a secte of vaine Philosophicall diuines, who as our late scholemen did corrupt the scripture with Aristotle and Theophrastus, turning all into curious and subtile questions.

15. Calixtus the first.

CAlixtus borne at Rauenna, when persecution began to wexe hotte againe, did like a constant Christian, hide him selfe with many moe in a certaine place on the farther side of Tiber. In these daies saith Platina, al thinges were kept close and hidden, because the persecution was so great euery where, yea, their churches and places of assembly, were in corners and caues for the moste parte. But Anno 226. this Calixtus was apprehended by the commaundement of Alexander Seuerus, and was beaten with roodgiels, pent in prison, afterwarde hurled headlong out of a wyndowe, and then his bodie was drowned in a depe pitte.

16. Vrbanus.

Vrba-

Urbanus a Romaine, liued vnder that moste lasciuious wreatche Heliogabalus the Emperoure, and with his sinceritie of life, and excellencie in learning, he drewe many men on all sides to the Gospell. He was oftentimes banished the citie for the Christian faithe, but being secretlye brought in againe by the faithfull, he was martyred by cõmaundement of Seuerus, Anno. 233.

17. Pontianus.

Pontianus a Romaine, in the time of the sayde Emperour Seuerus, being one of Christes ministers, and a distributer of Gods misteries, suffered both banishement, & punishement for the Gospell, and the churche sake. For when they ran thicke to him to heare him preache ye worde, by the princes commaundement, being set on by the Idolatrous priestes, he is caried frõ Rome to the Isle Sardinia, where after many miseries and sore tormentes, he was put to death, Anno. 239.

18. Antheros.

Antheros was borne in Grece, a man of God if any wer: he preached Christe stoutely, euen vnder the tyranny of Maximinus the Emperour. This byshop prouided first of all that the actes of martyrs should be diligently writtẽ by notaries: least the remembraunce of Gods hardie souldiours should be lost with their liues. This Antheros in the yeare 243. did with his bloude beutifie the churche, whiche with his woorde he had fed before.

19. Fabian.

After him came Fabius a Romain borne, who (as Eusebius witnesseth) as he was returning home out of the fielde, and with his contrimen present to electe a newe by-

C ij   shop

The first Booke of the

shop, there was a pygeon sene standing on his head, and sodenly he was created pastour of the churche, whiche he loked not for. While he liued, he him selfe sawe that the recordes of martyrs should be written, and that burying places should be prepared for them: who afterwarde vnder Decius (that afterwarde dealt cruelly with his owne brethren) ended his life with most glorious death, Anno.150.

20. Cornelius.

Cornelius a Romaine, being in the time of Decius, accounted the seueth persecutour of Christe & his church, had a Godly care ouer ye safetie of his neighbours. He entertayned curteously, and restored to the churche, as many as hauing denied Christe in tormentes, did yet repent the of their deede afterward. O the aboundant spirite of Christ that was in this byshop. O worthy minister of the Gospel, for although this man of God Cornelius, was caried away into banishement, yet he neuer fayled the churche of Christ. But as a valiant champion in the maintenance of the truth, did yelde his necke vnto the sworde of Decius.

21. Lucius.

Lucius a Romain, being a faithful seruant in the lordes house, and driuen into banishment by Gallus Hostilianus, the persecutour of Christianitie, was comforted of S. Ciprian by his letters. And at the length after Gallus death, euen by Gods wil retourned to Rome, & enriched ye churche with healthful doctrine, and afterward being purified in the lambes bloud, he pearced the heauenly paradise, being put to death at Valerianus commaundement.255.

22. Stephen.

Stephen a Romaine borne, a man in al pointes iuste and good

Pageant of Popes.　Fol. 19

good and one that was counted worthy to haue the eccle=
siasticall function. Whereupon (as VVicelius saithe) the
churche gaue vs many worthy examples of Prelates, so
longe as they were called but bishops of the citie of Rome.
While Galienus a wicked Emperor raged, Steuen, Anno
257. after he had conuerted many of ye Getiles to the faith of
Christe, loosing his head, was with many other sacrifices
to God, receiuing the crowne of iustice.

23. Sixtus the seconde.

Sixtus the seconde was a Grecian, borne in Athens, he
being of a worldly Philosopher, become Christe his di=
sciple, and of an earthly man, made an heauenly stewarde,
did shine like an ornament of the churche, & as an example
worthy to be folowed. This man also enstructing the peo=
ple in Gods holy woorde, was slayne with many thousands
of martyrs, in the persecution of Decius and Valerius, An.
267. S. Laurence claue vnto this holy byshop vnseperably,
euen to the last tormentes of his life, of whiche twoo the
one was slayne with swearde, the other burnt to death.
Whereof Mantuan in the 8. of his Fast. saith.
These men whose vertues florished by Decius dire decree,
VVere hid with other lockt in chaynes and dungeon
  darke to bee.
In time of this bishop about the yeare of our lorde 260.
one Paule being terrified with the vnmercifull persecutiō
of tyrantes, gat him into wyldernesse and solitary places,
and so became the firste Eremite. For at that time, as Euse=
bius saith, many Christians for feare of death denied their
fayth. Upon this Monkery had his beginning, as Hie=
rome shewes in the life of the same Paule the Eremite.

The beginning of Eremities and Monkes.

24. Dionysius.

Dionysius was a Grecian, whome Pope Damasus cal=
　　　　　　C iij　　　leth a

The first Booke of the

lette a Mouke. He was a worthy man in preaching the faithe, and a notable encreacer of the Christian churche vnder Claudius the seconde. Neither did he want other churches, whiche with the doctrine of truthe did reforme heresies that sprange in those dayes. As appeareth by the churche of Antioche, which calling a counsell in the yeare of our Lorde 273. did conuince of errour Paulus Samosatenus, notwithstanding he him selfe coulde not be there present, because he was olde. Dionysius conuerted to Christianitie the daughter of the Emperour Decius, and Triphonia her mother, with 46. thousand other: And at the length was martyred with them & many other at Salarie gate Anno. 277.

25. Fœlix.

Fœlix a Romain, being a good man and of perfect conuersation, florished in preaching the Gospell, at suche time as Aurelianus did persecute his brethren: While this accursed manslear exercised his tyranny, Fœlix among other martyrs, departed moste happely vnto Christe, that is to saye, from death to life. But to saye that this martyrdome (working their glory) caused temples to be made, & yearely sacrifices to be done therein in their names, it is to open blasphemy. Who will beleue that these holy fathers of the priniatiue churche, would so charely haue suche regarde to kepe stockes and stones, or dead mens bones, in time of so many persecutions, and heresies, as if they had nothing els to doe. But such forgeries vse our Romauistes to maintayne their idolatry.

26. Eutychianus.

Eutychianus borne in Thuscia, being geuen wholy to Godlynes, and commended to the churche for his learning and vertue, sauced many people by preaching the Gospell. This spell. This man (by report) did bury with his own handes, 342. martyrs, and appointed an order for the burying of martyrs, and in the ende he him selfe was made a martyr, Anno. 283. It appeareth that this man did nothing to establishe the fantasticall topes of our age: but the Papistes foarge of him, that he blessed vpon the altar grapes and beanes, and that he buried the dead in purple vestimentes, a deede meete for a Christian martyr.

27. Gaius or Caius.

Gaius borne in Dalmatia, cosen to Dioclesian the Emperour, succeded Eutychianus in preaching the comfortable Gospell, and was a moste worthy president in the churche of God. Carsulanus and Platina, the Popes clawbackes, reporte of this man, that he encreased the dignitie of the Clergie marueilously, by making difference of degrees among them, so that from one degree to an other, they should arise to the estate of a bishop. Furthermore they prattell that he commaunded, that a man in holy orders should not be sewed of prophane men, Pagans, or Heretikes. But who is so fonde to beleue that ye bishops power was so great at Rome at that time, when Pagans them selues bare all the sway, & executed the ciuill lawe? Gaius was in the time of the raigne of the foresayde Dioclesian, vnder whome cruell persecution continued, so that for a great time he lurked in caues and hoales vnder the groud, and had no pontificall pallaice or stately temple. And in the ende being plucked out with his brother Gabinius a maried priest, he was slayne with a sworde.

28. Marcellinus.

Marcellinus was a Romaine, who in the tenth persecution after Nero, was cruelly vexed of the tormentours

The first Booke of the

cours under Dioclesian and Maximinian, being terrified with feare of the paynes, he offered unto the Idols a graine of frankinsens. In those dayes, as Gildas writeth, the scripture where soeuer it was founde, was burnt in the streate, and the chosen shepeheardes of Christes flocke, were slaine with their innocent shepe. But Marcellinus immediatly after his dede, remembring him selfe, reproued Dioclesian to his face, and offred him selfe willingly to death for the truthe of Christe, and striuing valiauntly he preuayled, receiuing the crowne of martyrdome, Anno 303. Hereunto agreeth Mantuan in the life of the sayde Basill.

29. Marcellus.

MArcellus a Romaine, was pastour of the churche, feading it with wisedome and doctrine. And (as I maye saye with the Prophete) a man accordyng to Gods harte, & full of Christian woorkes. This man admonished Maximianus the Emperour, & endeuoured to remoue him from persecuting the sainctes. But the Emperoure being more hardened, commaunded him to be beaten with cogiels, and to be driuen out of the citie, wherefore he entred into the house of one Lucina a widowe, and there he kept the Congregation secretly, whiche the tyrant hearing, made a stable for cattell of the same house, and cōmitted the kepinge of it to the byshop Marcellus. After that he gouerned the churche by wryting Epistles, without any other kynde of teaching, being condemned to suche a vile seruice: And being thus dayly tormented with stinke and noysomenesse, at length gaue vp the ghost, Anno, 308.

30. Eusebius.

EVsebius, a Grecian, being a very Godly man, a doctour and teacher among the Christiās, gouerned the church in the great storme of persecution. He traunpled stoutly in the worde the worde of the Lorde, as well at Rome as els wheare through his countrey, in the time of Maxentius that horrible tyrant, vntill he were destroyed by martyrdome, as Massæus writeth, Anno 309. whereupõ as Mantuan writeth an Aungell sayde to Basill.

Of thinges that are reueald to me Ile make the vnderstãd,
The ioyful dayes of peace draw on, the time is nie at hand
That tyrants rage shal shortned be:er many years be rõne,
This cruel kind that ioyes in bloud shal wasted be & done,
Rome hath beheld her prelats al ẽbrewd in their own gore
Three cruel ones yet shal she se:and then shalbe no more,
The death of next Melchiades shal ende the bloudy age,
His karkas being buried, then peace shal all assuage.

31. Melchiades.

Melchiades an Aphrican, being a man very religious, and a leader of the Christiã flocke, proceaded in preaching the Gospell, and in the affaires of the truthe so farre, vntill he spent his bloud for it vnder Maximinianus Galerius: And in the profession thereof died Anno, 314. Reade the Ecclesiasticall history of Eusebius bishop of Cæsaria, concerning manifolde and vnaccustomed cruell deathes of the sainctes of that time: Cursulanus, Platina, Stella, and other the Popes flatterers, doe falsely father vpon these martyrs whole loades of decrees and lyes, that the lewde inuentions of their ceremonies, might be established by the authoritie of these men. For they are not afraide, for the aduauncement of the Popes crone, with these vnclenly dregs to staine the bloud of sainctes, and defile this beautiful face of the primatiue churche, being through continuall persecution euer agreable to Christe the head therof. But what wyse man can thinke that suche simple ministers and pastours of Gods worde as the bishops then were: dwelling in holes, dennes, and corners, and looking for nothing but

dayly

The first booke of the

dayly death vnder tyrantes, should haue minde of pontificall pompe, stately buildinges, or Papisticall solemnities, when as they had neither churches, nor dwelling houses. The churche as yet obtained no peace: they liued not yet in vnprofitable idlenes, neither had they the chiefe pleasures of the worlde. But those were ye imaginations which, false prophetes, according to their custome, deuised for their bellies sake. But Sabellicus speaking of the saluage persecution of the churche vnder Dioclesian, saythe (allcaging it out of Eusebius) that the Christian flocke was plaged at this time by the iudgement of God, because sinne began to growe vp in the churche aboue measure, and the priestes seemed nowe rather to sauour of tyranny, and not humilitie: and therefore when this persecutiō came, it was rather a reformation of the churche (corrupted by ease and peace) then a scattering thereof: Whereby it semeth that euen then God geuing but a pause of persecution, and whyle tyranny did but staye to breathe it selfe, they began to decline, and growe crooked: yet is it not to be thought that they were caried so farre away, as yet to newefashiō, and transport with maglinges & addicions the Christian religion as the Papistes dreame they did. And thus is the popishe synagoge grōded on vntrutye. But it were a fond matter to beleue these scoffes & toyes contriued for priestes aduauntage, as our forefathers haue done: we should rather trie of what spirites they be, as S. Iohn commaūdeth, whether they be of God or no. Iohn.4. For many false prophetes haue crept into the worlde. Hetherto the pastors were starres shining in the firmament of the churche, as well in life and manners, as in doctrine: and preserued in his right hande, who walked in the middest of the seuen candelstickes. Apocal. 1. Hetherto they were counted Angels, reuealing the euerlasting wyll of almighty God, purely without mans diuices.

.32 Syl-

32. Syluester the first.

After that Melchiades was put to death, Syluester a Romaine, succeded in the ministery of the woorde: but because that the tyrant Maximinus continued his bloudy persecution against the Churche, Syluester was fayne to hide him selfe, and to lyue solitarily in the hille Sóracte. But at the length it pleased God to laye his terrible hand vpon the persecutour Maximinus, forcing the tyrant to reclaime his cruel decrees against the Christians. Touching the death of Maximinus, who among other tyrantes was a Scorpion to the Christians, it is to be noted that Eusebius writeth first in the eight booke and 28. chapter of his ecclesiastical history thus. First in the secrete partes of his body arose an impostume, then in his bowels grewe a fistulowe, within the whiche a great swarme of woormes and magettes, gnawed and deuoured his guttes, wherof arose a noysome stinke, so ranke that no man could by any meanes abide it, beside the ougly & loathsom sight of the soare it selfe: so that some of his phisicions not able for the horror of it to endure to dresse him, were put to death by his cõmaundement. Afterward the disease increasing, all his body was swollen and rankled with it, so that with extremitie of his panges and fainting through honger, he fel down and lay spawling on the grounde. Then all his body by the hande of God, was terribly enflamed and burned exceadingly odious to beholde, so that the scorched fleshe being by little and little eaten awaye, pyned and consumed, he was so disfigured and deformed, & his feauter so baded that a man could discerne no resemblance of his former shape. His gastly and naked carkasse was euen as an image of drye bones. And yet the glowing heate boyled more feruently, so that the marrowe fried out of his bones, and his eyes (all moisture being wasted) dropped out of his head. Thus his limmes and members through scalding heate &

ranke

The first booke of the

ranke disease, rotting one from an other, his body laye miserably as it were a graue to the soule: vntil the tormentes thereof wrested out from his cancred harte to acknowledge Christe Iesus, and to repent his bloudy persecuting the cause of this his woful ende, the last persecutour. Eusebius lib. 10. cap. 8. Furthermore it pleased the almighty to worke so graciously in the hart of the noble Emperour Constantine, that by his procurement the churche at the length obtained peace vniuersally, so that euery mā might safely returne to his owne countrey and citie, whereupon Syluester returned to Rome, and was the firste Romaine byshop that escaped martyrdome. There are many, some indifferent, but moste detestable grosse and fonde decrees, falsely fathered vpō this Syluester, as halowing of Chrismes, geuing of orders, confirming of children, decking of churches, couering of altars, making masse priestes, annoynting and attiring of them: and of making the howsell to be God, called deifying the host, of worshipping and preseruing it. Also touching copes, hoodes, corporals, albes, mitars, palles, cloathes, churching kerchiefes for women, rochettes, sacrifices, ceremonies, chappels, anoyling of the sicke, with a rablement of diuers other Iewishe and Heathen ceremonies. Platina, Polidor Virgill, and other the Popes parasites, slaunder this Syluester, that he tooke vpon him in steade of a golden crowne to weare a mitar, after the Phrygian fashion. Touching certaine miracles whiche are also with like credit, sayde to be done by this Syluester. Mantuan wryteth thus. Fast. lib. 12.

Men talke of many miracles that Syluester hath wrought
But authour yet sufficient hath neuer forth ben brought
Nor witnesse good to proue the same: therfore I let alone
Such things as fables fondly faind: for our religion
Condemneth toyes, and doting dreames: and listeneth
   not to lyes. &c.

This Syluester died a confessour, Anno domini. 334.
                                          Mantuan

Mantuan in his thirde booke of the life of S. Blase, bringeth in an Angell talking with the sayde Blase among other martyrs of the Empyre of the foresayde Constantine, and of the estate of the churche for the time folowyng, of the wickednes that should raigne, both among the Clergie and the people, and finally of the vengeance that should ensue. His wordes are these.

¶ The woordes of the Angell to Blase, concerning Constantine.

THe tyrātes being daunted now a gracious prince shal raigne
In Romain empier, vnder whō the world shal peace obtaine,
And worship Idols olde no more: the mighty Constantine
Shall kepe his court in Thracia, and to the Lorde diuine
Christe Iesus Italy he leaues, and Rome with mountaines seuē.
Then shal the crosse despised earst aduaunced be to heauen,
And far excel the Romain mace, the scepter, & the crown. &c.
¶ Of the euels to come vpon the churche.
But euen vpon this gentle calme there shal alas ensewe
Destruction, such as wel thou mayst with woful wepings rewe,
And poyson ranke shall surely from the hony swete procede,
The sound of ease, the name of peace, are plesant words in dede:
But out alas more wretchednes, more villany, and vice,
More greuous woūds, more shame & wo, shal to the church arise
Euer of this peace, then did of all the bloudy broiles and warre,
For auncient vertue shal decline: and pleasure vaine shal marre,
And spoile the bodies chast of mē through wātonesse & welth,
The lazy mīde shal quayle, & droupe, neglecting heauēly helth
O leude delightes, O wicked guise, O cursed time: I se
The people of their Lord and Christ forgetful quite to be:
I se their vnbeleuing hartes doth treade down and defie
The faith, & hedlong into sinne by thousandes thick they flie,
I se how men are beastes become, and Rome is now transport
Into a stable. &c.
¶ Of the plagues that folowe.
Then shal we heauēly gostes at length most wrathfully be bent
And

The first booke of the

And God shal frowne against those lãdes, whẽ vp to him is sent
The shew of this their wicked age: heauẽ shal shut vp his grace,
And al reliefe frõ earth, whom hell with horrour doth deface.
At wrath of God the noysome starres shal altogether conspire,
And fling down fearcely frõ aboue most fearfull flakes of fire.
And heauẽ shal make his wrath away to daunt & driue to dust,
This saluage kinde of faithlesse folke, and people most vniust.
And mẽ with grim & grisely lookes, with stern & gastly mind
To rise vp from the Northren poale, shalbe by God assind.
The Hunnes, the Gothes, the Vandals, Turkes rude creatures lacking lawe,
Of God and mã to guide and kepe their saluage hartes in awe.
The Christiãs eke amõg thẽ selues shal wrangle braule & iarre,
And as mad dogges one eate anothers hart through ciuil warre
The Romaynes shal destroy the Greekes, the Almaynes waste the Frenche,
VVith more then deadly hate: that one the others power may quenche.
They shall forbeare the Saracens and Turkes.

And thus muche concerning this matter: Nowe let the reader consider that whiche foloweth, whether it agree not to this that Mantuan hath written: If it be true as Mantuan saithe, that Blase had this reuelaciõ, then the estate of Rome folowing this time, was condemned as detestable by the Angell. But if it be but fayned by Mantuan and other, then we se howe they (noting howe farre this latter churche of Rome in her pompe and royaltie swarued from the former in persecution) iudged of it, and yet was Mantuan an Italian Carmelite or whyte Fryar. Thus hath it pleased God, that some of the braunches shoulde both discerne and bewray the loathsomnesse of this wicked tree.

But it shall not be amisse here to adde the saying of Sleidan, talking of this time of Syluester, in his seconde booke of the iiii. Monarches. Then (sayth he) the byshops of Rome began first to be in safetie, for hetherto they were almoste all put to death. From Peter whom they will haue to be the first to this time, they accompt xxxiii. Their decrees are set downe among the

generall

generall counsels, but the moste of them are suche trifles, suche toyes, and so diuers from the scripture, that it is credible that they were deuised by other that came long after. But if it were true that they came from these former prelates, saint Paules wordes may be well applied hereunto being verysied, saying in prophecy, That lost childe and mā of sinne, did euen then beginne to worke the mystery of iniquitie. Coloss. 2.

Anacletus, as some saye, the fourth frō Peter, hath this decree extant in his name, That the Churche of Rome should by the commaundemēt and institution of Christ, be the head of other Churches. Also to Alexander is attributed, that he commaunded that water should be hallowed with salte, to purge the people of sinne, and to dryue awaye the snares of the deuill. But howe muche do these vanities differ from the maiestie of the Apostles doctrine, & from the wryting of Iohn the Euāgelist, who liued almost till the time of these bishops. These two decrees may suffise for wyse men to iudge of the reste, being euen of the self same mould, for the moste part bearing with them an open shewe of ambition. But to returne to the purpose, this Cōstantine, for the loue and zeeale whiche he bare vnto the Churche, did endewe the pastors thereof with many large benefites, rychches, and possessions, that they might with better oportunitie addicte them selues to preache the Gospel. But where as he gaue them an inche, some haue since stollen an elle; fathering vpon him the forged donacion for their supremacy: But of his liberalitie toward the church, Eusebius wryteth at large. He sommoned the first generall counsell at Nicea, wherein the detestable heresie of Arrius was condemned, though it could not be with all so vtterly quenched, but that it did yet afterward enflame again, so ỹ some of the sparcles therof did alight euen in the pontificall seate of Rome sone after, as shall appeare by some of these that follow.

Finis libri primi.

THE SECONDE SORTE OF ROMAINE BIshops, from Syluester to Boniface the thirde.

¶ These bishops persecution being ceased, began to take estate more vpon them then the former, for Constantine and other Christian princes, began of deuociō and zeale to aduaunce the prelates to wealth, and therupon they liuing in wealth and ease, began also to aduaunce thē selues in dignitie aboue the former estate, putting riche mytars on their heades, taking vpon them the name of Archebishops. Also they began by litle and litle to adde their own deuices to Gods seruice, to alter, chop, and chaūge, and make Canons, as liked euery ones fantasie, and so pecemeale began to plante and sowe in Rome the seade of Antichriste, which afterwarde grewe vp to so great pride and abhomination: Thus at the firste in the churche, deuotion bredde wealth, but the doughter choaked the mother, and engendred the mōster ambition, who also like the cursed impe of the bastard her morher, did in the ende deuoure her grandmother Religion.

THE PRELATES or Archebishops of Rome.

1. Marcus.

Marcus a Romaine, bestowed a pall vpon the bishop of Hostia, who had consecrate the bishop of Rome before other. He also cōmaunded that the people and the clergie should on Sondayes after the Gospell were redde, singe the Nicean Crede. He builded churches, and gaue many

many giftes vnto them & died a confessour in the yere. 335.

2. Iulius the first.

IVlius the first a Romaine, appointed that a priest shoulde (as they forge of him) not aunswer his cause any where, but before an ecclesiasticall iudge: and he reprehended the bishops of the east, (onlesse they slaunder him) because they had helde counsels without his authoritie, but they scorned him for his pride, he caused churcheyardes to be made, and at the length died a confessour in peace, Anno. 351. Platina sayth, that this Pope appointed certaine notaries to wryte the actes of other men, the whiche office sayth he, is yet about the Pope remaining: But these notaries of our time saith he, are such doultes for the moste parte, that for wante of learning they can not wryte their owne name in Latin: of their maners I will not speake, because these offices are bestowed on bawdes and flatterers, vnmete to wryte the actes of other men.

3. Liberius.

Liberius a Romaine, for ambition (as Hierome witnesseth) falling into the Arrian heresie, forsooke the trew faith, and subscribed to Arrius articles. And yet this man died a confessour also, Anno. 366. though in dede taynted with damnable heresie.

4. Fœlix the seconde.

Fœlix the seconde a Romaine, was preferred by the Arrians, who thrust out Liberius, and aduaunced him, because they hoped he agreed with them in opinion. But in the seconde yeare after he was dryuen from his seate, and Liberius restored: And in the yeare of our Lorde, 359. He with other spirituall persones, was slayne in a tumulte.

D   This

The second Booke of the

This man sayth Isidorus, made lawes for the defense of the Clergie. Also Sozomenus, lib. 4. ca. 10. Eccle. histor. saith, that he being bishop, did both admitte Arrian heretikes to the ministery, and also vsed their communiō, though els he yelded to the counsell of Nice.

5. Damasus.

Damasus a Spanyarde, being made Pope in a certaine faction, and vehemently accused of adultery, did condemne Liberius his dedes, he builded temples, and beawtified them with iewels, he gaue landes, and bathes to the Clergie, he encreased strange seruice in the churche, he added Confiteor to the seruice: he appointed the singing of the Psalmes, and allowed Hieroms translation of the Bible: For then the myndes of the Prelates began to bee more puft vp with ambition. Afterward Damasus (as they saye) being a diligent gatherer of thinges doone in times past, wrote the lyues and decrees of his predecessours the byshops of Rome, enterlacing them with many open and manifest vntruthes. And in the yere 384. died a confessour.

Socrates, in the eight booke of his ecclesiasticall history, and the 24. chapter, sayth: that when this Damasus was chosen bishop, one Vrsinus a Deacon of the same churche, did stande in suite against Damasus, but whē he sawe that Damasus was preferred, for anger he began by all endeuour to gather congregations to him selfe, seuered from the churche. Also he perswaded certaine obscure and abiect byshops, to chose him bishop secretly in a corner. And so he was created not in the churche, but in a close place of the pallaice called Sicona: Whiche being done, the people began to wrangle. And hereof arose a bitter contention and deadly sedicion, not touching religion, but whether of these two Prelates should be bishop. Of this grewe so many assemblies, and so often brawlinges, that in the end the tumulte

was so

was so great that many were slayne about it. And therfore Maximinus then lieuetenant of the citie, did punishe sharpely a great numbre, both the Clergie and layetie, & so suppressed Vrsinus and his faction. Thus it appeareth that bloudy ambition is not a newe thing in Rome.

6. Siricius.

Siricius a Romaine, medling and making decrees in many matters, remoued those from saying seruice, that had bene twyse maried, & was the firste that admitted monkes into orders for pretence of single life, who before, were neuer reckened to be as clarkes. He mingled ye Antiphones with the Psalmes, and appointed that orders should be geuen, some at one time, some at an other, he died a confessour, Anno 399.   38

7. Anastasius.

Anastasius a Romaine, appointed that whyle the Gospel was reading they should stand, & not sitte. He exempted from the ministery those that were lame, impotent, or diseased persons, and slept with his forefathers in peace being a confessour. Anno. 404.   39

8. Innocentius.

Innocentius borne in Albania, aduaunced the sea of Rome aboue all other, and would haue it to be iudged by none. He commaunded the faithfull to faste on the Saturday, to bewayle with Mary Magdalene our sauiour Christe that was buried; euen as on that daye. He deuised that at masse time the Pax should be geuen about in the church, and commaunded that the church (a wayghty matter) being ones consecrate should neuer be consecrate any more. He made certayne decrees concerning Iewes, Pagans, & Monkes,   40

D ij   and made

The second Booke of the

and made the anopling of the sick to be a sacrament: And is counted among the dead confessours, Anno. 416. The yeare before being the yeare 415. Alaricus king of Gothes, ouerranne Italy, wan Rome, wasted, spoyled, and burnt it miserably. And sone after him his cosen Athoulfus, came thether againe and spoyled all that he had left.

9. Sozymus.

41   SOzymus a Greke, appointed that tapers should be blessed on the holydaye, and that the Deacons in saying seruice should haue their lefthandes couered. He forbad that clarkes should vse tipling in opē place, or haunte tauernes, and that no bondmen should be admitted to be of the Clergie: And died a confessour. Anno. 420. Also this Sozymus suppressed the Nouacian heretikes, whiche in time past had borne great swaye in Rome. But nowe they were kept vnder, for sayth Isocrates, the byshop of Rome, as well as the byshop of Alexandria, had stretched his power beyond the limittes of priesthood stepping into temporall authoritie. Socrat. histor. eccle. lib. 7. cap. 11.

10. Bonifacius.

42   BOnifacius a Romaine, the sonne of one Iucundus a priest, was chosen Pope, at suche time as there was great sedition among the Clergie. He made decrees that were very necessary, God graunte they proue so: as þ a woman (yet though she were a hooded nonne) should not openly touche the altar cloth, nor the holy vessels, nor smell to the incense: And that none should be made priest till he were thirty yeres olde. After he had decreed that sainctes eueninges should be kept, he died a confessour, Anno. 426.

11. Cœlestinus.

Cœlestinus

Pageant of Popes. Fol. 27

Cælestinus borne in Campania, patched the Popishe masse vp with these thinges, Introitum, Graduale, Responsorium, Tractum, & Offertorium, as his owne deuices. And gaue straight charge that the priestes shoulo be perfitte in the Popes decrees. He sent these bishops, Germanus into Englande, Palladus into Scotlande, and Patricke with a certaine Segetian into Irelande, to roote out the Pelagian heresie. He died Anno. 435. being put in among the number of confessours.   43

12. Sixtus the thirde.

Sixtus the thirde a Romaine, called the enricher of churches, he builded the churche of S. Mary the greater after a miracle of snowe: and enriched it with great giftes, and garnished the pallayces with golde. At the persuasion of a woman called Eudoxia, he did hallowe Peters chaynes, and appointed a yearely feaste daye in honour of them to be kept at Midsommer. He died a confessour. Anno. 440. and was buried in the citie.   44

About the yeare of our Lorde. 456. Genesericus came out of Aphrica, into Italy with a great armye against Rome, and cōming thether, he finding the citie empty, inuaded it. And for the space of xiiii. dayes continually caried out the spoyle of it, and toke away many pryfoners.

13 Leo the first.

Leo the first a Thuscane borne, added to the masse these wordes to name it Sanctum sacrificium, Immaculatā hostiam, hanc oblationem, whiche cannot be without blaspheming God haynously. He like an Idolatour, builded a pallayce in the honour of Cornelius a byshop, and appointed clarkes to kepe the Apostles sepulchres. He decreed that men should worship the images of the dead, & allowed the   45 An holy sacrifice an vnspotted offering and oblacion.

D iii

The second Booke of the

the sacrifice of the masse, he died a confessour. Anno. 462.

14 Hilarius.

HIlarius borne in Sardinia, a man daily exercised in building and beautifying of churches, decked the post of
Christe his crosse with golde and precious stones: He made
decrees by synodes, proclayming them to be kept through
the whole worlde. He made a lawe that euery minister
should be put from his calling, whiche maried either a widowe or deuorced woman, and not a mayde: He died a confessour, Anno. 469. In his time Mamertus Claudius, bishop of Vienna, made the Letanies or procession to be saide
thrise a weke, whereof Mantuan sayth Fast. 4.

By Rodanus there standes a towne Vienna men it name,
Sore noied while one Mamertus, was bishop of the same:
And suffred many sturdy stormes: for oft with firy flake
Of thonderclap it burnt, & while the trebling soyle did
   shake,
The grounde did gape as torne in twayne, whereby the
   daungerous dell
VVith yawning mouth stoode open downe to glowing
   goulphe of hell,
Among the dungeons depe of Ioue: and rauening wolues
   vvithall
VVere driuen to madnes, through the haggs of hell that
   vp did crall.
The fraticke neat begā to murther mē in field, & tovvne,
VVherevvith mens hartes amazed vvere, that thus the
   Lord should frovvne.
And so cōstraind they asked aide and succour frō aboue,
And vvith their humble prayers sought Gods mercy for
   to moue.
And hereuppon the Letanye at first deuised vvas,
And aftervvard it did from thens to other people passe.

In the

In the time of this Pope about the yeare of Christ 476. Odoacer with an army of Herulās & Turcihugians, came from Panonia and wanne Rome and all Italye, and raigned there xiiii. yeres. About this time Rome was so terriblie shaken wyth earthquakes, that manye houses fell downe wythall.

15. Simplicius.

SImplicius a Tiburtinian borne, did dedicate Pallaces and deuided the towne into fiue parts for the priestes to serue, and appointed the sacrificing priestes their weekes: hee shewed ye the Church of Rome was the chiefe Church of all. He vsurped auctoritie vppon the people of Rauenna like a tyraunte, and commaunded that none of the Clergy should acknowledge, that he held any Ecclesiasticall benefice of a lay mā. And this mā dyed a confessor. Anno.484. 47

16. Fœlix the third.

FOElix the thirde a Romaine the sonne of one Fœlix a priest, decreed that onelye a bishoppe, and no priuate priestes should dedicate the Churches, and allowed a feast for the dedication of them: Hee hallowed Agapetus hys Pallaice. He decreed that the Clergye being accused of a nye matter, should haue dayes graunted to returne theyr aunswere, and dyed in peace a confessor. Anno.494. 48

17. Gelasius.

GElasius an Aphrican sonne to Valerius a bishop, burned the bookes of the Manichies, hee made hymnes, prefaces, graduals, collects and prayers, hee seuered ye Apocrypha from Canonicall Scripture: and allowed maryed wydowers after they had maryed their seconde wyfe to be priestes, if they toke his dispensation. He encreased ye 49

D iiii   Clergie

The second Booke of the

Clergye, he dedicated Pallaices: and decreed that priestes orders should bee geuen foure times in the yeare, he added to the Masse the conclusions of the prayers Et te igitur: & at lengthe auouched ẏ he & his successors should be iudged by no bodye. And dyed a confessor. Anno. 497.

18. Anastasius the second.

50   ANastasius the seconde a Romaine, leaned to the Eutichians and Nestorians, he did comunicate wyth heretikes: he excommunicated the Emperour. And in the yere of our Lorde 499. on the stoole of easemente his bowels issued out of his bellye. He dyed a confessor, so wryteth Volaterranus.

19 Symmachus.

51   SYmmachus borne in Sardinia was chosen bishop wyth much dissention among the Clergye. He ordayned that birgins which had once professed chastitye, shoulde neuer marrye afterwarde, and that none of the Clergye shoulde keepe in house wyth anye woman, but such a one as were his kinswoman: He builded many Pallacies euen out of ẏ grounde. He brought the masse into fashion, hee commaunded to singe Gloria in excelsis vppon the byrth dayes of sainctes. And if any man may trust Gregoryes Dialogues, he comitted to Purgatorye the stubborne soule of one Paschasius a deacon after his death. And yet this man dyed a confessour. Anno. 514. Vspergensis sayth that whē this Pope was chosen, one Laurence was also chosen by some, wherevppon manye slaughters both of the people & Clergye were made in Rome during the space of iii. yeres, but Symachus preuailed.

20. Hormisda.

52   HOrmisda borne in Campania, did set quietnes among the Clergie, he appointed that the Psalmes should be song by

longe by courſe enterchaungeable: He commaunded that the decrees of counſels ſhould be kept, and beſtowed many thinges to ý furniture of churches, he lefte a wedge of ſylver waying a thouſande & fourty poundes in ſaint Peters churche: and commaūded that no aultar ſhould be builded without the conſent of the byſhop. He added ceremonies to publique mariages: and excommunicated Anaſtaſius the Emperous, becauſe he ſayde that it was an office dewe onlye to the Emperoure to commaunde, and not to be at a byſhops commaundement: ſuche then was the courage of the ſpirite of Antichriſte. Iuſtinus the Emperoure, as Iſiodorus wryteth, made this Hormiſda a Patriarch of Rome being before but an Archebiſhop: who died a confeſſour, Anno. 523. From the time of Sylueſter, the Romaine prelates were Archebiſhops, for the ſpace of twoo hundreth yeares, that is from the yeare 320. untill this yeare 520. at what tyme they were firſt made Patriarkes by the Emperour Iuſtinus. I declare this more diligently, whereby the attentiue reader may knowe by what degrees the Romain biſhops crept up to the Popedome it ſelfe, and what crafte the deuill wrought in them before the great Antechriſte came, and was reueaſed to the full. So that as ye ſee the biſhops of Rome. Here againe altered their name the ſeconde tyme, to title of greater dignitie, that is frō Archbiſhops to Patriarkes, and ſo the reſt folowing for a ſeaſon were called.

21. Iohn the firſt.

IOhn the firſte a Thuſcane, whome Theodoricus kyng of Italy ſent, (for then they were ſubiect to Princes) as his oratour, with certaine other, unto Iuſtinus the Emperoure. This biſhop being the worthieſt man of all this latter company, gaue a teſtimonie of his pure life, by ſuffring paciently undeſerued death. He decreed, and that very godly, that

53

The second booke of the

ly, that if any man were robbed of any thing, he should haue all restored againe. But I take it to be false that he should restore three churcheyardes, enriched the churches with giftes, or decked the altars with golde, siluer, or precious stones, as Platina and other wryte, least he should seeme nothing to haue encreased the kingdome of Antichriste. There is to be seene comfortable Epistles of his to the byshops of Italy, whereby he warneth them, that they should not shrinke from their purpose, but stande to it stoutly, although that the said king Theodoricus, fowly tainted with the Arrian heresy, had threatened to destroye them and all Italy. For the whiche at the tyrannous commaundement of Theodoricus, Anno. 527. hee perished at Rauenna through famine, stinke, & noysomnes in the pryson. As touching Arrius, thus Mantuan wryteth of him.

This Arrius, euen the deadly bayne infecting mankinde,
And borne to breake Gods lawe, and quenche the faithe
   of Christian minde,
Had venomd sondry nacions infecting all the world.

22. Fœlix the fourth.

54   Fœlix the fourth was borne in Samia, being not verye carefull in his pastorall charge, and casting of the office of preaching, builded the churche of Cosma and Damianus, he restored Saturninus temple, and repaired other temples of the dead. He commaunded that masse should be said only in halowed places. He made a partition betwene the Clergie and the people in the churche. He excommunicated the Patriarke of Constantinople, misdeiued of heresy: he commaunded that if a priest died, another should succeade him twoo dayes after, and commaunded precisely that they that lye a dying, should be annoynted, with hallowed oyle, and died a confessour, Anno. 530.

                                           Boniface

23. Boniface the seconde.

BOniface the seconde a Romaine, was made bishop, whē the Clergie were at great iarre, ready to go together by the eares: He made canons, especially this one, that within three dayes after one bishop were dead, another should be appointed in his rowme. He following Fœlix, did seuer the Clergie frō the layetie, by making the quier in the church, and that for double pollicie, the one was, that by this meanes he might at length take frō the people both their place, and their voyce, whiche they had in chusing the bishops, & that it might not be lawefull for any of them to sewe a byshop, or any of the Clergie in any cause, ciuill or criminall, before a temporall magistrate. But marke what happened these wretches through their pryde, as I thinke, Whyle euen like the Pharisies they wilbe counted holier then other; with their shauen heades, their annoynted fingers, & seuered chauncelles, deuiding them selues from the faythfull, that were redemed with the bloud of Christe.

It is to be feared, least hereby they become the Goates that in the last day shalbe deuided frō the lambes. Math. 25 as not pertaining to the misticall body of Christe. It is easy to iudge howe muche these men swarue from Peter the Apostle, of whome they boaste so muche, to whome it was not lawefull in the tenth of the Actes, to decree of Cornelius, that he should be either a layeman, or a prophane persone: Boniface died a confessour, Anno. 532.

24. Iohn the seconde.

IOhn the seconde was a Romaine, who otherwyse for his eloquencie was called Mercurie or Iuppiter, his embassadour. Iustinianus the Emperoure, sent vnto this man a cup of gold, of sixe pound waighte beset with precious stones, and

The second booke of the

nes, and two syluer cuppes of seuen pounde weight, and twoo syluer chalices, waying fiftene poundes, for a present from Constantinople, after he had condemned Athenius the Patriarke of heresie, and the sayde Emperoure commaunded his bishops, as (Crantzius witnesseth) to talke with the byshop in his name, moste friendly vnder benediction: this byshop died a confessour, Anno. 534. And as VVicelius saith, he did nothing of any balewe.

25. Agapetus the firste.

57 Agapetus the first a Romaine, sonne of a priest, called Cardinall Gordian, was sent by Theodatus kyng of the Gothes, as his Embassadour, to pacifie Iustinianus the Emperour; for the cruell murther of Amalasimitha a noble queene, and an excellent learned woman: whose worthy vertues the same Emperour reuerenced highly, who also procured his peace with spending saint Peters treasure: He decreed that on the sonday they should go in procession in the churches: And died a confessour, Anno. 535.

26. Syluerius.

58 Syluerius borne in Capania, sonne of Hormisda a bishop of Rome, when Agapetus was dead, as he went on his voyage to the Emperoure, this man by the commaundement of Theodatus kyng of Gothes, was placed in his steade without the Emperours consent. Therefore by the prouocation of Vigilius a Deacon, who also did accuse him, that he would betraye Rome to the Gothes, he was banished into the Isle Pontus, by Theodora the Empresse, and Antonina the wife of duke Bellisarius. So that it appeareth, the Popedome at that time was a thing but of small countenaunce, when they were sent as Embassadours at the commaundement of inferiour princes. & could
be depri-

be depriued of their authoritie, put from their seate by women. At length Syluerius died miserably in his banyshement being an hooded confessour, Anno. 537.

27. Vigilius.

VIgilius a Romaine, the crafty accuser of the sayd Syluerius, compassing the bishoprike by subtiltie, was aduaunced into the sayde place by the forenamed women. Whereby Rome had then twoo bishops, one made by the Gothes, another by the Grekes, or rather by those Grekishe dames. And were vsed vrgently, but not vnworthely of them: for either of them receiued the reward of his rashnesse, for the one attayned the Popedome by crafte, the other by might, and yet the Papistes will haue them bothe reckened among martyrs. Theodora did sue Vigilius, because he brake promisse with her, and caused him first to be brought to Constantinople, there to be reuiled and beaten, and afterwarde with an halter about his necke to be drawē through the streate, and last of all, bee driuen into banishement. This man made certaine lessons of his owne for the holydayes to be redde in the churche. He woulde haue the church of Rome to be taken for the mother of other churches: He appointed Candelmas daye to be kept holy daye, and that the masse should be sayde, the priest standing with his face into the East: He died a confessour, in the yere 554. in Cicilia. In these dayes was one Maurus, who preached and taught the hipocriticall life of mōkes. Also in his time Anno. 542. there was a terrible earthquake ouer all the world, as Vspergensis sayth.

28. Pelagius.

PElagius a Romaine, aspired to the pontificall dignitie, in that time when the tyrant Totila, called Gods scourge, to the

The second booke of the

to the great comfort of the Goathes being their king, inuaded Italy, as Procopius wryteth. This Pelagius to please Totila and his companie, made a publique decree, that it was nedeful to haue the authoritie of the prince, and consent of the people in creation of byshops. He in the middest of troubles of that time, hauing more regarde to aduaunce the Popedome, then Christianitie: decreed that the Clergie should mumble euery daye seuentimes, the canonicall howers. Abbots should be chosen by order, one magistrate should be sufficient to punishe an hereticke: that in Lent priestes might say masse at nine of the clocke: and that euery Prouince should contayne twelue or tenne cities at the least. This man first auouched that the premacie of the churche of Rome was fette from Christe himselfe, and not from men nor generall councels. He buried together the bones of the firste Martyr Stephen and S. Laurences carkasse. He allowed solemnities in remembraunce of the dead, and for loue of gaynes he mingled them with the masse. And because he sometime him selfe was accused in a libell, that he had geuen occasion why Vigilius his predecessour was troubled, and depriued, therfore he prouided that such libelles should not be harde. But it is reported that he purged him selfe from the infamy of that libell by takinge an oathe, and kissing the crosse. He liued in the extreame tyme when Rome was besieged, & died a confessour, Anno. 566.

About the yeare of our Lorde 557. Totila king of Gothes, besieged Rome, whiche being miserably oppressed with extreame famine, was compelled to yelde it selfe to the slauery of the saluage people, vnder whiche it continued tenne yeares.

In the time of this Pope, a Pestilence raigned ouer all Italy, beginning in Liguria so contagiously, that the contreye was almoste destroyed of the inhabitours thereby. Vrspergensis.

19 Iohn

29. Iohn the third.

IOhn the thirde a Romaine, was an especiall friende to Narsetes the Eunuche, gouernour of Italy, when the Gothes were ouercome: for he recouered his fauour towarde Rome, when it was in displeasure, and obtayned that hee was made consull, for then the bishop had almoste all the swaye in Rome. This man decreed contrary to his predecessour, that none ought to be called chiefe priest, or vniuersall bishop, Distinctione 99. Nullus. Furthermore, taking away from the bishops chauncelours the laying on of handes, graunted it only to bishops, as Isidorus writeth. Afterwarde turning his minde, and taking delight in building, he finished Philip and Iacobs churche, whiche Vigilius had begonne, and restored the Sainctes tombes in the citie. Finally being a very olde mã, & taking great thought vpon occasion of straunge tempestes, he died at Rome, Anno, 577. In his time the Armenians became Christians.

30. Benedict the first.

BEnedict the first a Romain, was bishop when the Lombardes spoyled Italy. And was a good bishop, because he did nothing worthy memorie: as Barnus and Functius write of him. But yet whiche is to be noted, for the worthinesse of the dede, he forbad that mē should treade on crosses made of marble, stone, or woode: And when there was great dearth in Rome, he or at the least wife Tiberius Augustus in his steade, brought corne out of Egypt, to succour them withall. He died for sorowe to se so many miseries in the citie, Anno. 582.

31. Pelagius the second.

Pelagius

PElagius the seconde, while the citie was besieged, without the Princes comaundement, cotrary to the custome was made bishop. Therefore to pacifie the Emperoure, he sent one Gregory a monke, to Constantinople: afterwarde he made the clopster of Hermes a martyr, and builded vp S. Laurence pallaice from the foundacion. He renewed the Canon for saying the howers, and commaunded Subdeacons, either to forsake their wiues, or els their ecclesiasticall functions, and appointed nyne prefaces to be song in the masse before the Canon: Pestis inguinaria, arising of great tempestes, and the contagiousnes of the aire tooke awaye this bishop among many other: This pestilence was cause of many supersticions, for then they firste began to thinke that Gods wrath was to be pleased: and the Letany of seuen partes was made by Gregorie. The occasion hereof saith Vspergensis was, that a great part of Italy was drowned with great flouddes.

32. Gregorie the great.

GRegorie the great a Romaine, was made byshop being before but a Monke and a Deacon. He was the best mã of all these Romaine Patriarkes, for learning and good life. He succeded Pelagius, vnwillingly refusing it, and in the ende copelled thereunto: he (though otherwyse he was learned and Godly) yet because he was a Monke, burthened the churche, and religion of God aboue all other, with more ceremonies, then had the Iewes. He turned his parentes houses into Monasteries, and dedicated the firste of them to S. Andrewe the Apostle. He made Scholes of quiresters, and made certaine songes for the church, accordiug to Ambrose maner, which we call Anthemes: He appointed one to be chaunter for the daye, another for the nighte. He gathered together the lawes of the holy fathers. He did deuise the order of masses, & linked the Cannons ther-
uf toge-

of together, he caused the masses to be begonne with peces of Psalmes. He commaunded to saye Kyrieleison nine tymes, and to chaunt Alleluia after the Graduall hee ioyned the same Alleluia, for Easter tyme to the Offertories. Hee added three peticions to the Cannons of the masse: That is, Dies nostros in tua pace, &c. He comaunded that the Lordes prayer, should be either song or sayde, with a loude voyce over the communion bread. He commaunded that masse shoulde be saide over the dead carkases of sainctes: And added to the Canonicall howers, Deus in adiutorium, with Gloria patri: He devised Letanies, and processions, & devided thē into these seuen orders, Clarkes, Monkes, Nonnes, Boyes, Laymen, Widowes, and maried wyues. He suffered the Image of the blessed virgin Mary to be caried about withall, But not to be worshipped: Furthermore this Gregorie (as they shamefully imagine) compelled an Angell to put vp his terrible swerde into his sheathe. By his indulgences he established certaine stacions, and pilgrimages vnto Images in the citie, according to the peoples deuocion. He solemnized the feast of the Purification of our Lady with wex candels, (whereof it is called Candelmas daye) and appointed the solemnitie of Palme Sondaye to be kept with processions. He added iiii. dayes to Lent faste, and hallowed the beginning thereof with Ashwednisdaye. He forbad those that should faste to eate fleshe, milke, butter, chese, or egges, because they seme to beare a taste of fleshe, and suffered them only to eate fishe, excepting also the greater sorte of fishes, whereof Mantuan sayth Fastor. 2.

Yet was it not against the lawe to fede on fishes small:
For Gregorie forbad the great, but time misordred all
And stately tables combred are with fishe of larger sort
So Gregories laws ar kept wher nede doth bear a siple port
That in the shallowe brookes and floodes to find his fare:
As for the great grown fulsom fishe in depth of seas they are.   E   But

The seconde booke of the

But holy peers that do with Peters line and gredy hooke,
Down to the bottom angle: can eche sort of fishes brooke.

Gregorie gaue tapers to the churche, and furnished it
with quier Psalmodis, Canticles, Oades, Hymnus, and o-
ther Heathen ceremonies: He buylded sire Monasteries of
his owne coste in Sicilia, and dedicated Agathas churche:
He forbad that women should resorte to abbeyes, or that
Monkes should resorte to Nonneries. Also he woulde not
haue Mōkes baptize, neither Nonnes to be Godmothers.
He forbad him that had bene twise married to bee made
priests: And that priestes should geue testimony of honest
life by taking an oathe: He was an vpholder of pardons,
but not a seller of them. He was the first that gaue pardons
vpon certayne dayes, to suche as frequented the churche.
He entertayned straungers at his table. He apded the Mōkes of Hierusalem with necessaries, and gaue stipendes to
three thousande maydes: He allowed by decree the first fiue
counsels: He forbad that sainctes Images should be broke,
or that one of the Clergie should at the Emperours commaundement serue in the warres, or that there should bee
twoo Metropolitanes in one Prouince: He would haue a
bishop to be consecrate, but ones, and would haue the laste
will and testament of euery man to be ratified. He made
foure bookes of Dialogues, to boulster vp Purgatorie: He
allowed hallowing of ashes, washing of feete, worshipping
of the crosse, and masse to be saide for the dead, and (wherin the Papistes horribly belie him) he deliuered Traian the
Emperours soule from hell. He cōtemning the Britaines
sent Augustine a Monke, to reclaime the English Saxons
to the churche of Rome: He reft from London the right of
the Archebishopprike, and translated it by the same Augu-
stines meanes to Caunterburie. Al these thinges did Gregorie as Patriarke of Rome, and died a confessour, Anno.
604. But although he doted in many superstitions, yet
more is falsely fathered on him thē euer he did or thought.

33 Sabi.

33. Sabinianus.

SAbinianus borne in Thusca, was a Prelate of no value, who for the hate he bare to his predecessour Gregorie, after he had published certaine slaunders against him, commaunded that his bookes should be burned. This man being the last of the Romaine Patriarkes, commaunded that the howers of the daye shou'de bee deuided by ringing of belles for the ecclesiasticall offices: & that they should haue continuall burning lampes in the churche: At length he died an infamous death through feare that he conceiued of a terrible vision, which he sawe in the night time, An. 606.

The Christian deedes of Gregorie.

NOwe to say somewhat touching the Christiā sayinges and doinges of the foresaid Gregorie: he fought stoutly against the supremacie of the Popishe kingdome, in the very entraunce of the Popedome, and hewde in pieces with sharpe tauntes the title of vniuersal Patriarkeship, saying that suche an one was the forerōner of Antichriste, an hipocrite, a tyraūt, and Lucifer the vsurper of Gods power. He commaunded certaine Images that were of wonderfull excellent workemanship, to be throwen into the Riuer Tiber, least religion should be corrupted by them. He commaunded prayer and fasting for the asswaging of the pestilence. He reclaymed the Gothes from the Arrians, to the vnitie of the church. He wrote Homilies in a pleasaunt stile following S. Augustine. Hee expounded the moste part of the holy bookes of the Bible. He by common consent defacedthe name of vniuersall byshop. And professed him selfe in his wrytinges Seruus seruorum Dei, seruaunt to Gods seruauntes, whereby he mighte shewe, howe farre he was

E ij   from all

The seconde booke of the

from all ambicion and desire of souerainctie: This title his posteritie hath continued, bearing the name, but forbearing the humilitie that belongeth therunto. At the length Gregorie did greatly lamente to se that bowling and chasing in the church had so taken place, that preaching of the Gospell was neglected. Beholde (quoth he among other sayinges) the worlde is full of priestes, & yet in the lordes haruest are founde fewe labourers: We haue taken vpon vs the office, but we do not discharge the office. Brethren, I thinke that God suffereth dishonour of none more then of priestes (for the moste parte). If they se any liue in lowly estate, or liue continently, they scorne them. Consider therfore what becometh of the flocke, when Wolues are made shepeheardes. These take charge of the shepe, who are not afrayde to endaunger the liues of the Lordes foulde, but they chaunge the office of their blessed function to the encrease of their ambicion. We leaue Gods cause, & ronne to worldly affaires: we enioye the place of holines, and are entangled with earthly matters, so that Baptist Mantuan saith of him in the thirde booke of his Fastor.

In speache he was ful eloquent, his workes are yet in store,
He speaketh still, and by his workes he shall do euermore,
He taught the quyristers to sing, in sōgs was his delight.

Huldricus bishop of Angusta, sheweth a wonderful story of this bishop, in his Epistle to Nicolas the first, the eff. of whereof is, that this Gregorie did first cōmaunde priestes to liue single life: but afterwarde when he perceiued, that they were geuen secretly to fleshly pleasure, and that hereupon many children were murthered, hee disanulled that commaundement, and sayde that it was better to mary, thē geue occasion of murther: For whē on a time he sent a certaine woman vnto a fishepoole to take fishe, there were founde in the same poole sixe thousande heades of infantes, that had bene drowned therein: whiche he perceauing to procede of forced single life, with sighing and sorrowing,

he reuo-

he reuoked that Canon. For as that Huldericus sheweth, they accompanied not onely with virgins and wyues, but also euen with their owne kindred, with mankind, yea and that whiche is horrible to be sayde, with brute beastes. After the tyme of this Gregorie, ensued more blindnes then was before. The puritie of doctrine decayed, & the churche was darkened marueloussy with mans tradicions: For Monkery with his manifolde supersticions waxed great: Herewithall sprang vp sale of masses, and praying to the dead, and the Lordes supper began to be an offering for the dead. Bishops also being deluded with visions of spirites, or rather of diuels, began to reuolte from the doctrine of faithe to put affiance in good workes, and mans satiffactiō, as appeareth of Gregorie.

As it is euident of Gregorie, who in his Dialogues to Theodolinda, a very supersticious woman, telleth of dead men that appeared and craued to haue prayers and suffrages. This while Christianitie began to fall to ceremonies forthwith blinde supersticion, by meanes of Monkery began to crepe in. Gregorie as is mentioned before, sent Augustine a Romaine Monke, and other his compaignions, to the Englishemen, Anno. 596. not to preache Christe vnto them, whose doctrine the Brytaines had receiued more sincerely of Ioseph & the churches of Asia, But to thrust vpon them the Romain religion, patched vp with mans diuices and tradicions. The Britaynes had alwayes the preaching of the truthe, syncere doctrine, and the liuely faith and such seruice as was deliuered to the Apostles by Gods commaundement: They had Christian churches, whereof Godfrey of Munmuthe, in the eight booke and fourth chapiter of the actes of the Britaines sayth thus: In the contrey of the Britaines, Christianitie florished hertherto, which neuer failed among them since the Apostles time. But when Augustine came hee founde in their prouince seuen bishoprikes, and one Archebishoprike maintained by

E iij   Godly

The second Booke of the

godly Prelates, and many Abbots, liuing by their handy labour, among whome the Lordes flocke kept true waye. It appeareth also that there were sheperdes among thē that were diligent to preserue the puritie of doctrine, as was Dionotus, Anonius, and his fellowes, who in contēpt of the Romaines ceremonies stacke stoutly to it euen to the death. Augustine entred the lande, not with the Gospell of Christian peace, but with the banner of his Apostleship, with his syluer crosse, his Letanie, his procession, images, painted puppettes, reliques, canticles, and bookes of ceremonies. But when by the authoritie of the king in the west part of England he sommoned the byshops and doctours, that they accepting and communicating the Romaine customes should submitte them selues to him, Anno. 602. They going to the synode, did firste demaunde of a certaine wise man, that liued solitarely, whether it was laweful to followe his commaundement, and forsake those traditions whiche they had receiued of their fathers: to whome hee aunswered, If he be a mā of God, followe him. They further asked howe they should proue that. Ye knowe quoth he, that the Lord commaunded saying: Take my yoke vpō you, and learne of me because I am gentle and lowlye of harte. Therefore if this Augustine be suche an one, it is credible that he also beareth Christes burthē, and offereth it to you to beare: but if he be proude and cruell, it is euidēt tha he is not of God, and ye ought not to regarde his talke. And howe shall we knowe that quoth they, Let Augustine (quoth he) and his company goe firste to the Synode: And if when ye come, he ryse vp to salute you, knowe ye that he is Christe his seruaunt, and obeyye him. But if he dispayue you, or make smale accompte of you, and shewe no token of curtesie in his countenaunce, seing ye are the greater number, doe ye likewyse contemne him. Therfore when they came to Augustine sitting ambiciously on his stalle, and sawe that he gaue them no token of frendship, they by

and by

Pageant of Popes.   Fol. 36

and by conceiuing displeasure, & noting him to be a proude person, did forthwith ouerthwart euery thing that he put forth: For he charged them that they did many thinges contrary to the custome of the catholicke churche, especially in keping their Easter, in ministring of baptisme, and in their preaching, and that they regarded not mans tradicions: and he commaunded that in these and other thinges they should followe the vse of the church of Rome. But they aunswered that they would do none of these, neither take him for their Archebishop. Whereupon he promised them warre should ensewe, and threatned them fiercely to reuenge it by death, whiche immediatly ensued. Reade Beda in his ecclesiasticall history of Englande, the seconde booke, and the second chapter, and likewyse the sayde Godfrey. But I wonder muche of this crueltie of Augustine: For Gregorie before had so discussed it, and wrote vnto him that it was not nedefull in all churches to haue the same order of ceremonies: but that euery churche might ordaine the beste for it selfe. But suche was wonte to be the tyranny of hypocrites: whereof Mantuan saythe.

The fathers of the Latin churche to taxe they enterprise,
And make them fondly force the Britains bend vnto the
  guise
Of Romish church against al right: with foolish hardines
They rashly cause the auncient league of amitie to cease.
As touching peace they saye that Rome should rather
  make then marre,
To kepe mans lawe: so that Christes lawe therby do neuer
  Iarre.
And faith with doctrine whiche allowed by the firste Sy-
  node was
As it from Christe the light of life to all mankinde did
  passe.
And to speake in fewe wordes, the Romaine bishops were
starres euen hetherto, yet but falling from Christes right
                              E iiii   hande

The second Booke of the

hande to the graunde, from whome the heauen departed, Apocal: 6. and they are prefigured by the redde horse, vnto whose ryder power was geuen to take awaye peace from the earth, and to murther to and fro, whereupon as in the firste order the Romaine Prelates called bishops by their true ministring the worde of God, and constant faith, were starres abiding in Christe his right hande: so in this second sort vnder the name of Archebishops and Patriarkes, by the neglecting of the same worde, and their earthly affections, they were starres falling to the earth, Apocal. 6. But in the thirde ranke, whiche shall followe vnder the name of Popes and Antichristes, for their absolute reuolting from Christe, and open idolatries they shal be the starres falling from heauen to the earthe.
Apoc. 9.

THE THIRDE Booke.

¶ Nowe enſueth the thirde ſorte of Romaine biſhops cōming from euill to worſe: For as the former company in the ſeconde booke ſhewed, declining from pure Chriſtianitie, and enclining to Antichriſte, ſo now appeareth in theſe, that the ſeede ſowed by the forainer is growē vp, & Antichriſt as it were appearing aboue the grounde: who grewe ſtill forwarde frō greneneſſe to ripeneſſe, as ſhall appeare by theſe that followe, and ſo from ripeneſſe to rottenneſſe, which is to be hoped for in that already he is wexed ſo mellowe, that if he be not plucked from the tree, if it pleaſe God to ſende a ſmale blaſte of winde, he will fall of him ſelfe. Note therfore diligently gentil Reader what fruite enſueth and ſpringeth of the former grayne. Reade, conferre, and then iudge, whether theſe men ſhewe them ſelues to be the vicars of Chriſte, or deceitful and miſcheuous Antechriſtes, for by their fruites ye ſhall knowe them whether they are ſuche as they would be accompted.

Abadon or the Latin Antichriſte.

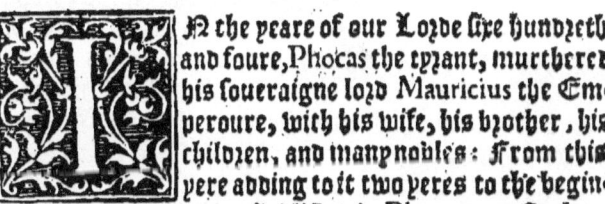

In the yeare of our Lorde ſixe hundreth and foure, Phocas the tyrant, murthered his ſoueraigne lord Mauricius the Emperoure, with his wife, his brother, his children, and many nobles: From this yere adding to it two yeres to the beginning of the Popedome, eſtabliſhed by Phocas, are ſixe hundred ſixty ſixe yeares, from the cōſulſhip of M. T. Cicero, and An-

The second booke of the

and Antonius, as Bibliander Funccius, and other do euidently recken it, at whiche time the Iewes (while their bishops iarred for supremacie) lost their libertie: For Christe (as Bibliander gathers) in his reuelation (whiche by his dearely beloued Apostle Iohn, he deliuered to the church) foare tolde, that a certaine tyrannicall Empier should afflicte the true church: as Nero and Domician, with others did. And calleth the beaste hauing two hornes like a lambe the ennemy of Christe, whiche neuerthelesse should speake like a Dragon, like an euill spirite, and should rage as vnmercifully as the firste beast did, whiche destroyed Peter and Paule, and great companies of sainctes: whiche with her charmes, should so bewitche the worlde, and with monstrous workes should growe into suche admiration, that none might by or sell, but such, as had the seale or the name of the beaste in his forehead. But as touching the name of the beaste, he shewes it mistically by these letters, χ ξ ς. Ch, X, St, & reciteth it to be discussed. This (saith Iohn) is wysedome, let him that hath vnderstanding accompt the number of the beast, for it is the number of a man, and his nuber is this. 666. Apocal. 13. What meane these markes but that wee should searche the time wherein this beaste should arise from the earth and the bottomlesse pitte, and should destroye the Christian common wealth: But howe shall a man apply it, if he haue not the certaine time, when Pompeie toke the scepter from the Iewes, according to the notable prophecie of Iacob, & entring the temple, prophaned the Sanctum sanctorum. But that was done as Iosephus wryteth, in the time of Tullius consulship, the 60. yeare before Christe was borne. To these three score yeares adde six hundred, vntill after the death of the sayd Gregorie the great, who prophecied that he should be Antechriste, whiche would be compted vniuersall bishop, or head of all churches. Therefore marke well what kinde of times happened in the 666. yeare after Hierusalem was taken by the

Romaines

Pageant of Popes. Fol. 38

Romaines, Pompeie being their general, and you shall se
straunge matters fal out, at the time that this Phocas was
Emperour, of whome V.Villiam Stantphurdius wryteth
as foloweth.

The Empier Phocas chokes, and doth the Popedome first
    aduaunce,
By wicked writts about his Empier sent, for to enhaunce,
And to confirme moste sure for ay vnto the after age
The premacy of Rome, and of the dragon that doth rage
Against Gods power.

   Furthermore applie this misticall number of 666. con-
taining highe wisedom in it frō the time of Christes birth,
or from the tyme of his passion, or from the xb. yere of Domician, at whiche time the reuelation was written, and stil
ye shal finde some mōsterous thing wrought in the church.
But to returne to the matter of Englande: In the yeare
of Christe 593. Colman, Harding, and Fabian saye, that
the raigne of the seuen kinges at one time began: whereby
1735. yeares after Brutus their first king, the royall estate
of the Brytishe king ceased. For as Paulus Diaconus writeth in his fourth booke, the Britaines founde that the Saxons were in steade of succourers, suppressours and cruell
eunemies, vntrusty, warring rigorously vpon them, who
had entertained them for ayde. Anno 596. the foresaid Augustine sent from Gregorie, came into Englande, who at
his comming did not reproue, but maintaine, and vpholde
the wicked treasons, the horrible robberies, & the slaughters more cruell then were Neroes, whiche the Saxons cōmitted. Anno 600. Gregorie gaue to Augustine his byshops pall. Thereby as was sayde, London was spoyled of
her right without all order; to the destruction bothe of the
commonwealth and of religion, and finally the vndoing of
the Brytishe kingdome, and thereupon are sumptuous tē-
ples builded. Before that time the Britains had their churches dedicated to eternall God the father, and to our Sa-
                                                uiour

The thirde booke of the

uiour his sonne Iesus Christe. But afterwarde the Saxōs did colecrate their temples to Images, and dead sainctes. Anno. 604. the Christiā Emperour Maurice being slaine, Phocas an adulterer and a murtherer, obtayned the seate imperiall, and in him the maiestie of the Cæsars, and the moste noble Empire of the Grekes decayed together. As for the Romaine Empire that was weakened and empaired, yea and at length brought to nothing, by meanes of the Popedome whiche he had graunted and established. Anno 606. in Nouember and December, as Paulus Diaconus writeth in his 18. booke, euen at the rising and beginning of the Popedome, there appeared a wonderfull great blasing starre: There were straunge sightes and monsters of the Sea, shewed them selues to the terrour of many. Thus in ye time of this Phocas murderer of the Emperour (whiche is to be noted as a misterie concerning the Popes) Papistrie and Mahumets religion began bothe together at one time, which corrupted, darkened, and weakened the doctrine of the sonne of God in many regions. For in another yeare of the same Phocas, as Bibliander writeth, Mahumet recited the Alcoran, so that (saieth hee) the Egles three heades awaked all at ones, according to the heauenly vision in the fourth booke of Esdras: that is to saye Phocas him selfe, Pope Boniface, & Mahumet the Arabian, now followeth the thirde troupe of Romishe Popes, whiche is deuided into fiue partes.

The firste parte of this thirde troupes of the Popes or Romaine Antechristes, prophecied of by the names of Sodome or Egypt. Apocal. 11. vntill the time of Pope Iohn the eight.

1. Boniface the thirde.

About this time the bishoppes of Constantinople endeuoured to obtaine the title of vniuersall bishop, and to haue their Church called the head of all Churches, vsing these

these fonde reasons, that because the Emperour beinge chiefe of all Princes kepte at Constantinople, therefore ye shoulde be the chiefest Church, and there the chiefe bishop: This ambitiō enflamed many to speake and wryte against it, but especiallye the late Gregorye who in this wyse reproued John bishop of Constantinople for the same: Sayinge, None of my predecessors (although the Emperours began first in Rome, and were wont to byde there onelye, and yet do keepe the title thereof) durste take vppon them this title of vniuersall bishop. And againe Gregorye sayd plainlye that such a one was the forerunner of Antichrist. Yet notwithstanding that the Church of Constantinople with great insampe preuailed not herein, because that Antichrist or the whore of Babilon accordyng to the 13. of the Reuelation should be in the Citty builded on seuen hilles, that is Rome it selfe, For so diuers auctors testifye that onelye Rome is knowen to be builded on vii. hils: and certaine it is that when this Reuelation was written, Rome was then the greatest Cittye being built on seuen hils, as Mantuan testifyeth in the life of Syluester, speaking of S. Blaze at the ende of the first booke. And the fulnesse of ye time prophecied of, now drawing nighe, this Boniface the thirde Anno 607. by the meanes of Phocas the Emperour an adulterer, traytour, and murtherer of his Lorde and soueraine Maurice the Emperour with his wife, and children) was aduaunced to be bishop of Rome with much hurley burley and greate tumulte, and in despite of manye bishops and Churches standinge against it, he is extolled, confirmed and worshipped as Lorde and Prince of all bishoppes: By great sute (but greater bribery) he obtayned of the sayde bloudye Emperour, that Rome should be called the head of all Churches, partlye by the same reasons that Constantinople vsed (as Platina sayth) ye where the heade of the Empyre was, there shoulde be the heade Church, againe the Emperours had their beginninge in

Rome,

The thirde booke of the

Rome, againe though some of them kept at Constantinople, yet euer they bare the name of Rome, as Romaine Emperours: finally Peter deliuered to Rome þ keyes of heauen and hell, A feeble reason thoughe it had bene true. Thus at this time as an aoulterer by treason and murther vsurped the Empyre, so of the same man this ambitious Boniface obtained by briberye to be vniuersall bishop, and consequently by the saying of his owne predicessour to be the forerunner of Antichrist.

He decreed in a Synode that vnder the paine of excommunication one Pope beinge deade, another should not be chosen before þ third day after: Also the same penaltye for such as sought to be bishops by fauour or briberye, he decreed that a bishoppe should be chosen by the voyces of the clergye and the people together, and þ election to be good if it were ratifyed and allowed first by the Prince or chiefe parson of the place, and last of all confirmed by the Popes auctoritye, and wyth these woordes of his, Wee will and commaunde. From this time forwarde the puritye of the Gospell decreased and superstition increased: Likewise þ Empyre was at this time mightely weakened, for Fraunce Germanye, Lombardye and Spaine reuolted and forsoke the Empyre, & beside Cosdroa kinge of Persia inuaded and wanne away many countreys and Cittyes in the East, and among them Hierusalem. Boniface hauinge enioyed his auctoritye scarce a yeare dyed: From this time sayth Vspergensis the Romain Empyre was neuer without great trouble, miserye and misshap.

2. Boniface the fourth.

BOniface the fourth borne in Marcia, obtained of Phocas the Emperour that a Church in Rome called Pantheon, which the heathen had dedicated to all their gods and idols, should be translated from the worshipping of Idols

to the

to the seruice of Christ, and be dedicate to al Sainctes, and so called allhallowes Churche: An vngodly and blasphemous alteratiō, and contrary to S. Paules doctrine, that Christians should turne that to Gods seruice, which was dedicate to idols. He appointed ye feast of alhallowes day, and that the Pope on that doye should say a long masse: he also appointed the corps cloth to be had at masse: he gaue moncks leaue to baptize and absolue. In this Popes time God punished ye wickednes of Phocas, who was reft both of Empyre & lyfe, by his successour Heraclius, for hauinge his handes and feete cut of, he was throwne into the sea.

3. Theodatus.

THeodatus the first was a Romaine, the sonne of one Steuen a subdeacon: he deuised a newe founde alliance betwene the Godfather and ye goddaughter, and betwene the godmother and her godsonne, calling it spirituall cōsanguinitye; and therefore he commaunded that neyther ye godfather nor his godsonne should marrye the goddaughter, and so of the godmother likewyse: which is one token giuen to know Antichrist by, forbiddinge and makinge vnlawful (as Tacianus Montanus, and other heretikes do) honest mariage, which God hath made lawfull. At this time raigned such a straunge lothsome kinde of leprosye disfiguring men in such sort, that one coulde not discerne another by the face: Theodatus died Anno 618. in ye thirde yeare of his Popedome. Here note by the waye that none of the Popes from this time liued longe, which wroughte not some notorious acte for the maintenance of the tiranny of the Sea of Rome.

4. Boniface the fifte.

BOniface the fifte was borne in Campania, he decreed ye holye places shoulde be rescewes and maintenaunce for theeues.

The thirde booke of the

theeues, murtherers and leude parsons, making the churches, churchyards, chappels & such others to be sanctuaryes for them, and that no man should draw them away by violence that fled thether. He commaunded that none but deacons shoulde handle the reliques of Sainctes: furthermore that a will and testament being made by commaundement of the Prince should stande in force, which prerogatiues his successors did afterwarde vsurpe to themselues, that no testamente should be good, vnlesse it were allowed by them. He dyed Anno. 623.

5. Honorius the first.

70 HOnorius borne in Capania was a good Pope (as Vvicelius saith) for diligēce in building Churches, deckīg them with golde & siluer, but a negligent pastor for ought that is read of him in feeding Christ his flocke. Amonge other temples and monasteries that he founded, he bonge S. Peters Church w<super>th</super> cloth of Tissew, which with þ Emperours consente were taken out of Ianus Capitol or Romulus temple: hee deuised holye roode daye, and added to the Letanye the prayinge vnto dead saintes, Sancta maria, sancta Gregori &c. and commaunded to go about the streates in procession euery Sabboth day. This Honorius died Anno 634. in whose time Mahumet arose, the auctor of the Turkishe religion.

6. Seuerinus the second.

71 SEuerinus or Zepherinus the secont, was cōfirmed Pope in the name of Heraclius the Emperour, by Isacius his lieutenaunt in Italye. This Pope also was very carefull to build vp Churches of dead saints, but carelesse of buildinge vp the Gospell: whereuppon Isacius brake into the Church treasurye, and perforce toke away the great heapes of

Pageant of Popes. Fol. 41.

pes of riches, ỹ priestes to their power defending the same: for then (euen by Gods iust punishment) the Sarracens wan from the Romaines, Damascus, Arabia, Phœnicia, Egipt, and other kingdomes of the worlde, Mahumets power encreased still against them: and as for the Emperours souldiers they were driuen to great pouertye and wante of all thinges, and the houge heapes of the Churches hourded treasury encreased to no bodies profit. For (sayth Platina) in this daūger of Mahumet, the priests loked that the laitye shoulde beare the charge of this, to withstand the ennemies of Christendome: againe the laitye looked that the clergye for defence of Religion shoulde promise, and giue their money for the maintenaunce of the warre, and shoulde not waste their wealth prodigallye to worse purposes, as for the most part they doe, spendinge plentifullye their riches gotten by almose deedes and with the bloud of martyrs, vppon statelye and massye plate of siluer and golde: hauinge little care of the worlde to come, defying God and mā, whom they serue only for luker sake. Plat. in Boniface the 5. This made Isacius with his souldiours to burst into the Churches treasurye. Seuerinus dyed Anno 636.

7. Iohn the fourth.

IOhn the fourth, learning by his predecessours harmes howe to vse ryches better, did redeme out of captiuitie with that money, whiche Isacius lefte in Lateran, his contreimen the Assirians and Dalmacians, whome the Lombardes had taken prisoners in battell. And yet least the like deede shoulde be attempted against the churche anye more, euen sone after in the beginninge of his Popedome, he decreed, that the churche goodes being so purloyned, shoulde be recompenced fower times double. He wrote to Englande concerning the keping of Easter, and against the Pelagian heresy: Hee transported from Dalmacia to
F. Rome

The thirde booke of the

Rome, the dead bodies of two martyrs, Vincentius and Anastasius, rather to hurt liue Christians with committing Idolatry in worshipping them, then that the saluage people should harme the dead bodies. Hee died ere he had raigned Pope two yeares, Anno. 638. Platina reporteth that in this mans tyme, a certaine priest robbed the tombe of Rotharis in S. John Baptistes church: for (sayth he) they were wonte to burie certayne precious thinges with kinges bodies. The like thing happened of late tyme to Cardinall Allouisius, Patriarke of Aquilia, for his graue being burste vp, he was robbed by those, whome he from very base estate had aduaunced to the dignitie of priestes and better calling.

8. Theodorus.

73

Theodorus the firste was a Grecian borne, the sonne of Theodorus byshop of Hierusalem, hee builded manye churches in Rome, and golden shrines for sainctes. He set vp the reliques of Sainctes in golde & siluer in the church. He forbad that mariage made after a single vowe, shoulde be broken. He depriued Pyrrus byshop of Constantinople, for heresy: He appointed that tapers should be halowed on Easter eue for Easter time: He died, Anno. 646.

9. Martin the first.

74

Martin the first a Tuderdinian borne, made lawes for keping holy dayes, and decking of churches, suche as the Idolatours before were wot to kepe: He gaue straight charge that priestes should shaue their polles, and that bishops should make euery yeare as they call it, an holye Chrisme, and sende it to euery churche in their Diocese: He burthened the Clergie with vowe of single life, and appointed that a couple being married, ere they lay together,

the

the brydegroine & bryde, should haue the priestes blessing. He commaunded also, that priestes houses should be buylt next to the churche: That Monkes shoud not go out of the abbies without the Abbots leaue:& in a Synode at Rome that bishops should not transpose the churche goodes to their owne priuate vse. He died Anno, 656. VVicelius sayth, he was very vehement against certaine sectes, excōmunicating them whome he ought by the scripture to haue admonished. He deposed Paule Patriarke of Constantinople, not admonishing him first once or twise, according to S. Paules rule: for the whiche he was bounde in chaynes, and so brought to Constantinople, by the Emperour Constātinus, wher in banishmēt he died in great miserie. An.653.

10. Eugenius the first.

EVgenius the firste was a Romaine, commended for his manners. But VVicelius saith, this Pope did neuer any notable deede: but decreed that bishops should haue prisons to punishe priestes. Thus by little and little, they encroched the power of temporall swearde: certaine letters were sent vnto him from Constantinople, contayning heresie, whiche were so detested, that saith Platina, the Clergie it selfe toke vppon them to forbidde the Pope to saye masse in S. Maries churche, vnlesse he would firste burne the letters; then might the Clergiz controll the Popes slackenes or errour in religion.

75

11. Vitellianus.

VItellianus borne in Campania, being an excellent musician, wrote the ecclesiasticall Canon, he broughte singing and organs into the churche. He accused one Iohn minister in a certaine churche in Crete, vnto the bishop of that place, for hauing a wife. He made the Latin howers,

76

F ii songes,

The thirde booke of the

songes, masses, idolatry, and ceremonies, adding and turning all into Latine, about the yeare of Chistes incarnation. 666. which was the number of the name of the beast spoken of in the 13. of the Apocal. Here therefore is to be noted, that the nūber of the beast agreeth vnto this time, secondly the number of the yeares conteined in the name of the beaste, is founde out in this woorde λατεινος: as who would saye, that Antechriste shalbe a Latin, or in the Latin churche, who shall come to his perfection in the yeare. 666. Also the letters of his name shall amounte to this number, and last of all is to be noted how that beside this Lateinos expressed the Latin bishop, and the time of Antechriste, it agreeth with the straunge doinges of this tyme, that all thinges were turned into Latin in the churche. And because that this mistery of sixe hundred sixty sixe, spoken of in the Reuelation, may appeare euen to the moste simple to agree vnto the churche of Rome, as in this place is saide: it is first to be considered that the auncient father Irenęus, being immediatly after the Apostles, reading this place, and considering of the woordes of S. Iohn, saying: Let him that hath wisedome counte the nūber of the beast, for it is the number of a man, and his number is sixe hundred sixty sixe. Irenęus I saye, considering of these woordes, did at the length finde out that this number agreed to this Greeke name λατεινος and therefore he sayde, that surely Antechriste shoulde be a Latin and in the Latin churche: for the Grekes, in whose tongue the Reuelation was written, do expresse their numbers by their letters, as we do by figures. And in their numbringe this letter λ the firste letter of that name, standeth for thirty: the next letter α standeth for one: the thirde letter τ for three hundred: the iiii. letter ε for fiue, the fift letter ι for tenne: the sixte letter υ for fiftie: the seuenth letter ο for threescore and tenne: and the eight and last letter, ς standeth for twoo hondred. So that if these eight numbers, that is: thirty, one, three hun-

dred,

Pageant of Popes.   Fol. 43

dred, fiue, ten, fifty, seuenty, and two hundred, be it two togegether, they make fixe hundred sixty sixe iumpe. Againe number so the letters in this worde εν Λληcιαcοττωλικα Ecclesia Italica, that is the Italian Churche, and ye shall finde it also make iump sixe hundred sixty sixe. For in the former worde of these two, there are eight letters: whereof the firste is ε standing for fiue, the second κ is value twenty, and so the thirde is κ that is twenty, the fourth λ that is thirty, the fift η that is eight, the sixt σ that is two hundred, the seuenth is ι that is tenne, the eightis α and that standeth for one: All whiche numbers added together, make 294.

Nowe to come to the latter worde ιοοκκ Italica, in it are seuen letters, the firste is ι and is euer set in the Grecian numbers for ten, the seconde τ for three hundred, the third α for one, the fourth λ for thirty, the fift ι for tenne, the sixt κ for twenty, the seuenth and last is α for one, all whiche seuen numbers amounte to three hundred seuenty and two, then vnto this adde the nuber of the former worde, whiche was two hundred thirty foure, and the whole somme is iumpe sixe hundred sixty sixe. Furthermore, in the same thirtene chapter, and the firste verse thereof, S. Iohn speaking of this beaste, saith that the beaste had seuen heades. And in the seuententh of the Reuelation, the Angell doth expounde this mistery vnto Iohn saying: the seuen heades were vii. mountaines vpon which the woman (meaninge the forenamed whore of Babilon) doth sit and afterwarde againe he saith that the same woman whom Iohn saw sitting on the beast with seuen heades, is that great Cittye which hath rule ouer the kinges of the earth : At which time it is manifest to all the world, that Rome had the soueraigntye and Empyre of all the world, and that it was then the great Cittie, and none but it, of whom this might be said: neither is it knowen that anye other Cittye is, or hath bene built vppon seuen hilles. And that Rome is so, it appeareth by diuers writers Romaines and other, that

F iij   report

The thirde Booke of the

...that they haue ſowen it. Knowe other Munſter in his Topographie declareth in the deſcription of Rome teſtifie that there are ſeuen hilles but alſo ſheweth the names of euery one, which are theſe: Auentinus, Capitolinus, Palatinus, Cælius, Exquilinus, Viminalis and Quirinalis hill. Propertius the Poet confirmeth it likeſely, in a verſe ſaying thus of Rome, Septem vrbs alta iugis toti quæ preſidet orbi: the like hath Virgil in his Georgiekes, Septem quæ vno ſibi muro circundedit arces, ſpeakinge it of Rome. Mantuan in his Faſt. li. 2. doth in like maner deſcribe Rome, calling it Romulea ſeptem ſu Collibus vrbem. So of the Grekes it is called Heptalophos, wherin Hepta ſignifieth 7, and lophos an hil, head or top.

9. This Vitellianus commaunded ſhauings and annointings of the clergye to be vſed, geuing vnder theſe markes licens to buy and ſell pardons in the Churche, as was propheſyed of Antichriſt: & after he had choaked the Church with much valerybe vſed. At this time at the fulneſſe of Antichriſt, mokery grew into ſuperſticious ſtimation. At this time alſo theſe two ſtraunge thinges were wrought, Abbeis were firſt founded for monkes, kinges were ſhaued and made monkes.

12. Theodatus the ſecond.

Theodatus the ſecond a Romaine borne, was made Pope beinge but a monke: he beſtowed great coſt to make a ſumptuous abbey of that, from whence he came: he gaue licence to mōkes to tranſport Benedict Nurſia patriarche of his own order with a ſcholeſiſter of theirs, from Caſsim mount into Fraunce. At this time were manye ſtraunge thinges as a blaſinge ſtarre appearing 3. monethes continually, with great raine & often thonders, with a ſtraūge Rainbowe and earthquakes, ſuche as the like were neuer heard of. And ſome ſay that the corne being beaten downe with

with these straunge tempestes of raine, slo spzāng vp againe
and grew to ripenesse. For these thinges Theodatus caused prayers often to be said, and dyed Anno 675.

13. Donus the first.

Onus the first, was made Pope in a miserable tyme
when the fieldes and the corne were burnt vp with thō-
der, lightninges and showers. He as (Popes vse) beautified S. Peters porche with pillers. And after he had punished certaine Nestorians hereticks, he scattered thē in other
abbeis in Italy. He restored to repaire olde churches. He deuided the Clergie into diuers orders, and adorned them
with seuerall kindes of honour, and dignitie. After muche
controuersie he made subiect to Rome Rauennas churche,
Theodorus the Archebishop therof, agreing to it through
the Popes flattery, whiche churche before was called Al-
liocephalis. After he had done many such deedes he dyed
Anno. 679.

14. Agathon the first.

Agathon the first, as Gratian witeth Distinct 19, being
a Monke of Sicill, cōmaunded that the Popes decrees
should be taken for as canonicall and authenticall, as the
Apostles wrytings. So he gaue as great auctoritie to the
masse, whiche was clouted together by sondry Popes. But
wickedly he cōdemned the marriage of ministers of the Latine churche: He sent one Iohn a Monke and Archdeacon
of Rome, into Englande, Anno 679. to teache them here
the manner of their reading, singing, & ceremonies in their
churches. And the better to vtter his knackes of celebra-
tions and sacrifices, as Beda wryteth in his fourth booke
18. chapter, de Gestis Anglorum. He sent his Oratours
Iohn bishop of Portua, and Iohn Deacon of the Romaine

F iiii churche

The thirde Booke of the

churche to the sixt Synode of Constantinople, and against the Monothelites he sent one Agathus. In the whiche Synode the Clergie of the Greke churche, were allowed mariage, and the Latin churche forbidden it. Also among other thinges then done the eight daye after Easter, Anno 681. the said John of Portua, did first of al say ꝑ Latin masse openly before the Prince and the Patriarke, and people of Constantinople, all men allowing it for novelties sake, as a new founde thing, whiche taking roote hereupon, was received in all churches, whiche helde vpon the Pope. In this Popes time after straunge Eclipses, both of Sunne and Moone, with a Pestilence so contagious in Rome, that the Pope him selfe died thereof. The seate then was voyde a yeare and a halfe.

Leo the second

Leo the seconde was a Monke very learned, as well in Greke as in Latin, and so skilfull in Musick, that hee brought the notes of the Psalmes and Hymnes to better harmonie. He confirmed the sixt Synode partly to establishe the masse, partly because by it also the Clergie of the West churches, were forbidden mariage. He translated into Latin the statutes of mariage. He appointed that the Pax shoulde be borne about, and be kissed of the people, while masse was saying. Also, if neede did require there shoulde be Christening every daye. He would have (for their sake of Rauenna) no election of any bishop to stande in force, vnlesse hee were first confirmed by the bishop of Rome: But (sayeth N. Vicelius) without paying for his poll, or anye other money, which saith Platina, I woulde were kept still in Rome: for out of this bribing at this day, many mischieues aryse. For as yet there durst none enterprise wholly such polling, as they did afterwarde about 1000 yeares after Christes. For in time past the vi. Princes of Italye did con-

firme

Pageant of Popes. Fol. 45

firme the bishops of Italy: yea, and the Pope him selfe: Afterwarde the Emperour Constantine the fourth, agreing thereunto, the election was againe ratified in the handes of the Clergie and the Laitie. But the Prelates of Rauenna, being emboldened becauſe that the court of the ſixe ſtates was among thē, would not obey the churche of Rome, but auouched that they were egall in dignitie. And thus Fœlix being their biſhop after Theodorus, went about to ſhake of the Popes yoke, and to recouer their loſt libertie. But the Emperour that was then Iuſtinian, ſonne of the ſayde Conſtantinus, being ſet on by Leo, withſtandeth the purpoſe of Fœlix, and after he had by aſſaulte wonne the towne, he boared out the byſhops eyes with a whot burning iron. Leo before the ende of his tenne monethes died Anno. 685. in which time the moone was in a monſterous and ſtraunge Eclipſe, appearing as redde as bloud all the night long, diuers nightes together.

16 Benedictus the ſecond.

Benedict the ſecond, whoſe holineſſe (they ſaid) moued the Emperour Constantine the fourth (if they father not a falſehode on him after his death) to decree, that heneeforth the Pope of Rome ſhould haue authoritie ouer the people without the licence of the Emperoure, or the ſixe ſtates of Italy, whiche laſted not long. He reedified diuers temples enriching them with veſſels of golde, ſyluer and guilt, with copes of cloth of tiſſue, and cloth of gold, and other iewels, according to the Iewiſhe ceremonies: and this Pope was the firſte that toke vpon him to be called Chriſtes vicar on earth. Out of Veſuuius hyll in Campania, ſuche aboundaunce of fier ſpouted, that it burnt vp all the countries, men and cattell rounde about: after whiche it is euident that there enſued, Anno 686. bloudſhed, burning, ſpoyling, and the death of Princes, and eſpecially of this

Benedict

82

The thirde booke of the

Benedict a Pope of tenne monethes.

17. Iohn the fift.

83 IOhn the fifte was borne in Siria, he first of all toke consecration of three bishops, of the bishop of Hostia, Portua, & Veliterne, whiche custome be appointed to be kepte of his successours. And his posteritie do kepe this vse euen vnto this daye in our Sauiours church at Lateran. In his Popedome he fell sicke, in the whiche time he wrote a vayne and vnlearned booke, touching the dignitie of the pall of an Archebyshop.

18. Conon.

84 COnon a Thracian, was made Pope after much wrangling betwene the Romaines, who would haue elected one Peter an Archebishop, and the host, preferring one Iohn a priest. This Conon being established, fell sicke and died, Anno 689. He made one Kilianus being before a Scottishe Monke a bishop, and sent him with other into Germanie, to winne the East part of Fraunce to þ church of Rome. But this Kilian & his company, were at the first slayne of their Auditours, and buried at Herbipolis. One Paschal an Archedeacõ, and Treasurer to the said Conon, in this Popes life bribed Iohn Platina, one of the sixe princes of Italy, to make him Pope after the death of Conon. Platina tooke the mony, but he perfourmed not the couenaunt, neyther restored the money.

19. Sergius the first.

85 AT this time was great hurlie burly about the election of the Pope: Some chose Theodorus a priest, some Paschal an Archedeacon. And whyle euery one did ambitiously

tiouflye maintaine his owne faction, either partie with the men of his owne side kept possessiõ in some part of Lateran pallaice: But when the chiefe of the clergye, the Romaines, & the army sawe, that this sedition would wexe bloudye, they agreed to appease this tumult, & reiecting both ye other they chose Sergius an Assyrian borne, & brought him to Lateran Church, and brasting vp the doores they driue oute the seditious electors, and compelled Theodor & Paschal to salute Sergius as Pope. He bestowed great cost in trimming the temples with guilding, images, golden candelsticks, and curious masons worke, riche clothes, & such stuffe: He (they say) founde a peece of Chrst his Crosse in a brasen cofer: He repayred the images of the Apostles being worne out with continuance: He set a new patche vpõ the masse, commaunding that Agnus Dei should be songe thrise whẽ the priest is breaking the bread. And on the day of the annuntiation of the virgin to sing procession: He reclaymed the Church of Aquilia which began to decline from Papistrye. He also by his monks allured the Saxons & Frisians to the same superstition: While Aldhelmus an Englishman waited at Rome to be admitted to a bishopricke, he hard the Pope accused of adulterye, the childe being new borne which was fathered vppon him, Aldhelmº therefore did secretlye admonishe the Pope of this wickednes. Sergius dyed Anno. 701.

20. Iohn the sixt.

IOhn the sixt a Grecian borne, beinge much delighted in vanityes as his predecessors were, was very curious in deckinge the temples. In the time of famine and warre, he noutished a great nomber of poore men with the treasures of the Church (being in deede the worthiest of al Popes, for such almes deedes) also he redeemed diuers prisoners oute of bondage: And with threatninge caused Gisulphus cap-

taine

The thirde booke of the

taine of Beneuent (who then wasted Campania) to returne home. This man (as it appeareth) was because of Sergius adultery elected only Pope, and not confirmed, Sergius being restored againe; and therfore he is not rekened amōg the Popes. Peter Premonstratensis sayth, that Iohn was thrust out againe because of his vnlawful entrance, & therfore he is not enrolled among the Popes.

21. Iohn the seuenth.

87   IOhn the seuenth a Grecian, was delighted in nothinge but superstitious garnishinge Churches and images of Saincts, for which he is muche commended: but not one worde spoken of him touching preaching the Gospell. Hee dyed Anno. 707.

22. Sisinius the second.

88   SIsinius & Sozymus after great contention with Dioscorus about the Popedome at length obtayned it: Hee was so sore sicke of the goute, that hee liued Pope but xx. dayes, being neither able to sturre, nor to eate any thinge: Nauclerus wryteth that he was poisoned by the said Dioscorus in the same yeare that Iohn the seuenth dyed.

23. Constantine the first.

89   COnstantine the first being sent for by Iustitian ỹ Emperour to come to Constantinople, was the first that euer offered his soueraigne to kisse his feete. At his returne home he condemned Philip Burdan of impiety, because he coulde not abide the abhominations of Idols, and toke the Images out of the Churche. Furthermore he commaunded that the picture of the Emperour (counting the good Prince a wicked heretike) should not be receiued, thoughe it were

it were engrauen in golde, or siluer: he cursed all the Emperours coyne: And holdinge a counsell at Rome, he decreed that Images should be had in the Church, & should be worshipped with great reuerence contrary to al Scripture. After this bee moued one Anastasius a mainteyner of images against the said Philippicus, who apprehending him, reft him of his kingdome, and put out his eyes: when the bishop of Ticinum rebelled against his Metropolitan the Archbishop of Mediolan, the Pope would not reconcile him, but falselye made him tributary by stelth to the Sea of Rome, whereby that bishopricke hath brought it selfe to perpetual bondage. Kinredus and Offa two kings of the Englishe Saxons for their pleasures made a voyage to Rome, and when they were there, the Pope made theym forsake their kingdomes, & turned them into monkes: hee dyed Anno 715. He was the first that gaue his feete to be kissed of Emperours.

24. Gregory the seconde.

Gregory the second bestowed his time in repayring and building spirituall houses & Churches with great coste: Hee forbad a nonne, a nouesse, an abbesse, a deaconesse or a spirituall Godmother to marrye: He ordained that masse should be said euery friday in Lent: and caused prayers often to be said because of straūg sightes in ÿ ayre : He would haue masse said no where but in an hallowed place: He persecuted euen to death, those that woulde not worship images. By his authority he compelled Luith Prandus king of Italye at the first withstanding it, to ratifye, Arithpertus donations beinge vniuste, onely to maintaine the totac of the clergye: He moued the subiectes of the Emperour Leo to breake into opē rebelliō, because their images were taken away: He caused Spaine, A Emilia, Luguria, Italye and other countreys to reuolt, and defye their obeysance to

the

The thirde booke of the

the Emperour. The Emperour would haue no worshipping of images in the Church, and therefore the Pope did both excōmunicate him & put hym from his kingdome, & threatned him eternall damphation. And thus the Emperours of the East lost their title in Italye. Gregory dyed Anno 731.

25 Gregory the third.

Gregory the third was a stout champion for the Church of Rome and their ambitiō. He did excommunicate his soueraigne the Emperour Leo, because he destroyed images. He ioyned to him Carolus Metellus ye bastard lieuetenaunt of the Frenchmen, to maintaine the estate of the bishop of Rome against the Lombardes: By helpe of the Lombardes, he draue the Grecians out of Italy. And afterwarde oppressed the Lombardes them selues by the helpe of Fraunce, and absolued all Italy from the oath of their dewe alleageance sworne to the Empire. He busied him selfe in taking care, and bestowing costes on churches, abbyes, celles, altars, & Images. In a Synode at Rome, he maintained that the Images of dead Sainctes should be worshipped, decreeing excommunication against those that would do the contrary. He layde up in Peters Pallayce ye reliques of sainctes, and commaunded that on euery daye masse should be said there to them. In the Cannons whereof hee addinge certaine clauses, clowted it with this pece, Quorum solemnitates hodie. &c. Hee forbad to eate horse fleshe. He translated the tuiciō of the churche, from the Grekes to the Frenchemen: He set the Apostles Images in churches seuerally by them selues. He wrote to Boniface an Englisheman, that their priestes ought to haue shauen crownes, that should pray for the dead at masse, and that they ought to praie, and to offer sacrifice for the dead. After these and like dedes he died, Anno 742.

26 Zacha-

26. Zacharias a Grecian.

ZAcharias emplied his witte and wealth in pompeous and gorgeous buylding: Among other vaine sumptuousnes, he was the first that gaue golden coapes decked with pearles and stones, to the churche for holy vses. He gaue a stipende to the churche towarde the charge of the lampe oyle. He deuised the manner and fashion of priestes apparell: He deuided the East churche from the West churche. He translated out of Latin into Greke, Gregories foure bookes of Dialogues, to the entent to plante the opinion of Purgatorie among the Grecians, which they neuer receiued yet. He made it vnlawefull to mary the vnkles wife, the vnkle being dead, although Gregorie the third allowed it. He comaunded gosseps (as we call them) in no wyse to marye together. He commaunded the Venetians (a Godly dede) that vpon payne of curse they should not for lucre sel their children of Christians to the Saracenes. Taking vpon him the power of God after a sort, he presumed very churlishly and cruelly, to depose kings from their estate, and to make kynges. He was the firste that attempted to release subiectes of their alleageance. For Pipinus, sonne of the bastarde Charles Martell, a traytour to his Prince, by his messengers obtained of Pope Zacharye, that he woulde depose king Childericus from the crowne of Fraunce, and geue it to him and his heyres. The Pope remembring the late dede of Pipinus his father, in the Popes behalfe against the Lombardes, & thinking by this meanes that he should be the better able to encounter the Emperoure of the East, graunted this trayterous request. And sent straight charge and highe commission to the estates of Fraunce, that they shoulde depose their present king Childericus, shaue his head, put him into an Abbey, and so make him a Monke: And after this they should acknowledge Pipin beinge cōfirmed

The thirde booke of the

firmed and annoynted by the Archebishop Boniface, to be their soueraigne and kyng. Furthermore he chaunged Lachis king of Lombardy, Charolomannus, and other from their royall estate, and made them Monkes. After tenne yeares raigne, he died, Anno 752. One Steuen a Deacō, was chosen to succede him, who being wakened out of slepe to go about his affaires, being taken with the falling sicknesse, died presently, and therefore is not accompted Pope.

27. Steuen the second.

Steuen the seconde, immediatly stept in after this other Steuen, who for his superstitious and ambitious dealing in their religion, is compted of the Papistes a Godly byshop: But note the misterie of his iuggling, he hauing thus by craft and guyle obtayned the Popedome, he immediatly subdued to the sea of Rome, all the dominion of Rauenna, which had wrought the Popes so much displeasure, and beside many other countreys in Italy, thereby to obtaine the kingdome of Italy. He craued of Pipin importunatly to reuenge his quarell against Aistulphus kyng of Lombardy, for demaunding subsidie of him and his Prelates. Pipin to gratifie the Pope, in consideration of the kingdome of Fraunce gotten by his meanes, after he had longe besieged, & often assaulted, the dominion of Rauenna, at the length deliuering it from the garison of Lombardy, gaue it as a present to the Pope, with al ye townes thereof, euē to the goulph of Venice. And thus they robbed the Emperour of that dominion, and withal pulled down the thirde part of the strength of the Romaine Empire, empairyng thereby the East Empire: And so for the west Empire, which then was arising, it lost his strengthe likewise. But Pope Steuen hereupon annoynting bastarde Pipin and his two sonnes agayne, and getting him a pardon for falsefying his oath of alegeaunce, did more ratifie

him and

him and his, in the kingdom for euer, cursing all those that at any time should speake against him. Also he shaued Childericus againe, and made him newely Monke, and so put him afreshe into an Abbey, to make all sure. Pipin for this fel downe flat on the ground & kissed the Popes feete, held his stirropes, and toke the bridle in his hande, and played the osteler, and vowed perpetuall fealtie to the Pope. The Pope to thanke God for this benefite of so great honour, whiche nowe began, caused procession to be song through all Rome, and the Apostles tombes and other sainctes reliques to be borne about and shewed openly, and him selfe to be caried triumphantly through the middes of the people on his porters shoulders in his Pontificalibus. Which vse of being borne on mens shoulders, his successours haue estemed as a moste holy thing. He confirmed by his auctoritie, that all Popes tradicions should be taken for good. He forgaue all treasons against Princes: for the hatred he bare the Grecians, he studied to chaunge the Empire frõ them into Fraunce. He furnished the churches in Fraunce with pricke song and descant. And whatsoeuer henceforth could be wrested from the Empire, he cõmaunded it should be S. Peters fee, and so dedicated to the churche of Rome: he died Anno 757.

28 Paule the first.

Paule the first was brother to the said Steuen: hee after wrangling and iarring betwene him and one Theophilact, succeded: and followinge the daunce that his auncetours had ledde him, threatningly and fearcely he restored the images, which Cõstantine Emperour of Cõstantinople had abrogated: but Constantine stãding stoutly in his opinion, and despinge his vaine curses and threates, wythstoode images wyth all his power euen to his death. This Paule honoured much the body of one Petronilla ỹ daughter of

The thirde booke of the

ter of S. Peter, and toke her karkasse out of the grounde, remouinge it to another place, and enlarged and repayred diuers Churches, adding manye ceremonies to them: At length he dyed through the extremity of the heate of sommer Anno 767. In his time (as Peter Premonstratensis sayth) starres fell from heauen to the earth, accordinge to the 6. of the Apocalips: And immediatly after this Charles the great begā to raigne, who builded 24. monasteries.

29. Constantine the second.

COnstantine the seconde being but a layman, by strong hand was made Pope (though manye other stoode for it) through the doinges of his brother Desiderius kinge of Lomberdye, and through Totho duke of Nepesia: but this hastines at lēgth is brought to none effect, because Cōstantine had not taken Ecclesiastical orders. Whereuppon arose great discord amōg the clergye: in which tumult one Philip was chosen, but because he wanted artilary & power to mayntaine his parte, hee was forced to depose himselfe againe: Constantine obtayned the Popedome a yeare, and that pontificallye: but in the ende a councell beinge gathered of Italian and Frenche bishops, in their great rage & furye they put him out, and with great reproch clapte him in an abbey as in a perpetuall prisō, hauing both the Popedome taken from him and his eyes put out Anno. 708. Some do not count him among the Popes because he was a laye man, and disalowe all his doing, sauinge Baptisme and Chrisme: But the next yeare after, his brother Desiderius comminge to Rome vnder pretence of prayinge, got those that put his brothers eyes, and rewarded them with the like punishment.

30. Steuen the thirde.

Steuen

Steuen the thirde is commended to be a stout maintayner of Romishe traditions and auctoritye: for in a Synode in Lateran hee did disanull all that his predecessour Constantine had done: The bishops by him created were disgraded, if they had no absolution, bee commaunded ỹ vppon paine of excommunication no lay man should presume to be Pope wythoute ecclesiasticall orders. Hee condemned the seuenth councell of Constantinople as hereticall: And did againe establishe setting vppe of Images, which by that counsell was condemned: He taughte that images shoulde be worshipped, and encreased the worshipping of them, and commaunded that they should be hallowed wyth Frankinsence. Hee broughte to his subiection Mediolan Church, which euer before had beene free. Hee sued to Charles the Emperour, & obtayned to depose Desiderius of his kingdome. Hee appointed those that brake theyr Canons, to sing Gloria in excelsis on Sōdayes: and that in the solemnitye of the masses it should be song on S. Peters altar by seuen bishops being Cardinals: He went one time (to counterfaict Christ in his doings) barefooted in procession. He dyed Anno 772.

31. Hadrian the first.

HAdrian the first was a meete champion to maintaine ỹ digintye, which his predecessours had enroched: Hee bestowed cost on altars, dead mens tombes, dead mens bones, and Churches: Hee attributed more worship to images then euer any did, and wrote a booke of the honour and profite of them: and pointed them in steede of Scriptures to be laymens bookes: He condemned in a coūsaile those that detested images, as one Foelix & other: By the ayde of Charles the Emperour, he delyuered the Sea of Rome from the perill of all other Princes: He was the first that with his leaden Bull did honour theyr decrees, dispensa-

G ii   tions, and

The thirde booke of the

tions, and priuiledges. Hee forbad that anye infamous parson should be promoted to priesthoode, & that the clergye should not be sued oute of theyr owne court: Charlemaine kinge of Fraunce and brother to Charles the Emperour being deade, his wyfe Bertha came wyth her two sonnes vnto this Hadrian, suinge to him that he would annoint and establish these her sonnes in theyr fathers kingdome: But this holye sire lest he should offende theyr vncle themperour, cast of the orphanes, despised theyr sute,& refused to do it: & finally committed to perpetual slauerye, both the children and theyr mother, w̄ Desiderius king of Lombardye, his wyfe, his children and his kingdom, whō Charles caryed into Fraunce wyth hym, where they liued long in care and miserye, vntil they dyed. And thus Gods vicar vseth orphanes, wydowes and poore Princes : To cloake all this hee fedde in the porche of Lateran pallaice, a hundreth poore folke euerye daye. But Charles in recompence hereof after he had kissed the Popes feete, cōfirmeth to the Pope his fathers gift, that is the townes pertaynīg to the Dominiō of Rauenna: and like an vniust pyrate, he added to the Popes possessions, Venice, Histria, the dukedome of Fotriiulenia, the dukedome of Spolet, & Beneuēt, and other lands. Also he made Hadrian Prīce of Rome & of Italy & ratifyed ẏ Popes Empyre, by spoyling the king dom of Lombardy, and ioyning so in league w̄ the Pope, ẏ who so delt wyth the one, shoulde be enuempe to both : Agayne Adrian caused Charles and his successors the kings of Fraūce, to haue the title of most Christian king, and like a subtill fox hee gaue him power to chuse the Pope, and to make bishoppes through all his dominions, but that lasted not long, and so vsed him, that in deede he had but the bare name of the Romaine Emperour. This Hadrian cloathed the bodye of S. Peter all in siluer, and couered the Altar of S. Paule, with a pall of gould. He dyed Anno 796.

32. Leo

32. Leo the thirde.

Leo the thirde as sone as he cought the Popedome, by & by sent S. Peters keyes and the banner of Rome with other giftes to Charles the Emperour, desyringe him to binde the Romaines by an oath, to become subiecte to the bishop of Rome. Charles to pleasure him, sent one Agilbert an Abbot, who compelled the Romaines by his commaundement to sweare allegeaunce vnto the Pope. Hereupon the Pope purchased such deadly hate among the people, that as he was ones going on procession, certaine furious parsones fell vpon him, and beate him from his horse, and stripping him starke naked out of his pontificall roabes whipped him very sore: But at length when Charles came, they (knowyng his good will towarde the Pope) turned their former hatred into loue and fauour, and durst not auouche the faultes layde against him. Therefore when he asked of his conuersation, they aunswered with one voyce that the sea Apostolicall, ought to be iudged by no layman. After the whiche aunswere the Pope affirming, and swearing him selfe to be giltlesse, the Emperoure being pacified, doth absolue him, and pronounced him innocent: For with curtesie the Pope desirous to be thankefull, with a great voyce proclaimed Charles Emperoure, & ioyned him with himself, & set the Diademe on his head, y Romaines in y meane time cried, God graūt life & successe to Charles our mighty Emperoure. Thus was the name of the Romaine Emperoure restored, so as the Popes aucthoritie should not be empaired. Hereof the custome continued that he who should receaue the scepter of the Empire, shoulde be ioyned in auctoritie in Rome by the Pope. From this time, being in the yeare. 801. the honour of the Romayne Empire, was first translated frō the Grekes to the French men by the Pope, and after at his good pleasure, from thē

G iii   to the

The thirde Booke of the

to the Germaines. This Pope also pronounced Pipin of Fraunce sonne to the same Charles, king of the same parte of Italy, whiche neither he nor any of his predecessours could euer subdue: whiche he did for this pollicie, that the kinges of Fraunce hauing ye title Emperial, should neuer suffer him to lose his maiestie. For this cause (saith Hieronymus Marius) ye Pope wrought perpetual dissentions betwene the Emperours of the West, and of the East, to the great spoyle of Christian bloud. Thus vpon condition that Charles and his, should sweare perpetuall homage and fealtie to the churche of Rome, he made him Emperour. He first appointed to hallowe the altar with frankinsense. He made the Popes decrees to be of greater auctoritie then al the writinges of the doctours. Also he caused that a certain counterfeit bloud made by a conueisaunce to ronne from a wodden roode, should be taken to be the very & true bloud of Christe: And caryed it to Mantua where to this daye it is preserued, reuerenced, and worshipped. He by his auctoritie allowed it to be so, appointing for it yearely a solemne holyday. Such was the dotage of the time, wherof Mantuan bewitched with this enchauntement, writeth to the Emperour Charles, of the Popes iourney.

VVhyle Leo hearing of the brute
   of counterfaited blood,
VVhiche founde was lately streaming from
   a crucifixe of wood,
He hieth him to Mantua:
   where he perceiuing well
The wonderous woorkes wherein this bloud
   so straungely did excell,
He thought wee should it as the bloud
   of Iesus Christe esteme,
That earst was shed vpon the crosse
   our soules for to redeme.

An abhominable elusion and blasphemy to say, & teache that the that the glorified bloud of Chriſte ſhould ſhead it ſelfe in a rotten idoll, whiche as the Apoſtle ſaith, was ones ſhed for all, & that out of his precious body. But the Popes auctoritie in this matter, cauſed this to be beleued, almoſte of all men. But ſo Paule prophecied the cōming of Antechriſt, to bee in falſe ſignes to deceiue the vnbeleuing: Leo died, Anno. 816. Vſpergenſis ſaith, that in this time of Leo, the Sunne was darkened and loſt his light for eightene days, ſo that the ſhippes ofte on the ſea wandred to and fro: Alſo that in an other yeare it was twyſe in the Eclipſe, firſte in June, ſecondly in December: Likewiſe the ſame yere, the Moone was twyſe in the Eclipſe, in July and in January.

33. Steuen the fourth.

STeuen the fourth, the thirde moneth after he had taken the Popeſhip vpon him, made a voiage into Fraunce to Lewis the Emperour, to purge him ſelfe of election, wherby he was made Pope, becauſe he was choſen, and confirmed by the Clergie, and the people, contrary to the decree made by Hadrian and Leo. And thus their owne decrees whiche the former predeceſſour made, the next ſucceſſour broke. But to flatter and dally with the Emperoure for a while, he brought with him a fayre crowne of Remis, and put it on the Emperours head, & put another on the Empreſſe head, naming her Auguſta. When he had receiued his rewarde of the Emperour, & ſhould returne, ẏ churche of Reata wanted a biſhop, and yet Steuen very ſubtelly would electe none, onleſſe he might firſte knowe, whether the Emperour would allowe his doing: but note the ſequele. As ſone as he was returned ſafe to Rome, he began to conſider that the prerogatiue which was geuen to Charles and his ſucceſſours, might be a bridelling to the ſea of Rome: being embouldened the more, becauſe Lewis was a gentle perſone, and a tractable man: he diſanulled al that

G iiii   aucto-

The thirde Booke of the

auctoritie and right, and affirmed that it ought to belonge to the Clergie, the people, & the senate, to electe the Pope. But to auoyde the Emperours displeasure, he vsed this interpretation, that it was lawefull for them to chuse him without the Emperours auctoritie, but not to consecrate him, but in the presence of him or his embassadours. And thus the Emperours were a litle shouldered out from the election of these prelates. And beside this because he raigned but eight monethes, he coulde not any further enhance the pompe of his seate, dying, Anno. 817.

34. Paschal the first.

99   PAschal the first a Romishe monke, was chosen withoute the consent of the Emperour, according to the glose deuised by Steuen: but when the Emperour complayned, y᷉ he founde himselfe agreeued with the election, Paschall verye craftelye wrote vnto him purging himselfe therof. In processe of time when he perceyued y᷉ the Emperour (vpō blinde zeale to religion) was a greate maintayner of the Church of Rome, he thinking that it were daungerous, if he shoulde delaye the enlarging of his auctoritye: did so craftelye charme and enuegle the Emperour, that he yelded whollye to the Romaynes all his auctoritye touching the election of the Pope, which was giuen to Charles, and he confirmed by wrytinge hys auncetours presentacions, which they had wrongfully purloyned. This did the Emperour confirme with hande and seale, not knowing theyr crafte. But after y᷉ when this Emperour Lewes minding to haue his sonne Lotharius ioyned w᷉ him in the Empyre, and for the more coueniēt doing therof sent him to Rome, to be crowned there by the Pope king of Italy: which after y᷉ the Pope had done, whiile Lothari⁹ (because of a certaine tumulte and sedition there arysing) fled to his father for aydeto suppresse it, leauing behind him one Theodorus

and

Pageant of Popes.   Fol. 53

and Leo, chiefe officers aboute him, who stoode stoutlye in theyr maisters quarrel, the Pope secretly and trayterouslye caused certaine seditious persons to pul out theyr eyes, and afterward to strike of their heades. And when he was accused to the Emperour both of the sedition, and of this murther, he picking out for his purpose a counsell of Prelates, purged himselfe by his othe: notwithstanding he absolued and pardoned those that were giltye and knowen offenders, he accused them that were slaine to be giltye of treason against the Emperour, and finallye auouched, that they were lawfully put to death. This Paschall they say (if they ouer reach not in the nomber) did take vp ii. thousand saincts karkases, that were buryed in Churchyards, and bestowed more honourable tombes vppon them in other places: He commaunded to worship and reuerence ye reliques of Saincts: He was beneficiall to stone walles, as Churches, and altars diuerslye. Last of all he gaue commaundement to the clergye, that they should not take any benefice or Ecclesiasticall lyuinge at the handes of a layeman. He dyed Anno. 824.

35. Eugenius the second.

EVgenius gat the Popedome with much brablinge and strife among the fathers of the election, for first one Zizimus had it graunted him: but the discorde beinge ended Eugenius gat it both for his curtesye & eloquence (as they say) who as Premonstratensis sayth, ye while he was Cardinal of S. Sabines, bestowed on the Church a siluer cuppe and a stately picture, but now in his Popedome, he so busied himselfe aboute corne matters, as if he had bene borne to feede manye men: and yet some saye that his eyes were put out by the Romaynes, other say by the priests that hated him. In this mans time Lotharius the Emperour appointed magistrates in Italy, to gouerne and brydel the

100

Romai-

The thirde booke of the

Romaynes, because they abused their libertye very much which they had vnder Charles: which deede as manye thincke hastened the death of Eugenius. Michael ÿ Emperour of Constantinople sent Embassadours to Lewes ÿ Emperour, desyringe to be resolued concerninge Images, whether they should be worshipped or abandoned: and Lewes sent them to Pope Eugenius to be instructed, but Eugenius aunsweare was neuer knowne. He raigned 4. yeares and then dyed. Anno. 8 2 7.

36. Valentine the first.

101   VAlentine the first being yet but deacon & not ful priest, was made Pope, he was a man of a quicke wit, able to perswade and diswade. And some write that there was in him such excellent hope, that he would haue raigned more happelye and in better order then the rest, wherby the fathers aboute, feared the decaye of theyr former holynesse, for he neuer did any thing that was not liked. He dyed the fourth day of his raigne, and as some thinke poysoned.

37. Gregorie the fourth.

102   GRegorie the fourth would not take the Popeship vpon him (fearing the sequeale) vntill that ÿ Emperour had allowed the election, and by this man the Emperours had restored to them theyr right of cõfirming the Pope, which yet lasted but a while. In this Popes time there was a counsaile of bishops held by the commaundement of Lewes at Aquisgran, where it was decreed (Gregorie being president of the counsaile, that euery Church should haue reuenewes of his owne, wherby the clergye might be maintayned, and not be constrained to forsake their cure and office, and giue themselues to occupations of lucre. And it was concluded that none of the clergye of whatsoeuer degree,
should

should weare anye precious or purple garmentes, neither weare any ringes, nor iewels, vnlesse it were a ring at saying masse. Againe that they should not kepe a great traine and familye, neither horses, dysing, nor vnhonest woinen, and that monkes shoulde not exceede in glottonye and feasting, and that the clergye should weare neither golde nor siluer in theyr shoes, slippers, nor girdles, which (sayth Platina) are far disagreeing with religion, and most manifest tokēs of incōtinencye. Yet such was theyr royat then, which continued so that Platina in ÿ life of this Gregorie cryeth out in these wordes.

O Emperour Lewes I would thou were liuinge in oure time, the Church nowe wanteth thy holye lawes, and thy iustice, for Ecclesiasticall persons do so wallow in al kind of lust and royat: Ye might now see thē pranked in crymson, with bruchies and Iewels, and that not men onelye, which perhaps might seeme tollerable, but also their horses and beastes. And while our prelats passe abroade, a lustye troupe of youthes, go ietting before them, & a knot of chaplins following behinde: and they themselues not ryding on sillye asses, (as Christ the author of our religiō, and onelye paterne of good life in earth did) but vppon their neyeng and trampling horses, al betrapped as if they roode in triumphe after a conquest of an ennemye Touchinge their siluer plate and statelye furniture of houses; and delicate fare, it booteth not to speake: vvhen as their dainty diet excelleth all that euer was in Sicilli, their roabes passe all the pompe of Attalus, their vessels staine all the plate of Corinth; but what wil come of this intemperancye, I saye nothing. Thus complayneth Platina.

But to returne to Gregorie, he made diuers holy dayes for sainctes, as Bartholmew, Gregorie, Sebastian & others, he was beneficiall to Churches and deadmens bons. By the Emperours helpe he draue the Moores out of Italye: he procured tenthes to be giuē to the Churches, and deui-

The thirde booke of the

sed solemne erection of Sepulchers. He dyed Anno. 843.

38. Sergius the second.

103 SErgius the seconde was before called hogs snoute, he being made Pope did first bringe up this use that the Popes should chaunge theyr names. To confirmation of whom the Emperour sente hys sonne with auctoritye Emperiall to Rome, and manye nobles to attend on him: which kinde of confirmation they were wonte all to attende uppon, untill Hadrian the thirde told the Romaines, that they oughte not to loke for the Emperours good will in creatinge the Pope. This Sergius was the first that of himselfe renounced his Christian name given him in baptisme: He appointed that Agnus Dei should be said thrise at masse, & the oste the while to be deuided into 3. partes: He bestowed paines as other did on dead mens tombes. He dyed. Anno 846.

A nevv patch set on the masse.

39. Leo the fourth.

104 LEo the fourth toke the Popeship under Lotharius the Emperour, and bestowed manye ornamentes on Romain cities & churches, for he builded a tower in Vatican, he repayred the wall and towne gates, and raysed about them euen from the foundation xv. fortresses, whereof hee planted two verye well at the ende of the riuer Tiber, to beate backe the force of the ennemye. He builded a newe S. Martyes Church, and gaue an Alter of iiii. crownes for martyrs bones, he repayred the Castell of S. Angell, and made seates of Marble in the porche of Lateran. Hitherto he played the baylisse of husbandrye, but after this he became a warrier and captayne of an armye. For when the Sarracens made manye a roade into Italye and spoiled the countrye, first he promised them heauen that would fight for the defence of his state, then mustring the Romaine garrison

Pageant of Popes.   Fol.55.

rison he making the signe of the Crosse, encountereth the ennemies, and with this prayer (as they say) O God whose right hand &c. at Hostia gate he put them to flight and ouercame them. Afterwarde he summoned to a counsaple 47. bishops, wherein hee condemned one Marcellus of diuers crymes: But afterward he gaue sentēce that a bishop should not be condemned without 72. wytnesses. He first began (contrarye to the counsaile of Aquisgran) to decke the Popes Crosse with precious stones, & commaunded it to be caryed before him: Hee toke vppon him to profer his feete to be kissed, and decreed that none of the laitye should abide in the quier at masse time, but onely he which attended on the Alter. He appointed sondrye hollyedayes, and seueral prayers and solemnityes to them. He was accused of many crymes, but speciallye that he went about by auctorie of a counsell, to translate the Empyre from Fraunce into Germanye, but he purged himselfe by his oath. He dyed Anno 854. In this Popes time Anno 847. Ethelwolphus beinge first a monke of single life, hauing a dispēsation from the Pope, left his monkery and became kinge of Englande, making his dominion tributarye to the Sea of Rome, appointing a certaine taxe of money to be leuied yearely of euerye house, and payed to Rome: And thus all Englande became thrall to Rome, to the fulfillinge of the saying in the 17. of thapocalips concerninge the x. kinges, These haue one counsell and power, and shal giue their power vnto the beast.

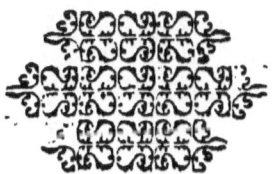

THE

THE FOVRTH BOOKE

cōtayning the third order of Popes, in whō Antichrist appeareth to be come toward fulnesse of hys wickednes specifyed in the 17. Chapter of the Reuelation, speakinge of Antechrist in the kingdome of the greate whore of Babilon, vvhich sitteth vppon the beaste vvith seuen heades: and that Prophecye seemeth to maister Baale to containe these 41. Popes following to Siluester the second.

Ytherto from Phocas the Emperours time for the space of 247. yeares, Antichrist like the beast raigned in the Church of Christians without iudgemente, or consideration of heauenly spirite. Hytherto the Popes euen to the fortieth Pope cast theyr eyes on earthly things, forgetting Gods euerlasting testament, as if they onely regarded but the fleshe, and not the soule. All theyr delight was in newe traditions, ceremonyes, buildings, pleasures, pompe, warres, treasons, and translations of kingdomes as appeareth, so that they seemed to liue in the glorye of this worlde, and in contempte with Christ: so that the Church vnder their gouernment is at length become the strompet of Babilon according to the whole discours of the Apocalips. The truth whereof the Lord hath most euidently reueiled in this next Pope þ followeth, who was a woman and an harlot, whereby al men may vnderstand the misterye reuealed by Christ.

THE

THE POPES OR ROMAINE ANTI-CHRISTES.

40 Ioan the eight.

IOan the eight, being a woman, was made Pope, and because of her bringing vp vnder a certeine Englishe mā a Monke of Fulda, (whome she loued tenderly) her name was altered, and she was called Iohn Englishe: She sat as Pope in the pontificall seate at Rome two yeares, and syxe monethes: She was a Germain of kindred, and borne in Mens, called at the firste Gilberta, who the more to enioye her louers company, and the better to auoyde suspiciō, dissembled her kinde, and put her selfe into mans apparell, & so trauailed with the Monke her peramour to Athens: where after she had profited in all the sciences, her louer being dead, she came to Rome disguising still her selfe, and counterfaiting to be a man. For through the promptnesse of her wit and ready tongue, shee talked eloquently in publique lectours and disputations: And many had her in admiratiō for her learning: She grew into so great credit, & was so wel liked of al, that Leo the Pope being dead, they chose her Pope: In whiche office as other Popes did, shee gaue orders, made priests and deacons, promoted bishops, made abbots, sayde masses, hallowed altars and churches, ministred the Sacramentes, and gaue men her feete to kisse, and did all other thinges belonging to Popes, & her doinges stode in force. But in the time of her Popeship, Lotharius the Emperour being an olde man became a Monke. And Lewis the seconde came to Rome, and receiued of her the scepter and crowne of the Empier with Peters blessing: whereby the whore of Babilon shewed her

selfe so

The fourth booke of the

self so mighty that she made kinges stoupe vnto her. Apo. 17. Also as Houedenus saith in her time Ethelwolphus king of Englande gaue the tenth part of his kingdome to the Priestes and Monkes to praye for his soule. And his sonne Ethelwaldus maried Iudith a wydow, and lately his owne fathers wyfe and his stepmother. But as touching Pope Ioan, she was gotten with childe by one of her familiar chaplaynes a Cardinall, to whome her fleshly appetite caused her to disclose her selfe. As she was going on procession solemly to Lateran churche, in the middest of the way, and in ye open streate betwene Colossus & Clement church, she was deliuered of childe in presence of all ye people, and died of her trauell in the same place. And for this wickednesse she was stripped and spoyled of all pontificall honour, and buried without any pompe or solemnitie: Whereof Mantuan wryteth describing hell in the thirde booke of Alphonsus thus.

Here honge the dame that erst disguised would seme a mā to be

VVhose head the Roman miter ware with crest of crownettes three,

VVho playde a shameleſſe strumpettes parte in place of Popes degree.

Lo this is that seate that can not erre, being endued with the holy Ghost by succession, or rather an euident argument of the seate of Babilon. But ye Popes since that time in their procession do shonne that place, where she was deliuered as odious for the hap thereof. Funcius sayth boldely that this was suffered by Gods especiall prouidence, that this woman should be made Pope being also an harlot, euen then when she should bring kinges as she did Ethelwolphus and Alphredus in subiection vnto her, whereby Antichrist might be knowen: for then it was the Lordes pleasure, to bewraye the whore of Babilon in a Pope being an whore. Whereof the holy Ghost foretold, Apoc. 17. that

the clerg

Pageant of Popes. Fol. 57.

the elect might beware of her. But to auoide the like inconuenience of a woman for the time folowing, they deuised that who so euer should be chosen Pope, should be serched very narrowely to be tryed a man, shamefull to be reported, but vsed without shame among suche shamelesse shauelinges. But nowe commonly they nede not when they chuse them Popes, mistrust them to be women, for whyle they are Cardinals they playe suche Carnall partes that they are able to bring forth bastardes of their owne begetting to proue them selues men, whereof one Iohn Pannonius wrote a mery Epigram in foure Latin verses: testifying the truthe of this their doing, of the whiche I omitte the two first verses for ciuilitie sake, it may be gathered by these latter two what is ment.

Cur igitur nostro mos hic iam tempore cessat
Antè probat sese quilibet esse marem

How hapneth that this groaping them is vsed nowe no more,
Because eche one doth try him selfe to be a man before.

41. Benedict the third.

Benedict the thirde, being first tried vpon the porphyry stoole to be a man, was made Pope. Massæus saith he howled out and cried miserably, that he should be promoted to so great dignitie, whereof he was vnworthy (a rare thing among them.) But some thinke he did it but of hypocrysie, because (As Platina saith) he offred his feete to be kyssed, and suffred him selfe to bee worshipped lyke an earthly god. Then came Embassadours from Lewis the Emperour, to confirme the election of him done by the Clergie and people. Among many superstitious and vaine ceremonies he appointed that Dirige should be sayde for the dead, & that the Clergy should go soberly, & honestly. He died Anno, 859. In this time (as Sigebertus and Vin-

centius

The fourth booke of the

gentius testifie) in Mens as a certaine Priest was casting holy water a certayne Diuell lurking vnder his Cappe, as if he had bene a familiar to him, did accuse him, that he laye with a Proctours doughter that nighte.

42. Nicolas the first.

107 Nicolas the firste was made Pope in the presence of Lewis the seconde Emperour after his father Lotharius. But as sone as Lewis was departed out of Italy, hee began to consider howe he might aduaunce the dignitie of the Popedome whiche before (that the Emperour might counte him holy) he refused. He put downe John Archebishop of Rauenna, for maintaining the olde libertie of his byshopryke: and brought that churche into perpetuall bondage. Among many decrees he concluded, that no seculer prince, no not the Emperour him selfe, should be so hardye as to come in among the Prelates in their counsayle, onlesse they were debaiting matters of beliefe, then the Emperour should execute those, whome the Pope iudged to be heretikes. Also he decreed, that the layetie should not take vpon them, to iudge the life of the Clergie, neither to dispute of ye Popes auctoritie & power. Also he decreed that Christian magistrates should haue no auctoritie ouer a prelate, because saith he, ye pope is called God, Auton. Tit. 16. He comaunded that the Clergie should not be warriours but study, howe to talke, and perswade. He commaunded agayne that diuine seruice should be sayde in Latin: But yet graunted the Sclauonian and Polonians, to haue it in their owne tongue by dispensation. He added the Sequencias to the masse. He added Gloria in excelsis, to be songe to the masse on Maundy thursday. He added the terme of Apostolicall auctoritie to the Popes decrees: He commaunded mariage to be openly solēnised: he allowed that the sa-

cramentes

cramentes might be receiued of euill ministers: He firste bounde the Clergie to single life. But Huldericus bishop of Augusta, controlled his wickednesse herein by a sharpe epistle: he died Anno. 867.

43. Hadrian the second.

HAdrian the seconde, the sonne of Talaris a bishop, was by the people and the Clergie made Pope, before the Emperours Embassadours could come thether: For then the Romaines did by force take vpon them the election of the Pope: whiche when the Embassadours tooke in euill part, they were thus aunswered, that the wyll of the multitude could not be brideled in such a tumult. But yet they had done happely, because they had appointed such a good man. The Embassadours euen of compulsion seing there was no remedie to abrogate the election, did against their willes pronounce him Pope: being confirmed, he bestowed muche on the poore. He sent three Legates, bishops all, Leopart, Syluester, and Dominicus, (that were bredde and brought vp in his kitchin) to kepe the Bulgarians and Dalmacians within his dominion, whom Nicolas had brought to the yoke before. But the Bulgarians hauing had proofe of his tyranny draue out the Italian priestes, and receiued the priestes of the Greke churche. This enkindled hotte coales betwene the Latins and the Grecians. Hadrian died Anno 873. Before whose death it rayned bloud three dayes at Brixia, and all Fraunce was miserably troubled with Locusts. Alfredus king of England, toke his crowne of this Pope, and was anoynted, whiche neuer any king of Englande did before: But afterwarde he was called the Popes adopted sonne.

44. Iohn the ninth.

H ii   Iohn

The fourth booke of the

IOhn the ninth was excellently learned, bothe in Latine and in Greke: He in his soueraintie crowned three Emperours, Charle the bauld, Charles Balbus, and Charles Crassus. Carolus Caluus vnderstanding that the Emperour was dead, hied him to Rome to Pope Iohn, whome with his bribes he allured to satisfie his desire, and so was made Emperour by him, and receiued the crowne Emperiall. But about a yeare after he was poysoned at Mantua by one Sedechias a Iewishe phisition & an enchasiter. Iohn hearing of his death, bent al his force to make Charles Balbus to succede his father, but the Romaine Lordes withstoode him, and made Charles Crassus Emperour. The Pope standing obstinatly in his frowarde purpose, was taken of the citezens & put in prison, because he would not relent: but being released by his friendes helpe, he fled into Fraunce. And bestowing the imperiall crowne on Balbus, saluteth him Emperour. In the meane time Crassus hauing gotten the citie of Rome, causeth Iohn with terrour to retourne from Fraunce: Who returning to Rome, willeth the Emperour to let him returne in safetie, & maketh him Emperour, and setteth the crowne on his head. Iohn at his being in Fraunce, sommoned a counsell at Treca, wherein he condemned certaine contentious persones, and made many lawes to the aduauncement of Popery. Afterwarde he wrote to Lewis Balbus, that the priuiledges of the Church of Rome could not be abrogate without a prescription of an hundreth yeares. Also he made it sacrilege, to take any holy thing of any vnholy persone, or any vnholy thing of an holy persone. He excommunicated these that were gilty of sacrilege, but in suche sorte that for money they might be dispensed withall. Hee gaue to many men sainctes reliques for great iewels. He confyrmed the liberties belonging to ecclesiastical persones, cloysters, church goodes, monasteries, and clarkes. He prepared an army against the Saracenes, and droue the out of Italy and Sicil.

He died

he died, Anno. 883. At this time the Empier was translated from the Frenchemen to the Germaines, by Carolus Crassus.

45 Martin the second.

Martin the second was a Frencheman, whose father was a Necromancier, and coniuring prieste, he gate to be Pope, not by honest meanes, but by crafte & ill artes. They saye that by this mans subtell enticement, the foresayde John was apprehended, and layde in pryson, and so constrayned by his frendes, ayde to flye into Fraunce, to saue his life. At the electiõ of this Martin, the Emperours auctoritie was not loked for, nor demaunded to his administion. Thus proudly by little and little, the Popes shooke of the Emperours power, whereby they might the better treade them vnder their feete. But he raigned not longe, about a yeare and certaine monethes, he died Anno. 884.

110

46 Hadrian the third.

Hadriã the third was of such a proude stomake & hawty courage, that as sone as he had gotten into the Popedome, he made a decree, that the Emperours auctoritie should no more take place in creating of Popes: but that the voyces of the people and Clergie of Rome, should be euer free to do it. The Emperour at that time warred against the Normans. Thus saith Cranzius, these Prelates and the lewdenesse of the Romaines, durst contemne their Empier, vntill the force and strengthe thereof decayed. Whereby this one Pope was now deliuered and brought to bedde of that monster at ones trauelling, wherof so many of his auncetours had traueled: that is to cut cleane of the Emperours auctoritie: For Nicolas the first had attempted it, but brought it not to effecte. Lo here good reader, how

111

H iii

The fourth Booke of the

ter, howe by this decree all the Emperours right and title whiche they had ouer the Pope and citie of Rome, is wrest from them, whereby the Pope with great triumphe hath gotten the victory, and vpper hande: Thou shalt se him yet creepe hier, and attempte greater matters, ceasing not vntill he haue aduaunced him selfe aboue all that is called God, or that is worshipped, 2. Tit. 2. Whereby his flatterers may saye: Who is like the beaste, or who is able to fight with it. Apoc. 13. But after this he lyued not longe: he died sodainly, Anno. 886.

47. Steuen the fift.

STeuen the fift gat to be Pope, at such time as Fraunce was inuaded by the Normans, England by the Danes, Pannonye by the Hunnes, and Italy by the Sarracens. He liued in much trouble and anguish of the mind all the time of his being Pope, because Italy was so vexed with warre and the Romaines were not at his commaundemente enoughe: yet he employed himselfe to the most of his endeuour, daily to encrease their Babilonical trumpery, and that none of his decrees might be defaced: for as Gratian writeth Distinct. 6. Enimuero, he decreed that all the Canons of the Church of Rome ought of necessity to be kept. The same Pope (sayth he) forbad anye Chriftians to condemne any to be put to death with hot iron or scalding water, which was then vsed, Cau. 2. quest, 4. He caused a lawe to be made, howe to order such parents as do either ignorantly smother their children in theyr beddes with thē, or els do choake them, or murther them. He dyed Anno 892.

48. Formosus the first.

FOrmosus the first being bishoppe of Portua fearing the crueltye of Iohn the ix. forsoke Rome, because hee was thought

thought to be giltye of Iohns impꝛisonmente: this name Formosus signifying beutifull, whiche beinge made Pope he choose and toke vppon him, sheweth (sayth Cranzius) ꝥ he was a pꝛoude parson. This Formosus foꝛ those foꝛmer causes vowed and sware an oath, that he would neuer returne to his bishopꝛicke, noꝛ to Rome, both which he had foꝛsaken: & so he gaue ouer his oꝛders, foꝛsoke pꝛiestcrafe, and became a lapeman, but the nexte that succeded, did absolue him frō the oath, which he had swoꝛn to Pope Iohn, and foꝛ monye did restoꝛe him. After the death of Steuen this Formosus so monied the matter, that hee purchased Peters chayꝛe, but as not with out bꝛibes, so not without great bꝛauling, by meanes that one Sergius a deacon wꝛestled foꝛ the same place. Foꝛ the appeasing wherof he calling Arnulphus sonne of Carolomannus into Rome made him Emperour, who to gratify him foꝛ his curtesy, stroke of the heades of them that were his chiefest aduersaries. He raigned vi. yeres & did almost nothing, he died Anno. 896. And at the length foꝛ these quarrels cōtinuing amōg his successoꝛs, his bodye and bones were taken vp by Sergius the third, the ninthe Pope after him and thꝛowne into the riuer Tiber. After this Formosus, the Popes did so dispatch one another, that within nine yeaꝛes, there were xi. Popes.

49. Boniface the sixt.

BOniface the sixte was Pope but a while after Formosus, and therefoꝛe he could not shew of whether faction he was in such great debate among the Cardinalles & the people: He liued but 25. dayes Pope, & as Anselmus saith to be remembꝛed foꝛ nothinge, but foꝛ his quiet election, & happye in nothing but in raigning but a while.

114

50. Steuen the sixt.

The fourth booke of the

then forthwith wickednes hauing gotten libertie, brought forth and yelded vs these Popes, being as it were mōsters and mongrels, which encroche Peters place by ambition and bribery. Benedict dyed Anno. 904.

55 Leo the fift.

120 Leo the fift being made Pope, euen in his dignitie was taken by strong hande and cast into prison violently by one Christopher, seeking to make him selfe Pope, being but a priest and chapleine to Leo, & one whom he had brought vp in his owne house. Whiche thing sayth Platina, coulde not be done without great seditiō, and the slaughter of many. And of what auctoritie the place was now, it may wel appeare, when as firste harlottes bare sway and ruled the Popes, then a priuate persone durst, and could thus within so short a space as fourtie dayes, driue out the other, and kepe the place him selfe. Leo seing him selfe reft of the renowne, and thus defaced euen by his owne famulias frend, on whome he had heaped so many benefites, conceiued so great thought that immediatly he died thereof.

56 Christopher the first.

121 Christopher the first, was of so base linage, that neither his countrie, nor his fathers name was knowen. Hee hauing shoued out Leo, and his concubines adding him thereto, wan the Popeship by strong hande. But as he gate it naughtely, so was he shamefully thrust out again by one Sergius, the peramour of one Marozia, a notable harlotte and beautifull concubine, who sought to place him selfe in it. So Christopher was put downe, the vii. moneth of his Popeship: And as Platina sayth, compelled to be a Moke, whiche thing was then become the refuge of all captifes. And afterwarde he was againe pulled out of the Mona-

sterie by

sterie by the same Sergius, and caste into a straight pryson, where at length in muche misery and sorowe he died. Anno, 905.

57. Sergius the third.

SErgius the thirde, when as he was but a Deacon, gaue a proude attempt to aspire to the Popedome, and was in dede chosen thereto with great tumult among the people, when Formosus was chosen. But taking the foyle, he fled into Fraunce, but nowe espying his oportunitie by the aide of Charles Simplex king of Fraunce, and Adelbert Marques of Thuscia, he returned by stelth into Rome. And as it is sayde, he deposed Christopher, apprehended him, and clapte him in pryson, & inuaded violently the Popes place: Being setled, and remembring his ranke mallice againste Formosus, not withstanding the long time that had since passed, and eight Popes betwene Formosus and him, yet freshly to reuenge his olde grudge, Hee the seconde tyme toke vp the karkasse of the sayd Formosus out of his graue, after it had lyen thus long, & setting it in ye Popes chaire, did drawe him from thence agayne, and as if he had bene a liue strake of his head. And where as since his laste mangling, he had but three fingers remaining on his right had, Sergius chopped of those also. After all this, he caused his body and all these peeces therof to be hurled into the riuer Tiber, as if he had not bene worthy to lye amõg Christiãs. And yet not satisfied with this reuenge, hee defaced, condemned, and disanulled al his actes, so that it was then nedefull, to admitte them a newe to their orders, whome he being aliue, thought mete to make priestes. He compelled the Romaines to subscribe to this, for feare of the Frenche king. This Sergius among other newe ceremonies appointed that the people should beare candels on the daye of the purification of the Virgin Mary, whereupon it is yet called Can-

The fourth booke of the

led Candelmasse dayes, to geue their bodies vnnecessary light at noone daye, because their soules wanted their necessary light at all times. This lasciuious Pope begat a bastarde, which was afterwarde Pope Iohn the twelfth, whome he had by the moste shamefulle harlotte Marozia: So Luthprandus testifieth in the thirde booke, and xii. chapter, De gestis Imperat. This and other like prankes, among harlottes and bawdes he practised, euen in his Popeship: At the time of whose death Anno. 913. there were sene in the element great flakes of fier running to and fro.

58 Anastasius the third.

123 Anastasius the thirde, after Sergius (all their vnclenlye ceremonies being obserued) was elected Pope. But some write of him that he did neither good nor euill in his time, and therefore is he more commendable. They wryte that in his time the bodye of Pope Formosus was founde by certaine fyshers in the ryuer Tiber, and so taken vp, and with great worship buried in S. Peters pallaice, and as some are not ashamed to sayne, the Images of the church did salute it, whyle it was burying: A notorius vntruthe, and grosse blasphemie against God, although in the tyme of suche blindnesse, God might suffer Sathan to moue and styrre the Idols, before these idolatours, as in times past the diuell hath doone when he spake and gaue oracles and prophecies out of Idols: Anastasius died Anno. 915.

59 Laudo the first.

124 Laudo the firste being a fruytfull Prelate in begetting children, as Petrus Premonstratensis sayth, hee begat Pope Iohn the xi. in detestable adulerye. This Popes life sayth Platina was so obscure that some do not recken him among the Popes, especially Vincentius. This Laudo as
it appea

Pageant of Popes.   Fol.63.

it appeareth, spent the more parte of his chast life (as charitie went then) among harlottes, till at the length he was
destroyed among them: For one Theodora, the Lady that
gouerned Rome, a shamelesse curtezane, could not longer
forbeare the company of her louer, Iohn Archbishop of
Rauenna, who was apparent sonne to this Pope Laudo.
Rauenna (sayth Luthprandus) was two hundred myles
from Rome, whereby Theodora could not so often enioye
the byshop her louer, and therefore she caused him to giue
ouer Rauenna, and to vsurpe the Popes place in despite of
the auncientes of Rome. Here sayth Funcius, a man might
demaunde which of al these Popes did erre from the truth,
seing they were all called holy fathers, and heads of the
vniuersall churche. Let the Popes partakers aunswere if
they can.

60 Iohn the eleuenth.

IOhn the eleuenth borne at Rauenna, the bastard and adulterous sonne of his forefather Laudo, as sayth the Præmonstratensis, he obtained the Popedome by right of inheritaunce, though whoredome were his ayde. For thus
wryteth Luthprandus in his seconde booke, and thirtene
chapter of Emperours. Theodora an impudent harlot and
the Lady of Rome burning in fleshly lust, was so enflamed
with the comlye countenaunce of this Iohn comming to
Rome, that she did not only request him, but compelle him
to satisfie her carnall desire. For the whiche afterwarde she
made him byshop, firste of Bononia, secondly Archebishop
of Rauenna, and thirdly to obtaine her filthy pleasure more
conueniently, she made him Pope of Rome. Thus at this
tyme was the holy mother churche subiect to an harlot, &
ruled only by her, and is made an whore, according to the
xvii. chapter of the Apocalips. This Iohn hauing a warlike courage, played rather the warriour then the byshope

For

125

The fourth booke of the

For when the Sarasins wasted Calabria, Apulia, and Italy, he putting him selfe in armour, slew a number of them in these countries, & draue them cleane out. As concerning the ende of this man, thus wrpteth Luthprandus in his thirde booke and rii. chapter: In the meane time Guido Marques of Thuscia, began to conferre earnestly, and diuise with his wife Marozia (the doughter of the saide Theodora) howe he might depose this Iohn. Guido had many souldiours gathered together at Rome, the which apprehending Pope Iohn in Lateran pallayce, Anno. 928, cast him in prison, and holding a pillowe to his mouthe, did smother him to death very miserably: After his death they set vp Iohn the twelfth, the bastard sonne of this Marozia, whome she had by Pope Sergius. Thus the young harlot Marozia, for the aduauncement of her misbegotten sonne, murthered the louer of the olde harlot her mother Theodora, by the helpe of her husbandes seruauntes. But because the people of Rome and the Clergie, had not agreed vpon the election of this suborned Iohn the rii. the selfe same yeare of his election, he was deposed againe. And thus the same Iohn of whome (being set vp by force, & by and by thrust downe againe) Carsulan, Platina, Stella and others do make mension, because they knew not the true story of him, whiche Luthprandus wrote; the ignoraunce whereof bredde muche cofusion, for some toke these twoo Iohns to be both one, and some the one for the other.

61. Leo the sixt.

Leo the sixt, after that Iohn the rii. bastarde of Marozia the harlot and Sergius the Pope was deposed, obtained to be Pope by the election of the Romaine people and clergye being in great tumult. This Pope did nothinge commendable, but the establishing of peace in Italye: after he had raigned vii. monethes he was poysoned by Marozia, whereby

Pageant of Popes.   Fol. 64.

wherby she might establishe her sonne againe Anno 930.

62. Steuen the seuenth.

STeuen the seuenth did as Leo had done, he medled with nothing: for after he had liued Pope ii. yeares in peace, securitye, and liberty of the fleshe at his owne ease, hauing the blinde worlde readye to bende at his becke, he toke his death in a cup, wherewith (as they saye) he was poysoned. For sayth Crantzius it is a straunge thinge that so manye Popes at this time dyed so soone in their dignityes, which is a great presumption þ they were poysoned, as the moste part of them were knowen to be.

127

63. Iohn the xii.

IOhn the xii. the bastard impe of Pope Sergius þ third, and of the famous concubine Marozia, was now againe made Pope after much sedition. At this time a fountaine in Genua flowed with bloud very plentifully, prognosticatinge the wrath of God that immediatlye followed, for the Aphricans, Sarracens and Hungarians, wasted and spoiled all, and slue a houge nomber of people. There are some wryters (as is said before) that make ii. Iahns of this one, the one going before Leo and Steuen, who they said neuer enioyed the Popes Albe or Rochet, & the other this which nowe was set vp after Steuen, of whom (they saye) the bishoppes write nothing. Againe there are other some, that make this beinge borne in Rome & the other borne at Rauenna all one: amonge whom Platina sayth, that either of them was sonne to Pope Sergius, but Anselmus deceiued by Platina sayth the one was brother to the other : but other writers do make him a seuerall parson from the other two, saying he was not knowne of the Cronographers, because he did nothing worthie of memorye. But Luchprandus in

128

The fourth booke of the

dus in his thirde booke and iij. Chapter wryteth thus of the mother of Iohn. Marozia a shameles concubine and mother to Pope Iohn, after the death of her husbād Gui, doth send messengers to his brother Hugh king of Italy a Burgundian borne, to desire him to come to her, and to receiue of her the noble cittye of Rome: vvhich (she sayd vvithall) she could not do, vnlesse he would take her to be his vvife. For whiche her incestious desire Luthprandus wrote thus against her in Verse.

VVhye broyling thus vvith Venus brand Marozia doest thou raue?
Thy lavvfull loue and vvilt thou of thy husbandes brother haue?
Dare buckson, dame Herodia tvvo naturall brethren vved,
Lo Ladye blinde, Iohn Baptists layve is quite out of thy hed.
VVho did forbid that brother vvith his brothers vvyfe should mell,
And Moses Larve doth not allovve thy doing to be vvell.
VVho did commaunde the brother rayse vnto his brother seede,
If that the former by his vvyfe had issue none in deede.
But that thy husbande children hath by the can be declarde,
Tis so (saye you): but dronken loue doth nothinge it regarde.
Kinge Hughe euen as an Oxe to death, for thy desire is brought,
Vvhose mind not for to gaine thy loue, but rather Rome hath sought,
VVhat boteth it thou cursed dame this noble man to spoile,
For seeking thus by sinne to gaine a Queenely place a vvhile,
Iehouah iudge doth make thee leese both Rome and all the toile.

Vppon the said message the king leauing his armye a loose, came to Rome who being honourably receiued passed forth vnto the stronge houlde S. Angels castell, and so into the bedde chamber of Marozia. After he was established in vncestous mariage with her, he began to cōtemne and despise the Romaines: at which time Marozia had a sonne named Albericus, brother to Pope Iohn, but begotten by Marques Albericus. While this Albericus at his mothers bidding gaue water to king Hugh washinge his handes, the king because he did it not handsomelye, gaue him a blow on the face: Hereupōn Albericus to reuenge this iniurye, callinge the Romaines together spake thus vnto them. The honour and dignity of Rome is brought

to suche

to such doultishnes and follye, that it is nowe controlled euen by harlots? For what is more abhominable, what more shamefull, then that Rome should be brought to obeysaunce, throughe the incest of one woman; and that the Burgundians whilom slaues to the Romaines, shoulde now be lordes ouer them? If he beinge yet especiallye but a new come gest take vppon him to dashe me on the face, being his verye sonne in lavve, hovve thincke you vvil he deale vvith you in processe of time? Knovve ye not the pride of a Burgundian &c? This being sayde, without any delaye the Romaynes all defyed king Hughe, & chose the same Albericus to be their Prince. King Hughe being dryuen into this terrible feare, was compelled to forsake Rome, and leauinge Marozia fled to his owne companye: Then Albericus and his mother Marozia did only enioye the Monarche of Rome, and his brother the Popedome, who spendinge fiue yeares in Popishe practises dyed Anno 937, while the harlotte his mother ruled as well the estate temporall as spirituall in Rome.

64. Leo the seuenth.

LEo the seuenth succeedinge Iohn because hee desired to liue quietlye, medled wyth no matters, but as a slouthfull parson did nothinge worthye remembraunce. In his time sayth Luthprandus, the said kinge Hugh forsaking his wyfe Berta loued especiallye three concubines Bezola, Roze, & Stephana: and because they were such notorious harlots, hee gaue them the names of three Goddesses, callinge Bezola Venus, Roze Iuno, and Stephana Semele: by Bezola he had a sonne called Bozones, whom hee made bishop of Placentia, by Stephana he had Theobaldus made Archdeacon of Millain Churche, and by Rosa he had another greate prelate of the Churche, and a doughter besyde. In those dayes many sawe bloude rayne oute of the

Sunne,

The fourth booke of the

Sunne, as Masseus wryteth, and after it followed a great pestilence amonge men. Leo dyed. An. 941.

65. Steuen the eight.

130 Steuen the eight a Germaine obtained ye Popes chayre after this Leo, yet this seemeth straunge to many, how it should be doone, because no Emperour out of Germany procured it. But Steuen being notwithstandinge Pope, was so vexed with ciuill seditions among the Romaynes, that he coulde do nothinge worthy remembraunce: for hee was so shamefullye wounded, and foulye mangled and defaced amid the peoples, that for shame of his soule disfigurings, he durst neuer shewe his face abroade: So litle reuerence had ye Popes at that time, for their litle holinesse. Steuen dyed Anno 944.

66. Martin the third.

131 Martin the thirde being Pope gaue himselfe onelye to repayre the Church, not in Religion, but in building: not in reforminge ceremonyes, but encreasinge the dignitye and pompe of the Church. He was very beneficial to the poore, & bestowed plentifully on their bellyes. He was diligent in reformation of outward manners. In the first yeare of this Pope a great blasing starre was seene in Italye, after which saith Vspergensis followed an extreame famine: and againe saith Masseus the Sunne appeared verye terrible, threatninge the sequeale of Gods vengeance. Martin dyed Anno 947.

67. Agapetus the second.

132 Agapetus the seconde being Pope ruled Popelike in the time of one Berengarius a Marques of Italy, who was
the last

the last of that name, that had that dignitye after Hughe. This Berengarius is reported to haue dryuen many Monkes oute of their cloysters, whiche liued idellye, and gaue them selues to the pleasures of the worlde. The Pope perceiuing howe he could not rule Berengarius in these and such other spiritual matters, & that he would not restraine his soueraignitie, according to the wil of him and his: Hee sent for Otho the first king of the Germaines, to come into Italy, promising him the kingdome of the Romaines, to fight with Berengarius, and so saith Sabellicus, troubled the estate of that countrey: And except it were the settinge of these princes together by the eares, he did nothing worthy memory till his death, being Anno. 954.

In his time was a counsell holden at Ingelhaim, but suche was the negligence of the time, that no man can tell what was done there, or wherefore it was.

68 Iohn the thirtene.

IOhn the thirtene, being the sonne of the foresayde Albericus sonne to Marozia, obtained to be Pope partly by the bribery, partly by the threatning of his father Albericus, being Prince. He being Pope liued not like a bishop, but altogether like a ranke ruffianly roister, geuing him selfe wholly to all kinde of pleasure, as to whoredome, adultery, incest, masking & momming, hunting, maygames, playes, robberies, fyring of houses, periury, dyce, cardes, blading, robbing of churches, and other villanies euen frō his youth: he misused his cardinalles in cropping their noses, thrusting out their eyes, chopping of their fingers and handes, cutting out their tongues, gelding them, and vsing diuers diuersly. For before the Emperour Otho, in an opē Sinode it was layde to his charge (as Luthprandus wryteth) in his sixt booke, that he neuer sayde Mattins, that in celebrating the masse he him selfe had not communicated,

I ii   that he

The fourth booke of the

that he made Deacons in his stable among his horses, that he had committed incest with two harlots being his owne sisters: That hee played at dice, prayed to the diuell to sende him good lucke, that for money he admitted boyes to be bishops: He had rauished virgines, and straunge wome: He had made the holy pallaice of Lateran a stewes & brothell house: That he had defloured Stephana his fathers concubine, and one Rainera a wydowe, besyde one Anna an other wydowe and her niece: that he had put out the eyes of Benedict his ghostly father, vsed common hunts, that he woare armour, and set houses on fyre, brast open dores and wyndowes by night: that he tooke a cup of wyne & dranke to the diuell, and neuer blessed him selfe with the signe of the crosse: these and many more odious articles were layde to his charge: Whereupon the Emperour by the consent of the Prelates deposed him. And Leo the eight was set vp in his steade. But as sone as the Emperour was gone, those harlottes that had bene his companiōs, inueigled the nobles of Rome, promising that the treasures of the church to depose Leo, and place John againe: whiche they did out of hande, and so Leo whom the Emperour appointed, was deposed, and John established againe. Who in his Popeship decreed that the Emperour should euer be crowned at Rome by the Pope: But as he was solacing him self without Rome on a certaine night, with the wyfe of one that was a valiaunt man, he was taken by him euen in his adultery, and so sore and deeply wouded with a dagger, that he died thereof within eight dayes, in the tenth yeare of his Popedome, as Mantuan witnesseth. Of this Pope John S. Dunstanea Nicromancier and a coniuring Moke Archbishop of Caunterbury in Englande, receiued at Rome cōfirmation and pall to be metropolitan, Anno. 960. This Dunstane did shamefully snaffle king Edgar: For the king had deflowred a certaine Noonne, for the which cause Dūstane did so taunte and rate him, that the king fell downe

flat be-

Pageant of Popes.   Fol. 67

flatte before him, offering to submitte him selfe to any satisfaction, and obayed this that was commaunded him by Dunstane, first because he was yet vncrowned, he charged him that he should not take the crowne vpon him for seuen yeares, and that during this time he should fast twyse in the weeke, distribute his treasure to ye nedy, builde a Moonnery at Shaftesbury, and last of al, that he should driue out all maried ministers, calling them adulterous priestes. Cronicon Saxonicũ ecclesię VVigornienfis. But as other stories testifie, they were shortly after restored againe, & the mōks who had encroched their places were depriued. Also he purchased of him for a great somme of money, a cōmission, to disanulle and condemne the mariage of the Clergie, and to constrayne them to single life, or els to depriue them of ecclesiasticall benefites: So writeth Iohn Capgraue, and Polidor Virgil, in his sixt booke of the history of Englande. Hereupon he being emboldened by the auctoritie of king Edgar, ioyning to him selfe in the same commission, Oswalde bishop of Yorke, Ethelwalde bishop of Winchester, and Monkes of the like disposition, did violently thrust out of the cathedrall churches the Curates and Ministers, whiche would not forsake their wiues: and planted in them Monkes with their counterfaited chastitie, whiche they kept vntill the time of the moste renowmed Prince kyng Henry the eight. But many there were that stoutly stoode in defiance of this wicked doing, especially a certayne Scot did bitterly speake against it. Of this Pope Iohn came this prouerbe, As mery as Pope Iohn.

69. Benedict the fift.

BEnedict the fift, after the departure of Otho the Emperour with his armye, and depriuing of Leo, being but a Deacon, and Cardinall, was made Pope by Iohns frends in a tumultuous time. But Otho would not suffer Leo, 134.

I iij   (whom

The fourth Booke of the

(whome he had appointed) to take this iniurye, and therefore returning to Rome with his armie, hee plonged the Romaines diuers wayes, to make them yelde this Benedict into his handes, and to restore Leo. Therefore after they had kept the gates lockt twoo monethes, they yelded Benedict vnto the Emperour, and receiued Leo, and established him solemly in the Popes chayre. But when as Otho should returne into Germany, he sent Benedict to Hambrough to his Chauncelour Adaldag the Archebyshop thereof, where he liued in exile, and for very thought and anguishe of minde died, and was buried in the Cathedrall churche, Anno. 964.

70 Leo the eight.

153. Leo the eight, citizen of Rome, and chiefe secretary of Lateran churche, was made Pope by Otho the Emperour, in steade of Iohn deposed for his vilany. Who being established in his Popedome (& Benedict deposed) because he perceiued the lewdnes of the Romaynes, how that with threatninges, with bribes and euill meanes, they were still aduauncing their owne: He crowned Otho and made hym vniuersall Emperour. Afterward by decree of a Synode, he bestowed on Otho the whole and absolute aucthoritie, to electe the Pope, taking it from the people and Clergie of Rome, whiche (saith Gratian) Charles the great had geuen vnto them. This he did to auoyde those seditions, which vsed to arise in the elections. Otho desirous to be thankefull for this curtesie, restored to the sea of Rome, all whiche they forge, that Constantine gaue them, or that Charles or Pipin toke from the Lombardes. And had bestowed on them: He restored sayth Barnes, those thinges whiche hee neither possessed nor was able to defende. But Leo after he had raigned a yeare and three monethes, died Anno. 966.

71 Iohn

71 Iohn the. xiiij.

IOhn the xiiii. sonne of one Iohn a bishop (or as some saye of Pope Iohn the xii.) obtained the Popedome, as it wer by his fathers righte. This Pope was quietlye chosen, whiche was a rare thinge, and yet Peter the Liuetenaunt of Rome with the twoo consuls and twelue senatours, cōspired against him, because he fauoured the Emperoure, they apprehended him in Lateran churche, and kepte him prysoner in Angel castell the space of eleuen monethes. This being knowen, the Emperoure hasted to Rome with his armie, and dealt sharpely with the offendours, some he banished, some he made to forfaite their goods, some he hāged on the gallowes. But the Pope hauing Peter the president, yelded to his will, deliuered him to the hangeman, who according to the Popes cōmaundement, stripped him out of his apparell, shaued his bearde, and hong him vp by the hayre of the head for the space of an whole daye. Afterwarde he commaunded that he should be set vppon an asse with his face to the tayle, and his handes tied vnder the Asse tayle, and to make him a laughing stock to all men, to leade him thus about the citie, and withall to scourge him with roddes, this being done to dryue him out, to be banished into Germany. This Pope Iohn allured ye kingdome of Poleland to Popery, and sent thether Giles Cardinall of Thusculan to confirme the people therein, to deuide dioceses, to annoynte bishops, and consecrate them, and to accompte the Pope as supreme head of all churches. After this he died, Anno. 973. At this time they began to Christen belles, and to geue them proper names: For this Pope called the great bell of Lateran after his name.

72 Benedict the sixt.

I iiii   Benedict

The fourth Booke of the

137 BEnedict the sixte succeded Iohn as well in misery as in place, for he was cast into Angell castel as prisoner (for certaine offences) by Cynthius a Romaine, a man of great power. And within a while after he was strangled to death with a roape in the same pryson: or as some saye, pyned to death. I cannot but marvell (saith Platina) that his death was not revenged, neither by the Romaines, nor by Otho the Emperour, who so tendered the estate of the church of Rome: but I feare saith hee, that Benedict deserued as Cynthius rewarded him, seing no man reuenged his death.

73 Donus the second.

138 DOnus the seconde, succeding Benedict, learned by him to be more wyse, and therefore did nothing at al worthy to be written. Only this is mencioned, that when the Polonians desyred they might be made a kingdome, and haue a crowne graunted to them, he denied theire sute. Crantzius sayth, he gouerned indifferently, deseruing neither great prayse, nor dispraise; for a yeare and sixe monethes, he dies Anno.975.

74 Boniface the seuenth.

139 BOniface the seuenth was of so base birth, that neither the name of his stocke, nor of his countrey was knowen, he getting to be Pope by lewd meanes loste it lewdly again. For hauing obtained the seate, the magistrates conspired against him, whereby he was compelled to hide him selfe: But perceiuing he could not tary at Rome safely, hee filched and robbed Saint Peters Pallaice of the moste precious and richest treasure and iewels, and so by stelth fled to Constantinople: where after a whyle selling them all, he made a great somme of money, and returned to Rome, knowyng that mony could obtaine any thing. But in his

absence

absence the Remaines made cue Iohn the fifteth Pope in his steade: But he returning enriched the citezins with money, and allured to him euery rascall, whereby he toke Iohn, and thrust out his eyes, put him in pryson, pined him to death, and so gat his place againe, wherein shortly after he died wretchedly of ye falling sickenes: Whereuppon his body (hauing a roape tied about his heles) was haled through the stretes, and despitefully stabde in with daggers, pikestaues, iauelinges, and suche like thinges: and at length commaunded by the Clergie to be buried in a common place.

75 Iohn the fiftene.

Iohn the fiftene a Lombarde, was made Pope by the citezins and the Clergie, while the former Boniface robbing the treasurie, fled to Constantinople secretly. This Iohn was a Deacon Cardinall, and of great auctoritie, & fauoured not Boniface, but (as Platina saith) he with certaine other honest citizens stoode against Boniface his doinges, whereupon (as is aboue mencioned) he was made Pope, the other being fled, and so cōtinued eight monthes, till the other returning, did put out his eies, imprysoned him and murthered him there, with the rāke stinke of the pryson, and famin, and griefe of mynde together. Yet some thinke that Ferrucius the father of Boniface slewe him, because he withstode his sonne to be Pope: so saith Anselmus.

76 Benedict the seuenth.

Benedict the seuenth, after these was made Pope by the Layetie and Clergie, he by the Emperours ayde, dyd apprehende a great company of conspiratours in the citie, and for their haynous offence, he put them in pryson, and punished them cruelly. He helde a coūsell at Remes against

Lotharius

The fourth booke of the

Lotharius king of Fraūce, wherin he restored Archebyshop Arnulphus, who was violently deposed, and he deposed & condemned of heresie one Gilbert a Monke, being a coniurer, whome the king for his money and sorcerie, had aduaunced to be Archbishop. This Gilbert notwithstanding, did yet afterwarde obtaine of the Emperoure Otho the thirde, whome he had taughte to coniure, that he might be Archebishop of Rauenna, and afterwarde he was promised by the Diuell, that he should at length be Pope of Rome. Whereupon saith Polidor Virgill in his sixt booke of his storie of Englande, Monkes and priestes at this tyme, declining from the trade of their elders in all places begā, euen as it were by their owne right to scratche together howge heapes of ryches, to compasse honour by ill artes, (coniuring and sorcery) and to exercise tyranny. Benedict after he had raigned nine yeares died, Anno. 894.

77 Iohn the sixtene.

142. IOhn the sixtene, sonne of one Leo a Prieste, succeded by election of the people and Clergie. As sone as hee was Pope he began to beare deadly hatred against the Clergye, so that he was abhorred not onelye of them, but of all the people: and chiefelye because he neglecting the dignitye of the Romaine Sea, bestowed the riches & treasures therof vppon his kinred, his harlots and bastards. Which fault (sayth Platina and Stella) hath continued among the clergye vnto our time, for an ill president to the posteritye: Then the which custome nothing is more perillous, when our clergye (sayth Platina) shall couet spirituall dignities, not for loue of Religion, & to serue God, but to maintaine
14. the prodigality, gluttonye & rauenousnes of their kinred, and frendes, their concubines and bastards. Of the like complayneth Mantuan of his tyme.

Sanctus ager sturris venerabilis ara cynædis,
Scurrit horrendæ diuum Ganymedibus ædes.

At this

Pageant of Popes.   Fol. 63

At this tyme appeared a Comet, after which followed both famine & pestilence with terrible earthquakes, which shooke both Beneuent and Capua: which plagues moste men iudged, were sent for the pride, ambition, greedines & ryoat of the Popes, and for the contempt of God so greate at this time. This Iohn dyed in the viii. yere of his raigne. Anno, 985.

78. Iohn the 17.

IOhn the 17. was verye experte in feates of cheualrye, he was made Pope with the goodwill of the clergye & laietye. He was excellentlye well learned, & published diuers bookes. He beinge troubled with the sedition of one Crescentius the Consull, going about to make himselfe king of the Cittye, gaue place vnto Crescentius conspiracye, and banished himselfe into Hetruria: but Crescentius knowing of Iohns displeasure, and that he went about to call the Emperour wyth his armye into Italye against him, hee sente those frendes and kinsefolke which Iohn had remayning in the Citye, to entreat him not to sende for the Emperour, but himselfe to returne to Rome wyth his autoritye, and he promised to be obedient to him in all thinges. Iohn being entreated by his frendes, and fearing that the Emperours comminge would do more hurt then good to him and his clergye, returned to Rome: Against whose comming Crescentius with all the rest of the cõspiratours came forth to meete him, who with ẏ other people (a great multitude) wayted vppon him into the Citye, & in ẏ porch of Lateran Church, Crescentius and his company falling downe before the Pope, kissed his feete and craued pardon. This Iohn dyed Anno 995.

79. Gregorie the fift.

Gregorie

The fourth booke of the

Gregorie the fift a Germaine borne, but a Saxons sonne was first called Bruno: He after wranglinge and iarringe was made Pope by the Emperours auctoritye, because he was his cosen. But after Otho the Emperour was departed, the Romaynes despyinge chaunge of state, did aduaunce Crescensius to be Consull againe, and committed the estate of Rome to his gouernment. This Crescentius and the people of the Cittye toke it greuously, that Gregorie beinge a Dutchman shoulde by the Emperours auctoritye be made Pope, and therefore they deposed Gregorie: after which the people and clergye of Rome established one Iohn yt rothe beinge before bishop of Placentia, an excellente learned man and very well stoared wyth money. Gregorie in fine went to the Emperour to complaine of his great iniurye, the Emperour takinge it dispitefully, went into Italy with his armye, besieged Rome, assaulted it, and toke Crescensius the Consull and Iohn the newe Pope, and as for Iohn he had his eyes put out and so dyed: Crescensius was put on a vile beastes backe wyth his face to the taylewarde, hauinge his nose and his eares cut of, & to be seene of al men was caryed about the Cittye hauing his members quartered, he was honge vp about ye walles of the Cittye. Then Gregorie (his enemyes beinge punished) was restored, who perceyuing that the estate of kingdomes were fickle and wauering, through the ambition of Princes and couetousnes of the clergye, while there followed great warres hard vpp{on} his restoring, be sommoning a coūsaile at Rome, made a decree for the election of the Emperour. Hee decreed that ye election of the Emperour shoulde continue from hencefoorth amonge the Princes of Germanye, that is the Archbishop of Mens, of Treuers & Collen, the Palsgraue of Rhein, the Duke of Saxonie, and the Marquesse of Brandeburge. To these also he added ye king of Bohemia, to be an vmpier, if the voyces were euen: which decree Anno a thousande & ii, the Emperour Otho
did al-

Pageant of Popes. Fol. 71.

did allowe and confirme, but the kinges of Fraunce were highly offended that ye Germaynes had this prerogatiue. Gregorie dyed Anno 998. ye third yeare of his Popedome.

80. Iohn the xviij.

Iohn the xviii. a Grecian borne (of whom is spoken in ye former Gregorie) obtayned the place by brybery, sedition, and hurlye burlye. This man was before bishop of Placentia, an olde man, learned & ryche, but proud, couetous, and desirous to be Pope, which wrought his horrible and mischeuous ende: For hee broughte so muche moneye to Rome wyth him from Constantinople, whereby he was able to drawe and tempt vnto him aswel the wyse & wary, as the simple sort, to be of his faction: whereby he corrupted Crescentius the Consul, violently to abuse Pope Gregorie, & to driue him out being a Germaine, and so purchased the Popedome and the sequele thereof. But of those thinges that he and his traine set to sale in his Popeshippe Mantuan wryteth thus:

 Pernices mercantur equos, venalia Romæ
 Templa, sacerdotes, altaria, sacra, coronę.

I maruaile (sayth Platina) that the Chronographers would recken this Iohn amonge the Popes, seing he vsurped the place while Gregorie liued, vnlesse in wrytinge the Popes liues they thincke to do as they doo in a continuall historye: For the peeuishe deedes of tyrants are set among the great exploites of good Princes, that the readers may discerne the good from the euill, and so by the example of good men be moued to vertue, & by the example of the ill terrifyed fro vice, and so liue happilye vpon earth, which happines this Iohn wanted being a theefe & a robber euen in his Popedome. So much sayth Platina of him. At the lēgth this Iohn w̄ his Crescētius perished, hauing his eyes digged out, and his bodye foulye mangled: Crescentius for

his

The fourth booke of the

his doing was set vppon a vile horse (as is saide before) hauing his nose cut of, and was so led through the Citye, his face being turned to the horse tayle, and afterward hauing his members cut of, he was hanged vppon a gibbet. Here will I alledge the wordes of Gualther out of his third homelye as touchinge Antichrist, and so ende this booke. Nowe (sayth hee) let anye noble harte iudge vvhether so manye good men haue vppon sufficient cause, complayned of the tirannye and vniust dealinge which the Popes haue vsed: seing that seate of Rome hath sustaind within so fevve yeares so manye leude persons, tyrantes, theues, filchers, robbers, rebels, adulterers, and open purloyners of Church goodes. And who in Gods name vvill reuerence that as holye, which receiueth so many plagues, but as yet the nomber of the wicked ones is not fulfilled as shal follow immediatlye &c.

(*.*.*.*)

The ende of the fourth Booke.

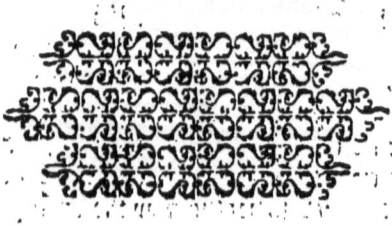

THE

THE FIFTE BOOKE
contayninge the thirde diuision of the thirde order of Popes or Romaine Antichristes in the kingdome of the greate Dragon, which is the deuill and sathan Apocalips 20. vnto the time of Innocentius the fourth.

FRō Ioan the eighte (who was an harlot) for the space of 146. yeares to this yeare being the thousand yere from Christe his incarnation, Antichrist raigned like an harlot in the Churche of Rome, pretending chastity in the meane time. Yet we see howe here the prophecye in Daniel 11. concerninge Antichriste was fulfilled, contayned in these wordes: And Antichrist shalbe in the cōcupiscence of women. We see in these former histories howe these Popes haue liued in wantonesse, royat, whoredome (and worse thē whoredome) incest, pride, ambition, robbinge and rifling Churches, coniuringe, treason, rebellion, dissention, murders, poysoninges & such other detestable enormities. So that accordinge to the sayinge of Esaie they deserue rather to be called the Princes of Sodom, thē the elders of the Church. Consequentlye after the thousande yeare after Christes byrth, it was prophesyed that the deuill should be let loose, and this shalbe called the kingdome of the great Dragon: wherin the actes of the Popes do wonderfully aunsweare vnto it, both in Syluester the second, who wyth his Necromancye raysed the deuill from hell, and hauinge coniured him vp, did compounde wyth him for the Popedome. And againe in Benedict the ix. who made sacrifyce vnto the deuill in woodes, and vppon mountayne toppes: In Hildebrand

The fift booke of the
brand or Gregorie the seuenth, who toke counsaile of euill spirites, and vsed other diuelish charmes, beside other.

81. Syluester the second.

Syluester the seconde was a Frenchman, in profession a monke, and called Gilbert, before he was Pope. He was of S. Benedicts order in an abbey at Florence, where he being a yonge man and addicted whollye to deuilishe artes, betoke himselfe to the deuill both bodye and soule. Afterward forsaking that abbey he went into Spaine delighting much in prophane sciences, & came to Hispalis vnto a certaine Philosopher being a Sarracen and expert in Magick, of whom he learned much both sorcerye and ambitiō, and began to deuise howe he might attaine to greate honour & riches: and thought in deede that coniuringe and Necromancye were the meetest wayes to come by hys purpose. He had espyed before in the house of his host a certaine cōiuring booke, and did his endeuour to steale it awaye, but the Magician kept it so deuoutlye, that Gilbert coulde not come by it: therfore he inueigled the Magiciās doughter, (wyth whom beinge in þ house he had good acquaintance) to steale her fathers booke, and let him haue a sight therof, þ may be fulfilled his request, & so he obtayned his purpose. He hauing þ booke went about to depart by stealth, but fearing least this might endaunger his life for stealing the booke, he gaue himselfe to the deuill vppon this condition, þ he should warrant him to passe safelye into Fraūce, and to obtayne great dignityes. He came into Fraunce & taught the liberal Sciences, so as many had him in admiration, wherby he had a nomber of scholers and auditors, some of great calling that learned þ former artes of him, as Cōstantine abbot of Maximin, Lotharius Archbishop of Seuen, Otho the Emperours sonne, Roberte kinge of Fraunce, wyth sondrye other bishops, prelats & priestes of
Rome.

Rome. By the procurement of these parsons he was made first bishop of Remen, afterward by his lewde artes he obtayned to be Archbishop of Rauenna: Last of all he obtayned to be Pope of Rome by the helpe of the deuill, whom he in coniuration raysed out of hell according to the xx. of the Apocalips. For Peter Præmonstratensis & other wryters saye, that he was made Pope in the Thousande yeare of our Lords Incarnation: In the which yere sayth Masseus, was a great and terrible earthquake, and a blasinge starre horrible to loke vppon the xiiii. day of December. In his Popedome he concealed his coniuring, and dissembled that familiarity which he had with the deuill: but yet he kepte in a certaine secrete place a brasen heade, of which when he demaunded anye thinge, hee receyued aunsweare of an euill spirit. At the length in his pontificality he would needes demaunde of the deuil how longe he should be Pope: the deuill aunswered doubtfullye and mistically, sayinge he should not dye, vntill he sayd Masse in Hierusalem: He therfore conceyuing good hope of longe life began to waxe carelesse, thinking to take heede enoughe of comminge in Hierusalem. But the vse was that on a certaine day of stations in the Lent time, ye Popes should say masse at Rome in the Pallayce of the holy Crosse, which was called Hierusalem: whereuppon Syluester not fearinge his life, nor heedefull enoughe to forecast the deuils despite according to custome said masse in the same Chappel, And by & by, a terrible shyueringe and quakinge came vppon him wyth a great feuer, and by the rumbling noyse of deuils (as Peter Præmostratensis & Platina say) he perceyued his death was at hand, and that he must paye the deuill his fee. And thus bewayling & lamenting openly the abuse of his charmes, he confessed his fault, til he perished miserablye. And (sayth Benno) he commaunded his tongue and his handes to be cut of, wherewith he had blasphemed God in sacrificinge vnto deuils: thus he dyed Anno 1003. The reporte

K is that

The fifte booke of the

is that the tombe of this Sylueſter doth euer ſince prognoſticate the death of the Pope, by the ratlinge of the bones and the guſhing out of water that ryſeth out of the grounde about it: as alſo (ſayth Platina) is teſtifyed by ý Epitaphe written on his graue.

82.   Iohn the 19.

147   Iohn the 19. an Italian, did likewiſe ſucceede Sylueſter, and gat to be Pope by ý deuils ayde: for (ſayth Benno) the ſcholers of the ſayde Sylueſter being coniurers, euerye one gaped for the Popedome. This Iohn did take from ý people the election of the Pope, ſayinge in behalfe of his doing, that the clergye muſt teache the people, but not followe them: And againe, the lawe which is ruled by Gods ſpirite, is more worthye then that which is mans lawe. He allowed & commaunded to eſtabliſhe in all Churches the feaſt of al ſoules, at the motiõ of one Odiloc abbot of Clunic: whoe dreamed that ſoules were deliuered oute of Purgatorye by vertue of the maſſe, and ſayd that he harde the deuils houle and roare, while the ſoules were takē frõ them, through dirges & trentalles. After he had raigned 5. monthes, he was poyſoned by his owne frendes. In his time the name of Cardinals began to grow to eſtimation, and many ſtraunge monſters were ſeene, and diuers terrible earthquakes.

83.   Iohn the 20.

148   Iohn the 20. called Faſanus after ý Iohn the 19. was poyſoned, by magicke & coniuringe gat to be Pope. For from the foreſaid Sylueſter till Gregorie the ſeuenth (a notorious parſon) all the Popes were famous enchaunters: by theyr charming they ſtirred vp walking ſpirits, bugs, goblins, fierye ſightes, & diuers terrible goaſts & ſhapes of thin-

of thinges, with howlinges and groaninges aboute deade mens graues, perſwadinge the ſimple people ẏ they were deade mens ſoules. And thoſe ſpirites beinge coniured vp by prieſtes, deluded men, deſſemblinge that they were the ſoules of the dead, complayning theyr intollerable paynes in Purgatorye fyre, and craued to be releaſed by the meritorious deedes of theyr frendes & kinred, beſtowinge dirges, maſſes, and trentalles on them. But to returne to this Pope Iohn, hee (ſayth Platina) beinge giuen to idleneſſe, did nothinge worthye remembraunce. He dyed after he had beene Pope. iiii. yeares Anno 1009.

84 Sergius the 4.

AFter this Iohn, came Sergius to be Pope by the like meanes, who alſo in his Popedome exerciſed the ſame ſorcerye ſkill, by which he obtayned the ſeate: Yet ſome of the flatterers of Rome do highlye commende him, as one that in all his Popedome did no one thinge to be miſliked. An vnmeete mayle for the prelates of that corrupte time, wherein the light of the Goſpell was extinct: without the which nothinge can be pure and perſite. Amonge other prayſes this is one that he had, he was a very pleaſãt, meerye, and familiar companyon: In his tyme was great peſtilence and famine in Italye, and in Loraine a fountaine turned into bloud. He dyed Anno 1012.

149

85 Benedict the eight.

BEnedict ẏ eyght was borne in Thuſca ẏ ſonne of George biſhop of Portua, brother to Albericus and Iohn, & was a layman: He had a nephew called Theophilactus, which was the ſcholer of Sylueſter, and by the magical charmes of this Theophilact, Benedict gatte to be Pope: and obtayned the place ſo longe as Henry Bauarius liued, whoſe

150

K ii

The fifte booke of the

apoe defended him, because he had bestowed on Henrie the crowne Emperiall. But after his death the Cardinals enuyinge him, deposed him and set vp another: and hereuppon arose a cruel debate. Yet afterward he compounded for money with his aduersaries, and so the vsurping Pope being put out again, Benedict is restored to great pompe: He graunted to the foresaid Henrick (as Barus testifyeth) to make at Bamberg builded by Henry a cathedral Church, but with this condition that the same Church should paye to the Pope yearely vnder the name of tribute, an hundred markes in siluer with a white horse furnished with trappings. He dyed Anno 1023. Peter Damianus cardinall of Hostia sheweth, as it is also written by Platina, Carion, and others, that this Benedict (or an euill spirit in his likenes) appeared rydinge on a blacke horse, and came vnto a bishop of his familiar acquaintaunce, who amazed at this sight asked him, Art not thou Pope Benedict whom wee know to be dead? He aunswered I am the same vnhappy Benedict: And howe do you sayd the bishoppe? I am cruelly tormented, but I may be eased quoth Benedict: And therefore go to my brother Iohn, who nowe is Pope, and bidde him repayre to such a place (naming it) and take the treasure that is there hidde, and distribute it to the poore: And likewise he appeared to Pope Iohn, saying I hope to be deliuered, and I would to God that Odilo would pray for mee. Thus the deuil deluded this age, bearing them in hande that the distribution of moneye, and not the death of Christe might bringe saluation to soules, to the great aduauncement of Purgatorye and masses.

86. Iohn the xxi.

Iohn the xxi. brother of the former Benedict, and sonne of Gregorie bishop of Portua beinge as yet but a lay man, yet likewyse by the enchauntmente of his nepheiwe Theophilact,

philact, gat y Popedome, as Benno a Cardinall wryteth. For the coniuring and charmes of these men Theophilact, Iohn, Gratian, Laurence, Malsitan, Brazutus and other like, wrought and ruled all thinges at Rome accordyng to the deuils appointmente, the aucthor of theyr artes: For (sayth Benuo,) Theophilact vsing to do sacrifice to deuils in woods & on mountaynes, caused women to runne after him, whom he with his enchauntments bewitched to loue him: And this appeareth to be true by certaiue bookes of his, which after his death were founde in his chamber. This Pope Iohn crowned Conradus Emperour, and was by him defended from the violence of the Romaynes, who had longe troubled him: y Emperour threatned to destroy the Romaynes vtterly, if they should practise ought agaist the Pope, and by this meanes he continued Pope xi. yere. The latine Church doth highly commend him, but shewe no good workes that deserued it: He commaunded Princes to keepe a solemne kinde of geuinge almes, he appoynted priestes to say masse, and the people to fast: In his time began the superstitious fastes of S. Iohn Baptist, & S. Laurence. Of the counsell of Triburia Anno 1030. began in Fraunce a sect of fasters, who said that it was reueled to them from heauen, that to fast Saturday with breade and water was sufficiente for remission of all sinnes, if so that they had made a vowe to keepe it: But the bishop of Camera did ouerthrowe this blasphempe, as derogatorye to the passion of Christe. Pope Iohn dyed Anno, 1034.

87. Benedict the ix.

Benedict the ninth who before was called Theophilact, the sonne of Albericus and nephewe (as is said) to the former Pope Benedict & Pope Iohn: as he by coniuring and diuelishe artes did first aduaunce his vnkles, so nowe by his magicke he brought to passe that he succeded them.

K iii   Hee

The fift Booke of the

He be̔ing Pope did greatly aduaūce euē next to himselfe as his chiefe and secret counsellers, Laurence, & Iohn Gratiā, for that they were notorious coniurers, broughte vp with him vnder Pope Syluester: he with these companiōs had vsed before he was Pope accordīg to ye cursed ceremonyes of their sorcery, to call vppon theyr euill spirites in woods and forrests, and to bewitch by his cunning any woman ye liked him, to couet his carnall companye. But (sayth Benno) as on a time he wyth these his mates was comming from the woods to the Church, a nomber of birds beinge together, a sparowe made a merye and pleasaunt kinde of chirping: This Laurence being both captaine coniurer, & also a southsayer, curious in the obseruation of byrds, was demaunded what it was that the birde prated? The byrde (quoth hee) calleth other birds to the great gate, where a countreymans carte is broken, and his meale spilte, which was caried in it: and therefore she wyth her much chattering biddeth them to come thither to eate, and fil themselues. Which being harde, diuers of them ye stoode by ranne in all poast hast to the gate to try the matter, and whē they came there they found it so in deede as Laurence had sayd. Theyr cunninge in southsaying and coniuringe was such, that they knew what was done both East, West, South and North, & in the corners of the world, eyther touching warres, or the death of Princes. And therefore many had theyr cunninge in greate reuerence, and did attempt dilligently to learne of them, and gatte theyr skill, especiallye one Hildebrand: Who forsaking an abbey where he was placed, did so follow this trade, that he excelled his maysters, and was wonderfull busye in pestilent practises, by meanes of his magicall artes, as the Church by the fruite thereof did afterwarde feele, sayth Benno. But to returne to Benedict, who after the death of Conradus conspired wyth his former counsellers, to disherite his sonne Henry the thirde of the Empier, and to plant in his steede

Peter

Pageant of Popes.   Fol. 76

Peter king of Hungarie, and therefore he sent the crowne of the Empier to him with this Uerse.

Petra dedit Romam Petro, tibi Papa coronam,
The roche to Peter gaue Rome the towne,
The Pope to thee Peter giueth ye crowne.

But Henry at the first conflict ouercame Peter, and toke him prisoner, and purposed to set forward to Rome, which beinge heard Benedict being terriblye afraide, soulde his Popeship to his companion Iohn Gratian, who payed for it fiftene hundred poundes, & was afterward called Gregorie the sixt. But in the meane time the Romaynes deposinge Benedict for his negligence and slouth Anno. 1045. did place in his steede Iohn bishop of Saba, callig him Syluester the thirde: For this sale (sayth Platina) Benedict was accused of all men, and condemned by deuine sentence, and at the length by Gods iuste iudgemente he was strangled to death by a deuill in the woods Anno. 1056. The Historiographers write, yt this Benedict or Theophilact, was seene of a certaine Hermite in a most ouglye and gastlye shape hard by a Mill, for his bodye was all rough and hairye like a beare, wyth head and tayle like an asse: And being asked of the Hermite how he was thus trasfigured? He aunswered, I wader in this shape because in the time that I was Pope, I liued without reason, without lawe, without God: and defiled the sea of Rome with all kind of villanye. In his time the Cardinals that began of little, grew to be great in dignitye.

88. Syluester the thirde.

SYluester ye thirda Romaine, first called bishop of Saba obtayned to be Pope, partly by his owne briberye, partly by the tumult and vprore of his countreymen after the expulsion of Benedict, as some say, but as it is rather to be thought by the magicall sorcerye of his father Laurence ye

K iiii   famous

The fift Booke of the

famous coniurer: For thus sayth Benno. After Benedict was driuen out and ỹ Popeship sould, Iohn Gratian being in the place, Iohn bishop of Saba was thrust in vppon him, and called Syluester the thirde, and thus these .iii. Popes beinge at once, it rente the Church of Rome a sonder, and deuided it into diuers factions: thus wyth cruell warres and great bloudshed the Church was torne in peeces, foulye mangled with sciesmes, & choaked with errors, while vnder the colour of wine it gulled in poyson: Thus wrote Benno of that wretched time. But (sayth Platina) Syluester enioyed the rowme but a while, for within xliꝯ dayes the frendes of Benedict with great tumult restored Benedict to that, which he had first both lost and soulde. The Popeshippe (saith Platina) was now brought to this passe, that he that was of greatest wealth, and beste able to giue bribes and most ambitious, & not most goodlye or best learned, he onelye (good men being oppressed and reiected) obtayned that dignitye: which trade (sayth he) I woulde to God they had not continued euen vnto our time, but these are but small matters, for we are like to see worse vnlesse God amende it. Thus muche doth Platma complayne of theyr leude liues, who otherwise flattered ỹ Sea of Rome and extolled theyr doctrine. But as touching Syluester, the Emperour Henry draue him from the Popeshippe, & caused him to returne to his owne bishopricke, wherein he continued (as before he was,) Cardinall and bishop of Saba. In the time of the foresaid Benedict the sixte daye of April Anno 1039. there was seene a mighty beame of fire burninge in the Element, as Masseus wryteth in his sixte booke. Anno Domini 1041. Pope Benedict made one Cazimirus a monke in Clunade abbey and a deacon, kinge of Poleland, on this condition, that for euery head in Poleland, he should pay yerelye to the Pope and his successors, an ordinary summe of money: And furthermore that they should not let the heyre of theyr bearde so grow longe, and

that

Pageant of Popes.   Fol. 77

that they of Poleland shoulde remember for euer, howe ỹ this polling had giuen them a shaue king out of an abbey.

89. Gregorie the sixt.

GRegorie ỹ sixt an Italian first called Iohn Gratian, learned the magicall sciences of Syluester the seconde: he bought the Popeship of his kinseman Benedict the ix and at the length obtayned it. He after sicknes and sedition being made Pope sayth Premonstratensis, perceyuinge ỹ certaine filchers purloyned the goodes of the Church, & that straungers were robbed on all sides, began to haue a regard vnto the riches, and first admonished them, afterward he excommunicated them, and last of all he warred on them that contemned his threatnings: and thus he did both recouer the Church goodes wyth encrease, and also executed, and put to death the masters thereof. The Cardinals being moued with this cruelty called him Simonist, murtherer and bloud sucker: and on a tiime while he was sicke, they saide hee was vnworthye to be buryed in the Church: Whereunto among other thinges he aunswered thus: I haue warred vppon other, that wyth the damage of the laietye I might purchase glorye to the clergye, and thus ye recompence mee? and sone after he recouered his health. The troublesome & tragical broyles which these Popes wrought at this time, are thus described by Otho, Frisgensis, Godfri Viterbiensis, and other auctors: While (saye they) Benedict the ix was Pope, Syluester the thyrd, and soone after Gregorie the sixt did inuade the seate. And in the 7. yeare of the Emperour Henry the third, these 3. Popes made themselues 3. seueral seates in Rome: wherby they brought in a detestable scisme, & euerye one endeauoured that he might not yelde to other in sedition, impietye and villanye. Benedict he sate as Pope in Lateran Pallaice, the rest, the one at S. Peters, ỹ other at S. Maries

154.

made

The fift booke of the

made his pontificall throne. While these three Popes did at once (to the perill of the whole estate) possesse & comber the Citye, Iohn Gratian a priest came vnto them, perswading them euery one to take a peece of moneye and giue ouer their title of Popeship, and so it came to passe: and for this cause the Romaynes created Gratian Pope, as one y had saued the comon wealth. Henry the Emperour hearing of these sturres, in haste came to Rome & helde a Synode, wherein those three Benedict, Sylvester & Gregorie were condemned, and the fourty Pope created in theyr steede called Clemens the second. And thus sayth Benno the Emperour made Theophilact to flye, he put Gregorie in prison, and afterward he banished him wyth Hildebrad into Germanye, and compelled the bishop of Saba to returne to his bishopricke: So Gregorie dyed in Germanye, of whose falsehood and money together (sayth Benno) Hildebrand was made heyr, who after his death returned to Rome.

90.   Clement the second.

155. Clement the seconde was made Pope in a Synode at Rome by the Emperours commaundement while the other three Popes were yet liuinge. Hee caused the Romaynes to giue ouer to the Emperour theyr title in electing the Pope, for the auoydinge of those broyles which arose there vppon: But some saye that it was the Emperour who made the Romaynes sweare, that they should neuer name anye to be Pope. But the Emperour beinge gone into Germanye, they forgettinge theyr oath, did poyson this Pope Clement, because he was chosen wythoute theyr consente, the ninth monthe after his creation: which poyson was tempered by Steuen, who succeded him called Damasus the second, or as some thincke that Brazutus being commonlye practised in these thinges, and companion to Theophilact and Hildebrand, was auctor therof. At

this

Pageant of Popes.   Fol. 78

this time were great and straunge contencions about the Sacramente of the alter, and by the deuils doinge manye wonders and myracles were wroughte, but ye Pope forbad manye to vtter their conscience hereof, least it shoulde be preiudiciall to the masse: And therefore manye of the doctours as appeareth by theyr wrytings, wrote doubtfully.

91. Damasus the seconde.

DAmasus the second otherwise called Steuen Bagniarie, gate the Popeship by force at the Emperours comaundement, with consent of the clergye and laitye: for (sayth Platina) it was now a common thinge for euery ambitious parson to prease into Peters seate violentlye, but he kepte it not long, for the thirtenth day after he was poysoned by the sayde Brazutus Anno 1049. This Damasus beinge chauncelar to Clement his predecessour did poyson his maister, and therefore dranke worthely of the same cuppe. After this (sayth Benno) Theophilact who before was fled returned to Rome, and there wyth his olde acquaintaunce Laurence, wroughte much mischiefe, and by the letters of his scholer Hildebrande beinge then in the Emperours Court and a traytour about him, he knewe all the Emperours secretes. While he thus did greatlye vexe the Romaynes, they by the counsell of Cardinals sent Embassadours to the Emperour, desiringe him to assigne one to be Pope. And therefore one Bruno, afterwarde called Leo ye ninthe was made Pope, and ye force againste his wyll brought to Rome: In whose company through ouermuch gentlenes of the Emperour, Hildebrand was suffered to returne to Rome, who afterward wroughte such mischiefe in the worlde, as neuer was harde of, both againste Emperour, Church, clergye, and common wealth vnder colour of religion: meaninge not to keepe his oath longe sworne to the Emperour, So sayth Benno of him.

156

92 **Leo**

The fift booke of the
92. Leo the ninth.

Leo the ninth a Germaine borne of the countrey of Dasburg, being also himselfe countye Etistheim and bishop of Tulledo he became Pope in this maner. Because the Romaynes (not for the loue of the Emperour) but beinge wearyed wyth those ambitious and seditious prelates that straue for the Popeship, desyred him to appointe one to be Pope: he sent them this Bruno bishop of Tulledo, a man of a simple witte, for none of the other Germaine bishoppes durste aduenture to come amonge the poysoned cuppes of Rome. He goinge on forwarde in his pontificall roabes, had wyth him in companye the abbot of Clunace, & Hildebrand the monke, the clergye of Rome meetinge him & seing him come on this manner, altered his Popes vesture, did most dispitefullye charge him wyth apostasye, because he had receyued his auctoritye from the Emperour, therefore they perswaded him to put of his pontificals, and to returne to Rome in his wonted apparell: Saying, the election of the Pope was not graunted to the Emperours, but to the clergye and people of Rome. Bruno obeyed theyr commaundements, and came to Rome in his owne priuate apparel. And through the counsaile of Hildebrand did confesse openly before the auncients, that he had offended, and therefore because he ascribed the auctoritye to them, they chose him Pope more willinglye, and for this deede called him Leo or Liō, whose courage argued him rather to be a sheepe. Afterward he made Hildebrand a Cardinall, and partner of his Popeship with him, committing to him the charge of S. Peters Churche, whereof Benno wryteth thus. As sone as he came to Rome (meaning Hildebrād) he obtayned of Leo to be made one of the keepers of the alter of S. Peters Church, and within a while he filled his cofers: and to the end he might put out his money to some

mar

man for dailye entereſt, he became familiarlye acquainted with ye ſonne of a certaine Iewe, who though he were latelye become a Chriſtian, yet he left not his Iewiſhe trade of vſurye. And before this hee had well acquainted himſelfe wyth the famous worker of miſchiefe Brazutus frende to Theophilact: who is reported to haue poyſoned by his cunning theſe Popes wythin xiii. yeares Clement the ſecond, Damaſus the ſecond, Leo the ix. Victor the ſecond, and Nicholas the ſeconde. Pope Leo held a counſell at Vercella, wherin he condemned the doctrine of Berengarius, who helde opinion againſt tranſubſtantiacion, and the real preſence of Chriſt in the Sacrament: Likewiſe he held another counſell at Maguntia wherein was concluded that prieſts ſhould not keepe hounds nor haukes, neither medle with any ſuch profane things: Alſo ye mariage of ye clergye was vtterlye condemned by ye procurement of Hildebrād: And it was decreed to be ſimonye, for a prieſt to be preferred to an eccleſiaſticall lyuing by a layman. By the enticement of Hildebrand and Theophilact, this Leo not knowinge their diſpoſition, moued warre againſt the Normans, whoſe power was thē great in Apulia. But Theophilact meaning to worke the Pope miſchiefe ſecretelye (becauſe he durſt not openly do it) bewrayed firſt al his ſecrete counſell, and finally with Hildebrands aduiſe, betrayed the Pope himſelfe to the Normans, from whom (his men beinge ſlaine) he himſelfe eſcaped narrowly: who yet returninge to Rome was poyſoned by Brazutus the fift yeare of his Popedome.

93. Victor the ſecond.

VIctor ye ſecond a Germaine borne in Bauaria was made Pope, not by free election, but becauſe the Romaynes did ſo much ſtande in awe of Henry the Emperour, that they durſte do nothinge againſt the oath made to the ſayde

Henry

The fifte booke of the

Henry in the time of Clement the seconde. And therefore to gratifye the Emperour, they sent Hildebrād as Embassadour to him, to know his pleasure in the election, and by this meanes this Victor beinge a Germaine came to be Pope: In this Embassage Hildebrande toke vppon him by vertue thereof, to make Henry the Emperours sonne heyre to the Empire. This Victor helde a great Synode at Florence, wherin he condemned all those priestes of Symonie, who had bene presented to their spirituall liuinges by any temporall parsons. Immediatly after the establishmente of this Victor, Brazutus repayred to Rome at the procurement of Hildebrande to poyson him, or anye other (sayth Benno) that should steppe into the Popeship before Hildebrand, and so Victor sone after he had raigned two yeare was poysoned by the same Brazutus. Anno 1057.

94. Steuen the ninth.

STeuen the ninth borne in Loraine, the duke of Loraines brother, was made Pope after Victor with generall consent of all, but withoute the Emperours agreemente. This Steuē caused ẏ Church of Millain (which almost 2. hundreth yeares had defied ẏ supremacye of Rome) to become subiecte vnto it: he also before he came to be Pope, had accused the Emperour Henry of heresye, because hee somewhat abridged the vsurped auctoritye of Rome. Also he helde a counsell in Florence against mariage of priestes, countinge it fornication, and therein concluded many thinges against dualities, pluralityes, and totquots. But at ẏ length in the tenth yeare of his raigne Hildebrand caused his olde companion Brazutus to giue him such a drinke, ẏ the Pope dyed thereof Anno. 1058. At his death Hildebrand was not at Rome, but returned in all hast vppon it, and at his comming he commaunded all the clergye to appeare before him, and bounde them with an oath to suffer

A note for gredye beneficemongers and nonresidents, that euen Antichrist himselfe is like to be a vvitnes against them, vvho thus condemned that vvherein they offende obstinatlye.

none

none to be Pope, but such a one as obtayned it with the consent of euerye one.

95. Benedict the tenth.

Benedict the x. borne in Campania was first called Mincius, while the Romaynes were in an vprore and cryed oute to haue one of their owne countreymen to be made Pope: this Benedict had the name generally, and so was made Pope, contrary to ye oath which ye clergye had made to Hildebrand at his departure lately. Hildebrād therefore taking it despitefully thus to be deluded in his absēce, deposing Benedict, was very importune with the clergye, to make one Gerhard bishop of Florence, that came wyth him, Pope in his presence, as they promised him at his departure. The clergye because they coulde not with safetye chose another in Rome went therefore to Senas, and there they chose this Gerhard Pope, naminge him Nicolas the seconde. Gerhard beinge Pope held a Synode at Sutrius againſt Pope Benedict, who vnderſtanding of this conspiracye wroughte by Hildebrand, was content for quietnes sake to forsake Rome, and to liue like an outlawe priuatly in Veltra, after he had bene Pope ix. monthes. Christian Maſſeus reporteth, that this yeare a great company of snakes about Tornaie fought cruelly together, vntill the people beſet them with fier and burned them.

96. Nicolas the second.

Nicolas the seconde was made Pope as is mentioned in Benedict. After he had helde the councell of Spire against Benedict, hee returned to Rome, and ſommoned a councell at Lateran by ye craft of Hildebrand for his owne purpose: wherein was decreed, that he should be condemned for an apoſtata, that should be Pope eyther by fauour or mo-

The fifte booke of the

or money without the whole consent of the Cardinals. Also he gaue the Cardinals, the priestes and laitye, power to excommunicate any such Pope, & to hold Synode against him any where, and to driue him out. In this Synode Berengarius was forced to recant his opinion against the real presence: for he had long maintayned, that in the breade & wyne was nept the body and bloud of Christ really, nor naturally, but a signe and figure thereof, as Platina, Muclerus and other write of him. This Pope Nicolas established and strēgthened the Popedome, wyth sondrye and diuers strañge forgeryes, fables, and vntruthes, terrible bizards, and gastlye countenaunces of excommunication, and dreadfull threates of cursings. The wordes of the excommunication and curse are these, in the 23. distinction as Barnes testifyeth. In the name of God. Amen: If any man do breake this oure sacred decretal sentence, and presumptuously attempt to hurt or disquiet against this statute the Church of Rome, let him be accursed for euer, & damned by excōmunication: Let him be repúted amōge the vvicked, that shall not rise againe to iudgement: Let him feele the wrath of the Almightye against him: Let him feele the rage of Peter and Paule vppon hym in the life to come, that spurneth against their Churche in this life: Let his dwelling be in the wildernes, & let his house be left desolate for none to dwell therin: Let his children be orphanes, and his wife be a widowe: In his trouble let him be troubled: Let his childrē beg their bread, and be cast out, and be vagabounds driuē out of their owne houses: Let the vsurer rifle all his goodes, and let straungers spoile the labour of his handes: Let the whole world fight against him, and let all the Elementes be contrarye vnto him: Let the merits of all saincts confound him: Let him spende this life prisoner fettered in chaines: and let the saincts powre their open vengeaunce on him. But our grace defende them that keepe this &c.

Such

Such thonderbolts did the Pope shoote abrode to terrifye the worlo, which yet wrought so in mens hartes, that for feare thereof they yelded themselues subiecte to the Pope, against their owne natiue and Christian Princes. But to returne to the bishoppe concerninge the sturre that Hildebrand kepte at this time in Rome, Thus wryteth Benno: Nicolas beinge Pope, Hildebrand perceyuing he could not yet gette to be Pope, deuised to get an archdeaconshippe by hooke or by crooke. At the length he set vppe one Mancius archedeacon of Rome, whom he tossed and disquieted with diuers iniuries: who beinge ouerlayed wyth the reprochful dealing and craft of Hildebrand, and beguiled w his moneye, at the length graunted him to surrender vnto him his archedeaconship. This being graunted, Hildebrād commeth to Pope Nicholas ere he were aduised, and very impudentlye, partly by vnreasonable request, partlye by ye threatnings of armed souldiers hired for the purpose, who gaue him watchworde to yelde or to dye, hee made Hildebrād archdeacon. This being done euen immediatlye after Brazutus ministred the same cuppe to Nicolas, that he had done to the other Popes. Nicolas beinge thus poysoned, ye Cardinals being so well acquainted with the ambition of Hildebrand, besoughte the Emperour earnestlye to assist them in the behalfe of Cadolus his bishop of Parma, whō they had chosen Pope: which thing so strake Hildebrand to the hart, that from thence forward he professed himselfe an vtter ennemye to the Emperour: He brake his oath of fealtye and allegeance. And makinge a conspiracy wyth ye Emperours ennemyes, and with the Normans, he beguiled Anselmus bishop of Lucia, causinge certaine Romaynes to chuse him bishop, and call him Alexander the secōd, as one whom hee would set vp against Cadolus chosen by the Cardinals. And thus Hildebrand brought trouble as much as he could, both to Anselmus and Cadolus, who in deede wayted to succede them both, &c.

L   97 Alex-

The fifte booke of the
97. Alexander the second.

Alexander the seconde was as yee reade made Pope by Hildebrands craft, for his owne purpose against the Emperours minde: and therfore ye Lombards by the Emperours consent, did set vp another against him called Cadolus, (as is before mentioned) who came to Rome and besieged it wyth a great armye, and after one or two battailes was wyth his companye put to flight. The Emperour willinge to ende this sciesme, sent to Rome Otho archbishop of Collen with his auctoritye, to debate the matter: who comming to Rome began with a sharpe oration to reproue the intrusion of Alexander, & to amplifye the Emperours auctoritye in the election of the Pope. But the mischeuous Hildebrand puft vp with his late victory, did interrupt Otho, and stoutly defended the Popes doing, a uouching that the election belonged onely to the clergye: whereunto Otho the bishop in this case more fauouring ye Pope, then his maister, did easelye giue place, and desired to haue a councell at Mantua to appease ye matter: Wherin was decreed that a man oughte not to beare masse of a priest ye laye with a concubine: that maryed priests shoulde leese their liuings: And yet their children wyth the Popes dispensation might take orders: That the Pope shoulde be chosen onely by Cardinals. But this Alexander perceyuinge at the length (sayth Benno) ye it was but for a pollicye of Hildebrand, that he was made Pope by the Emperours enuemyes to spite him withall, began to mislyke of it with himselfe: and on a time as he was preach'ng to the people, he tolde them that he would not any longer enioye the Apostolicall seate without the Emperours good will, and professed opely that he would send letters to the Emperour, for the same purpose. Hildebrand hearinge this was forthwith so enraged, ye presentlye he began to mumble,

ble, curse, and fret, and could scant keepe his hand from ye Pope till masse were done: Masse beinge done, he toke the Pope, and wyth a troupe of armed souldiours he led him into his chamber, where with his fistes he buffeted and be- pommelled him shamefullye, rating and taunting him wyth rayling and reuiling wordes, because he would go aboute to seeke the Emperours fauour. And from that time for- warde Hildebrand (because he saw him so simple) allowed him but fiue shillinges a daye to spende, and the rest of the reuenues he retayned to himselfe, and casting Alexander into prison he purloyned a great masse of money. Alexan- der beinge thus in the miserable bondage of Hildebrand, in an euening dyed God knoweth whereof, and the same houre Hildebrand was enstalled Pope by his garrison of souldiours, without consente of the people or clergye: be- cause he feared yt if he had delayed it, another shoulde haue bene chosen. None of the Cardinals subscribed to his elec- tion, vnto the which when the abbot of Cassia came, Bro- ther (quoth Hildebrand) ye haue lingred ouer longe, & you quoth the abbot haue hied you ouer fast, who ere your mai- ster the Pope be yet buryed, haue vsurped his place con- trarye to ye Canons. Hildebrand being thus chosen, how he liued, howe he draue the Cardinals from him, howe he tormented them miserablye, how he poysoned the world wt heresyes, how often he committed periurye, howe great & many conspiracyes he raysed, it is harde for manye men to vtter: But most of all, the bloud of many Christiās which by him and his meanes haue beene miserablye shedde, do crye oute vengeaunce on him. Thus and much more doth Benno the Cardinall wryte of him.

98. Gregorie the seuenth.

Gregorie the seuenth was first called Hildebrand borne in Hetruria, a notable coniurer and great Magician, he
gatte

The fifte booke of the

gat to be Pope by his saluage sorcerye, & bloudy meanes. He forsaking ye abbey wher he was monke, gat to one Laurence an archpriest of whom he learned his notorious enchauntments, which ye sayd Laurence had learned of Pope Syluester the seconde. There was greate familiaritye betweene this Laurence, Theophylact, Iohn Gratian & Hildebrand, being archpriests or Cardinals of Rome: wherby this Hildebrand by his subtiltye bare all the swaye in Theophylact, while he was bishop vnder the name of Benedict the ninth, and so he cōtinued in his factious dealing in al other Popes times, till he came to the place himselfe. Benno Cardinall wryteth of him, that when hee listed, hee would caste of his sleeues, and skip and daunce in forme of sparkles, or flames of fyer, and with these myracles he deluded the eyes of the simple people, bearing them in hande it was a signe of his greate holinesse. And (sayth Benno) because the deuill could not openlye persecute Christians by Pagans, he practised craftelye to ouerthrowe the name of Christe by this counterfaite monke, vnder the colour of religion. Diuers auctors do write that this Hildebrand or hellybrand rather, by the helpe of his companiō Gerardᵒ Brazutus poysoned vi. or vii. Popes, so to open himselfe a gap to come to be Pope: and yet hee in these wroples behaued himselfe so subtellye, that no man could charge him therewithall, ye it was rather thought he sought to shonne the Popeship. And yet when in name he was not Pope, yet was he the onely instrument, and contriuer of all their doings and deuises: and began to worke by litle and litle vnder other, which he brought to perfectiō in his owne time. Under coulour of religion and godlines, he practized all treachery and mischiefe. He accused Pope Alexander his maister, because he had craued the Emperours assistaunce against his aduersaries: His accusatiō was this, ye he was vnmcete to be Pope according to the Canons, who cōtrary to the Canons had craued ayde of a prophane Prince: &

caste

cast him into prison, where he wrought his death, & forth-with ere he was buryed vsurped his place: He imparted his treasure (sayth Benno) to Brazutus and to a certaine Iewe, that were his companions, and by theyr meanes he purchased the voyces of diuers, who ere that Alexander was buryed cryed out amayne: Peter þ Apostle hath cho-sen Hildebrand to be Pope, & so they set him in the Popes throne callinge him Gregorie the seuenth. And this was done in the thousand yeare after the destruction of Hieru-salem, in the which yeare the Popes began to challenge & take vppon them the name, office, and power of Christe: for it was proclaymed at the enstalling of this Gregorie, þ he was created þ true vicar of Christ, & Gregorie applyed vnto himselfe those thinges that are spoken in þ 7. Psalme of Christe: Hee altered the lawes of God, for where the Scripture licēceth al estates to marrye, he barred þ cler-gye therof, forcing thē to vow single life aboue their abili-tye. Now was þ Scripture in him fulfilled prophesyinge of the warre of Gog and Magog, which this Gregorie bro-ched so perillouslye to all Christendome, as the like neuer happened, which his companion Vrban the second did exe-cute. Gregorie at the first entrye to his Popeship began to vrge such canons, as he had in his auncessours time pro-cured against priestes mariage, and the bestowinge of be-nefices by temporall men, which hee did not of purpose to take away the abuse of byinge and sellinge of ecclesiasticall lyuings, but with a fayre showe to abridge Princes and o-ther estates, of their preeminence in that matter, whereby he might binde all the bishops and clergye to be more sub-iecte to Rome, who now depended more on their Princes, because of the bestowig of the lyuings, wherby the Popes strength encreased, & the tēporal Princes were weakened, and neglected of their clergye. And the better to atchieue his purpose, because Henry the Emperour was chiefe of temporall Princes, he attempted it first againste him: for

L iii   this

The fift Booke of the

this matter he sommoned a councell at Rome, wherto the Emperour could haue no regarde, becaufe of his warlike affayres then prefente. And yet this matter fo delighted ye Pope, that for compaffing it he fpared neyther treafon nor murther, but in manye places he procured ciuill warre, & fedition, with al kinde of mifchiefe that might be. For firft feekinge ye Emperours death he attempted it diuers wayes, as thus amonge other euen in ye Church: The Emperour (faith Benno) vfed to go to prayers to S. Marpes Church in Auentine hill. Hildebrand therefore hauinge his falfe efpyes caufed the place to be wel noted, where the Emperour vfed to kneele or fit in the Church all feruice time: & hyred one to go and laye certaine great ftones fecretelye in the roofe of the Church righte ouer the fame place, in fuch fort as he might throwe them downe vppon ye Emperours head, and fo flaye him: which as this fellowe went aboute and was bufye wyth a great ftone, the waighte thereof ouerwhelmed him, fo as he fell downe to the pauement and the ftone vppon him, which brufed him fo as he dyed of ye, which hee had prouided to flaye the Emperour withall. This thinge being knowen, the Romaynes bound his heeles to a roape, and drewe the dead carkaffe through Rome ftreats three dayes together for an example. Againe (faith Benno) Iohn bifhoppe of Portua who was of Hildebrands priuye councell, faid in his preachinge before the people & clergye in S. Peters Church: what meaned Hildebrand and we to do this thig wherby we fhould be burned aliue? (meaninge that violence which they had vfed towarde the Sacrament of Chriftes bodye:) Becaufe Hildebrand demaunding of it (as ye heathen vfed to do of their idols) what fucceffe he fhoulde haue againft the Emperour, & becaufe the Sacrament fpake not and gaue him no aunfweare, he threw it into the fyre, maugre all the Cardinals that were about him, and faid to the Sacrament moft blafphemouflye: Could the idoll Gods of the heathens giue them aun-
fwere

Pageant of Popes.   Fol.84

swere of theyr successe, and can not thou tell mee? He excommunicated the Emperour being a cōformable Prince, withoute lawfull accusation, without canonicall citacion, or iudicial order: and caused his peeres to reuolt frō him, and soughte by secrete traytors to murther him. Also hee caused the bishops to sweare them selues vtter ennemies against him, wresting & wringinge places of the Scripture to make a shew to maintaine his purpose, But (sayth Benno) as sone as he roose vp from his chayre, being newly framed of wood, by Gods workinge it claue in pecces & was rente terriblye into diuers partes.

When he sawe that his secrete treasons toke not effect, he brast out into open outrage and enmitye: he excommunicated the Emperour, and discharged all his subiectes of theyr allegeaūce, & gaue his crowne vnto Rodolpho duke of Sueuia, which he sent to him with this poesye.

  Petra dedit Petro, Petrus diadema Rodolpho.

This moued the Emperour very sore, in so much that hee stripped himselfe out of his royall roabes, and puttinge on wollen apparell, came with his wyfe and his sonne a litle child in the depth of winter, a cruel and perillous iourneye to Canusius, and stoode barefooted at the gates of the Citie, fasting from morning to night, suing humblye for pardō at Hildebrands hand, and for three dayes suffered with lamētable miserye to be laughed at, and flowted by Hildebrand amonge his paragons and monkes. He desired often to be let in to come to the Pope, but hee was still aunswered for three dayes together, that p Pope was not yet at leasure to speake with him. The good and gentle Emperour toke it paciently to be thus delayed, and because he could not be let into the Citye, he abode in the suburbes tō his great inconuenience, for the frost was verye extreame more then ordinarye: and yet he endured it continuallye 3. dayes, least by taking his ease he should haue offended my Lorde bishops grace, and still he sued to be pardoned. At

L iiii   the

The fift Booke of the

the length the fourth daye by the intercession of the Countesse Mathilda, who for loue, not for honesty was in fauour with the Pope, & the abbot of Cluny, and Adelaus Earle of Sauoy he was admitted to come in. And thoughe hee craued pardon on his knees, & offered vp his Crowne, yet would the Pope neither pardon him nor absolue him, vnlesse hee woulde promise that accordinge to the Popes appointment he would purge him of his fault in the councel, with other vnlawfull conditions. All which he promised and confirmed with hand & seale, and yet was not restored to his estate. This being knowen, the Princes & Lordes of Italye were highlye offended that the Emperour Henry in such maner with so great dishonour, and so shamefullye had submitted himselfe to recouer the fauoure of this Hildebrand, who by treachery purloyned the Popedome, and defiled all thinges with slaughter and harlotrye. But the Pope and his Cardinals beinge puffed vp with this ẏ they had brought the Emperour to this seruile yoake, began to attempt further matters: but Henry reuēged this dishonour sone after vp the sworde, and after sharpe battelles he ouercame Rodolpho, who hauinge his hand cutte of commaunded to bring vnto him the bishops and auctors of his rebellion, before whom he sayde thus hauing his hand layde before them. I am (quoth he) iustlye plagued, lo this is the hand wherewith I pleighted my allegeaunce to my soueraigne Lord Henry, and by your enticements I haue often time fought against him to my losse, and falsifyed my fayth, and therefore haue receyued the rewarde due to my periurye: Consider therefore whether ye haue guided me righte or no: Go ye therefore, and stand to your first fayth vowed to your king, for I must go to my father: this being said, he dyed. After his death at the Popes commaundement they set vp another to be Emperour, one Harman a Saxō County of Lucelburg: who while he was assaulting a certaine Castell in Germanye, was slaine by a certaine

great

great stone, which a woman hurled downe vpon him. And yet the Popes malyce ceased not, but he raysed vp a thirde traytour againste the Emperour euē his kinsmā Egbertus a Marquesse, who also being taken in a Mill by the Emperours frends, was miserably slaine. In the meane time the Pope did solace himselfe with the companye of Mathilda, who forsaking her husbande Azon Marquesse of Esta kept continually by the Popes deare side, whereby she was called S. Peters doughter: and so of one ieast another sprāg, for (as Lambert Hirswaldēsis saith) the talke was how S. Peters doughter liued in secret incest wt S. Peters heyre, and that he that had deuorced other men from theyr wiues and honest matrimonye, liued in whoredome with another mans wyfe. Also this Gregory iudged to death three men before they were conuict or confessed theyr cryme, without the sentence of anye seculer Iudge, and caused them to be hanged forthwith. Another time he cast Centius the sonne of a Senatour into prison being his especial friend, & caused him to be tormented & rolled in a barrel of sharpe nayles till he was almost dead: But Centius escaping apprehended the sayde Hildebrand and mighte haue quitted his quarrel, yet the people disappointed him, but the Pope ere he were deliuered sware openlye yt he would forgeue him, and the rest yt had apprehended him. But being at libertye contrarye to his oath he reuenged it, causing Centius and ix. of his company to be hanged for it, yt other he condempned to banishment, and among them the sonne of a widow, who after the yeare of his banishment was expyred did returne & was led with an halter about his necke by his mother to Gregorie, whō yt mother for full satiffaction desired to take her sonne and deliuer him againe as a new purged mā: But Gregorie had hanged him but yt the Iustices cōsidering the penaunce that he had done were more iuste and wyse, and refused to do it, and therefore Gregorie in a rage commaūded one of his feete to be cut of, wherof the yongman

The fift booke of the

mā dyed wythin fiue dayes, to the great griefe of the poore wydowe his mother. Abbas Vspergensis & other write thus: It is manifest (say they) that this Hildebrand was not chosen by God, but intruded himselfe by money & guile, who tossed the ecclesiasticall estate vpside downe, and troubled the kingdome of Christen Empier, practised to murther the quiet Prince, defended oathbreakers, fostred debate, sowed discentiō, raysed offences, made deuorcemēts, and disordered euery thing that seemed to be well among the godlye. He was the first that put the ministers of the Church from their wyues by excommunicatiō: He moued broyles through Fraunce, Germany and Englande, tedious to be tolde. This deuorcement of ministers wiues, did offende a great nomber of learned men at that time: for in Germanye and Fraunce there were yet xxiiii. and more bishops, who wyth the clergye of theyr Diocesse were then maryed, and did stoutly maintayne theyr mariage still, beside those that were in England & Italye. Amonge other things Gregorie commaunded the Saturday to be fasted. He canonized Pope Liberius sainte, who was an Arriā heriticke, also he apointed an holye daye in reuerence of him. He toke awaye the Crowne from the kinge of Poland. He condemned Berengarius opinion againste reall presence, & was the first that is noted to haue established the doctrine of transubstantiatiō. He condemned a layman of sacrilege, that should reape the commoditye of tenthes as of impropriat parsonages, but condemned him of heresye, that inuested a priest, and him of Idolatrye that should take a benefice of a layman. These and other like attemptes gaue Hildebrand, whereby hee made the Popes leaden blade, to hew asonder almost the Emperours iron sworde. Many of ye clergye as 14. Cardinals beside diuers bishops & other, did so abhorre ye detestable treachery of this coniurer Gregorie, ye they forsoke him for shame, his villanyes were so manye, and so monstrous encreasinge daylye: In steede of God of God he serued the deuill, & of Princes whom he shoulde honour hee made worse then slaues: finallye as his name was Hildebrand so in deede he was an belly brande to all Christendome, tormoyled by his meanes with rebellions, treasons, murders &c. But at the length Henry ye Emperour began to set himselfe against the Popes practises, and in the yeare of Christ 1083. in a Synode at Brixia, layinge his treacheryes to his charge hee did depriue him of his place, and appointed another in his steede, whom hee called Clement the thirde. He sent his armye to Rome to driue out Gregorie, and to establishe this Clement, and by his longe siege he brought Rome to so great penurye, that they were compelled to sue for peace. But Hildebrand because he would not come in the Emperours sighte, beinge reiected & forsaken of the Romaynes fled to Salerne, wher he ended his wretched life in great miserye Anno 1086. Antonius and Vincentius shewe that this Hildebrande euen at the latter gaspe called to him a certaine Cardinal, and confessed to him yt he had haynouslye offended, because at the deuils enticemēts he had sturred vp hurlye burlies, hatred, and warres among many, and bad the cardinal go to desire the Emperour to pardon him. Diuers mē wrote against him & his vile life, as Cādidus a Cardinall, VValramus bishop of Niemburg, Venericus bishop of Vercellen, Rowland priest of Parmen, Sigebertus Gemblacensis. Also of this Gregorie it is said that he neuer wēt without a booke of coniuring about him.

99. Victor the thirde.

VIctor the third abbot of Cassa was made Pope, not by the election of the Romaynes or Cardinals, but was thrust in by the ayde of his harlot Mathilda, and the Normans that were of his faction. He being establiched began to defende Gregories prankes against the Emperour, and

164.

Clement

The fift booke of the

Clement appointed by him, but the hastines of hys death shortened his mallice: who as Hermannus, Contractus, Carsulanus, Præmonstratensis and sondrye other testifye, was poysoned by his deacō, who at masse time put the poyson into the challice, against þ Pope should receiue it. Diuers wonders are reported to haue happened at that time, as of tame birds, geese, cockes, hennes, pigions, & pecocks flewe into the mountaynes and became wild, houge store of fishe died in the Sea: diuers Cityes were so shaken in earthquakes, so as the greater Pallas at Syracuse falling downe, did slaye all that were then in the Church, sauing a couple.

100. Vrban the second.

165. Vrban the seconde an Hetrurian borne called Otho before, was made Pope by the harlot Mathilda, and the Norman Lords in Apulia in dispite of þ Emperour. This is a scholer of Hildebrand, whom for followinge his maisters steppes, Benno calleth a blind guide, a sciesmaticke, an hereticke, and companion of Liberius the Arrian hereticke: He watred those graftes of mischiefe which Gregorie had planted, and was therfore called the turmoyler of the world, by descantinge of his name and in steede of Vrban calling him Turban. He excommunicated Clement þ seconde established by the Emperour, and also the Emperour for establishinge of him, & procured manye forsworne rebels both nobles and commoners, to conspire againste him: and likewyse the same Clement as being Pope, did againe excommunicate him as an vsurper, whereuppon it moued many reasonings amonge both spirituall & temporall, who should be right Pope: And these controuersyes were tossed both in Germanye and other countryes. But when Vrban would absolue none, whom Gregorie had excommunicated, he was fayne for feare of his life, to flie by

stealth

Pageant of Popes.　Fol.87.

wealth from Rome, he held fiue coūcels in sondrye places, and all for the establishing of Gregories decrees, and to cōfirme that auctoritye which the Church had gotten. Amonge many other enormities he cōcluded that no priests sonne shoulde be capable of orders. He made þ archbishop of Toledo primate of Spaine, vppon condition þ he should sweare fealtye to þ Pope, & so by that meanes he broughte Spaine vnder his winge. He cursed the kinge of Fraunce for imprisoning a bishop. He caused all that should take order to sweare with this clause, So God helpe me and the holye Euangelistes: finally he standing in awe of one Iohn Pagan a Romaine, did hide himselfe for two yeares in the house of one Peter Lion, where he dyed Anno 1099. And his bodye was conueyed by nighte ouer Tiber for feare of his foes, the same yeare also dyed Clement the thirde, who had seene in his time the death of three Popes.

Of the former Hildebrand and this Vrban his schooller, Theodor Bibliander writeth thus to Princes of al estates: Hildebrand (sayth he) by sturringe vp the Greeke Emperour against the Turkes, did sowe the seede of the voiage of Gog & Magog, vppon whom the bloude of the Church cryeth vengeaunce, that was shed wyth the sworde of his tongue. But this Vrban by causinge Christians to goe warre vppon Pagans, with vaine colour of fighting for þ holye Lande, & for Christes Sepulcher, hath caused more Christian bloud to be shedde of all Nations, then can be esteemed: and did it onelye to oppresse Clement the second and his faction, the while to restore himselfe to be Pope. In the time of this Vrbā, VVilliam Rufus kinge of England was sore combred with the proude prelate Anselmus archbishop of Canterbury, who whē he was commaunded to aunsweare to his misbehauiour, did auoide it in appealinge to the Courte of Rome, both against the liking of al the bishops in Englande, and in spite of the kinges harte went to complaine to the Pope.

101 Pas-

The fifte booke of the
101. Paschal the second.

PAschal the seconde was an Italian called before Rainerus, hee was made Cardinall of S. Clements by Hildebrande his Scholemaister, & succeded Vrban. He when he sawe he shoulde be chosen, woulde not take the place vppon him vntil the people had cryed thre times S. Peter choseth thee worthie man Raynarde: Then hauinge a purple robe vppon him, and a Miter on his head, he was brought vppon a white horse vnto Lateran, where hee recepued the Popes Scepter, and had the gyrdle put about him, wheron are hanged seuen keyes, and as manye Seales. All the time he raigned he was continually busyed in warres, and seditions, attemptinge by all meanes possible to aduaunce yet hier the estate of the Popedome. He draue out furiously from their places all those bishops and abbots, y were established by the Emperour. At this time there was a certaine prelate called Fluentinus, who seinge the greate enormityes that presently choaked the Christian Church, held opinion that Antichrist was incarnate and borne, and that he was reueaued herein. And therefore (sayth Sabellicus) the Pope held a councel against him, with the bishops of Italy and Fraunce, in Rome: amonge other canons he concluded it heresye to denye obedience to the Pope, and made a canon for paying of tenthes to priestes, concluding it sinne against the holye Ghoste to sell the tenthes. He renued and published the excommunication against the Emperour, and caused the bishop of Mentz, of Collen, and of VVormes, to thrust him frō his estate, taking his Crowne from him with al princelye title, dignitye and honour. Yea and which is horrible to be heard, not content with this he did prouoke and arme his onelye sonne Henry the fifte, to rebell against him being his naturall father: A lamentable and pitifull case, to see the onelye child of so good & nu-
ble a

ble a father, not beinge prouoked by any iniurye on the fathers part, not onely to despise, to forsake and reuolt from his father, denying to ayde him, but also to assault hym by force of armes, & to enclose him with his armye as he did, and toke him entrapped by treason, spoyled & robbed him of his royal estate, and forced the wretched and miserable man captiue to his owne child, to dye a double and dolefull death. Thus could the Pope put the sworde in the sonnes hand, forsing him to sheath it in his fathers bowels: Neither could this vnnaturall death of ye good olde man, cause the vnnaturall rancour to dye in the Popes breast, but for further reuenge he cōmaunded that the Emperours carkasse should not be buryed, but first be cast out of ye Church and be caryed from Leodos to Spira, where it rotted fiue yeares without any Christian burial. But lo what a wonder God wrought in the meane time. To testify (sayth Abbas V. spergensis) the Popes tyrannye, it rayned bloud at Spira. It were a lamentable thing to tell at large the maner of the Popes vnmerciful dealing with this good Emperour. For first the forenamed bishops comminge to him to Hilgeshem, they cōmaunded him to deliuer vp his Diademe, his Purple roabes, his Signet and other like ornaments belonging to the Empyre. Whē he required a reason thereof, they aunsweared partly for sellinge spirituall liuinges, but chiefely for the Popes pleasure. Wyth that the good Emperour sighing saide: Ye know you receyued your bishoprickes at my hande, that I gaue them freelye and am giltye of no suche cryme, and yet do you thus quite my curtesye? But the vnthankful prelates moued neither with allegeaunce, oath, nor benefite, prosecuted their purpose: and first yelding him no reuerence, they plucked frō him (sitting in his place of estate) his Crowne Emperial, and his Purple roabe, and his Scepter. He beinge thus stripped out of his royaltye and forsaken, sayde pacientlye Let God see and iudge. They leauing him, bestowed these

thinges

The fifte booke of the

things vppon the sonne creating him, & causing him forth with to pursue his father, forcing him to flye but wyth ir. parsons to the Dukedome of Limborough, where ye duke beinge his deadly ennemye did also make speede to apprehende him. The Emperour percevuing himselfe thus entrapped and fearing death, submitted himselfe to the duke, beseaching him rather to shewe mercye then vengeaunce: Hereupon the noble harted duke, thoughe the Emperour had whilom displaced him of his Dukedome, yet pityinge his miserye he both forgaue him & entertayned him curteously in his Castel, and w an armye conducted him to Collen, where he was well receyued. But the sonne hearinge thereof besieged the Citye, but the father fled by night to Leodium, where so manye louinge hartes resorted to him, that he bad his sonne a battaile and ouerthrewe him, and still desyred that if his sonne were taken, he should be saued harmelesse. Yet the sonne ceased not, but renuinge the battaile preuayled and so dispossessed his father: whoe in the ende was brought to such penurye, that he craued of the bishop of Spire to giue him but a prebende to liue vppon in ye Church: But the carle forgetting the benefites receyued of him in his prosperitye, denyed him flatlye and said, by ladye ye get none here. Thus after he had raigned 50 yeare in his life he lacked lyuinge, and after death he wanted a graue throughe the malice of the Pope.

Pope Paschal held a councell of Princes and bishoppes about matter of gaynes, as homages and fealtyes due vnto him, also he spoiled the bishop of Rauenna of his lands, and toke them into his owne handes: But afterwarde because he refused to confirme certaine bishops appointed by the Emperour Henry the fift, the Emperour (though late before he had kissed the Popes feete) apprehended him, and cast him into prison, where he continued vntill he had cōfirmed them all, and should by his Seale restore the priuiledge of ratifying a bishop, which was graunted to Char

les the

les the great, and confirme him to be Emperour. While (sayth Masseus) the Pope sate in his chayre after Masse, beholde the souldiours cryed vnto him and his clergye, Giue vnto Cæsar that which is Cæsars: and forthwith apprehended both him and all his clergye, and caryed them out, and stripped them out of their apparell so naked, that they lefte them not theyr breeches on, and ledde them thus hadled to Soractis mount, wher they put them in prison &c. This broyle being ceased, and Henry being crowned Emperour, Paschal renued vnto him the auctoritye of appointing bishops, and pronounced openlye in the Church, that they were all held accursed, who soeuer would disanul the preuiledge which he had graunted: Then thy sange Gloria in excelsis, because of this peace betwene ye Emperour and the Pope. But as sone as the Emperour (this being done) was departed into Germanye, the Pope brake al his oathes, and went from his word in euerye thinge, saying ye hee did it not freelye and of his owne accorde, but that for feare hee yelded to the Emperours desire. Then was the priuiledge condemned, and the Emperour excommunicated, and terrible tragedyes sturred, which were all blazed throughe diuers countryes. Also hee by a councell diuorsed the clergye of Fraunce from their wyues, as Gregorie had done in Germanye, and draue diuers bishops frō their Seas, because they would not leaue theyr wyues. Againe to encrease the regiment of Rome, he reuiued the strife for the bestowig of bishoprickes, which wrought great slaughter and bloudshed in all countreyes of Europe. Anselm⁹ archbishop of Canterbury, wyth sophistrye and cauillinge vpheldc this Popes doing, as he did Pope Vrbanus being both their councelour at Rome, & their Vicar here in Englande. This Anselmus did depriue kinge Henry the first of all auctoritye in Ecclesiasticall causes, and denyed to do homage to the kinge, thinking and auouching it to be vnlawfall, because it was due in the clergye vnto the successours

M.　　　　　　　　　of S.

The fifte booke of the

of S. Peter. Also he condemned in England the mariage of ministers: Pope Paschal dyed Anno 1118.

Matthæus Parisiensis wryteth in his Chronicle, ý when Anselmus accused his soueraigne kinge Henry the first of England, before the Pope at Rome for medling with the appointing of bishops and ministers, VVilliam VVarelwarst the kinges Proctour did aunsweare stoutlye in hys Princes behalfe, and amonge other thinges sayd, that the kinge would not for the losse of his kingdome leſe his auctoritye in appointing of prelates. Whereto the Pope said: If as thou sayest thy kinge to hazarde his crowne, wil not forgoe his giuing of Ecclesiasticall lyuinges, knowe thou precisely, I speake it before God, ý I will not suffer him without punishmẽt, no not for the price of his head. Which beinge heard, Anselmus besought the Pope, to laye hands in despite of the kinge on those whom he had disgraded, & so (sayth Matthæus) the holye seate readye to yelde fauour to all, restored them to their former dignities by the intercession of White and red. But kinge Henry did depriue Anselmus of all his goodes, and confiscated his Archbishopricke and desyed the Popes auctoritye. Anno 1110. the Moone was darkened, as if she had lost her lighte, the yeare following it rayned bloud at Rauenna in Italy, & at Parma in the month of Julye. Anno 1114. in December the Heauen appeared sodenlye of a very fierye and ruddye colour, as if it had burned, and the Moone suffered an Eclipse. The same yeare the riuer of Thames was drye for two dayes. Anno 1117. there were thonders, hayle, great windes, horrible dreadful and houge earthquakes, that ouerthrewe Churches, Towers, walles, buildinges, and destroyed men.

102. Gelasius the second.

Gelasius

GElasius the second called before Iohn Caietanus of a noble house, was sometime a monke, he succeded Paschal but not without great discention. For because he was chosen withoute the consente of the Emperour, one Cincius a mā of great power in Rome would not suffer this iniurye, but went with a troupe of souldiours to Palladiā minster, where the Cardinals were gathered together: and breakinge the gates open he rushed in vppon them, and stroke at euerye one that he mette. And as for the Pope with his necke wrong doe awrye he threwe him on the ground, stamped on him wyth his feete, and cast him into prison: and as the Cardinals were running away, he hopsed them of their Mules and horses to the grounde, and vsed all the despite he could toward them. But ye Romaynes would not suffer this, and therfore by the ayde of the Normans they deliuered the Pope, & made his ennemyes to submit themselues, and to aske pardon wyth kissinge his feete. The Emperour hearing this sent a great armye out of Germanye to Rome, which Gelasius fearing, fled by shippe wyth his companye to Caieta, and there was made a priest, for he was made Pope before beinge but a deacon. Henry the Emperour comming to Rome in the absence of Gelasius, created Maurice Burdinus archbishop of Bracharie Pope, and called him Gregorie the eight, and thē he returned frō Rome. Gelasius hearinge therof returneth priuilye to Rome, and takinge harte to him he commeth into Praxis Church to saye masse, where he was so hindred by the contrarye syde, that he scant saued himselfe by runing away: From thence he fled into Fraunce, where at the length he was entertayned by an abbot, in whose house hee dyed of a pleuresye in the seconde yeare of his raigne. In his life by a Legat that he sent, he held a councell in Collen, where he excommunicated the Emperour, and decreed yt the Popes of Rome should be iudged by none.

M ii 103 Ca-

The fifte booke of the

103. Calixtus the seconde.

Calixtus the second being before called Guido of Burgundy came of the kinges of Fraunce and Englande, he succeded Gelasius. And after he was confirmed at Rome, he sent a messenger to the said Conon in Germanye, to continue the excommunication of his predecessour against the Emperour. Hereupon ye Emperour was compelled to summon a councell of Princes and bishops at Tybur, to make peace betweene him & the Pope: and least the Popes part shoulde haue spoyled his dominions, he toke peace vppon vnequall conditions. He confirmed to his great dishonour the electiō of this Calixtus, who was chosen Pope at Cluny in Fraunce by a fewe Cardinals, whom Gelasius had brought wyth him: and yet was the other Pope Gregorie aliue, whom ye Emperour himselfe had first created. And when the Popes Legates demaunded of the Emperour to giue ouer his auctoritye in Ecclesiasticall causes, and bestowing spirituall liuinges: he desired respit to deliberate thereon with the Princes of Germanye, who councelled him to seeke for the fauour of the Pope, (to such puissancye was ye Pope then start vp ouer the mightie Monarches.) Finallye Embassadours meetinge at VVormes in Germanye for eyther parte to debate the matter, after greate controuersyes and sharpe reasoninges on cyther syde, the Pope bare awaye the victorye: for the Emperours Proctours were the bishop of Spire and the abbot of Fulda, by theyr callinge bounde to fauour the Popes part, who perswaded the Emperour to yelde ouer his righte for feare of the excomunication, which would cause his subiects to reuolt from him: And so he obeyed. This beinge done the Popes Legates did absolue him, and gaue him licence to repayre to seruice in the Church, which Gelasius had denyed him. These compositions were drawne in wrighting

for both

for both sydes, and therfore the Popes part euen to triũph of their victorye, and shewe how the Emperour was vanquished, caused theirs to be read with open Proclamation, and hanged them vp at Lateran to be seene openlye. Calixtus after he had thus maistred the Emperour, persecuted Pope Gregorie his aduersarye that stoode against him for the Popedome, by the Emperours meanes: Gregorie hearing of this fled from Rome to Sturium, where Calixtus caught him, and to make him a laughing game euen to the Emperours reproche, he caused Gregorie to be set vppon a Camel with his face toward the Camels tayle, & so to be brought to Rome: afterward he caused his heade to be shauen, & so sente him into a Monasterye. Amonge manye Canons that Calixtus made, one was, that it should be adulterye if a man in his life time shoulde forsake his bishoprick or Church, wresting this place of Paule vnto it: The wyfe is bound to the lawe of her husbande, while he liueth &c.. He appointed to fast foure times in the yeare, whereas before it was but thrise., and said it was not lawfull to fast anye otherwise then accordinge as the Church of Rome did, addinge this reason: For (sayth hee) as the sonne came to do the will of his father, so muste Christians do the will of their mother the Church of Rome. He dyed of a feuer which he toke by the trauell of a greate iorneye, Anno 1125. One Simeon an Englishman borne in Duresme in the 2. booke of his historye of the Kinges of Englande wryteth, that this Calixtus held a generall councell in Fraunce, wherin he forbad priestes, deacons, or subdeacons to haue wyues: and first to leese their benefices, secondlye the Communion if they woulde not yeilde herein. Whereuppon one in Englande wrote a sharpe Epigram against him, thus in effect.

O bone Calixte nunc omnis clerus odit te,
Quondam presbyteri poterant vxoribus vti:

The fift Booke of the

Hoc deſtruxiſti, poſtquam tu Papa fuiſti,
Ergo tuùm meritò nomen habent odiò.
O good Calixtus now the clergye doth the hate,
In former tyme the Churchmen might enioy their ſpou-
sal mate:
But thou haſt take this away to Popeſhip ſince thou came,
Therefore as thou deſerued haſt they do deteſt thy name.

104. Honorius the seconde.

HOnorius the ſecond before called Lambert being but of baſe byrth, was firſt made biſhop of Hoſtia for his lear-ninge, and so came to be Pope. But (ſayth Platina) his en-traunce into Peters place is not to be commended, becauſe he came in rather by the ambition of a few, then the cōſent of good men: for he was made Pope with great debate by the pollicy of one Leo Frangepain ÿ chiefeſt Citizen, who perſwaded that they ſhould not choſe ÿ Pope, before they knewe all the Canons concerning the electiō. While they ſtayed about this, Leo practiſed to ſerue this Popes turne by ſuch fetches as he could deuiſe: but the Cardinals per-ceyuinge his policye did create one Theobaldus (a Cardi-nall) Pope, callinge him Celeſtine, but the people ſtoode earneſtlye vrginge for another Cardinall that was a Saxō, which Leo ſeemed to like of, onelye to defeate the election of the Cardinals: and when by this meanes he had ÿ peo-ple ſomwhat indifferent to be ruled by him, he brought to paſſe by them to make Lambert Pope, and called him Ho-norius. This Honorius (ſayth Mattheus Pariſienſis) ſent out a Legat one Iohn Cremenſis a riotous Cardinal, to fil the Popes bagges: He cōming into England Anno 1125. wyth the kinges fauour paſſed from one Religious houſe to another, ſtill fillinge his pouches with moneye and hys paunche with delicate cheare. And when he had euen loaden
him-

himselfe meetely wel, he held a Synode in London, where he cōdemned all the clergye of adultery which had wyues, and euen the selfe same daye at night my Lord Legat himselfe euen his owne parson was taken in adultery. And yet Pope Honorius wrote in his behalfe to ye clergye of Englande thus: Wee desire you, charge you, and commaunde you, that ye receyue this Iohn as the Vicar of S. Peter with reuerence, heare him with humilitye and at his commaundement be assistant at his Synodes. &c. The like for him wrote Honorius to Dauid kinge of Scottes. There is a certaine statute made by the same Iohn, in ye said Synode helde at London to this effecte: Wee by our Apostolicall auctoritye commaunde that priestes, deacons, subdeacons, and canonists, shall not come in companye wyth theyr wyues, concubines, yea or any other women, except theyr mother, sister or aunte, or such womē as may altogether giue no suspition, and who so shall breake this, shall forfaite his orders. Wee commaunde that no mariage shalbe made betweene kindred, or affinitye to the seuenth degree. Honorius dyed Anno 1130. Platina sayth that in the time of this Honorius, one Arnulphus an Englishmā and a noble preacher of ye Christen Religion, was murthered at Rome by the treacherye of the clergye, because he did sharpelye reproue theyr ryot and wantonnesse, and rebuked theyr pompe, and greedinesse in gatheringe riches. Manye of the nobles of Rome did followe this man as a true disciple & Prophete of Christe, and onelye preacher of the truth.

105. Innocentius the second.

Innocentius the second after he was made Pope, coulde deuise no more charitable deede then to suppresse Roger Duke of Sicilia, for sayinge that he was kinge of Italye. The Pope broughte oute his armye, and marched forward stoutlye and manfullye ouerthrew his ennemyes but

M iiii   the

The fift Booke of the

the dukes sonne comminge vppon his backe with an army toke the Pope, and his Cardinals, and so Roger obtayned all besyde the title of Sicilia. In the meane time, the Romaynes created one Peter Leo his sonne Pope, and called him Anacletus, which being heard Innocentius desired to be set at libertye and obtayned it, and purposed to returne to Rome: but because he saw al was in an vproze at Rome, he turned frō thence, trauayling till he came into Fraūce. In the meane time Anacletus sought wyth spendinge and brybinge, to winne and confirme all mens good wills towarde him, that anye way seemed to fauour him: He made Roger kinge of both Sicils to be his freinde. Innocentius was buspe on the other syde, to recouer the Popedome, & therefoze held a councell in Fraunce and condemned Anacletus foz an ennempe of the Church. Afterward he went to Philip kinge of Fraunce, and crowned his sonne Lewes, then he wente to Carnotus, where he met with Henry the first, kinge of Englande, perswading with him to send an armye against the Sarracens that kept the holpe lande, but his purpose was to haue vsed that army foz the recouering of his Popedome. From him he went to Lotharius kinge of Germanye desyzinge him to see him restozed: Lotharius gyuinge his oath to the Pope, pzepared an armye to conducte Innocent safe to Rome. So Lotharius entred into Italye wyth a puissante armye to restoze Innocent to hys place, and comminge to Rome deuided his hoast, and entred into the Citye, ouerthzewe Anacletus with duke Roger, and set Innocētius safe in Lateran. Innocentius therefoze to shew himselfe thanckfull, crowned Lotharius Emperour, and gaue to Reginold his chiefest Captayne the Dukedome of Apulia, p was none of his owne to bestow, and all that Roger possessed in Italy. But Reginold dyed soone after, and then Roger claymed his right againe, and because p Pope withstoode him, he toke him againe, & his Cardinals sodenly ere p they wist, & would neuer let them

depart

Pageant of Popes. Fol.93

depart vntill they had graunted him his whole desire: yea to make him kinge of both Sicils, and so since that time the kingdome of Sicill is called S. Peters patrimonye. But (sayth Nauclerus) much mischiefe arose vp hereof, because the Pope woulde thus take vppon him the bestowinge of Princelye titles, robbinge the Emperours of that righte, which they had gotten by the sworde. Innocentius made a lawe, that whosoeuer should strike an annointed priest or shauen clarke, shoulde be excommunicated, to be absolued onelye by the Pope: after this hee dyed Anno 1143. In this Popes time Steuen Kinge of Englande Anno 1136. kept to himselfe and vsed in his owne power the inuesture of prelates. And Lotharius the Emperour would haue reclaymed that to himselfe, which the Pope toke from Henry the Emperour, but that S. Bernard being then of great credite disswaded him. About this time was VVilliam bishop of Yorke called S. VVilliam of Yorke, who was poysoned in his challice by his Chapleynes.

106. Celestine the second.

CElestine the second a Thuscan succeded Innocent by þ commaundement of Conradus: his life was so shorte that he could not play the Pope like other. At this tyme was a great contagious plague through out al Italy. Celestine dyed in the sixt month of his Popeship. In his time the bishop of VVinchester in Englande helde a councell, where was concluded þ if any man abused eyther Church or Churchyard or layde hand on an Ecclesiasticall person, he shoulde be excommunicate, to be absolued onelye by the Pope. 171

107. Lucius the second.

LVcius the second borne in Bononia succeded Celestine. He was the cause & auctor of much discension in Rome, for deposing and disanullinge a kinde of office called Patricianship, 172

The fift booke of the

cianſhip, which the Romaynes being weary of the Popes yoke had made in the time of Innocentius, becauſe the Popes toke vppon them all ſwaye within the Citye & abroade likewiſe. But this Pope Lucius becauſe he was not able to depoſe the Patrician alone, craued ayde of ẏ Emperour Conradus, whoe beinge otherwiſe buſied coulde not aſſiſte him. Lucius therefore ſoughte to attaine his purpoſe another waye: for when the Patrician & the Senatours were all gathered together cloſe in the Capitol, Lucius toke his oportunitye and came thither with a bande of ſouldiours in armour, meaninge either to deſtroye the Capitoll, or to driue them out. The Cityzẽs hearing hereof armed themſelues forthwith, and ranne to ſuccour theyr officer, wherevppon roſe a very bloudye fraye: Pope Lucius beinge in the middeſt of the broyle was ſo pelted with ſtones and other lumpes, that ſone after he dyed therof Anno 1145 ere he had raigned a yeare.

108. Eugenius the third.

EVgenius ẏ thirde ſometime an abbot, was made Pope by this meanes w̃ the conſente of the Cardinals. This Eugenius was ſcholer to S. Barnard, who for his learning was then in great reuerence, and conſidering the time how the Romaynes wrangled to haue auctoritye in the electiõ of the Pope, they thoughte it ſafeſt and ſureſt for the maintenaunce of the Popes auctoritye, to choſe none of the Colledge of Cardinals but this Eugenius, that it mighte be a cauſe why his ſcholemaiſter Barnarde ſhoulde aduaunce ẏ Sea of Rome in his wrytinges: and ſo it fell out as it appeareth in his 2. booke of Conſiderations. Eugenius at his firſt creation perceyued the Romaynes woulde be importunate, to haue the election of theyr Senatours ratifyed, and therefore hee fled wyth his Cardinals from Rome by night to Viterbium, where he excommunicated all the

Romaynes

Pageant of Popes.   Fol. 94

Romaynes, which caused ẏ Citizens to obeye Iordan chosen Patrician: then he ioyned his armye with the hoast of the Tiburtines, olde enemyes to Rome, & so compelled ẏ Romaynes to sue for peace: which he graunted at length vppon condition that they should fullye abolish the principalitye of the Patrician, and shoulde restore his deputye to his former place, and for hereafter shoulde be contente to take suche Senatours, as hee by his Papall auctoritye would assigne them. Peace beinge thus concluded he returned into Rome, but perceyuing afterwarde that falsehoode was mente towarde him, he slipt againe to Tiburie: the Romaynes pursued him forthwith, with bowes and bils, and draue him from Tiburie into Fraunce. And at length he returned to Rome and there dyed Anno 1152.

109.   Anastasius the fourth.

Anastasius of a Cardinall became Pope, wherein hee did nothinge worthye memorye, but that hee bestowed vppon Lateran a riche and massye Chalice, and bestowed cost in repayringe S. Maries Churche, and so dyed the seconde yeare of his Popeship Anno 1154. This Anastasius after the death of one Henry Mordachus a proud moke whom Pope Eugenius intruded, restored S. Willia͡ archbishop of Yorke, which William was afterward poysoned in the Challice comminge to receiue the Communion, as Mattheus Parisius sayth. In this Popes time ẏ Thames at London was so frozen, ẏ cartes and waynes passed ouer the ise, and a litle before were two Eclipses, one of the Sunne, and the other of the Moone, after which followed terrible tempestes, stormes, thonder, lightninges, raine and winde.

174

110.   Hadrian the fourth.

Hadrian

The fift booke of the

Hadrian the fourth was an Englishmā borne called Nicolas Breakespeare, ye sonne of one Dan Robert a mōke of S. Albanes: he was first a reguler priest, & afterwarde a bishop, then a Cardinall, and finallye Pope of Rome. He being chosen by the clergye at Rome, would not ascende & take the place untill they had consented unto him, that one Arnold bishop of Brixia whom he counted an hereticke, should be banished oute of Rome. This Arnold perswaded the Romaynes to recouer their libertye of choosinge theyr Maiestrates: and when the people withstoode the presumption of the Pope, it wroughte greate strife. This Hadrian a man of loftye courage forthwith did excommunicate the Romaynes, untill they should driue out Arnold, and compell theyr Consulles to leaue theyr offices, & yeild the gouernemente of the Citye freelye unto him. In the meane time Fredericke ye Emperour hasted him to Rome with an armye, to put downe the rebels: the Pope and his clergye went out to meete him, whereby ye Pope thought to get oportunitye to be reuenged by the Emperours ayde uppō his ennemyes. The Emperour meeting with ye Pope alighted from his horse and went on foote, and attendinge on the Popes parson when he should alight, ye Emperour helde the lefte stirope, for the which the Pope scorned him for mistakinge the stirope, and sayde unto him: Ye shoulde haue held mee the right stirope. The Emperour takinge it paciently aunsweared him similingly, I haue not (quoth hee) learned to holde a stirope, and you holye father are the first, to whom I euer did this seruice: And (quoth ye Emperour, because he sawe the Pope angrye that he aunswered) I would know of you whether this be my dutye to do it, of force, or of my owne curtesye: If a man offer it of curtesye, how wil you rebuke him for negligence? If it be not of dutye, what neede ye care on which side hee come unto you, that commeth to do you worship? Such sharpe talke passinge betweene them, they departed both full of wrath.

But

Pageant of Popes.   Fol. 95.

But on the morowe the Emperour beinge awaré of wisedome, neglected all that he had hearde and seene touchinge the Popes statelye and prowde minde, and sent for him desiringe him to come to his pauilion. The Pope came and ye Emperour went forth to meete him, and as he was tought the daye before againſt the Pope ſhould alight, he held the right ſtirope, and so conducted the Pope in. As they sate together, Pope Hadrian beganne to talke in this mener. Princes (quoth hee) in olde time which came to craue the Crowne, were wonte to recompence the curteſye of the Church of Rome wyth some excellente benefite, that as it were presenting the Popes bleſſinge and the crowne, that they ſhould receiue by their dutifulnes, might notifye themſelues to all men by their noble deede: For so Charles deſerued his Crowne by conqueringe the Lombardes, Otho his by aſſwaging the Berengarians, Lotharius his by ſuppreſſinge the Normans. Therefore your worthines may reſtore Apulia to be territorye to Rome, which nowe the Normans withholde, & then will we afterward ſone do ye which is our dutye. The Princes therefore perceyuing ye the Pope would not crowne Fredericke, vnleſſe he ſhould firſt winne Apulia from VVilliam kinge of Sicill by his owne coſte & charge, they promiſed it ſhould be performed with a newe armye out of Germanye, as sone as the other armye were growne out, if so be he would crowne ye Emperour. Thereupon the next daye he was crowned with ye Crowne Emperiall, by the Pope in S. Peters Pallaice: and afterward hauinge executed aboue a thouſande of the rebellious Citizes, he prepared to returne into Germany. After the Emperours departure, ye Pope beinge diſapointed of his ayde, purpoſed to ſet vpon Apulia to winne it fro the king of Sicill, with such force as as he could make: firſt he excommunicated the kinge becauſe he woulde not yelde it vp, and diſcharged his ſubiects of theyr alleageaunce, to make them to rebell againſt him. But becauſe theſe thinges pre-

The fifte booke of the

ges preuailed but little against kinge VVilliam, he set Emanuel the Emperour of Greece vppon him, because hee knewe that he had beene a mortal ennemye to king VVilliams father. VVilliam fearinge this sought for peace, & promised to yelde all to the Pope, but the Pope by the councell of certaine Cardinals (hopinge to gaine more by the warre then peace) refused the offer, & proclaymed warre against him. King VVilliam percepuinge this to preuent the daunger in time, gathered an armye in haste out of all Sicill, and sayled to Apulia wher he fought with Emanuel and ouerthrewe him. Afterwarde hee assaulted the towne Beneuent (where the Pope and his Cardinals weare) in such sort y they dispayring to escape craued peace: VVilliam graunted it, and so was reconciled to the Pope, who then pronounced him king of both Sicils, making him first to sweare that he should hurt nothinge that belonged to y Church of Rome. Thus the Pope returned to Rome in foule shame, where contrarye to his expectation hee was troubled with ciuill discention, for the Consuls began to reclayme their libertye and auctoritye which he had taken awaye: and because he coulde not preuaile with his vaine thonderboltes of excomunication, he departed to Arminy.

While these thinges were doinge, the Emperour abydinge at home, remembred with himselfe howe the Pope had taken from the Emperours the former right of inuestinge of prelates, and by his Legates had summoned all nations together, & had sowed y seede of rebellion through all his Empyre, taken homage & fealtye of all the bishops in Germanye. Hereuppon he commaunded, that if the Popes Legates came into Germanye without his commaundement, they should be kept out. He forbad that anye of his subiectes should appeale to Rome, he set his owne name in wrytinge before the Popes: whereuppon the Pope was so wroth, that he sente letters to the Emperour rebuking him sharpelye for it. The copye whereof for the better vn-
der-

derſtanding of it, it thus.

Hadrians letter to the Emperour.

Hadrian biſhop ſeruaunt to the ſeruaunts of God, ſendeth greeting to Frederick themperour, and apoſtolicall bleſſinge. As the lawe of God promiſeth longe life to them that do honour their parentes, ſo doth it threaten death, to them that diſhonour their father or mother. The truth teacheth vs that euerye one that exalteth himſelfe ſhalbe brought downe. Therfore right welbeloued ſonne in the Lorde, vvee do not a little marueile at your vvyſedome, that ye do not ſo much dutye as becommeth you to S. Peter, and the holye Church of Rome: For in your letter ſente vnto vs yee haue ſet your name before ours, whereby you do bewray your vanitye, I will not ſay your pride. VVhat ſhall I ſpeake, hovve little ye obſerue your fealtye, which ye are bounde by oath and promiſe to perfoime to S. Peter and vs? Seing ye requier honour and allegeance of them that are Gods, and of al our honourable ſonnes, biſhops I meane. And ye wrap their holye handes within yours, ſettinge your ſelfe manifeſtlye againſt vs: Ye ſhutte not onelye the Churches, but alſo the Cities of your dominion againſt the Cardinal ſent from our owne ſide. VVhat ſhall I ſaye? Repent therefore repent we aduiſe you: for we feare leaſt your noblenes whyle you deſerue of vs to haue both bleſſing and Crowne, vvill looſe that vvhich vve haue graūted you, by taking vppon you that which we haue not graunted. Fare ye well.

The aunſweare of Fredericke themperour to the Popes letter.

Frederick by the grace of God Emperour of the Romaynes Auguſtus euermore, to Hadrian Pope of Rome, and to al thoſe that (are vvilling to cleaue to that vvhich Chriſt began to do and teach)

ſendeth

The fifte booke of the

sendeth greetinge. The lavve of Iustice requireth to euerye man his ovvne, For vve do not dishonour our aunceftours, to vvhom vvithin this our kingdome vve yelde due reuerence, by vvhom vve haue enherited our Crovvne and regall dignitye. Is it knovvne that Syluester bifhoppe of Rome in the time of Constantine the Emperour, had anye kinglye poart? But by his godlye graunte the Church obtayned libertye, peace vvas restored, and vvhat soeuer your princelye pontificality is knovvne to haue, it came by the bountifulnes of Princes: VVhereby vvhen soeuer vve vvrite to the Pope, by good righte vve set our ovvne name former, and accordinge to the rule of Iustice vve allovve it to him vvritinge to vs. Loke ouer the Recordes and if ye marked not in readinge vvhich vve auouche, there ye shall finde it. But vvhy shoulde vve not require homage and royal oathes tovvarde our parson of them, that are Gods by adoption, and possesse the royaltye belonging to vs: Seing that he vvho taught both vs and you, takinge nothing of a Prince but geuinge al goodnes to all men, yet payde tribute to Cæsar, for himselfe and Peter, and gaue you an example that ye shoulde do the like. And so he teacheth you saying: Learne of mee, for I am humble and gentle of harte. Therefore let them eyther graunte vnto vs that belongeth to our royalcye, or els if they vvill challenge this for their more commoditye, then let them, paye vnto God that is due vnto GOD, and vnto Cæsar that is due vnto Cæsar. The Churches are shut to your Cardinals, and the Cityes are not open vnto them, and reason good, becaufe vvee see that they are not feeders but fleecers of their flockes, not kepers of peace, but catchers of pence: not thofe that amend the vvorld, but that deuoure it. But vvhen vvee shall see them such, as the Church requireth, bearinge peace, giuinge light to their countreye, affiftinge the caufe of the lovvlye in equity, vve vvil forthvvith succour them, vyith necessarye stipends and suftinaunce. But ye do much discredit your humilitye and curtesye, beinge the sauegarde of all vertues, vvhen ye moue to secular parfons such questions as do not much further religion. Let therefore your fatherlye vvisedome prouide, least vvhile ye sturre aboute such vnmeete matters, yee giue offence vnto those vvhich applye themselues to giue eare to the vvotds of your mouth, as it vvere to a shovver of raine after Haruofte. For vve cannot but aunfvveare to thofe thinges vvhich vve heare, vvhen vve see the deteftable beaft of pride to haue crept euen to Peters feate, fo long as vve purpofe God vvillinge continuallye to prouide for peace and the Church. Fareye vvell.

Here may

Here may you discerne somwhat the dealing and spirite of the Romain bishops, which I leaue to euery ones owne indifferent consideration. To returne to the matter, hereupon this Pope Hadrian did excommunicate ye Emperour, and by his Legates sent from Rome prouoked rebellions against him in Italye and other places: and brought it secretly to passe, that the conspiracye of the rebels should be made the stronger, by these lawes confirmed among them by oath, that none of them should take peace with him, withoute the whole consent of all the rest. And againe, that if this Pope Hadrian should dye, they should choose none to be Pope, but one of those Cardinals that were of the conspiracye against the Emperour. But shortlye after God punished this Hadrian very straungelye for (sayth Abbas Vspergensis in Frederico primo) it came to passe that this Pope Hadrian the fourth, going to Agnania to denounce the excommunication against the Emperour, after he had taryed there a fewe dayes, walked forth with some of his companye, to coole him selfe: And when he came to a certaine springe of water he drancke thereof, and forthwith a flye did enter into his mouth, and did cleaue to his throte in such sort, that no art of the Phisitiōs could get it away, and so he was choaked therew, and died therof Anno 1159. in the fift yeare of his Popeship. But the Italians being thus set on by the Pope, deuised continuallye treasons against ye Emperour, amonge other, practised to haue murthered him by a certaine counterfeit foole, beinge in deede an excellente Musician, who had surelye slaine him, but ye the Emperour driuen to his shift leaped out at ye fifte window downe into a riuer, which ranne vnder ye place where he was: The foole beinge taken was also throwne downe out of the same windowe, and so he brake his necke. After this they hyred an enchanter of Arabia, who poysoned his bridle, his spurres, his ringes, and his stirope, and such other thinges, that with ye onlye touching thereof he should

haue

The fift Booke of the

haue beene flaine: But he was bewrayed and hanged vp. This Pope Hadrian made king Henry ye second of Englande, Lorde of Irelande. Carion in his Chronicle wrytinge of Conradus the thirde, Emperour of Germanye sayth, that it is found written that this Pope Hadrian ye fourth euen a little before his death should say: that there is no kind of life vpon earth more wretched then to be Pope, and to get the Popedome by bloud is not to succeede Peter, but Romulus whoe for the kingdome slue his owne brother.

III. Alexander the thirde.

Alexander the third was borne in Hetruria called first Rolland Chancelour. After Hadrian ye fourth had his breath stopped, and was choaked with a flye, this man succeeded him beinge farre worse then the other. But because that all partyes coulde not agree to elect him, nine of the Cardinals that held on the Emperours part, did choose another Pope called Octauianus a citizen of Rome, being a priest and Cardinall of S. Clements, whom they called Victor the fourth. And after the death of this Victor the strife sine and discention beinge continued, three Popes succeeded in order, Paschalis, Calixtus, and Innocentius, all which withstoode this Pope Alexander and made greate turmoyles in the Church of Rome, and al perished, he yet lyuinge. But when the Emperour sommoned a councell at Papia wherby the strife might be ended, and the matter debated, that he might be confirmed Pope that had ye better right: this Alexander defyinge the Emperours Embassadours, aunswered proudlye that the Pope (as he toke himselfe to be) is to be iudged by no man, and thus sent awaye the Embassadours with great contempte: and sendinge his letters throughe all Christendome, he plagued both the Emperour and this Victor with excommunications.

tions. And because he might assure Rome to himselfe, hee sente letters forthwith to Iohn Cardinall of sainct Peters Church, who supplyed his roume there, who by briberye and flatterye so curriedfauor with the people, that he allured the most parte of the Citye to fauour Alexander, and to make those Consuls that did most leane to his part. In the meane time Alexander comminge out of Fraunce into Italy returned forthwith to Rome, and was curteously recepued: and ye Cityes of Italy being emboldned by his comminge, to shake of their allegeance to the Emperour contrarye to their oath, did forthwith reuolte from him, king Philip of Fraunce fauouring their part. The Emperour knowing of these rebellions & conspiracies against him, did forthwith gather a newe armye and went into Italye: but when he came to Brixia, one Hartman ye bishop thereof beinge of the Emperours priuye councell, (but a false hipocrite) did disswade him from ye warre. And perswaded him (by the Popes secrete councell) to make warre rather against the Turkes ennemyes to Christian fayth, then against the holye father and Christian men, addinge withal yt now the Soldan oppressed & enioyed Hierusalem, and al ye holy land, which his vncle had whilom conquered with greate power & charges. He prayed him to trye the force of his army vpon the Agarens & Saracens, and to recouer these landes therewith: furthermore he promised the Emperour to perfourme this, that ye kinge of Fraūce likewise should leuye an army to ayde to conquer the Soldan kinge of Aegipt. At his supplication the Emperour ledde his armye against the Paganes, which he had prepared against the Pope & his rebels. He traueyled throughe Hungary to Constantinople, and sendinge ouer his army he wan manye townes from the Turke, as amonge other Philomenia and Ionicus, & passed into Armenia the lesse, conquering all: pea God so prospered his victoryes, that ye Soldan himselfe feared the losse of his kingdome. At the length

The fift Booke of the

length he came to Hierusalem, where he suffred the Pagans to passe with life out of the Citye. At length hauinge gotten great victories in Iewry, he cōsidered how he might defende from the Turkes that which he had wonne, and repayre that which was wasted. But while he was thus busye here in the East, Pope Alexander was not yet quieten, but both he and his conspiratours stil feared him, if he should euer returne into Italye, and therefore Alexander still deuised how to haue him destroyed. He sent a cunning painter to go to the place where the Emperour was, who (the Emperour not knowing thereof) shoulde drawe his picture: this being perfectly done, he commaūded a secret messenger to conuey it to the Soldan, & wrote a letter wtall to the Soldan certefying him that it was the Emperours picture, and tellinge him that if he would liue quietlye, he must worke the feate to haue him destroyed by som traine. The Soldan hauīg receyued these letters & y Emperours liuely picture, deuised howe to gratifye the Pope, and to slay his ennemye: but he could neuer get oportunitye, neither in battell nor in his tentes to haue him slaine. But when the Emperour hauinge wonne Hierusalem retired wyth his army homeward, he hauing no feare of himselfe did deuide his armye into diuers partes, whereby they might returne the more conuenientlye for vittaile and lodginge one after another. But in Armenia being on a time in a great heate and sweatinge, partly with trauell, partly with the heate of the Sunne, mistrusting no daunger in y saluage country full of woddes, he taking a fewe horsemē with him & his chaplein, did step frō his armye. Beinge a litle gone a side he alighted from his horse, and was about to put of his apparell at a riuers side, where cōmaundīg his horsemen to depart he purposed by himselfe & his chaplen alone to baath himselfe, because he was exceding hot: where it so hapned that the Soldanes which had lyen in wayte for him as he trauelled negligentlye, came and toke him,

him, and ledde the noble Emperour prisoner through the woods to the Soldan: his horsemen not knowinge thereof attendinge for him in vaine, at length came and sought diligentlye for him till the nexte daye. The rumour was broughte to the armye that he was drowned, whereuppon all the hoast lamented, wepte, and mourned heauilye, and sought him alonge the floude almost the space of an whole month: but when they could not finde him they chose them newe Captaynes, and so marched homeward.

The Emperour being broughte to the Soldan did dissemble that he was one of ye Emperours chamberlaynes, but the Soldan perceyuinge by the picture which he had from the Pope, resembling his face that he was the Emperour, commaunded the picture to be broughte forth, and the letters to be read before him. The Emperour beinge astonished at this treason, sawe that it auayled not to denye himselfe, he confessed the truth, and besought the Soldan humblye to haue compassion on him. After the Soldan had talked much with him, and saw both by his wordes & deedes, that he was a worthie and noble gentlemā in whom there was no vertue meete for so princely a parsonage wanting, and hauinge him in great estimation for his wisedome, his good demeanour, his faythfulnes and vprighte dealinge, thoughte he should purchase himselfe great glorye and renowne to deliuer him. Therefore afterward he called the Emperour vnto him, offered him liberty vppon conditiōs, and curteouslye profered him that he should laye in hostages for his raunsome paying. And on this condition he let him go, that he shoulde make a perpetuall league of peace with him, and should paye an hundred thousand ducates, & should leaue his chaplen that was takē prisoner with him, to lye in pledge till it were payd: so writings were drawne of the conditions, and the Emperour prepared his iorney, and bad his chaplen be of good courage, promisinge him yͤ he would not take his rest in Germany, vntil the moneye were

The fifte booke of the

were sent and that he saw him returned thether. Then the Soldã bestowed giftes on the Emperour, prouided for his voyage, and with xxxiiii. horses & certaine souldiours conducted him to Brixia, and stayed there. The Princes vnderstandinge of the Emperours returne, for ioye resorted fast vnto him. The Emperour loadinge the Soldanes men wyth diuers rewardes sent them backe againe, and other with them to conduct them to the coast of the Empire. Afterward he held a Parliament at Norimberg, callinge together all the Princes of the Empyre, to whõ he detected the treason of Pope Alexāder, and read the traytours Epistle which he sent to the Soldan, and tolde them by what meanes he escaped. The Princes promised to assist him to performe his promise to the Soldan, and in great disdaine against Pope Alexander traitour to the Empyre, they offred to ayde him. The armye was gathered, hee came to Rome, and not a man through out Italye withstoode him: and sending his Embassadours into the Citye, he demaunded of the Romaynes (concealing his owne iniurye) that the Church might be brought to qnietnes by hearing both the Popes causes heard: and that the right bishop mighte haue his place, whereby the Church might be gouerned by one. If they would do this, he promised that he woulde graunte them not onely peace, but would restore them all their righte. Pope Alexander percepuinge that by this meanes the Emperour mighte obtayne his purpese to be reuenged on him, fled by night to Caieta, afterward to Beneuent: last of all in the 17 peare of his Popeship, he came to Venice disguised in the apparell of one that was his cooke, where lurking in an abbey he became a Gardener. A while after he was bewrayed and knowne, and there vpon calling a councell by the commaundement of duke Sebastian, he was recepued with great honour, and brought into S. Marges Church iñ pontificall pompe. The Emperour hearing that the Pope was at Venice, desyred the

Venetians

Venetians to yeld to him his ennemye, being likewyse the ennemye of the common wealth. The Venetians denyed to do it: therefore ye Emperour sente his sonne Otho with a naupe of souldiours to demaund Alexander of them, but he charged him withall that he should attempt nothing in any case, till he himselfe were come vnto him. But Otho being a lustye yonge Prince ful of courage and desirous of renowne, neglecting his fathers commaundement, would needes encounter the Venetians, whereby hee was ouercome, taken prisoner, bounde & brought to Venice. Hereupon Alexander began to set vp his crest and put out his hornes, and woulde not take peace with the Emperour in anye case, vnlesse the Emperour would come to Venice, & take suche conditions of peace, as hee woulde offer him. Whereuppon the good and carefull father to prouide for the infortunate miserye of his sonne, promised hee woulde come at the time appointed: and so came where they commoned vppon conditions of peace. But the Pope woulde not absolue the Emperour of excōmunication, till he came to S. Markes Church, where before all the people, Pope Alexander commaunded the Emperour to prostrate himselfe on the ground, and to craue pardon. The Emperour did as hee commaunded him: then the Pope trode on the Emperours necke with his foote, sayinge it is written: Thou shalt walke vppon the serpent and adder, and shalt treade downe vnder thy feete the Lion and dragon. The Emperour disdayninge this reproche aunswered: It was not sayd to thee but to Peter. The Pope then treadinge downe his necke againe sayde: Both to mee and to Peter. The Emperour then fearing some daunger, durst saye no more, & so the peace was concluded. The conditions wherof are these, that the Emperour should vphold Alexander to be true Pope, that he should restore all that did belonge to the Church of Rome, which had beene taken away in ye warres: Thus the Emperour departed with his sonne.

N iiii The

The fifte booke of the

The Pope to shew himselfe thankfull to Venice, bestowed af his liberality giftes vppon duke Sebastian & ye Senate. First he gaue them a white Taper which onely the Popes vsed to weare. Secondlye he lycensed them to seale theyr letters with leade: and he graunted theyr Duke the third seate in the Popes Theatre. Fourthly he graunted that on Ascention daye, they should haue whole and perfit pardōs for euer at S. Markes Church. Fiftly he gaue the Duke viii. banners of silke, and an attier for the head like an hat. Afterward Alexander depriued the bishop of Papia of his Pall, & exempted him of the dignitye of carying ye Crosse, because he toke the Emperours part. He made many Canons in a councel at Lateran, as that an archbishop should not receyue his Pall, vnlesse he had sworne first to be true and obedient to the Pope. And that a man should not marye his brothers wyfe beinge wydowe, that they that toke orders should vowe chastetye, that a bastarde should not be made a bishop, that the canonizinge of Sainctes belonged onlye to the Pope, & that such sainctes should haue deuine honour. Amonge other he made Thomas Becket archbishop of Canterbury, & a rancke traptour to his prince (but stoutlye vpheld therein by the Pope) a sainct. He bounde kinge Henry the seconde, of Englande (excusing himselfe of the death of Thomas) ye his sublectes should franklye & freely appeale frō him to the Court of Rome, & that afterward none should be king of England, vnlesse he were first called king by the Pope. This arose vppon the quarel betwene the king and Thomas Becket, who so vexed and disquieted his soueraigne prince, with all the nobles and prelates of this Realme, with cursinges, excommunications, interditinges, threatninges, mouing both French kinge & Pope to moleste the kinge in this behalfe: and finallye as then Pope Alexander played the incarnate deuill against the Emperour, so did Becket rage like a subdeuill against the kinge in England, till certaine not able to endure his

arrogant

arrogante, seditious and trayterous doinges, in great despite therof slue him at Canterbury. He decreed that a man shoulde not be devorced frō his wyfe, though she had ye Leprosye. Also that those ye could be proued vsurers, shoulde neyther be admitted to the Communion, nor buryed in the Church: after these & other like deedes he dyed Anno 1181, Robert Montēlis Chronicle hath, ye Lewes king of Frāuce and Henry kinge of Englande, wayted on Pope Alexander as his gentlemē vshers and footemen, the one leading his horse by the bridle on the right syde, and the other on ye left, through the whole City Taciacunto Legeris. In this Popes time the Sunne was Eclipsed, and earthquakes were euery where. Also there were certaine called VValdenses who defended manye articles against the Pope and his doctrine, as transubstantiation, Purgatorye &c.

112. Lucius the thirde.

Lvcius the thirde borne in Thuscia of an honourable stocke, succeded by consente of all the Cardinals. But the Romaynes so vexed him that hee was driuen oute of the Citye, and manye of his frendes and companye taken by the Romaynes, some were set vppon Asses with their faces towardes the tayle, and Miters on their heades, and so ledde throughe the Citye in mockadge, some vsed despitefullye otherwyse: Some had their eyes put oute by the Romaynes in a madnes, other some murthered: & for this cause onelye, that he wente about to take away the name of Consuls in the Citye. The Pope sufferinge this great shame wente to Verona, where in a councell he condemned the Romaynes doinges, and euen then when the Christians were persecuted in Asia (which pretence of holines wrought the perill of many) that they might be succoured, because the ennemyes were emboldned to wast the holye lande vnder their Captaine Saladanus, presuminge for that our Princes were at discētion. This Pope being

minde

The fifte booke of the

mindfull of his coūtrye Thuscia bestowed large giftes vppon it, and obtayned of the Emperour that the Hetruriās
should haue the selfe same coyne that the Lucēsians amōg
them had, euen as the Lombards had onelye the money of
Papia with the Emperours coyne. Valerius Anselmus
wryteth that this Pope contrarye to other, allowed the
Sacraments that were done by whoremaister chapleins,
he dyed in Verona Anno 1185. In his time were greate
earthquakes which did destroye diuers notable Cityes, &
in Sicil were destroyed thereby fiue and twentye thousand
parsons. The Armenians being at this time at greate debate with the Greeke Church, did for hatred thereof become subiect to the Church of Rome.

113. Vrbanus the thirde.

VRbanus who because of his troublesome dealings was
nicknamed Turbanus, was borne in Millen. He as
sone as he was made Pope, was carefull at the first to set
the Christian Princes at concord, least while they were deuided the Pagās should destroy them: but lo how it fel out,
for sayth Crantzius because the Emperour woulde not in
all pointes followe his minde, hee purposed forthwith to
drawe out his blade of excommunication against the Emperour, wherby he made the matter worse, but death toke
him away in time and preuented him. As some thincke he
dyed for griefe, because he heard daylye encrease of the miserye amonge the Christians, & how Saladinus triumphed
in victorye against them, with their great slaughters, Hierusalem beinge taken againe, and kinge Guido also, as he
was going to Venice to repayre his armye. In this Popes time on Midsomer daye at .vi. of the clocke in the morninge was an Eclipse of the Sunne, after which ensued a
greate pestilence in Polonia, Russia, and other countryes.
By the bolstring vp of this Pope the monkes of Canterbury

bury did in matter of cōtrouersye out swaye both the archbishop and king theyr Prince Henry the second, who were glad to yeld to the monks their desire for feare of the Popes threatning.

114. Gregorie the eight.

Gregorie the viii. borne in Apulia succeded Vrban. At this time the Popes seemed very carefull for the recouery of the holy land, Iudea and Hierusalem, beinge but a vaine and false colour of them to weaken the Princes of Christēdome, wherby they might the better maister them one by one: and by this meanes also being so holy a shewe, they so occupied the mindes of Christian Princes, ÿ they coulde entende to haue no regarde to the Popes doinges, whoe in the meane time while they had no eye vnto him, wrought his feates to the great enriching & aduauncinge of his owne dignitye. For so this Pope Gregorie euen at his first entraunce did send letters to the Princes of Christendome, to rayse their armyes to go to recouer Hierusalem, and to spend their bloude in a vaine quarel: but as he was going to stir vp the Pisans & Genuans in this matter, he was poysoned, and so dyed before hee had raigned two monthes. 179

115. Clemens the third.

Clemens the third a Romaine sonne of one Iohn Scholar. He at his first entraunce sent out commaundement to make warre vppō the Sarracens: wheruppon the Princes raysed theyr armyes, the chiefe wherof are these, Frederick the Emperour, Philip king of Fraunce, Richarde king of Englande, and Otho duke of Burgundye, and diuers bishops and archbishops, with sondry people of Denmarke, Fryzeland and Flaunders, but yet they did almost nothing 180

The fifte booke of the

nothing at all. King Richard of England comming nigh to Rome in his iourneye, met with one Octavianus bishop of Hostia, to whom he complayned much of the unsatiable and shamefull simony used by the Pope and his courte, for taking vii. hundred markes for consecrating the bishop Cenomanensis, also fifteene hundred markes of VVilliam byshop of Elye for his office of Legatship, beside an houge somme of money of the bishop of Burdeaux for absoluinge him, whē he should haue bene deposed for a crime urged against him by his clergye. Anno 1188. VVilliam king of Sicil dyed, and left no heyre, and therefore the Pope by and by would needes claime it to be tributarye to the Church of Rome, and belonginge to it. But the peeres of the Isle chose Tancred bastard to king VVillia. The Pope therefore determined to chalenge and try his right by the dinte of the sword, whereby he filled the world full of spoylings, and slaughter, and yet he obtayned not his purpose, and so left of. He made divers Canons and amōg other this one, that none but the Pope might remoue a bishop from one sea to another, or to an hyer dignitye. Also he decreed that bishops should be preferred in dignitye aboue Princes. He commaunded to celebrate the Masse with unleuened bread and wyne mingled with water, with many other ceremonyes. He sent a Cardinal into Poland to reforme ȳ clergy, who among other matters in a Synode there held, forbad them to haue wyues, and because the Danes decreed mariage lawful to their clergye, they were excomunicated by ȳ Pope, who dyed Anno 1191.

116. Celestine the thirde.

CElestine the third was borne in Rome, he being an old man at Easter time after the death of Clement, was made Pope by the bishops and Cardinals, the next day he crowned Henry the sixt Emperour. This Celestine grudginge

Pageant of Popes.   Fol. 104

ging that Tancred did enioye the kingdome of Sicilia, maryed vnto the sayd Emperour a Nonne out of Panormitā Nonnery called Constance, the doughter of Roger, vppon this condition, that he shoulde chalenge the kingdome of both Sicils for a dowrye, and should driue out Tancred and possesse it himselfe, alwayes prouided, that ye Pope should haue his yearelye tribute oute of it. And thus the Sueuian Captaynes became Lordes of Sicill, but thereuppon ensued bloudy warres. After ye death of this Henry through the greate diuision in the Empire, there arose such debate through all Germany (while the Pope was at defiaunce w'' the Sueuians for ye soueraignitye of Sicill which he sought ambitiouslye) so that one parishe was not at amitye with another: whereby the Popes purse was excessiuely fed to appease the scisme amonge those spirituall men. Such were the practises of these holye fathers, while they set the Princes of the world on worke to conquer the holye land. Of the attonement of this strife Abbas Vspergensis wryteth thus, which is worthy to be noted, therby to discerne the holines of Rome, and how it grew to this riche estate. There was scāt (sayth he) one bishopricke or Ecclesiasticall dignity or parishe Church which was not at a brawl, & the matter was brought to Rome to be determined, but not w'' emptye hands. Reioyce O mother Rome becau se the conduites of al treasures on the earth are opened, ye moūtaines and whole riuers of money might flowe into thy handes: Reioyce vpon the iniquitie of the sonnes of men, because thou art rewarded for so many mischiefes: Reioyce vpon thine assistante companion Ladye Discention, who hath burst loose frō the pit of bottomlesse hell, that she might heape vppon thee many gubs of goulde. Thou hast that which thou doest thirst after: because thou hast daunted the vvorld by the malice of mākinde, not by holy religiō. Men are haled and drawne vnto thee, not by deuocion or pure cōscience, but by treachery and working mischiefes

mani-

The fift booke of the

manifolde, and the deciding of controuersies gotten with bloud. Thus sayth that abbot euen in those times when & wher the Popes pride flourished ranckly euen in his ruff:. Pope Celestine perceyuing the aduauntage hereof for his estate, was still vrgent to sende out the Christian Princes to fighte for the holye lande, while he at home with theyr treasures builded for his ease & pleasure (as Platina mentioneth) diuers stately Pallacies and Temples. Amonge many decrees he made that an oath made by feare and compulsion, should be of none effecte. It is sayd before that this Pope Celestine did crowne the Emperour Henry the sixte, which because it was done after so straunge a sort as hath not beene hearde, it shall not be amisse briefely to declare the maner of it as it is reported by Rogerus Houedenus, Ranulphus, Rogerus Cestrensis and other, of whom the first liued at that time, reportinge it as followeth. The Pope was going frō Lateran to S. Peters Church, where the Emperour and his wyfe Constantia mette him in the way: but the Romaynes did shut the gates against the Emperour & Empresse, comming with a great troupe of armed souldiours. And Celestine standinge vppon the stayres of S. Peters Church, toke an oath of the Emperour (his armye being shut out) that he should defend and restore the libertyes and patrimonye of the Church to the vttermost, yeldinge to Rome the Citye Tusculanum. After this he did annoynte him Emperour and her Empresse in the Church: while he sitting in his pontificall chayre and holding the Emperiall crowne betweene his feete, caused the Emperour to stoupe and bowe downe his heade to his feete, & so put the crowne on: And it being thus put on, he caused the Emperour stil to hould downe his head, while he with his foote did spurne the Crowne of his head againe, sayinge: I haue power to make and vnmake Emperours at my pleasure: Then the Cardinals toke it vp and sette it vppon the Emperours head. And in like maner the Em-

press

Pageant of Popes. Fol. 105

preſſe was both crowned and vncrowned with the Popes foote. Celeſtine dyed Anno. 1198. In his time one Cyrill an Hermite had a ſtrange viſion reuealed vnto him as hee was at maſſe, as Mantuā writeth Faſtorum, lib. 5. (if a man will beleeue euery vaine fantaſye.)

   As Cyrill in his holye weede was earlye ſaying maſſe,
   Beholde a child with glorious ſhape before him preſent was,
   And houering in the ayre on hye with ſiluer plate in hand,
   Which he vppon the alter layde, where Cyrill ſtill did ſtand.
   And ſayd vnto him holye ſer, God doth to the diſcloſe
   Theſe ſecretes: and do thou reueale vnto the Romaynes thoſe.
   The written verſes out of Greeke he turnes to latine tongue,
   Which ſtraite were ſet in ſcholes and yet are cited by amonge.

But touching the truth of this fantaſticall dreame, it ſhall folow in Gregorie the ix. for that age toke into credit three ſtraunge & monſtrous myracles, ſo y then the worlde did greatlye eſteeme of y ſecte of begginge fryers, while Saſhan wrought in Antichriſt the full miſtery of his iniquitye. The myracles are theſe, firſt the vpholding of Lateran Church reuealed in a viſion to a Dominicke Fryer at Rome, the fiue Seraphical woundes of S. Fraunces in a certaine hill of Lauernia, and the Oracle of this Cyrill.

117. Innocentius the thirde.

After Celeſtine was Innocētius y third, who ſo boyled in anger agaſſt Philip the Emperour, becauſe he was made Emperour by the Germaynes contrary to his will, that he braſt out into theſe wordes: Eyther ſhall the Pope ſpoile Philip of his Crowne and Empyre, or els ſhal Philip take frō the Pope his Apoſtolical dignitye. After this hee ſtirred vp againſt y Emperour, one Otho a duke both boulde and raſhe, ſo that by this holye fathers helpe there grewe cruell bloudſhed and foule ſlaughter infinite, vntill that this Philip the Emperour was traytecouſlye and villanouſly ſlaine by another Otho, and this Otho whom the
Pope

The fift booke of the

Pope had set on against Philip poasted to Rome, and of him was made Emperour. But this bloudy league did not last long betwene them: for as soue as Otho began to reclaime & recouer such thinges as of right belõged to the Empyre, (which ÿ Popes by subtil practises had purloyned many yeres) he was excõmunicated by the Pope himselfe, and spoyled of all his royall estate: furthermore he discharged al his Princes of theyr alledgeaunce, which by oath they ought to Otho, and commaũded vppon payne of his cruell curse, that no man should take Otho to be Emperour, nor call him so, and caused the Princes to make Fredericke king of Sicill Emperour. Also this Innocent Anno 1212. sought to compasse three harde matters, that is the deposing of Otho, a voyage to Hierusalem, and a generall councel. Also the same yeare (sayth Vlricus Mutius) certaine noble men of Alsatia did condemne this Pope of impietye, because he would not suffer the clergye to keepe their wyues, & the bishops burned an hundred in one daye, because they taught that Christians might lawfullye eate flesh, and marrye at any time.

   This mischeuous Innocent did mischeuouslye contriue many cruell tragedyes against king Iohn of Englande: he euen in despite and defiance of the kinge, did thrust (an enemye to the Realme called Steuen Langton a Cardinall) into the bishopricke of Canterbury, and encouraged threescore and foure monkes to worke seueral treasons against him. Because the king would not suffer these treacheryes, he condemned him to be an ennemy of the Church, excommunicated him from the company of all Christians, interdited his kingdome vi. yeres and three monethes, deposed him from gouernment, toke from him the Crowne and ÿ Scepter, discharged his subiectes of their allegeaunce, gaue his Realme to Lewes the French kinges sonne, commaunded to spoile him both of goodes and life, with diuers other tyrannous dealinges. Kinge Iohn beinge dismayed

mayed with these stormes being otherwise a noble and valiant Prince, yet because he was forsaken of his nobilitye, his bishops and commonaltye, submitted himselfe full sore against his hart to ye Popes obeysaunce: compelled to acknowledge the Pope to be supreame heade ouer all Christendome, and God vppon earth, and bound himselfe with a solempne oath to stande to the Popes arbitrement, and yt his posteritye should do the like, to acknowledge themselues perpetuall tributaryes to the Popes of Rome. Also he kneeling vppon his knees to Pandulphus, yelded vp his Crowne in the presence of all his nobilitye, sayinge: Here I resigne vp the Crowne of Englande to Pope Innocent the thirde &c. Which Pandulphus kept for fiue dayes, during which time the king was as a priuate person: & then being bound to paye the Pope for his Crowne a thousande markes a yeare, with other shamefull conditions, he receiued his Crowne at the handes of Pandulphus, pardoning and restoring to full estate all those that had rebelled, conspired and wroughte treason against him. And yet by the procuremente of Steuen Langton Archbishop of Yorke, & other of the clergye and priestes of Englande, he was myserablye vexed with treasons and rebellions continuallye, for certaine of the nobilitye and priestes, had chosen Lodowicke to be their kinge, sonne to Lewes kinge of Fraunce: who entred the Realme and toke the estate vppon him by theyr maintenaunce against kinge Iohn, to the great hart breaking of the noble Prince, the spoyling of the Realme, and oppression of themselues, while this forren Prince bestowed all thinges vppon his owne countreymen, accomptinge the Englishe nobles that assisted him to be but traytours. In the ende after much miserye and sorrowe a certaine monke (as Caxton sayth) named Simō, of Swinested abbey in Lincolnshire did there temper a cuppe of wyne with the poyson of a toade, & drinking thereof to the kinge both hee and the king were poysoned and dyed: For which

D   doinge

The fift Booke of the

doinge, the sayde monke had a certaine masse songe for his soule confirmed by the abbots procurement for euer.

This Innocentius vnder the colour of recouering Hierusalem, held a councell at Lateran Anno 1215 against the Emperour to excommunicate him, & depose him, because he had inuaded certaine Cityes of ye Popes. In this councell the Pope first wrested oute Auricular confession, and robbed the laitye of the Communion cuppe. He condemned one Almericus a learned man for an hereticke, & commaunded his bones to be burned wt the rest of his sect at Paris: this he did (sayth Dominicus Soto in a certaine Sermon) because he preached that Images should be put out of the Church. Amonge manye other dotinge decrees, he disanulled the mariage of the clergye for euer, he required priuye tithes to be payde, and to maintayne warre in Asia, he commaunded the fourtye part of all reuenues to be paide. He toke from many Partriarkes, archbishops, & bishops, their ordinarye auctoritye in many thinges: He commaunded that the quarels of Princes should be brought before the Pope to be determined by him: and if the election of the Emperour could not be agreed vpon, then it should belōg onelye to the Pope. He deuised that the Communion cake should be kept in a boxe in the Church, and that when the priest shoulde visit the sicke, he shoulde go with a burninge Taper and a bell before him: He made the Canon of the masse to be equal in auctoritye with the Scripture, and that the Pope should haue power to correct and controll Princes, that none should be Emperour, vnlesse he were crowned by the Pope, finally he dyed Anno 1216. In his time Liuonia first recouered papistrye, & Peter kinge of the Arrogons was inueigled to yeild his kingdome & all his dominions tributarye to Rome, to purchase his saluation.

A certaine noble man in England hearing that this Pope had againe condemned priestes mariage in Lateran councel, did make a certaine rime thereof the yeare following,

which

Pageant of Popes. Fol. 107.

which one Iohn Pullan founde in an olde booke at Oxeforde as followeth.

> PRisciani regula penitus caſſatur,
> Sacerdos per hic & hæc olim declinatur:
> Sed per hic ſolum modo nunc articulatur,
> Cum per noſtrum preſulem hæc amoueatur.

Olde Priſcians rule doth whollye go to wracke,
Becauſe ſacerdos earſt declinde with hic and hæc,
Muſt be declined nowe but euen with hic alone,
Our prelat hath compelled nowe hec for to be gone.

> Ita quidam presbyter cepit allegare,
> Peccat capitaliter qui vult seperare:
> Quod Deus coniunxerat fœminam amare
> Tales dignum duximus fures appellare.

A certaine prieſt began in this wyſe for to reaſon,
Againſt the lawe of God he ſtaneth in hye treaſon:
Who parteth that which God hath ioynde as wyſe from man,
To call theſe robbing theeues full well auouch we can.

> O quàm dolor anxius, quàm tormentum graue,
> Nobis eſt dimittere, quoniam ſuaue.
> O Romane pontifex, ſtatuiſti praue,
> Ne in tanto crimine moriaris, caue.

Alas what paine it is, what torment, and what griefe,
For vs to leaue our wyues our comfort and reliefe?
Thou Popiſhe prelat doſt this wicked lawe beginne,
Take heede thou do not dye continuing in this ſinne.

> Non eſt Innocentius, immò nocens verè,
> Qui quod facto docuit, verbo vult delere:
> Et quod olim iuuenis voluit habere,
> Modò vetus pontifex ſtudet prohibere.

He is not Innocent but nocent may be termed,
That doth condemne by word that he by deede confirmed:
And thoughe that he himſelfe, in youthfull yeares did loue it,
Now he a doting Pope doth labour to impriue it.

D ii   Gignere

The fifte booke of the

Gignere nos præcipit vetus testamentum:
Nouum quod non retinet, nusquam est inuentum.
Præsul qui contrarium donat documentum,
Nullum necessarium his dat argumentum.

Should Testament saith multiplye and increase,
Which in the newe Testament is not found to cease:
The prelate that bidding the contrary, seemeth to abhorre it,
Of this his doing brings no lawfull reason for it.

Dedit enim dominus maledictionem,
Viro qui non fecerit generationem.
Ergo tibi consulo per hanc rationem,
Gignere vt habeas benedictionem.

For by the mouth of God the man is cursed and band,
Which hath not raysed seede and children to the land.
Therefore I do aduise you prouide you may haue issue
Whereby it may be so the Lord our God may blesse you.

Non ne de militibus milites procedunt?
Et reges à regibus, qui sibi succedunt?
Per locum à simili, omnes iura lædunt,
Clericos qui gignere, crimen esse credunt.

Do not men of warre of men of warre procede?
And kinges of kinges, that do vppon their throne succede:
So the similitude houldes, they do offend in dotage,
That thinke it is a fault the clergye should haue mariage.

Zacharias habuit prolem & vxorem,
Per virum quem genuit adeptus honorem.
Baptizauit etenim mundi Saluatorem:
Pereat qui teneat nouum hunc errorem.

Zachary had both a wyfe and a sonne,
By him whom he begat great dignitye he wonne:
Baptizing him on whom our soules health doth depend.
Then cursed be hee, that doth this error new defend.

Paulus rapitur ad coelos superiores,
Vbi multas didicit res secretiores.
Ad nos tandem rediens, instruens mores,
Suas (inquit) habeat quilibet vxores.

Up to

Pageant of Popes.　Fol.108.

Vp vnto the third heauen S. Paule was translated,
Whereas he hard many misteryes debated:
And after comming downe and teaching vs trade of lyfe,
Let euery man quoth he enioye his proper wyfe.

 Propter hæc & alia dogmata doctorum,
 Reor esse melius, & magis decorum,
 Quisq; suam habeat,& non proximorum.
 Ne incurrat odium vel iram eorum.

For these thinges and diuers doctours decrees,
With right and comlinesse I thincke it more agrees:
Ech should his owne wyfe haue, and not his neighbours borrow,
Lest thereby he procure wrath, malice, mischiefe and sorrow.

 Proximorum fœminas, filias & neptes,
 Violare nefas est, quare nil deceptes.
 Vere tuam habeas, in qua delectes,
 Diem vt sic vltimum tutius expectes.

It is a deadly sinne therefore be not beguiled,
Thy neighbours wyfe, neice, or doughter, to be of thee defiled:
Therefore take thee a wyfe in whom thou maist delight thee,
And at the latter daye more safely to acquite thee.

 Ecce iam pro clericis multum allegaui,
 Nec non pro presbyteris plura comprobaui,
 Pater noster nunc pro me, quoniam peccaui,
 Dicat quisque presbyter, cum sua suaui.

Thus for the clergye much I haue alleaged,
And also for our priestes largelye haue I pleaded:
Now all priestes with your prayers to God for me render,
A Pater noster for that I am an offendour.

FINIS.

118. Honorius the thirde.

HOnorius the thirde a Romaine borne was made Pope
at Prusium, at what time the Cardinals distressed for
want of foode, did there dispatch the election of him. Who
hyinge to Rome as fast as he coulde, toke order about the
warre

The fifte booke of the

warre in Asia, to maintaine it still, knowig how auailable it was to their matters wroughte heare at home in Christendome: forthwith John Columna a Cardinal of Rome was appointed to proceede as ambassadour with ye armye, which Innocentius had prouided for ye purpose: He crowned Frederick the seconde sonne of Constance the Nonne Emperour against Otho the fourth, whom notwithstanding afterward for vsinge his owne right in the coastes of Sicil & Apulia the Pope excommunicated. Yea this Honorius (sayth Marius) was so enflamed against this Emperour Frederick y^t hee did trayterouslye maintaine Thomas and Mathewe Earles of Thuscia with other rebels that put themselues in armoure against the Emperours maiestye, whereby the Emperour coulde not punishe them as they deserued: which (sayth Vspergensis) caused him much to complaine that the Sea of Rome did euer maintaine traytours and rebels, which presumed vpon that refuge. Also he discharged his barons of their fealty to their Lorde: which mischiefe was yet for a while stayed by the meanes of Hermannus, maister of the flemings of Zeland. He cõfirmed the orders of Dominican & Franciscan friers deuised in the time of Innocentius. He maintayned the white fryers and Augustinian fryers, that they should vphould transubstantiation against the Valdenses, who then began to defye the Church of Rome in many matters: for the Dominicans forged that Pope Innocentius a little before his death had a vision, wherin was reuealed vnto him that Lateran Church should fall, vnlesse their patron Dominicus shoulde bolster it vppon his shoulders: whereof Mantuan beluded with such fansyes maketh mention. Also he wryteth of another dreame for the Franciscan fryers, of which though they dreamed as necessarye, yet I omitte as vaine and fonde. In this Popes time while these thinges were doing, there were seene in the ayre strasig-sightes, testifying the horror of Antichrist encreasing in his members

Rome the sturrer and nourisher of rebels.

Signes of Antichrist in the heauens.

hereas shall appeare by the Popes following.

While the Christiā estates were turmoyled abroue fighting for Hierusalem, the Pope in pompe and ease at home, was at leasure to build sondrye sumptuous Pallaces and gorgeous Temples, dedicating them to diuers Sainctes. He published Epistles decretall: and decreed that vnlearned parsons should not be made priestes. He commaunded that when the singinge cake was heaued and lifted vp, the people should fal downe on their knees: and that it should be caryed in comlye order to the sicke, with a burning Taper before it. He graūted Archbishops power to giue pardons, faculties, dispensations, dualities, & pluralities win their diocesse. Anno 1223 one Adam Cathanēsis a bishop in Scotlande (as Boethius wryteth) was burned of his own neighbours in his owne kitchin, because he had excōmunicated certaine of them for withholding theyr tythes: the Pope knowing of this murther neuer ceased, till to reuenge the same foure hundred of these men were hanged, and their children gelded by king Alexander: A sufficient reuēge for the death of one man. Furthermore this Pope warred vppon the Emperour in Apulia: and condemned the Earle of Tholos for an hereticke, geuinge his landes to the French kinge, and finallye would not suffer his body to be buryed like a Christian. At length the Pope died Anno 1227. of whom Mattheus Parisius in the 8. booke of his Chronicle wryteth thus. Pope Honorius sent his Legate Otho to require to haue Prebendes giuen vnto him throughe all England: For (sayth the Pope) the naturall children must assist their mother in pouertye. Therefore he required ij. prebends of euery Cathedrall Church, one of the bishops stipende, and the other from the charter. And so he craued diuers porciōs out of the religious houses. At this time the Pope was sicke of the spiritual dropsye, so that by his Legat he drancke vp the treasures of the clergye, and cloysterimongers, and vsed straunge tyrannye amonge

Vvorshipping of the hoast at masse.

Nonresidenties and pluralities licenced by the Pope.

The Popes rigour on the dead.

The Popes pillage in England.

The fift Booke of the

amonge them: for Hugh Wells bishop of Lincolne to recouer his bishopricke paide an hundred markes to the Popes Legat, and a thousande markes to the Pope. At this time it rayned bloude for the space of three dayes in Rome: whereuppon one wrote these two Verses.

O pater Honori, multorum nate dolori,
Est tibi dedecori viuere? vade mori.

 O Pope Honorius borne thou werst,
  to mischiefe many men:
 Thou liuest with shame, conuaie with speede
  thy boones to deadly den.

119. Gregorie the ninth.

GRegorie the ninth borne in Campania, was nephew to Innocentius the thirde. He maintayned the quarell of his predecessour Honorius, against the Emperour. This Gregorie (as Marius wryteth) was more maliciouslye disposed toward y⁵ sayd Frederick: for he accused him because he woulde not fulfill that vaine promise, to the needelesse shedding of Christian bloud, which he made to Honorius for the unprofitable recouering of Hierusalem. And therefore this Gregorie did excommunicate him, before the Emperour coulde be hearde to speake, or were conuicted by reason: neither woulde hee suffer the Emperours Embassadours to come to his presence, nor heare them in the councell which came to alleadge good and reasonable excuses in y⁵ Emperours behalfe, as his owne sickenes at his settinge forward caused him to staye, besides the death of the Lantgraue. Therfore (sayth Vspergensis) this Pope like a proude man, began in his first yeare to excōmunicat and curse the Emperour for certaine foolish and false causes, neglectinge all order of iudgement, as the Emperour sheweth in excusinge himselfe in his epistle to the Princes of Almanye: openinge to them (becausethe Pope refused
             to heare

to beare it) his innocencye and vpright dealing. And therfore certaine noble men in Rome, namely of the house called Frangentes panem, when the Pope did the second time excommunicate Frederick, they caused the Pope to be driuen oute of the Citye with foule shame, so that he ranne awaye byding at Perufe al that yeare, & the yeare folowing. Yet no meanes could asswage his furye: but he prouoked Iohn kinge of Hierusalem, & the foresaid Earles of Thuscia rebels to the Emperour, and manye other Princes to trouble him. The Emperour appointed a day of assembly for diuers Christian Princes at Rauenna, and the Princes were making speede thether to obeye him, but by the Popes commaundement they went backe againe: and certaine souldiours wearing y Crosse by the Emperours appointment for the voyage to Hierusalem, were robbed and spoiled of all their prouisiō. The Emperour seing this sought to appeafe the Popes furye, and to get his goodwil prepared his iourney accordyng to his promise to Hierusalem: he tooke shippe and sayled into Cyprus, and afterward to Acon, and striued much against the Soldan for the Christian fayth, with great paine and trauell. In the meane time y Pope (seing the Emperours absence seruinge his turne) gat Apulia to be vnder his obeisance: and forbad that the souldiours wearing cresses shoulde passe ouer to assist the Emperour, but he draue them oute of Apulia, & Lombardye, shewinge himselfe a wicked and mischieuous man by many other meanes, in slaying those Germaynes that returned from the Emperour, moste cruellye. Thus while the good Emperour defended the flocke of Christe with y sworde abroade, the Pope deuoured and spoyled them at home. After the Emperour had wonne from the Soldā, Hierusalem, Nazereth, & Ioppa, hee toke a truce with him for tenne yeares, whereof he certifyed the Pope by his letters, looking that the Pope woulde haue shewed himselfe ioyfull therof, and all Christians likewyse: But the Pope

despi-

The fifte booke of the

despysing and reiecting the letters, commaunded the messengers that broughte them to be put to death, leaste they should make report of the Emperours noble successe. Also he spreade this rumour that the Emperour was dead, to this ende, to make such Cityes in Apulia to shrincke for feare, as had withstode to submit themselues to him. And both to stop the Emperours returne, and to obtaine Apulia at his pleasure, he wrote to the Soldan desyring him not to yeld the Holy lande to the Emperour, as he was about to do. But the Emperour finishing his matters with the Soldan, returned into Italye, whereupon the slaughter of his men done by the Pope as they returned stayed: and within a while he draue the Popes power oute of Apulia, and by the helpe of God recouered all his owne from him. Hereupon the Pope did excōmunicate him, and curse him anewe, and conspired with the Lombards and Thuscans to rebell against him, because he had made a league with the Soldan. But in the ende many Princes seekinge to set them at vnitye, the Emperour had absolution of the Pope, paying to him for it, ere (as Platina saith) he could obtaine it, an hundred thousande ounces of goulb. For (sayth Vspergensis) notwithstanding all these iniuries, yet so often as the Pope did excōmunicate him, he craued and sued for the benefite of absolution humblye, with all obedience, deuocion & yelding of iustice. Soone after the Emperour prepared to go into Germanye, to redresse certaine disorders doone by his eldest sonne Henry: the Pope hearinge thereof wrote to the estates of Germanye, commaundinge that they should make none of the Emperours family king of the Romaynes, because the kinge of the Romaines is heyre apparent to the Empyre. Frederick vnderstanding this treachery, and that the Pope had conspired a freshe wt manye Princes of Italy against him, did forthwith inuade Italy, suppressed the rebellious Lombards, wanne diuers townes in Vmbria and Hetruria, subdued to the Empyre

The price of absolution at the Popes hādes.

Lombar-

Lomberdie, Viterbie, Peruse, Fauentia, Cremona, Vicentia & Patauy, all which had conspired with the Pope. The Pope seinge this, cursed him againe. The Emperour hearinge of it, because the Popes couetousnesse, ambition, tyrannye and pride grewe so great, that it was no longer to be suffered, thought good to reueale the same to all Christians, to reclayme them from their errour and false Religion: and therfore helping in Patauy, commaunded a certaine learned mā wel studyed in the Scriptures to preach before him, concerninge the Popes curse, & of the Church of Rome. After the preacher had disclosed all the abuses of the Pope and his Church, the Emperour moued thereby wrote these 2. Verses to the Pope.

Roma diu titubans, longis erroribus acta,
   Corruet, & mundi desinet esse caput.
Rome that hath rulde long, and hath
   in errour farre beene ledde.
Shal come to nought, and cease to be
   on earth the supreame hedde.

¶ The Popes aunsvveare to
the Emperour.

Niteris incassum nauem submergere Petri,
   Fluctuat, at nunquam mergitur illa ratis.
To drowne S. Peters shippe ye spende
   your labour all in baine,
It tottreth oft, but sinks not so
   but it may floate againe.

¶ The Emperours replye.

Fata volunt, stellæq; docent, auiumq; volatus,
   Quod Fredericus ego maleus orbis ero.
Tis destinye, the starres of heauen,
   and flight of foules do showe,
I Frederick shalbe the club,
   to strike the deadlye blowe.

Fata

The fift booke of the

¶ The Popes aunsvveare.
Fata volunt, Scriptura docet, peccata loquuntur,
Quod tibi vita breuis pæna perennis erit.
Tis destenye the Scripture shewes
and thy offences tell:
Thy life is short, thy paine shall last
for euermore in hell.

Thus was the Emperour nowe the thirde time excommunicated by the Pope, and pronounced not Emperour: but at this time there were manye Cardinals ý disalowed the Popes doing, so that the Emperour had many frends in Italy, because he still sued and sought for the Popes fauour, and could not haue it, and now therefore he set all at defiance in maner afore shewed. Of this Gregorie (Mattheus Parisius sayth further) callinge him bloudsucker & couetous Pope, that he held a councell at Rome to depose the Emperour, who had maryed Isabel doughter to king Iohn of England: and ere the councell began, he caused ý Apostles heades to be borne aboute the Citye in a solemne procession, that the sighte thereof mighte astonishe mens mindes, and drawe their hartes from the Emperour. Also he gaue free pardon to euery one that would fight against him. The Emperour understanding it, stopped all passages both by Sea and laude, and taking many Cardinals & other prelates as they were sayling awaye, he put them in prison: hee drowned ii. Cardinals in the Sea, & of the rest some bishops, abbots and chaplins, and amonge them the Popes brother for their notorious and haynous treasons were hanged. The first excommunication ý was sent out against this Emperour arose of this grouñd: because themperour would not at the Popes commaundement daunger himselfe and many Christians with him, to go out to fight for the holy land. For ý Pope as it appeared by his actes, coueted to encroch the kingdome of both Sicils, Apulia, &

other

other landes, so that he sought meanes how to destroy the Emperour being inheritour thereof, which he mighte see come to passe by the chaunce of the warre: or els while the Emperour should there haue beene busye against the infidels, he in the meane time as chiefe prelate (hauing Christendome committed to his credite) mighte the more easely dispossesse ye Emperour. Furthermore this Gregorie was the cause of sedicion in Rome for banishing one Hannibal oute of ye Senate, because he sued to recouer the auncient e Romaine libertyes. Also he prouoked the Polonias to destroy the Prutenians being his foes. He made that cursed deuision in Italy, which to the great confusion of Christiā bloud, lasteth to this daye betweene the Guelphes and Gibelines: for these being two of the most noble and famous houses in Italye, whereof the one name whollye (that is the Gibelines) toke part with the Emperour, & the Guelphes ẃ the Pope, and this quarrel hath & doth last to this day, betwene all of the one name against all of the other ẃ continuall reuenge, as oportunitye serueth from time to time. Amonge diuers other his superstitious deedes these were some, he canonized S. Dominick, S. Fraūcis, S. Anthony of Padua and others, thereby to aduaunce the credite of the begging fryers, & of their holinesse. He decreed that the white fryers should possesse nothing but male Asses, and such foode as coms of certaine birdes and beastes as egges & milke, and all other thinges they should begge from doore to doore, as Paleonydorus sayth. He graunted the Iewes to be enfranchised for money in spite of all Christian Princes. He forbad any man to haue aboue one benefice. He commaunded out of Englande the fift part, & out of lowe Germany the twenteth part of all Church reuenewes. He appointed that to Aue Maria should be songe Salue regina, and the sacringe bell to be ronge then and at eleuation time. He decreed that no lay man should preach, and that no custome should take place, which leadeth to sinne.

The fift booke of the

sunne. And finallye he dyed for thought because the Emperours power preuayled so mightely against him. An. 1241. In his time Tiber in Rome brast out so hye, that manye were destroyed by it, after which ensued such a pestilence, that (sayth Platina) the tenth parson was scant left aliue: In his time also a certaine hill in Burgundy cleaued in twaine, and swallowed vp an houge multitude of people, and a litle before the Pope dyed, was such an Eclipse of the Sunne as hath not beene seene before.

Of the Oracle of Cyrill at Masse.

IN the time of this Gregorie Anno 1234. Cyrill⁹ a Grecian the thirde president general of ye white fryers dyed by report. They say that this man (accordinge as Moses & Iohn the Euāgelist did) recepued Anno domini 1192. a reuelation from heauen written in Tables of syluer with Gods owne finger in Greeke, concerninge the estate of the Church to come: and with this new delusion certaine captifes went about to put awape and whollpe to destroye the Reuelation of S Iohn in that time of deepe darkenes. Because at ye time in Italy, Germanye, England & Fraunce, many (through the doctrine of the VValdēses and ye preachers of Frederick themperour, prouinge it out of the Reuelatiō of Iohn) beleeued that Rome was Babilon ye great strompet, and ye the Pope was Antichrist himselfe: which opinion the vncle of Petrus Veronensis held, as his Legēd and Fasciculus tempōrū testifye. To such shiftes was ye totteringe estate of ye Pope then driuen, as to abrogate the olde Scripture and to forge new: for then Princes began to plucke from ye Church their temporalities, which maintayned theyr excessiue pride and pompe: Also they began to despye their transubstantiacion in the masse, and to worke diuers thinges that pinched the bellyes of the clergy, and

made

Pageant of Popes. Fol.113

made them keepe leaner kitchins. In moste thinges this reuelation of Cyrill, is cleane contrarye to the Reuelation of Iohn: many monkes and fryers haue written great commentaryes and fantasticall interpretacions vppon it, as Ioachimus Abbas, Guilihelmus Cisterciensis, & Iohn de rupe scilla. But who so euer preacheth anye other Gospell &c, let him be accursed. Gallathians. i.

120. Celestine the fourth.

Celestine the fourth borne of the house of Castilians, beinga learned, aged and crasyed man succeded Gregorie: who likewyse purposed to pursue the quarell againste Frederick, but that he was disappointed by a cuppe of poyson, whereof it is reported he dyed the xviii. daye of his raigne. One Thomas Egleston in his booke of the entraunce of ye Minorits into Englaūd, wryteth of an Englishmā called Robert Somerton Cardinall of Rome, who likewyse was poysoned harde before the election of this Celestine least he should haue succeded Gregorie: of the same Robert Somerton and his death, wryteth Mattheus Parisius comending him as a man who for the loue he had of all was worthy to be Pope. The same Mattheus wryteth of the behauiour of Legates at the same time saying, two of the Popes messegers remayned in Englād to gather vp his money, whose extorsion was so odious & shamefull, that it is better (saith he) to let it passe not to offende mens eares, then to defyle the ayre wyth the filthye reporte thereof. This Celestine vsed this sayinge commonlye: It is harder to keepe moderation in prosperity, then in aduersitye. After his death the Popedome was voyde xri. weekes, till the Emperour at the request of Baldwine Emperour of Constantinople, and Raimond Erle of Tholos, deliuered those Cardinals which he had in captiuitye.

185

FINIS.

THE

THE SIXTE BOOKE

and according to maister Baales order the fourth diuision of the third sort of Popes vnto Iulius the seconde, contayninge 260. yeares which he calleth the raigne of the Locusts vnder Abadon the destroyer, accordinge to the 9. Chapter of the Apocalips: For that in this time the Locusts which he enterpreteth the new found orders of begging fryers, inuented and ratifyed by the foure last Popes, deuoure, spoyle, waste and destroye all with their sophisticall and cauilling doctrine:

As did Thomas Aquinas, Ioannes Scotus, Occam, Gerardus Bononiensis, Aegidius Romanus, Magister Sententiarū, vvith other like subtill schoolemen and Sorbonistes, vvho with their gloses, allegories and distinctions, corrupted the true sence of the Scripture, and in maner toke it cleane awaye.

121   Innocentius the fourth.

After the Cardinals had long wrangled beinge reproued for it sharpelye by the Emperour, they agreed to chose this man callinge him Innocent the fourth borne in Genua, whose name before was Cynebaldus of the house of Flisci and the countyes of Lauany: who beinge in time paste the Emperours especiall freinde, became forthwith his deadlye ennemye, and did more annoye the noble Prince then any other before had doone. Marius reporteth thus of him, this Pope (sayth he) for hate he bare to Frederick, did forthwith summon a councell at Lions whither hee cited Frederick, purposinge himselfe to haue preached there: but the Embassadour

Pageant of Popes. Fol.114.

baſſadour of Frederick deſired he might haue a reaſonable dape graunted him that he mighte conueniently come to Lions, which the Pope did not onlye denye to graunt, but forthwith enflamed with wrath and rage did curſe themperour, depriue him of his eſtate Emperial, releaſe al his Princes of their alleageance and ſayth to him, and doth moue them to chooſe another to be Emperour. He charged ye godly Emperour with diuers falſe matters, as periurye, ſacriledge, empriſoninge certaine of the clergye and ſuch like, whereof though the Emperour had by wryting ſent to the Princes very honourablye purged himſelfe: yet this malitious man continued ſo importunate w the Princes with great promiſes, that they chooſe the Landſgraue of Thuringe: and rewarded all men with croſſes and pardons, giuen by Proclamation againſt the Emperour as againe a Turke or infidell. Furthermore he commaunded all biſhops and archbiſhops to publiſh euery where, how he had curſed, excommunicated, and depriued the Emperour: which was boldly doone in England, Fraunce, and Denmarke, but the biſhops of Germany fearing the Emperours diſpleaſure, beſoughte the Pope it mighte not be done. Which the Emperour hearinge did valiantlye ſet himſelfe againſt the Pope and all his tyrannous rebels, til he coulde not eſcape the Popes ſnares in Apulia. For the addition to Vſpergenſis ſayth: After the Pope had depriued and excommunicated both Frederick & his ſonne Cōradus; Frederick did ſo ſhake and worye the Pope and the Church of Rome, that ſome marked w croſſes ſet themſelues in battaile againſte him, when hee came to batter downe the gates and walles of Rome, where he encountred with a mightye armye of theſe croſſed fellowes. But ouercomminge them and takinge them priſoners, ſome of them he hewed a ſonder w foure ſquare woundes in forme of a Croſſe, of ſome he cleft their ſculs a croſſe in 4. parts, ſome he marked on the forhed with a croſſe cut: and as for

P.   the

The sixte Booke of the

the clergye hee caused their shaued crownes to be pared a crosse. When the said Henry Landsgraue of Thuringe was chosen kinge of the Romaynes, and Frederick deposed by this fourth excommunication, then the bishoppe of Strosborough like a peaceable prelate of ye time, to gratifye the Pope tooke part with the Landsgraue, and assisted him with such power & strength as he coulde, both against the father and Conradus the sonne: for he assaulted & wan diuers townes, some he sacked and razed to the grounde, some he burnt with fier, which townes and Cityes themperour had recouered to the Empyre in Alsatia. On the other syde Conradus ye sonne of Frederick gathered an armye against Henry, but was easely ouerthrowne and manye of his armye being slaine, diuers of his nobilitye were taken prisoners. But soone after this Henry beinge thus foysted into the Empire by the clergy, grew into cōtempt with them that liked not his election, whereupon he was in mockadge termed King of clarkes & Prince of priestes: but the Pope did straitly charge by his Legates al the Almaine Princes to obeye Henry as their soueraigne, and to defye Frederick & his sonne. In the meane time this Hēry dyed, and yet the Pope ceased not but sent a Legate into Germanye, one Peter Caputius a Cardinall, who summoninge the Princes at Collen, caused them to electe one William Earle of Holland, a readye man to maintaine any quarell by the sworde. In the ende the Emperour beinge in Apulia, one hired by the Pope gaue him poyson by meanes whereof he was daungerouslye sicke, but seemed to recouer it: but was smothered to death with a pillowe by Manfredus his bastard sonne, who as some thinke was allured by brybery and fayre promises of the Pope to do it. The truth hereof is written in fixe bookes of Epistles, written by Peter of the Uine.

Anno 1250, Frederick dyed, and as some write in his last will and testamente he gaue a summe of moneye for satisfaction

Pageant of Popes. Fol.115.

tiffaction to the Church of Rome, and bequeathed his eſtate and the order of all thinges to his ſonne Conradus. This Will was brought to the Pope to be approued, but ẏ Pope did whollye diſanull and fruſtrate the Will, ſayinge that the Prince whom he had depoſed, could make no Will and ſo it was voide. Within a while after a yonge Prince to whom the Emperour by his ſonne Kinge Henry was graundfather was murthered, but by whō no mā could tell.

About this time before ẏ death of Frederick, there were certaine preachers in Sweueland who ſtoutlye and openly preached againſt the Pope and his Cardinals, & iuſtifyed the doinge of Frederick and his ſonne Conradus, ſayinge bouldly that the Pope, his biſhops and Cardinals, had no auctoritye, becauſe they were al ſtayned with that one blot of ſimony, and ẏ their power depended not vppon Chriſt: & that a prieſt committing deadly ſinne, could neither binde nor looſe, nor conſecrate: that no man in the world might forbid a Chriſtian to execute diuine functions, & that they ſhould be hearde & celebrated without any difference. And in the ende of their Sermons this pardon (quoth they) which we do pronounce vnto you, wee do not declare it to you as forged by the Pope and his prelates, but proceedinge from Almightye God. Theſe preachers were maintayned by Conradus, and therfore he incurred almoſt danger of his life.

In the former councell helde at Lions it was decreed that the Cardinals ſhould ryde on their trapped Gennets throughe the ſtreates, and weare red hattes and crimſen roabes: to ſignifye (ſayth Pariſius) that they are readye to ſpend their bloud for the Catholicke fayth and the ſafetye of the people: but as (Platina ſayth) for the honour of their eſtate. Alſo in that councell Innocentius decreed amonge manye matters that the Pope mighte depoſe the Emperour. He did greatly fauoure the order of begging fryers, and beſtowed on them manye priuiledges and benefittes.

P ii He

The sixte Booke of the

He preferred the Dominicans to dignityes Ecclesiasticall: and aduaūced the Franciscās to be the Popes confessours: He adopted the White fryers and Augustine friers to be his sonnes: wher as they liued before in deserts he brought them into Cityes, teachinge them to begge their breade in idlenes. By the helpe of the Dominicans he reformed the rule of the Whitefryers, mitigated it, and finallye with his blessinge confirmed it, that (as the sayd rule sheweth) they should hope to be saued not onlye by Christ: He graūted these & the begging fryers lycence to preach, to dispute, and to shriue people. Also he exempted them from all power & iurisdiction of kinges and bishops: whereupon they crammed the worlde ful, and chaoked it with their gloses vpon Sentences, decretals, cannons, wich their commentaries vpon Aristotle, their Sophisms, Repertories, Sūmaries, Tables, Trinies, Quatrinies, Conclusions, Questions, Distinctions, Quidities, Quodlibets, Myracles of the dead, Legendaryes, Sainctes liues, Martyrdoms, Visions, Dreames, Reuelatiōs, Exorsisms, Concordances, Discordāces, Marials, perspectiues, Aphorismes, wyth a thousande vaine and combrous pamphlets, full of grosse & deceitful heresyes: and then nothing was counted deuinitye nor lawe, but their fansyes and canons. And in these dayes the world was fallen into such grosse blindnesse, ignorance, and barbarousnesse, that not onelye knowledge in diuinity, but also other learning was almost decayed, the knowledge of the tongues as Greeke and Hebrew buried in ignoraunce, & though some rubbishe of the latine tongue were left, yet it was rustye, corrupte, and broken stuffe, as appeareth yet by theyr wryptings, ye like barbarousnesse is not in any tongue. But to returne to Pope Innocent: he canonized diuers, makinge them sainctes that for his abnauncemente had played the traytours and rebels against theyr owne Princes, as one Edmond Archbishop of Canterbury, and other of sondrye places.

Till the

Till the time of this Innocentius the 4. (sayth Bibliander) it was not an article of fayth, nor a law of the Church that men should worship the breade and the wyne in ye Sacrament: therefore (sayth he) ye Pope as a creator brought forth a newe God Mauzis by transubstantiation. This Pope offred to sell to king Henry the third of England, ye kingdome of both Sicils to the vse of his sonne Prince Edmond, and yet Conradus kinge thereof was lyuinge. He vexed and polled the Churches of England with myserable exactions: for money he maintayned and licensed anye wickednes amonge the clergye, suffering worser matters in his bastards whereof he had diuers, especiallye one called VVilliam. One Robert Capito bishop of Lincolne, had a great controuersye with this Pope, for he detested & defyed both in preachinge and wrytinge, the Popes couetousnes, pride and tyrannye. He would not admit one of ye Popes bastardes because he was vnlearned and but a boye of yeares, to a canonshyp of Lincolne, but rebuked ye Pope for it in a letter, and withstoode the Popes pollinge & robbinge the Realme: and therefore the Pope recepuinge the sharpe letter from this Robert Grosted, for anger rayled not onlye on the bishop, but also brast into these arrogante wordes against his Prince king Henry the third, sayinge (as Mattheus Parisius testifyeth): Is not ye kinge of England our vassel, our slaue, & our page, who may at our pleasure to hamper him, put him in prison, & to vtter shame? And finallye because he coulde not tell howe otherwise to ease his rancke stomacke against the bishop hee excommunicated him: but he constantlye defyed and despised his excommunication euen to the death. He defended in disputation that ye Pope could do nothinge against iustice & truth, and that he was worse then Lucifer and Antichrist: at the length being cited to appeare in ye court, and condempned by the Pope wrongfullye, he appealed to the iudgemente of Christe. This good bishop after he had detected much

P iii of the

The sixte booke of the

of the Popes treachery, before his death vttered these two verses applying them against the Pope.

Eius luxuriç meretrix non sufficit omnis,
Eius auariciç totus non sufficit orbis.

One concubine could not suffice
his burning lust to quenche,
Nor yet his honger after golde,
one worlde serude not to stenche.

Also this bishoppe by diligent searche tryed it that this Pope and his clarkes had in reuenewes out of Englande aboue iii. score and tenne thousande markes, where as the reuenewes of the Crowne came not to 30. thousand. Cestrensis in his seuenth booke wryteth, that when this bishop of Lincolne dyed, a voyce was heard in the Popes court sayinge Veni miser in iudiciū dei, that is Come thou wretch to be iudged of God. And that the Pope was found deade in his bedde the next daye, and a blewe stroke in his bodye as if he had beene beaten wyth a staffe. This was done Anno 1253. he being at Naples and loking soone after to haue enioyed the whole kingdome of Sicill, where he lyeth buryed. Thaddition to Vspergensis sheweth, that the yeare before, as the Pope was going from Liōs to Millen, these straunge tokens happened: certaine bloudy cloudes were seene in the ayre, & streames of bloud gushed out of breade as oute of wounded bodyes. After his death the seate was voide two yeares.

124 Alexander the fourth.

189. Alexander the fourth borne in Campania, being Cardinall of Hostia succeded Innocent. He persecuted Ecelinus of Runcan, and Manfred king of Sicill, because they had beene enuemyes to the former Popes: thus he began his raigne. And first he craftelye admonished them not to stande against the dignitye of the Church in anye point, &

before

Pageant of Popes. Fol. 117.

before he gaue them this charge, he had prouided his army in a readinesse meaning to course them if they should seeke to preuent him and his Cardinals of the kingdome of Sicili: yet these Princes very couragiouslye with an oast of Saracens and other, fearinge not the Popes threates, did set vppon his army at vnawares euen in a trench ere they wist, and partly slue them, partly toke them prisoners. In the meane while Pope Alexander goinge to Anagnia excommunicated Manfred, and sent a Cardinal called Octauian to Naples, to make the Neapolitans to stand faithful to him against Manfred, promysing speedely to bring ayde to all Campania and to the Neapolitans: but Manfred not pacifyed with troubling Naples did also moue factions in Hetruria, but chiefely in Florence, where he brought in the Guelphis againe, who euer were at deadly foode with the Gibelines. Thus was al Italy in a myserable vprore, torne in sonder with cruell and saluage warre. But Manfred hauing poysoned Conrad king of Sicill, was proclaymed kinge at Panorme, and with an armye of hyred souldiours, he ouerthrew the Popes Legat with great slaughter. This Pope sent one Rustand Legate into Englande Anno 1255. to gather vp the tenthes in Englande, Scotland, & Irelād, to warre against Manfred. And saith Matthcus Parisius) manye mischiefes detestable, issued from y burning fountayne of Rome in those dayes, to the destruction of manye: for after the begginge fryers had preached the power of y Crosse, he required infinite sommes of monye, the exaction of the Pope was such (sayth he) that the like hath not bene heard. Whereupon Fulck bishop of Lōdon sayd with great griefe: Ere I giue my consent to oppresse the Church vvith such iniurye, seruitude and bondage, surely I will first loose my head: for although that Courte hath often in times past pinched euen to the bone the faithfull flocke of Christ, yet it neuer wouded in such deadlye sort all, and euery one of Christes seruaunts, as it

P iiii did this

The sixte booke of the

did this yeare and the yeare following &c. The money that was gathered for the holy land was transposed into Apulia against Christians, and (sayth Matheus) vnmeete mē are made gouernours of noble Churches, the prelates are sould as oxen and asses, this is the extreame point of seruitude &c. About this time the said Rustand the Popes Legate being Prebedary of Paules Church in Lōdon dyed beyond the sea, king Henry the third hearing therof gaue the same prebend to one Iohn Crakehale his chapleyn, but after the sayde Crakehale had full possession thereof, came one Iohn Grasse from Rome, wyth the Popes embulled letter to chalenge the sayde lyuing: Hereupon the matter being in controuersye, it was brought before Boniface bishop of Canterbury, who finding that the Popes gift was dated before the kinges, dispossessed the Englishman and inuested the Popes man, which was taken so in despite by certaine repyning to see the Pope and his Italian priestes in this and all such cases to beare more sway then ye king, and to reape all commodyties from the kinge and his subiectes, that the said Italiā and a cōpanion of his were murthered in a thronge, by whom no man knewe.

Rustand in a conuocation at London, alleaged that all Churches were ye Popes, to whom one Leonard an Englishman answeared modestly: yea sir in tuition, not in fruition, to defend not to expende. Seuell bishop of Yorke by ye example of the former bishop of Lincolne, did likewyse wīstande this Pope Alexander, and desyred him by letter to leaue of his wonted polling, & accordyng to Peters example to feede the sheepe, not to flece them, not to flea them, nat vnbowel them, neither as a wolfe deuoure them. Further it followeth in the sayd Matthews, that the Pope sente yet other Legates into England, namelye Arlot & Mansuet minorite fryers, who had power to pardon for money eyther lyers, forsweareters, vowbreakers, adulterers, and Sodomits, traytors, poysoners, murtherers, and

all

all suche: Whereuppon a certaine woman an anchoresse in S. Albons abbey had this terrible vision, she heard an old man of graue countenaunce crye thre times VVo, wo, to all that dwel on the earth, and then faded away againe.

Anno 1258. Richard Earle of Cornewall sonne to king John of Englãd was chosē king of Almany for his great treasure, and the Pope procured that he was chosen Emperour, but he did that closely, because he had likewyse for the same matter, taken a brybe of Alphonsus kinge of Spaine: Whereupon a certaine Poet made this Verse.

Nummus ait pro me, nubet Cornubia Romę,
   Thus money sayth for loue of me,
   Cornewal with Rome shal lincked be.

Beside these shiftes made for money, this Pope Alexãder vsed another notorious knacke, he abusing & deluding the simplicitye of the king of England, made him beleeue that he would make his sonne Edmond king of Apulia, if hee woulde sustaine the charges thereof to maintaine the warres appertayning to it: wherupon the king caused his sonne forthwith to be proclaymed king of Apulia, and sent to the Pope all the treasure and riches that he could make in his Realme. And thus was the king and his sonne deluded, and the Realme wonderfullye impouerished by the Popes craft. It were to long to discouer all the superstitious & wicked deuises of this Pope, who at length going to Viterbium Anno 1262. to make peace betweene the Genewaies & Venetians according to his owne fansye, and because he coulde not haue his will therein, he dyed there for anger.

125. Vrban the fourth.

VRban the fourth borne in Fraunce, and as some saye was first called Pantaleon being patriarch of Hierusalem. As soone as he was Pope by and by he commaunded
                      souldiours

The sixte booke of the

souldiours out of Fraunce to subdue Manfred the ennemy of the Church: & for the furtherance therof hee requested Lewes kinge of Fraunce to send his brother Charles & the Earle of Anteganor wtan oast into Italye, and made him king of both Sicils. After many conflictes ye said Charles ouercame and slue Manfred at Beneuent, and recepued of ye Pope against all lawe and right the kingdome of Sicill wt the dukedome of Calabrie and Apulia, whereuppon arose many great slaughters. While this Pope was frō Rome at Pruse, ye Romaynes coueting their olde libertyes made a newe kinde of officers, callinge them Branderesies, who had power of life and death in their handes: they chose one Brācaleo a pryuate parsō of Bononia to be Senatour, whō banished late before they restored. But touching Vrban it was not much more then this that he did, sauinge that hee ordayned an holye daye, namelye Corpus Christi daye, the fifte day after Trinitye sonday, vpon this occasion as some (and most likely) do write, namelye Arnold Bostro, & Petrus Præmonstratensis. Anno 1264. (as they saye) a certaine woman called Eue in a Religious house in Leodia, with whom the Pope in time past had beene well acquainted, had a reuelation which she signifyed by wryting to the Pope, beseeching him that the sayd day might be kept holye in the honour of the Sacrament of the altar, to whom the Pope according to her desire, returned his aunsweare with this Bull to confirme the holy daye.

The Bull of Pope Vrban to
Eue the Anchoresse for the establi-
shing of the holy day called Corpus Christi daye.

BIshop Vrban seruaunt to the seruauntes of God, sendeth greeting and apostolicall blessing to Eue our beloued daughter in Christe. VVe know O daughter, that thy

thy soule hath longed with greate desire, that a solemne feast day might be appointed for the bodye of oure Lord Iesus Christ, in Gods Church to be celebrate of all faithfull Christians for euer. And therfore for thy ioye we signifie vnto thee, that we haue thought it good for the establishing of the catholicke faith, that beside the dailye remembraunce which the Church maketh of so wonderfull a Sacrament, there should be more special and solemne recorde, appointing a certaine daye for it, namelye the fifte daye after VVhitsontyde next ensuinge, that on the said daye the faithfull flocke do gather together to the Churches deuoutlye and effectuallye, and let that daye be to all Christiās ioyfull with new holines, and holye with much ioye, as is more set out in our apostolicall letters, sente for this cause through the world. And know ye that we haue caused this feast daye to be solemnized with all oure brethren Cardinals, bishops and archbishops, and other prelats then being at Rome, to giue example of celebratinge the same to all that shal see or vnderstand the same. Therfore let thy soule magnifye the Lorde, and thy spirite reioyce in God thy sauiour, for thine eyes haue seene his saluation, which we haue prepared before the face of al people. Moreouer reioyce because almighty God hath giuen the thy hartes desire, and the fulnes of the heauenly grace hath not disapointed the of the will of thy lippes &c.

This Vrhan sate moꝛe then thꝛee yeares betweene the Guelphes & Gibelines, and pꝛouoked their quarrels to be tryed by the edge of the swoꝛde, to the confusion of manye thꝛough Italye. He being on a time vpbꝛayed that he was of base linage, aunswered that no man was noble by byꝛth, but that to be made noble by vertue is true nobility: finallye beinge at Prusc because in great attemptes he had not his desired successe, he dyed foꝛ griefe. Masseus sayth that a blazing starre appeared thꝛee nights befoꝛe the death of this Pope, and ceased the same night that he dyed.

126 Cle.

The sixte booke of the

Clemens the fourth.

Clemens þ fourth called before Gui Fulcodius borne in Narbonie, ere he came to be Pope was a maryed man, and had 3. children by his wyfe, a sonne & two daughters. He (as his predecessour began) continued in sheddinge of bloud: he sent for Charles Earle of Angeow to bringe an armye into Italye where he slew Manfred, and was made kinge of Sicill and Hierusalem, but vppon this condition that he should paye yearelye to the Pope fortye thousande Crownes. This bargaine beinge made betweene them, great slaughter & bloudshed was committed in diuers places, for the said Pope betrayed Conradinus sonne to Conradus kinge of Sicill, and inheritour of the kingdomes to þ former Charles, so that as he passed through the fieldes of Viterbie with an oast of Germaynes, wher his aboade was at that time, the Pope by report sayd: that the sayd Conradinus was as a lambe brought to the slaughter, shewing therby that he was of councell to the treason. Afterward when he foughte with Charles about Naples, & at the first conflict had sufficient victorye, yet then the treason reuealing it selfe, Conradinus & Frederick duke of Austria were taken: & being myserablye vsed in their captiuitye mocked and flouted, were in the ende beheaded by the Popes commaundement, because Conradinus claymed the kingdome which his auncetours possessed. Thus the kingdome of Naples came into the hand of the Frenchmen, and þ dukedome of Sweuia decayed and came to nought by þ wickednes of þ Pope. In the time of this Clemens one Octobon a Legate of his comminge into England, enrolled to perpetuall memorye the valuation of all Churches in the Realme so narrowly as he could possiblye gather the certaintye. Clemens dyed at Viterbium Anno 1270. & was buryed amonge the Dominickes, and the seate was voyde two yeares.

127 Grego-

127. Gregorie the tenth.

Gregorie the tenth borne in Placentia in Lombardye, of the house of the countesse of Millen, was first called Theobaldus. He being an archdeacō, after the Cardinals dissention (which had lasted almost two yeres) was ended, was chosen Pope: of whose election Iohn Cardinall of Portua wrote these Verses.

    Papatus munus tulit archidiaconus vnus,
    Quem patrem patrum fecit discordia fratrum,
    One archdeacon against his hope,
      by chaunce obtayned to be Pope,
    The iarringe of brethren caused the rather,
      that he was created of them the father.

This Pope amonge other thinges made peace betwene the Genewaies and Venetians: He excommunicated the Florentines for inuadinge such townes as belonged to the Popeship. Afterward he held a coūcel at Lions in Fraūce to the which came Michael Palæologus Emperour of Greece, to reason of the opinions of the Church of Rome, for vii. of his auncetours had in times past conferred with them, and euer departed dissentinge from them. In this councell was decreed that the Pope beinge dead, the Cardinals should be shut vp in a certaine closet without meate or drincke, till with one consente they should agree vppon choyse of another. He made many decrees for the helpinge of the Holy land, and the maintayninge of Religious mē. Many noble and great parsonages both kinges & Earles, made themselues apparell with the Crosse on it, to go the voyage to Hierusalem, to whom the Pope verye craftely, to further their purpose promised to come visit them there. He aduaunced diuers of the begging fryers to greate Ecclesiasticall dignityes, as to bishoppickes, archbishoppickes and Cardinalships. After the Empyre had beene voyde

                                      a longe

The sixte booke of the

a long time, at p length he made Rodolph Earle of Hamboroughe Emperour, because he shoulde maintaine ciuill discention: and after p Alphonsus kinge of Castile had bestowed houge summes of money in hope to be Emperour, (especially the Duke of Cornewail being dead) p Pope appeased him with wordes enoughe, but no recompence in money toward his charges. This Rodolph after he was chosen was charged by the electours that he shoulde go to Rome within a yeare to receiue the Crowne of the Pope, yet he neuer did it, excusing himselfe with pretence of priuate affayres: & vsed to saye oftentimes amonge his freindes, that the footinge of the Emperours goinge into Italye seemed glorious & triumphant: but in their returne out of Italye wretched, myserable, & ful of sorrow. Alluding to the fable of the Foxe, who being sent for to come to visit the sicke Lion, made aunsweare that he perceyued p footesteps of many beastes goinge into the Lions denne, but he could finde fewe or none comming from it. But Rodolph sente his vicegerent into Italye whom the Cities for the most part recepued: but the Pope returninge to Rome & iourneying hard by the Florentines, would not yet absolue them of their excommunication which had lasted almost 3. peares. At length he came to Aretium Anno 1275. & dyed in his iourney in the fift peare of his Popeship & is buried there, and neuer came to Rome nor sawe it.

128. Innocentius the fifte.

INnocentius the fift borne in Burgundie a dominican in profession, was chosen by the Cardinals at Aretiū: who beinge chosen Pope and crowned in S. Peters Church, went about to establish peace in Italye. Therefore he sent great Embassadours, who should compell the Hetrurians (entendinge to destroye the Pisans) to take peace: also the Venetians and Genewaies being at deadly enmitye, to fall to vnitye to vnitye vpon perill of his curse. Also he procured ye Embassadours of Charles king of Sicill to be present at ye peace makinge, the better to countenaunce his doinges: the Hetrurians obeyed, and especially the Florentines, and therefore the Pope did absolue them from the excommunitatiō of Gregorie: But the Genewaies and Venetians continued notwithstanding the slaughter of each other, whom yet Innocentius had broughte to his purpose if he had liued, he purposed it so earnestly. He dyed the same yeare that Gregoric dyed, in the second daye after he had raigned vi. monthes. This Pope (sayth Platina) did not a litle offende seculer priestes, because at Viterbium he did determine the dominicās should enioye the tombe of Clemens the fourth, for which they and the secular priestes had longe beene at sharpe debate.

129. Hadrian the fifte.

Hadrian the fifte a Genewaie borne before called Othobonus, was made Pope in Lateran porche: this mā was nephewe to Innocentius the fourth, and made Cardinall of S. Hadrian by him, and sent into England as Legate to gather vp the Popes money. But while he wente about to appease strife betweene the kinge & his barons, thereby to worke his owne matters more quietly, he was put into prison by the Citizens of London, and at length deliuered againe, Anno 1266. With a great trayne of bishops and priestes, he helde one councell at Northampton and another at London; where after he had dispatched his matters touchinge papistrye according to his owne minde, he made lawes whereby England did longe after maintaine Papistrye. Also he denounced all those bishops to be wicked, who had taken parte with the Princes against kinge Henry the third, and yet those same bishops were partlye absolued by him for money, partlye compelled to go for absolution

abſolution to the Pope. This Hadrian as ſone as he was made Pope went forth with to Viterbium, & ſente for Rodolphe the Emperour into Italye, to breake the power of Charles kinge of Sicill: this Charles is he whom againſte lawe and righte he had aduaunced before, who then ruled all at Rome accordinge to his luſte. But Rodolph beinge troubled with the Bohemian warre, could not ſatiſſye the Popes deſire: but Charles meaning to eſchue the mallice, tranſported all the power of his armye into Achaia, purpoſinge to make a waye to attaine to the Empyre of Conſtantinople. Hadrian (ſayth Platina) purpoſed to make the gouernemente of the Church to be ſafer from oppreſſours, & to alter the conſtitutiõ of Gregory his predeceſſor, touchinge the reſtraint of the Cardinals for the election of the Pope. He dyed at Viterbium ere he were conſecrate Pope 40. dayes after his election.

130. Iohn the xxij.

IOhn the xxii. a Portingale borne & a Phiſition by profeſſion called before Peter Portingale, was made Pope beinge firſt biſhop of Tuſculan. This man although he were counted very well learned, yet for want of ſkill in gouernment, & infirmitye in his maners (ſayth Platina) did more hurt and diſhonour to the Popeſhip then good. For he did many thinges that ſeemed to be both of a fooliſh and light minde: and was to be prayſed in this thinge onelye, that he ſuccoured with money and Eccleſiaſticall lyuinges yonge men that were toward in learninge, & eſpeciallye the pooreſt. At this time the Venetians ſpoyled the Anconitãs, becauſe they vſinge trafique into Dalmatia woulde paye them no tribute: & yet the Pope would not defende them as he ought to do, beinge tributaryes to the Church: and though in words he were haſty, yet in his doinges a ſlouggarde and baſtard. The Anconitans therefore being deſtituts

Pageant of Popes. Fol.122.

tute of the Popes ayde, gathering themselues together, brast out of the Citye vppon the Venetians besieging it, & draue them awaye with great damage. But the Pope vsinge the aduise of Iohn Caietan who then ruled all, because by his ayde he came to be Pope, he sent his Embassadours both to Michael Paleologus, & the kinges of the West, to moue them in his name to make peace amōge themselues, and to prouide to send their powers against the Sarracens: which if Paleologus would not do & keepe the vnitye promised, he woulde giue his Empyre from him to Charles kinge of Sicill. He prophesyed by the course of the starres that he him selfe should liue longe, and tould this to euery man in his vanitye, as one whose wante of discretion was euident to euery man. But beholde while he thus vaunted his cunninge in prophecyinge and constellations, openlye in a certaine chamber which for his pleasure bee had builded in his Pallaice at Viterbium the fourth day after fell downe sodainlye Anno 1277. After this ruine wherein he perished myserablye, he was founde the seuenth day after hauinge raigned viii. mouthes. Valerius called the place which fell downe Gamesters hall, and Stella calleth it the precious Chamber, for the Pope had builded it so gorgeouslye for his pleasure. After his death the seate was voide through great contention vi. monthes.

129. Nicolas the thirde.

Nicolas the third a Romaine, called first Iohn Caietan, after vi. monthes with great discention and brauling of the Cardinals obtayned the seate. Charles king of Sicil was as Senatour president in their consistorye, who was very vrgent to choose some Frenchman Pope: and therefore this Nicolas hauing gotten the place, purposinge to abate the power of Charles toke from him the Vicarship of Hetruria, & filled Italye full of broyles. And for his owne

Q.   lucre

194

The sixte Booke of the

there bee perswaded Peter kinge of Aragon to clayme the kingdome of Sicill, sayinge that it belonged to him, by the inheritaunce of his wyfe Constance, which liked Peter: but note the sequeale. Peter with a great navye went to Sardinia, and there wayted whē some motions should arise in Sicill, for the Sicillians making a conspiracy against Charles and the Frenchmen, appointed a daye that as soone as at eueninge a bell should be tould, the Frenchmen should be forthwith murthered both man woman & child, wherein they were so cruell ý they slue euen women with child. But this horrible deede was not doone vnder Pope Nicolas, but in the time of his successour Martin the fourth. Also this Nicolas toke to himselfe ý Senatourship, which Clement the fourth had bestowed on Charles: and forbad for euer that any Prince or kinge should be so hardy to desire or take vppon him that dignitye. By his falsehoode it came to passe that Flaunders, & Bononia, & the royaltye of Rauenna, which longe time were vnder the Emperour, became subiect to the Pope. Amonge other buildinges ý he made aboute Rome, he enclosed a warrante of hares in the walles, wherein euen in his Popeship he vsed often to hunt. He bestowed siluer cases for the Apostles heades: he was reproued of many for making his nephewe Berthold Earle of Romundiala, & for another of his nephewes beinge a Dominican & Cardinall because he sente him Embassadour into Hetruria. For Platina and Stella and other complaine that he loued his kindred to well, so that he bestowed withoute lawe on them that which he had filched frō other: for he toke perforce from some nobles of Rome, certaine Castels and bestowed them on his freindes. He made the Gibelines being seditious mē magistrats at his owne lust in Florence and els where, to defende and maintaine his tyrannye. Also he purposed to make two kinges of the stocke of Vrsines, the one in Lombardye the other in Hetrury, but while he purposed this he dyed sodenly of

an

an Apoplexye, without speakinge any worde Anno 1281. in the fourth yeare of his Popeship, and yet it was thoughte by his good complexion he should haue liued much longer. Some saye that one foretolde the death of this Pope by ý rysinge of the riuer Tiber, which then happened. The report is that of a concubine he begat a sonne that had hayre and clawes like a beare: it is written in Iohn Noucomagus in illustrationibus Bedæ.

130. Martin the fourth.

MArtin the fourth a Frenchman called before Simon, was nexte made Pope by the Cardinals of Fraunce, who then were the greater nomber. He woulde not be Crowned at Viterbium, because he thoughte that Citye was excommunicated, because they had made a tumult againſt the Cardinals, for the Viterbians entring into the consistorye apprehended the Cardinals, and put them in prison, spuninge out and contemninge the house of Vrsins: therefore Martin going to an olde towne called Oruietus, did there kepte all his solemnitye, & made viii. Cardinals the same daye to strengthen his power. Also hee did not onelye entertaine curteouslye kinge Charles comminge to him, but also restored to him the dignitye of Senatorship which Pope Nicolas had taken frō him: which thinge displeased many, because it should make seditiō in the Citye, the Vrsine being now returned and their ennemyes driuē out: for Charles for the hatred conceyued againſt Nicolas, was sore bente againſt the Vrsines. But Pope Martin meaninge to worke warelye, did much set by Matthew de Aquisporta a Franciscā, of the house of ý Vrsines, a Cardinal & bishop of Portua. He excōmunicated Peter king of Aragon, who went about to inuade ý kingdome of Sicil in his nauy againſt Charles: also he gaue his kingdome for a booty to one that did desire to enioy it: He released his subiectes

Q.ii

The sixte Booke of the

iectes from their allegeaunce, callinge him an vsurper of Church goodes. But Peter despinge all this did by the helpe of Paleologus obtaine the kingdome of Sicill: the Sicilians also beinge able no longer to sustayne the pride & lust of the Frenchmē, at the perswasion of Iohn Prochita, conspired against Charles, and ringinge the belles, did at once without anye regarde murther all the Frenchmen. Pope Martin amonge other thinges graunted to the Romaynes libertye to chose two Senatours of the nobilitye, and excommunicated Paleologus. He made warre against the Forolinians. He bestowed great pryuileges vpon the begging fryers: and as he was taking his accustomed recreation with his chapleins (as Carsulan testifyeth) a certaine secrete disease came vppon him, which after hee had sayd it panged him extreamlye, he dyed Anno 1285. and yet the Phisicions coulde finde no token of death in him. Some write that this Pope in the first yeare of his Popeship, receyued into his familiarity the concubine of his predecessour Nicolas: but to auoyde the like chaunce that his childe (if he shoulde haue anye by her) might not be like a beare, he commaunded all beares which were painted in his Pallaice by a Pope that was of Vrsine house, to be taken awaye or blotted oute, to auoyde in his concubine the sight thereof, which he thoughte wrought great effecte in conception.

131. Honorius the fourth.

HOnorius the fourth a Romaine of a noble familye was afore called Iacob, was next made Pope. He had a brother called Pandulphus a worthye man who at that time was Senatour in Rome, who did sharpely execute lawes against sensers, theeues, and murtherers. Honorius excommunicated Peter king of Aragon, because he helde at that time the kingdome of Sicill against Charles, & confirmed

firmed the curses and edict of Pope Martin, because for ye Popes lucre he woulde not leaue the kingdome. Also he raysed terrible warre against Gui Feltro who helde the towne Flaminia, and ouercomminge him, against all law and righte by tyrannye subdued the towne to Rome. Also he confirmed the sect of Augustine fryers which was refused at Paris, but withstoode by manye. Also he appointed to the Carmelites, that puttinge of their riche roabes, they shoulde weare white weedes, and commaunded they shoulo be called our Ladyes brethren. After which he died quicklye Anno 1288. in the second yeare of his Popeship. The seat after this was voyde x. monthes for pestilences and earthquakes. This Pope was much troubled wyth the goute, both in his handes and his feete, so that he was fayne to make certaine instruments fit for the purpose to saye masse. The Grecians in his time forsakinge papistrye returned to their old fayth.

132. Nicolas the fourth.

Nicolas the fourth a Franciscane fryer borne in Picene, after tenne monthes was chosen Pope, at which time the Cardinals did not yet agree vppon one. This Pope (sayth Platina) loued all men a like, and thoughte that he ought no more dutye to his kindred then to other. He did nothinge of any great waight, but busyed himselfe in erectinge superstitious buildinges, and makinge newe ceremonyes aboute fryers and monkes, which are not worth the mencioninge: finallye he seing Rome sore tormoyled in his time with ciuill dissentions, burninges, slaughters & spoylinges, dyed for very griefe and sorrow thereof Anno 1291. He beinge deade the Cardinals wente to Peruse, that they might vse the more libertye in choosinge a newe Pope: and yet they iarred so bitterly among them selues two yeares and 3. monthes, that they could neuer agree in ye election.

The sixte booke of the
Celestine the fift.

CElestine the fifte borne at Esernia beside Sulmo, by profession an Anchore called before Peter Moronens, after the Cardinals had scoulded two yeares, he by the procurement of Charles the seconde kinge of Naples and the latine Cardinals was chosen Pope, who as sone as he was created went to Apulia, & callinge all the Cardinals thether, he created xii. newe Cardinals wherof two were Eremites. Ptolomeus Lucensis wryteth, that at his Coronation were two hundred Thousande men: because (sayth Massæus) at the first time he sate in Consistory, he went about exactly to reforme the Church of Rome ý the clergy mighte be an example to other, he purchased such hatred that he doated & was a foole. Thereupon one of the clergye called Benedict, hyred one to set throughe an hoole in ý wall of the Popes chamber a greate hollow troncke, and throughe the same shoulde make an hydeous noyse manye nightes together, (as if it had beene the voyce of an Angell frō heauen) saying in the night time: Celestine, Celestine, giue ouer thy charge, for it is aboue thy habilitye. Beside this diuers perswaded him to giue ouer for his owne safetye. Kinge Charles vnderstanding of this spake with the Pope, desiringe him as earnestlye as he could, not to forsake that dignity, which came to him by the grace of God. But he gaue this answeare: I will do as it pleaseth God. And returning from Naples from the kinge, & perceyuing he coulde not be quiet, hee gaue ouer the Popeship on S. Lukes eue, and made haste to go liue an Eremites life in ý desert, sayth Massçus: but first of all he made a decree with the consent of al, that the Pope might yeld vp his dignity. But Boniface who had thus beguiled the simple man, and now gat to be his successour, fearing least ý people woulde followe the same Celestine as Pope, & desye him, he therefore put Celestine in close prison till he dyed, Anno 1292.

the f.

the x. daye of Maye after he had raigned one yeare and fiue monthes. Of this Celestine sprange a secte of monkes called Celestinians.

134. Boniface the eight.

BOniface the eight borne in Campania called before Benedict Caietan beinge chiefe councellour to Celestine, was set vp in his steade by a straunge kinde of treason at Naples. This Boniface while he was Cardinall of S. Martines in the mounte, did so honger after the Popeship that he spared no falsehood nor ambicious meanes y might further his desire. He was so proude that he did almost disdaine all men. And boyling thus wyth heate of ambition, he suborned (as is sayd before) certaine who should come in the night time, and wyth a still and straunge voyce in the Chamber of Celestine as it were from heauen perswade him (beinge a very simple man of himselfe) to yelde vp the Popeship if hee woulde be saued: which in the ende was brought to passe. But Boniface vsurping by craft against all right the Popeship, apprehending the sillye man Celestine (who was departing from Rome to some wildernes there to ende his life) put him in perpetuall prison: and yet (as Marius witnesseth) he professed he did it not for hatred against Celestine, but least the auctours of sedition shold make him their head, to trouble & disquiet the peace of the Church. And thus this vnthanckeful Boniface was not contented onelye to delude poore Celestine, and to beguile him of his dignity, but furthermore to cause the simple soule as if he had bene a malefactor, to dye for thought in prison. After this Boniface began to exercise such crueltye & he seemed to be another Nero: he sente for certaine Cardinals to come vnto him, but they beinge terrifyed th his falsehod and rigour, durst not come to him, and thereuppon they were proclaymed scismatickes by him, and depriued

Q. iiii

The sixte booke of the

pryued not onelye of their benefices and such dignityes as they had receyued of Popes, but also were berefte of all their landes, townes and goodes which they had by inheritaunce. Furthermore he gathered an armye, and pursued them with the Columnians and as many of the Gibelines as he met withall in any place. He destroyed & spoiled all mens places whether soeuer they fled: whereupon many of them seing they might be safe in no place, fled into woodes and forestes and taryed there, other some of the most noble houses of Italye, after they had euen in maner of wild beastes ranged longe aboute the Sea shore, did at length depart from Italye wyth saluage Pyrates and rouers: for they trusted more the barbarous Pyrates then this churlishe Boniface. He hated ye Gibelines with such rancour, that in persecuting them he heard saye that some of them were fled to the Genewaies, & therupon he posted thether to destroy them vtterly, & to roote out ye very name of them vpon earth. And when vpon Ashwednesdaye he should accordyng to the superstitious vse crosse al commers on the forheade with ashes, and saye vnto them thus: Remember man that thou art ashes, and to ashes thou shalte returne. Upon the same day & for the same cause, the archbishop of Porchet (who was a Gibeline) came vnto him, & kneelinge downe vnto the Pope put of his cappe, to haue the ashes put on his head, whō when Boniface had espyed, beinge neither ashamed for the time, nor the place, nor the people present, vttered his rancour towarde the bishoppe most shamefullye. For takinge vp an handfull of ashes, he threwe them spitefullye in the eyes of the bishop, sayinge reprochfullye wyth malicious chaunge of woordes: Remember man thou arte a Gibeline, and to the Gibelines thou shalt returne. And beside this depryued him of his archbishopricke, though in the ende he restored it.

In his time were great and cruell warres betwene the Sicilians and Robert duke of Calabria, which wroughte
much

much mischiefe to all Italye, and yet the Pope being oftentimes requested thereunto, would neuer with his auctoritye steppe in betwene them to pacifye the matter. But by the prouidence of God, they that before fled out of Italye with the routers, arriued in Italye againe, and gathering together a fewe (who fled and lurked here & there for feare of the rage of Boniface) came to Anagnia, ere the Pope mistrusted any such matter, they brast open the gates vpō him, apprehended him, and brought him to Rome, where frettinge and raginge in a great agonye most desperatlye for the space of xxx. dayes, throughe the extremitye of his malady, he dyed myserablye Anno 1304.

This Pope sent a commauudement to the king of England, charging him not to molest Scotland (as he did then) anye longer, because the Scottes were a priuiledged people belonging to his Chappell: but the kinge stoode stoutlye in the defence of his righte and quarrell, and claymed it as his right & not the Popes. After this the Pope moued kinge Edwarde to warre vppon the Frenche kinge because he had offended the Pope, but the kinge would not be so abused by him. After this when the kinge had bestowed the bishopricke of Canterbury vpon Robert Burnel bishop of Bathe, the Pope in spite of his teeth did not onlye place another called Iohn Peccam, but also sent downe his Bull to the spirituall men of England, for their discharge, not to paye one penye tribute to the kinge in any case, to his no small trouble: for vpon this the most of them were at defiaunce with the kinge and his Parliamente, especiallye the bishop of Canterburye. This is that Pope of whom it was comonlye said: He entred like a foxe, he raigned like a Lion, he died like a dogge. He thinking that kingdomes and Empires were all in his owne hande, did vsurpe the aucthority of both swordes, & woulde be counted the Lord of all the world. He gaue sentence p vnlesse kinges woulde receiue their kingdomes at his hand, they should be accursed, and

The sixte booke of the

sed, and oughte to be deposed. He excommunicated Philip kinge of Fraunce, because he would not suffer the treasure of his Realme to be transported oute to Rome: he cursed both him and his to the fourth generation. Also he would not confirme Albertus to be Emperour (whom before he had three or foure times reiected) vntill he woulde inuade Fraunce, and depose king Philip. He maintayned the discorde that was in Italye, and purposed to nourishe them continuallye. He forbad that the clergye should paye anye tribute to their Princes without his commaundement. He boasted that he bare the keyes of heauē, and published this Canon that he oughte to be iudged of none, althoughe hee shoulde drawe thousandes of soules to hell with him. He was the first that deuised the Iubelye, according to the Iewishe tradition. He gaue full remission of sinnes and pardons to all that shoulde come on pilgrimage to Rome. At the first daye of Iubelei hee prancked himselfe gorgeouslye in his pontificalibus. The seconde daye he being arrayed most royallye, with Emperiall insignes, commaunded a naked sword to be caryed before him, and said with a loude voice: Ecce potestatem vtriusq; gladij: Lo here is the power of both swordes. Finallye he being (as is said) apprehended, and offeringe rather his head to be cut of then he would yelde vp his Papacye, those conditions beinge put to him: his house was first spoyled of so much treasure, ÿ as it is reported all the kinges of the earth together were not able to make so much oute of theyr treasurye, as was caryed oute of his Pallaice, and from three Cardinals and a Marquesse that were with him. Then afterward he was set vpon an vnbroken coult with his face to the horse tayle, and so caused to ride a gallop & iaunted til he were breathlesse, and then was he imprisoned and there almost pined, by kinge Philips souldiours of Fraunce, till the people of the towne of Aragon where he was did releue him, and yet neuerthelesse for (thought of this misery and losse, he dyed.

He be,

he bestowed on S. Peters Pallaice a chayme of belles making a sweete and pleasaunt noyse, and encreased the reuennues therof: he yet encreased very much ye priuileges of the begginge fryers. He doubled ye idolatrous honour of the Apostles, the 4. Euangelistes, and the foure doctours of the Church. He gaue auctoritye to ye Ecclesiastical parsons generally in England, to excommunicate the people twise in the yeare. He caused one Hermanus of Ferraria to be taken oute of his graue, and burned xxx. yeares after he had beene buryed. He said that to be subiect to the Church of Rome is of the necessitye to saluatiō. He deposed diuers Cardinals: he deuested diuers kinges of their estate: he fostered harlots, he begat diuers bastardes, beside sondrye other lewde prankes. He sommoned kinge Edwarde the first to Rome vpon the cōplaint of Robarte VVinchelsey bishop of Canterbury after ye death of Iohn Peccam, both which Archbishops troubled the kinge, as almost all their auncetours from the time of Hildebrand had done to the Princes in their time: for so VVilliam Rufus and Henry the first, were troubled wyth Anselmus Archbishop of Canterbury: Henry the second also with Thomas Becket: King Richard and all England with VVilliam bishop of Elye the Popes Legate: King Iohn with Steuen Langtō bishop of Canterburye: Henry the thirde with Edmonde Archbishop, and now this kinge Edwarde wyth these two. The kinge beinge cited to Rome, was there suspended till he had purchased full dearely his absolution: but of the said Peccam this one thing is to be noted, that he caused to be ordayned ye no spirituall mynister should haue any more benefices thē one, which was also decreed by Octo and Octogonus, the Popes Legates in England at that time.

An Epi-

The sixte booke of the

An Epistle of Peter Cassiodorus to the Englishmen, reprouinge the extreame robbery, filching and slauerye vvhereby the Popes spoyled this lande about the yeare of our Lord 1302. to moue them to shake of the bondage of the Popes tyrannye, taken out of an ould booke in S. Albons Church.

TO the noble Church of Englande seruing in claye and bricke as the Ievves did in times past vnder the tyrannie of the Egiptias Peter the sonne of Cassiodore a catholike Souldiour and deuoute champion of Christe, sendeth greeting and vvishinge to caste of the yoke of bondage, and to receiue the revvard of libertie.

To whom shall I compare thee or to whom shal I liken thee O daughter Hierusalem? to whom shall I matche thee, O daughter of Sion? Great is thy perturbation, like vnto the Sea. Thou sittest alone without comfort all the daye long, thou art confounded and consumed with heauines. Thou art giuen vp into the handes of him from whence thou canst not ryse without helpe of one to lift thee vp: for the Scribes and Pharisies sitting vpon ye chayre of Moyses, thy enemyes the Romaynes are as thy heades and rulers, enlarging their garded phylacteries, & seeking to be enryched wyth the marowe of thy bones: laying heauie burdens, and not able to be borne, vpon thy shoulders and of thy ministers, and they set thee vnder tribute (which of old time hast beene free) beyonde all honestye or measure. But maruell not therat, for thy mother, which is the ladie of people, lyke a wydowe hauinge marryed and coupled her selfe to her subiect, hath appointed him to be thy father, that is to saye, the byshoppe of Rome, who sheweth no point of any fatherlye loue towards thee, the magnifyeth and extendeth to the vttermost his authoritye ouer thee: And by experience declareth himselfe to be ye husband of the mother. He remembreth oft wyth himselfe the propheticall saying of the Prophet, and well digesteth the same in the inward parte of his breste. Take to thee a great booke, and write therein quicklye with the pen of a man, take the spoyle, robbe quickly: But is this it, which the Apostles sayth, that he was appointed for, where he wryteth thus. Euerye bishop taken from amonge men, is appointed for men in those thinges that belonge to the Lorde: not to spoyle, not to laye on them

scarce

Pageant of Popes.   Fol.128.

yearelye taxes, not to kill men, but to offer giftes & sacrifices for sinnes: and to sorowe wyth them, that be ignoraunt and do erre. And so we read of Peter the fisher (whose successor he boasteth himselfe to be) that after the resurrection of Christ he turned with other Apostles, to the office of fishinge, who when he could take nothing of the left syde of the ship, at the bidding of Christ, turned to the right side, and drewe to the lande a net full of fishes. Wherefore the profitable mynisterye of the Church is to be exercised on the right syde, by the which the deuill is ouercome, and plentye of soules be lucrifyed and wonne to Christe. But certainlye the labourer on the left side of the ship, is farre otherwyse: for in it the fayth stumbleth, heauines beareth rule, whan that thing that is desired by seekinge, is not founde. For who is so foolishe to thinke that hee can both at one time serue God and man, and to satisfye his owne will, or to sticke to the reuelations of flesh and bloud, and to offer worthy giftes to Christ? And doubtles, that shepeheard that watcheth not for the edifyinge of the flocke, prepareth an other way to the rounge Lyon, and seeking whom he maye deuoure. And nowe behold, I say, O daughter, the deedes of him that is called thy father, such as haue not beene hearde of before: he dryueth away the good shepeheard from the sheepefold, and placeth in their steade bishops, to rule, but not to profyte (his nephewes, cosins, and parentes) some that knewe no letters, and other some domme and deafe, which vnderstand not the plaine voyce of the sheepe, nor curing their woundes that be hurt of the wolues: but like hyrelinges pluckinge of the fleeses a pase, and reaping that which other men haue sowen, whose handes moreouer be alwayes readye in theyr baskets and pouches, but theyr backes are turned from theyr burdens. By which thinge it is manifest ye the priesthoode is cleane chaunged at these dayes, the seruice of God decayed, almes diminished and broughte to noughte, the whole deuotion of princes, and kinges is banished. Maye not this be thought wonderful in the eyes of all men, that where as Christ commaunded tribute to be payd to kinges for him & for Peter, he nowe goeth about dominion of his stile, to subdue to him, both realmes and princes of realmes (against his will, whose Vicar he sayth he is, and who refused the realmes & iudgements of this world.) which this bishop contrarywyse chalengeth, clayming al that which he in his stile wryteth to be his. Blacke, O daughter, what doth he yet more against thee: marke, he draweth from thee what so euer pleaseth him, and yet he thinketh not himselfe content, to haue the tenth part onely of thy goodes from thee; except he

The sixte booke of the

he haue also the first fruites of the benefices of the Ministers, wherby he may get a newe patrimony aswell for himselfe as for his kynred, contrary to the godly wyls of the first founders. Ouer and besydes all this, he inferreth other execrable taxes and stipends for his Legates and messengers, whom he sendeth into England, which not onely take awaye the feeding and clothing of thee and thine, but also teare in peeces like dogges your flesh and skinnes. Maye not this prince be compared to kinge Nabugodonoser, which destroyed the temple of the Lorde, and robbed awaye the siluer and golde vessils therof? The very same doth this man also: he robbed the ministers of Gods house, and left destitute of due helpe. In like maner doth he: Truly they be better that are killed wyth the sworde, then they which be pined with hunger: for they are dead straight, but these are wasted with the barrennes of the earth. O daughter, all they that passe by the waye, let them haue pitye and compassion on thee, for there is no sorrowe like thy sorrowe. For nowe thy face is blacker then coales through much sorrow and weepinge, and thou art no more knowen in the streates: thy foresayd ruler hath placed thee in darcknes, and hath giuen thee wormewood and gall to drincke. O Lord heare the sorrowe and sighinges of thy people, behold Lord, and descende, for the hart of this foresaid man is more induraie then the hart of Pharao. For hee wil not suffer thy people to departe, exceepte in the fortitude onelye of thy hande. For he scourgeth them, not onely miserablye vppon the earth, but also after theyr death he intendeth to incroche the goodes of Christians vnder the name and title to dye intestate or making no will. Therefore let the chiualrye of Englande well remember, howe the Frenchmen in times past, directinge their greedy eyes on the Realme of England, laboured wyth all theyr power howe to bringe the same vnder their subiection. But it is to be feared, least the new deuises and practise of this newe enuempe, supply that which hitherto hath beene lackinge in them. For in diminishing of the treasury of the Realme, & spoylinge the Churche goods: the Realme shalbe brought into such inability, that it shal not be able to helpe it selfe against the enuempe. Therefore O daughter and you the ministers therof, suffer not your selues to be ledde any more into such miserable bondage. Better it is for the wealth of the & thine, that the Christian kinge and the powers of the Realme which haue indued thee with greate benefites, & you also which are inducd with their benefites, do labour wyth all your power how to resist the deuises, conspiracies, arrogancye and pryde, of the foresayd person: who

not ser

not for any zeale of God, but for the enriching of his parents, and for his owne kinred (exeltinge himselfe like an eagle) by these and such other exactions, goeth about after a new kinde of extorcion to scrape vp and deuour all the money and treasure of England. Now least the dissembled simplicitye of the Realme in this behalfe do bring vtter subuertion, and afterward be compelled to seeke remedy when it is to late: I beseech the Lord God of hostes to turne away the vale from the hart of that man, and to giue him a contrite and an humble mynde, in such sorte as he maye acknowledge the wayes of the true God, wherby he may be brought out of darckenes, and be enforced to relinquish his old sinister attemptes: and that the vyneyard which the Lord hath planted, may be replenished continnally with true preachers of the worde. Let the wordes of the Lorde prophesyed by the mouth of Ieremye stirre vp your mindes to withstand and resist the subtile practises of this man, by the which wordes the Lord speaketh: O thou pastor which hast scattered my people, and hast cast them out of their habitacions, behold I wil come and visit vpon thee, and vppon the malice of thy studyes: neyther shall there be anye of thy seede which shal sit vppon the seate of Dauid, neyther which shall haue power any more in Iuda. So that thy neast shall become barren, and vtterlye subuerted like Sodome and Gomor.

And if he being terrifyed by these wordes do not leaue of from this which he beginneth, and doth not make restitution of those thinges which he hath receyued: then let all and singular parsons singe for him being indurat, to him that seeth al thinges, the Psalme 108. Deus laudem &c. For truly as fauoure, grace, and benenolence, remitteth and neglecteth many thinges: so againe the gentle benignitye of man beinge to much oppressed and greued, seekinge to be deliuered & freed from the same, striueth and searcheth to haue the truth knowē, and casteth of that yoke by all meanes possible that greeueth him. &c. Hæc Cassiodorus.

What effecte this letter wrought in them, to whom it was directed, is not in story expressed. This by the sequeal may be coniectured, that no reason nor perswasiō could preuaile, but that the Pope retayned here still his exactions, what soeuer was said or written to the contrarye notwithstandinge.

135. Bene-

The sixte booke of the

135. Benedict the xi.

Benedict the xi. borne in Lombardy called Nicolas, a Dominican by profession of obscure parentage (whose father was a sheepeheard,) he after he had beene Cardinall and bishop of Hostia came to be Pope. He was of stature but a dwarfe, and at length waxed bauld, but of an excellent witte and very eloquent, and therfore in high fauour with Pope Boniface: who as soone as he was created, applyed his minde diligentlye to asswage all those broyles and seditious factions that wasted Italye. Leander Albertus reporteth, that when he was made Pope, his mother came to Peruse to see her sonne so exalted, & was apparelled by the Senate that she might come in seemely order to salute him: but he did reprochfulllye disdaine and would not acknowledge her to be his mother, til she had put on her former apparell againe. Then (quoth he) I knowe this matrone, for shee is my mother. He offered to S. Estorge Church in Millen a chalice of siluer of great waight, also a senser and a boxe of frankinsence, siluer candlestickes, & a silken curtein of ÿ price of an hundred Crownes, & gaue iii. hundred poundes ouce of the Popes treasurye to make another curtein about the Sepulcher of one Peter of Verona a dominican fryer. All that he gaue, coste viii. Thousand pounde accordinge to their computacion at Millein. He excommunicated all those that were the apprehenders of Boniface, vntill they had payde for absolution. He receyued into fauoure Iohn and Iames Cardinals of Columna, whom Boniface persecuted. He absolued Philip kinge of Fraunce who was excommunicated. He made three Cardinals Nicolas Pratensis of Hetruria, VVilliam Macklesfild & Gualter VVinterburne, being Englishmen. After he had appeased those braules which his predecessour had procured, he dyed Anno 1305. in ÿ fift month of his Popeship. The

Pageant of Popes.

hip. The report is that he dyed of poyson which was giuē him in a figge: Of this Benedict were made these two Verses.

A re nomen habe, Benedic, benefac, Benedicte,
Aut rem peruerte, maledic, malefac, maledicte.

136. Clement the fifte.

CLement the fifte was borne in Vasco, his father was one Bernard a noble knighte, he was first called Bertrad Goth, and was chosen Pope by the Cardinals after much strife at Peruse, he himselfe not beinge there. He agreeing to the election went from Burdigall to Lions, and sent for al the Cardinals, whither they came out of hand: where the Pope translatinge the court of Rome hether into Fraunce Anno 1305. continued still there threscore and ten yeares, to the great damage of the Romaynes. Philip king of Fraunce, and his brother Charles, & Iohn duke of Britaine, were at this Popes Coronation, where duke Iohn & xii. other mayned w a wall that was overthrowne by the wonderfull prease of people, dyed out of hand. Also King Philip was somwhat wounded with the fall therof. And the Pope himselfe in so greate an hurly burly beinge thrust besyde his horse, lost a Carbunckle stone oute of his Miter, valued at sixe Thousande Florences. The pompe & triumphe beinge ended, hee made manye Cardinals of the Frenchmen, but none of the Italians, sauing that he restored to Iohn and Iames of Columna their Cardinalships. He sente three Cardinals with Senatours auctoritye to Rome, to gouerne it and Italy. He graunted to Frederick king of Sicill, the Isle Sardinia (inhabited of the Saracens) vpon this condition, y as sone as he coulde he should driue out the enemyes and recouer it, but to the vse of the Pope. To these wordes of Platina, Marius hath added this: Clement the fift (sayth he) because he desired not to serue other

R as Christ

as Christe commaunded his Apostles, but to haue Emperours serue him, decreed by Canon, ỹ the Emperours appointed in Germany (although they bare ỹ name of ỹ king of Romaynes) should yet receiue of the Pope ỹ title, right, and name of Empire: and that the Emperour being dead, all the time the Empyre should be voide, the Pope should haue iurisdiction ouer those townes in Italye that are tributaryes to the Emperour. So much of Marius. Clement being an open whoremonger and maintayner of harlots, appointed the Popes Courte to be at Auenio for his owne pleasure. He rooted out ỹ Iewes called Templars, in a councell at Vienna Anno 1311. In the same councell he decreed that all religious orders exempted shoulde be subiect vnder the common lawes as other were, but the Cistercian monks did purchase of him to be priuiledged, and gaue large bribes to him for it. Also the Franciscan friers offered him fortye Thousande Florences of golde beside other siluer, that they might against their rule haue a dispensation for landes and possessions: the Pope thereupon willed them to bring the money, & hauing taken assurance for it of certaine marchaunts which they brought, he both toke the money & tould ỹ fryers ỹ he would not nor could not breake S. Fraunces rule for any money, & thus he beguiled ỹ fryers. He aduaunced S. Iohns knights called ỹ knights of the Roades, because they had won ỹ Roades frō the Saracens. He cōmaunded the master of the Templars to be burned w̄ one of his fellowes at Paris in presence of ỹ Cardinals, and made certaine decrees to bridle the disorder of the Iewes confiscating their goodes. He appointed punishmēt for such of the clergye as should busye themselues in secular affayres, or be costlye apparelled: and depriued monkes of hunting and hawking. He excommunicated the Venetians, the Florentines, and Lucians, and cōfirmed Corpus Christi daye for an holye daye. He commaunded ỹ the reliques of Saincts should be reuerentlye honoured.

He gouer-

Pageant of Popes. Fol.131.

He gouerned Italye by his deputyes two Cardinals: he made Celestine the fift a confessor Sainct: finally after diuers decrees of superstition, he dyed of the bloudye flixe, panged and pained sometime with a collicke, sometime payned in the guts, the sides and the stomacke, at Rocca Maura a tent vpon Rodanus Anno 1314. His body was caryed to Carpentorate in Vascony: the seate was voyde 3. peres. This same yeare also dyed Henry Lutsenburg the Emperour, poysoned by a monke called Bernad by the cōspiracy of the Guelphes, because he wēt about to take vpō him by force the kingdome of Sicill, beinge moued thereto by the Sicilians: for this cause the sayd monke (who had long dissembled frendship & good will to the Emperour) wrought his destruction in most sinfull and blasphemious manner: For against the good & godlye Emperour should come to receiue the Sacrament of the bodye of Christe, the cursed monke had prouided & tempered one hoaste wt such rancke poyson, yt the Emperour perceyued forthwith the horrible treason: and yet the godlye Prince as soone as he felt himselfe poysoned, gaue the trayterous monke warning to escape awaye with these wordes: Sir, conuaye your selfe awaye, for if the Dutchmen perceiue this and oure godlye frendes, ye shall dye the death. The monke therefore goinge to Sene, recepued ye reward which was promised him, and yet he did not by this treason deliuer his fryerlye brethren, for many of them in Thuscia, Lombardy and other places, both men & houses perished with fyer and sworde. This Pope Clement toke displeasure with the Venetiās, and furiouslye yelded them as a pray and spoyle to all that would make hauocke of them and theirs. They therefore sent to him a noble man of Venice called Dandalus, to sue for fauoure and for the safety of their Citye: and to obtaine pardon this noble Frauncis Dandalus was fayne to yelde himselfe bounde in a chayne about the necke, and to couch at the Popes feete vnder his table, and there like a dogge

R ii   to feede

The sixte Booke of the

to feede of the scrappes & bones that the Pope did cast vnto him, ere he could asswage the Popes fury, as Sabelicus declareth Enned. 9. lib. 7.

137. Iohn the xxiii.

IOhn the xxiii. a Frenchman borne, called Iacob Caturcensis bishop and Cardinall of Portua, after ye seate had beene voyde through ye discorde of 23. Cardinals ii. yeares, was chosen Pope at Lions: from thence remouinge his Court to Auenio he created viii. Cardinals, amonge whō was Iacob Caturcensis the yonger his sisters sonne, and Iohn Caietan of the house of Vrsine. He deliuered Hugh Gerard bishop of Caturcia, to a seculer Courte beinge disgraded and spoyled of his pontifical arape to be tormēted, his skin fleed from his bodye & then to be burned to death, because he had (as he saide) conspired against his parson. He was so new fangled that he made much chopping and chaunginge, erecting and supplanting of bishopzickes, abbeyes, and such like dignityes. He made two Thomasses Saiucts, the one bishop of Hertford in England, ye other Thomas Aquinas a Dominican, beside sondzye other. Hee ordayned that belles should be ronge thrise in the day, that the people fallinge on their knees euen as they go in theyr waye, shoulde saye Aue Maria thrise. He condemned them for obstinate heretickes, that defended that Christ and his Apostles possessed nothing priuatly, and sent commaundement to the Vniuersities that no scholers should presume to dispute therof. He condemned the wryting of one Peter a franciscan fryer, whō wente aboute to encourage men to follow the pouertye of Christe, for the which thinge many were condemned & burnte. He exempted the white fryers from all iurisdiction, reseruing them onelye to S. Peters auctoritye his deare children, and made diuers of them bishops: for (by the suggestion of Sathan, as surely it maye be well be well thoughte) he had a wonderfull straunge vision before he came to be Pope, as he him selfe testifyeth in a certaine bull, that is this: That the Virgin Mary deliuered him from his ennemyes amonge great debate of the Cardinals, and made him Pope, but vpon this condition that he should saue from Purgatorye these his bretherne. This Pope Iohn taught certaine errours, namelye that ye soules departed from the bodye do not see God till the day of Iudgemente: for so (sayth Massæus) his father taughte him, being deluded with the false visiō of one Tundalus an Irishman. He sent to Paris twaine, the one a dominicke ye other a franciscan, to preach ye same heresye: but one Thomas V Valleis an English fryer dominick, withstoode the Pope in his heresye, whom the Pope committed to prison. Durandus of S. Porcian, V Villiam of Callis, and other withstoode the Pope likewyse. Touching the errour & grosse heresye of this Pope Iohn, he was charged with it in the councell of Constance by these wordes: Pope Iohn sayde and stubbornely beleeued, that the soule of man dyeth together with the body, & is consumed to nothing like the soule of brute beastes: whereof he neuer would purge him selfe. Furthermore because that Thomas Vvalleis an Englishman was imprisoned by the Pope for reprouinge his heresye, the kinge of Fraunce sommoned a councell into his Pallaice in Vriciana sylua, where the whole assemblye subscribed against the Popes heresye: and therefore the kinge sent to Pope Iohn, willinge him both to reforme his heresye, and also to deliuer the prysoner, & so the said Thomas was set at libertye. This Pope reformed and transposed the orders & decrees of the Church at his owne pleasure, & made Colledges of Scribes accordinge to the nomber of the Apostles, who receyuing their fee, should write such letters as he should appoint. He condemned Iohn Poliacus a deuine, because he taught that men should not trust the begging fryers. He compelled certaine Nonnes called

R iii   Biginæ

The sixte booke of the

Biginæ to marrye, and detested pictures. He helde it for a grounded article that Chriſt gaue none other rule of godlineſſe to his Apoſtles then to other Chriſtians, and that ÿ Apoſtles neuer vowed pouertye. John Mandeuil in his firſt booke and ſeuenth Chapter, ſheweth that this Pope wrote at large to the Greekes that there is but onely one Chriſtian Church, and that he was head thereof and vicar of Chriſt, to whõ the Greekes aunſwered brieſely: VVee do aſſuredlye acknowledge your highe power ouer your ſubiectes, but wee cannot abide your high pride, wee cannot ſtanch your greedye couetouſnes: the deuil is with you but God is with vs. Thus briefely in a worde they reuealed the Popes eſtate. This Pope condemned Lewis Bauare a noble Emperour, to be a rebell to the Church, a ſciſmaticke and hereticke, becauſe he toke vpon him by the Electours choyſe the gouernment of ÿ Empyre, not bowing anye fealtye to the Pope. Thus wryteth Iohn Marius of this Emperour Lewis: Pope Iohn (ſayth he) hated vnto death Lewis Bauare, partly becauſe he beinge choſen by the eſtates of Germanye kinge of the Romaynes, did diſdaine to receyue at the Popes hand (accordinge to ÿ Canon of Pope Clement the fifte) the name and title Emperiall, partly againe becauſe he defended from the Popes power certaine monkes whom he had condemned for heretickes: therefore Pope Iohn auouched Lewis to be an hereticke. Lewis comminge into Italye, appointed his deputies in euery Cittye and came to Millen: and becauſe he deſired to qualifye the Popes diſpleaſure, he ſent Embaſſadours to him kepinge his courte then at Auenio in Fraunce, to require of him the ornamentes belonging to the eſtate imperiall, with freindlye affection as his auunceſtours had done: the Pope did not onelye denye the ſute, but ſent awaye the Embaſſadours with great reproche, and cited the Emperour him ſelfe peremptory wyſe (as they terme it) to come to Auenio, & ſubmit himſelfe to the Canons of ÿ Church.

The

The Emperour knowinge the Popes tyrannye vsed in his Church, & vnderstanding that he had his estate giuen him from God, desired to keepe and defende the same holye and vndefiled: and therefore woulde not submit himselfe like a slaue vnto Popes, and so denyed to come to Auenio. And yet being desirous of peace, he besought the Pope by Embassadours once againe, to bestowe on him with curtesye y ornamentes of the Empyre: the Pope stoode peuishlye in his wilfulnes, vaunting and boasting in his wrytings, y he had power to playe make & marre w Princes, and y at his pleasure he might set vp and depose whom he listed: and y the Empyre being voyde, the Pope is ful Emperour: And for malice against Lewis he excōmunicated the Uicounts, whom the Emperour had appointed to gouerne Millen. The Emperour perceyuinge the Popes obstinate minde, taking with him many Princes of Italye came to Rome, and was honourablye receyued of al the people, and required accordyng to the custome to receiue the solemnityes of the Empyre. The Romaine peeres and all the people sent Embassadours to Pope Iohn in Fraunce, and humbly besought him to come to visit his City Rome, & to bestowe vpon the king of the Romaynes the imperiall rites: which if he would not do, they said plainly that they them selues would keepe the ould law & pryuiledge of the Romaynes. Iohn hauing heard the Embassadours, vsing great threates and terrours draue them away with foule rebuke frō him. The Romaynes, seing this decreed to yeld to the noble Lewis his lawfull request: and so by the commaundement of the clergy and people, both he and his wyfe together were crowned by Steuē & Nicolas being Senatours, in the meane time the nobilitye shouted oute, saying: God saue Lewis Augustus Emperour of the Romaynes. The Pope hearing this (though the Emperour did nothing but that was lawful and godly) did accuse him for a traytour, and an heretick: he published sore processe against him, put

R iiii him

The sixte booke of the

him frō his estate imperial, depriued him of his kingdome, condemned him by vile and cruel curse of excōmunication, as a rebell and Captaine heretick againste the Church of Rome, by meanes whereof he enflamed all Christendome with such discord & deadly warres, as could not afterward be quenched in thirty yeres. Thus farre wryteth Marius.

Thus the Pope had nothing to defende his forged supremacye and auctoritye, but the dreadfull boultes of his excommunication. But there were certaine at this time as well deuines as lawyers, which preached that Christe and his Apostles did possesse nothinge properlye, and that the Emperour in temporall cases was not subiect to ỳ Pope: Amonge these men were Michael Cœsenus & VVilliam Occam minorites, Marsilius of Padua & Iohn of Iandane lawyers, with diuers other. Lewis the Emperour was so comforted by these, that he did stoutly withstand the Popes ententes, and published this his appellation about the coastes of his Empyre.

¶ The Emperours letters.

WE Lewis kinge of the Romaynes, doe pronounce againſt Iohn (who ſaith that hee is Pope) that he doth naughtelye execute the teſtament and will of Chriſte cōcerning peace, troubling the cōmon tranquility of Chriſtendome, neither is he mindfull that what honour ſoeuer he nowe doth enioye, was firſt giuen by the holye Emperour Conſtantine, to Syluester euen when he for feare lurked in forreſtes. Thus doth he ſhewe himſelfe vnthankful to the Romaine Empire, from whence hee reaped all the roialty which now he abuſeth &c.

Thus when Lewis and the peeres of Rome percepued well the iniquitye of Pope Iohn, and the people of Rome from the hyest to the lowest, did take it in euill part that ỳ Embaſſadours whō they had ſent were ſo mocked of him, they

they all agreed together that the oulde custome of chosing the Pope should be brought into the Church: that is, that he being chosen by the people of Rome, should be admitted and allowed by ye Emperour. Therefore one Peter of Corbaria a minorite was made Pope, and was called Nicolas the fifte: and as for Iohn they concluded of him that he was an heretick, and a tyrant of the Church, not a pastour but a breaker of the common peace of Christians. In the meane time Pope Iohn Anno 1335. in the fourscore & r. yeres of his age dyed at Auenio. About ye yeare of our Lord 1326. in ye time of this Pope Iohn, the prelats of England played a stout prancke: for the bishop of Hertford was by the kinges commaundement w other mo impeached of treason, & finally arrested in the Parliament house to aunswere to his endightments. Whereunto after long pauze he aunswered (claiming the priuiledge of the Church) saying thus: I am humble mynister of the holye Church &c. and cannot neither ought to aunswere to such matters, without ye auctoritye of the bishop of Canterbury my directe iudge nexte under the Pope &c. whereupon the other bishops stept up and sued to the kinge for this their fellowe. But when ye king would not yeld, the said bishops together w the archbishops and the clergye comming with theyr crosses, toke him away perforce, chalenginge him to the Church w out any other aunswere: charging moreouer under ye censure of terrible excommunication, none to presume to laye any further handes upon him. And yet the kinge encouraged herewith commaunded lawe to passe upon him, and he being found gilty his goodes to be confiscate: but yet the partye remayned safe under protection of the Archbishop of Canterbury.

This Pope lefte more abundance of treasure then euer any other did, namely fiue and twenty thousand thousande Crownes in gould, and yet but latelye before he ioyned in warre with Robert kinge of Apulia to defende Genua, in

which

The sixte booke of the

which warre (sayth Antonius Florentinus) eyther syde spente as much treasure as woulde haue boughte a good kingdome.

138. Benedict the xij.

BEnedict ý xii. borne in Tholos, in profession a white fryer (sath Paleonidorus) called Iacob or Iames of Furne, the sixtenth daye after ý death of Iohn he was enstalled Pope. This man (sayth Marius) was as vncurteous to the Emperour as euer was Pope Iohn: he renued the curses against him, he reft him of all regall dignitye, & by his sentence depriued him of the dukedome of Bauary. The noble Emperour wente into Germany, and called together (beboulde his vertue and wysedome) all the Princes electours, Dukes, Counties, bishops and the best learned, either in diuinitye or humanitye. And in presence of them all with open and solemne proclamatiō, he added and established his late confirmatiō with ould lawes: and very wisely proued that onelye the Princes electours & no man els, ought to medle wth the election of ý king of ý Romaynes, so that he that had most voyces amonge them was to be accepted berely, be it eyther king or Emperour; which in effect are al one though in name they differ. Because that he that is Emperour may take vpon him the gouernment belōging to his estate, without the confirmatiō of the Sea of Rome: and he being lawfullye chosen, ought after aduisemente giuen by the Princes to be annointed by the Pope. Which if the Pope refused to do, he might be proclaymed Emperour by any Catholick prelate as the vse hath long beene, for these ceremonyes enioyed by the Pope, are but imagined copes and solemnityes deuised by the prelats of Rome, who onely haue but the geuinge of the name, & not the thinge, for a signe of vnitye and mutuall helpe and succoure betwene the Empire and the Church. For the Emperour

Pageant of Popes. Fol.135.

perour bowed to the Pope not an oath of alleageance and fealtye, but of defendinge the Chriſtian faytb, for as much as the taking of this oath maketh not greater dignitye in temporall thinges. Furthermore the Emperour ſhewed how that the eſtate being voide, the righte thereof ſhould not belonge vnto the Pope, and ẏ to haue it ſo was againſt the libertye, righte, honour and maieſtye of the Empire: but by longe and allowable cuſtome notwithſtandinge the Clementine Canon, and by decree vnmoueable hytherto kept bie his auncetours, in the time the Empire is voyd, ẏ right of gouerning the Empire, the beſtowing of fealtyes and ordering of other aſſayres, belongeth to ẏ Palſgraue of Rhene. Afterward for his owne defence, he made proofe of his vpright and truſty dealing before them all, & plainlye confeſſed that he (as a Chriſtiã man ought to do) did beleeue the Articles of Chriſtian fayth, euen as the Church taught: and purged himſelfe of all thoſe accuſatiõs which Pope Iohn the xxiii. and Benedict the xii. had layed to his charge. Thus did the godly Emperour of his owne good motion, when as if he had not pitied the ſhedding Chriſtiã bloude, he might haue tryed the matter with the Pope, by the dint of the ſworde. At the length Pope Benedict began to conſider of the goodnes of this Emperour: for whẽ a certaine grudge happened betweene this Lewis & Philip kinge of Fraunce, by and by peace was made betwene the Emperour and the Pope. And the Pope loued the Emperour ſo entirelye, that he defended him againſt the Embaſſadours of the French king (which euer ſpake ſharpely againſt the Emperour) & ſtoutlye defended the Emperours innocencye. So that it came to paſſe that the Pope was by them called defēder of an heretick, whoſe words although Benedict for a while did much feare, for they threatned to ſet vpon him with all their powers if he abſolued the Emperour, yet in the end he abſolued him. And commaunded to proclaime throughe Germanye, that all the proceſſes of

Iohn

The sixte booke of the

Iohn whatsoeuer they were should voyde and of no effecte: and that it did not become Pope Iohn thus to deale with the Emperour, seinge their two functions as diuers, & testifyed openly that Lewis had in all thinges behaued himselfe, as mighte best beseeme so noble & Christian an Emperour. Yet it is to be noted that the Pope did not this of hartye good will to the Emperour, but vpon pollicye: for when he perceyued the king of Fraunce (within whose precinct he was then abyding) dealt vnfreindlye with him, he feared that if he should also haue the Emperour his enemye, he should haue no succour left, if the French kinge should go about to do him displeasure. And for this cause Benedict thoughte it stode with his commoditye to haue the fauour of the Emperour, hoping it would so fall out that he durst attempt nothing against the Pope. Such from time to time hath bene the pollicy of these prelats, to maintaine their estate. But to returne to the purpose (and leaue these wordes of Marius) Pope Benedict auouched the iudgmēt of his predecessour against Lewis. He appointed deputies in those townes of Italye that belong to the Empire: and toke to himselfe from the Emperour, the Senatourship of Rome. He deuised that euery thing did belonge to the Court of Apostolicall penitēciary. He appointing substodyes, gathered houge sommes of money out of euery nation. He first toke vpon him to vsurpe the presentments of all bishopricks, prelatships and benefices. He abridged vnlearned men of priesthoode. He reformed manye sectes of monckes. He commaunded that all his chapleins shoulde lye in one dormitorye together, and should haue none other renenues then for their diet and apparell. He with a great somme of money bought for his carnall desire, the sister of Frauncis Petrarcha a beutifull woman, of her brother Gerard: he denyed that the Pope had any kindred: he published certaine actes (as Leander testifyeth) against the dominicans: he left to the Church great store of treasure: he
kept

Pageant of Popes.   Fol.136.

kept diuers concubines: he dyed of an ague while he was hyring one Zotus a conning painter, to poztrature the storyes of martyrs in his newe buildinges Anno 1342. Of whom these Uerses were made.

Iste fuit vero laicis mors vipera clero,
Deuius a vero turba repleta mero.

About this time Iohn Stratford beinge bishop of Canterbury, did greatly abuse king Edward the thirde, both in defraudinge him of his treasure when he needed it most in his warres in Fraunce, and refusing obstinatly afterward to come at the kinges commaundement to aunsweare, vntill time & place serued accoding to his owne pleasure.

Benedicts comon sayings were these to be noted: Be thou such a sonne as thou desirest to haue cosens. The euil man dreadeth death: but the good man feareth him more. Those thinges that thou hast learned keepe by reading, and get by learning those thinges that thou wantest. It is as great shame to haue no freindes as to chaunge them oft. It is more dishonour to a Prince to be ouercome with benefits, then by force of armes.

139. Clement the sixt.

CLement the sixt borne in Lemonia by profession a Benedictine, called before Peter Rogers being abbot of Phisca, succeded Benedict at Auenio. This man with his faction troubled the Romaine Empire aboue measure: for he excommunicated (sayth Naucler) all the Princes, lordes and bishops, that consented to the doings of Lewis. To deface the Emperour he created Uicountes and made them Uicares of the Empyre: & Lewis on the other side appointed other Uicares to gouerne the Church. Ierom Marius in his booke called Eusebius Captiuus, doth thus set out the rigour of Pope Clement: Clement the sixt (sayth he) much giuen to women, honour and auctoritye, prouoked with

diuelishe

The sixte booke of the

diuelishe furye, set vp bills in wrytinge vpon Church dores, wherein he threatned the Emperour to be punished wt more cruell tormentes, vnlesse he woulde obey the Popes minde and that within three dayes, and would giue vp his right of the estate imperiall. Great was the cruelty of this Clement voyde of clemency. The Emperour cometh to Frankeforde, and preparing with all diligence to do all that was commaunded, besought the Pope by his Embassadours, to pardon him and to receiue him to fauour. But the Pope aunswered the Embassadours, that he would neuer pardon Lewis, vnlesse he would first confesse all his errours and heresyes and yelde vp the Empire, and put into the Popes hand both himselfe, his children, goodes & possessions, to dispose them at his pleasure, & would promise that he would neuer more enioy any part thereof without the fauour of the Pope, & deliuered a certaine fourme of of these articles in wryting to the Embassadours, comaunding them to carye the same to Lewis. The good Emperour least if he did not thus submit himselfe it mighte bee cause of slaughter and sedition, receiued the order taken by the Pope, and looking vpon it was content in such wyse to saue Christian bloud, and therefore he did not onely set his seale to it, but gaue his oath to performe all. Which when the Pope heard he waxed angrye. But note whether hee toke the Emperour to fauoure, and whether he shewed anye token of good will, by that which followeth. Lewis shewed that order to the Princes electours, and oratours. The Princes detested and abhorred certaine of ye articles, because they were deuised by the Pope to the confusion of the Empyre: and therfore they promised sufficient ayde to the Emperour if as he did before, he would maintaine the libertye and honour of the Empyre. They sente Embassadours desiringe the Pope not to exact those articles yt tended to the vtter subuersion of the Empyre: and ye oratours crauinge and doing nothing els came awaye againe. But

Clement

Pageant of Popes. Fol.137.

Clement blaming Lewis onelye for all, did purpose the destruction of him and his children: he cursed him cruelly euen at consecrating the Sacrament. He renued all the extreame processes which Pope Iohn had giuen out against him, he pronounced him to be an heretick and scismatick. He charged the Princes electours to choose another Emperour. He deposed the Archbishop of Mens both of his bishoprick and auctoritye of electorship, because he knowing the Emperours innocencye and vngiltines, woulde not abuse his maiestye. But the other electours being brybed with money by Iohn king of Bohemia, as the bishop of Colen who toke viii. Thousande markes, & the duke of Saxonye two Thousande markes) did appoint his sonne Charles to be king of the Romaynes: whō this vncurteous Clement did allowe afterward in open consistorye. But who is able to report the horrible bloudshed and warre that arose in the Empire by meanes of this mischiefe wroughte by Clement: for kinge Edward the thirde of England slue xx. Thousande Frenchmen, and Iohn king of Bohemia father to Charles was slaine with many nobles. But Lewis yet takinge thought because of the Popes processes, & not medling with the gouernment of the Empyre, was by the Popes procurement poysoned in a cuppe whereof he dyed. Thus wrpteth Marius: Lo by these kinde of treacheryes haue the prelates of Rome brought the Empyre to ꝑ low ebbe and poore estate, that it is at this daye: for the sayde Charles whom they against all lawe created, to make his sonne to succede him, did so corrupt the electours wyth bribes and fayre promises, that he morgaged to them the common reuenues of the Empyre, which they enioye to this daye, and therefore the Romaine Empyre cannot aduaūce it selfe againe. For then the Electours cōpelled Charles to take an oath, ꝑ these pledges should neuer be reclaymed: whereby at length it came to passe that the Empyre being thus decayed, the Turke inuaded the Church of Christ, & destroyed

The sixte booke of the

destroyed it wonderfullye, and it is by the especial grace of God, that Mahomets blasphemye doth not wyth fyre and sworde rage ouer all Chriſtendome &c.

This Pope Clement now at the fiftye yeare renued the Iubelie, & beinge abſent cauſed it to be celebrated at Rome Anno 1350. for his aduauntage: and (ſayth Premonſtratēſis) there were fiue Thouſande ſtraungers comuning in & going out at Rome, as might wel be counted dailye within the ſaid yeare. He made at ſeuerall times xii. Cardinals whereof ſome were monkes, ſome his nephewes and kinſemen: beſide he promoted diuers other to dignityes, & beſtowed coſt on diuers buildinges. He gaue licence to the biſhop of Bamberge to abſolue thoſe that toke parte wyth Lewis, but vppon theſe conditions: firſt that they ſhoulde ſweare fealty to him as to the Vicar of Chriſte: ſecondly, that they ſhould beleue that the Emperour hath no power neither to make nor marre the Pope: thirdlye that they ſhould acknowledge none to be Emperour whō the Pope had not confirmed. While his companiōs and ſeruauntes went to dinner leauing onely his chamberlayne with him, he fel downe ſodeinly & dyed of an impoſtume Anno 1352. This Clement (ſayth Marius) toke vpō him ſo prodigallp in his Popedome, ỹ he gaue to his Cardinals in Rome, biſhoprickes and benefices being then voyde in Englande: wherewith the king was offended and vndid all the prouiſions of the Pope within his Realme, commaūding vpon paine of impriſonmente and life, that no man ſhoulde be ſo hardy as to bring in any ſuch prouiſions of the Pope within his Realme any more, and vnder the ſame puniſhmente charged ỹ 2. Cardinals forthwith to auoide the Realme. Anno 1343.

Certaine blaſphempes gathered out of the Bull which the ſaid Pope publiſhed for the yeare of Iubelie.

VVhe

Pageant of Popes. Fol.138.

WHofoeuer purpofeth for trauel fake to come to Rome, maye choofe that daye whereon he fetteth forvvarde a confeſſour or confeſſours, or els in his iourneye by the waye, or in any other place: Vnto the which confeſſours or ghoſtlye fathers wee giue ful power to giue abſolution in all caſes that concerne ẏ Popes owne prerogatiue, in as ample maner as if our owne parſon were preſent. Item we graunt that if anye being confeſſed dye by the waye, that he ſhal be free and diſcharged frõ all his ſinnes: And furthermore we commaunde the Angels of Paradiſe (that his ſoule beinge fullye deliuered from purgatorye) they receaue it into Paradiſe.

☞ And in an other Bull he wrote thus.

WE will not that anye man be tormented in him ſelfe with the paine of hell: and alſo vve graunte to all thoſe that weare the Croſſe, 3. or 4. ſoules at their owne pleaſure whom ſoeuer they will to deliuer them oute of Purgatorye.

Againſt theſe hereticall blaſphempes, the Uniuerſitye of Paris did then openlye deteſt and reproue.

There were an hundred Thouſand poore men of ẏ clergye in that yeare reſorted to Auenio to obtaine pardons out of all countryes, and to be byred confeſſours.

140. Innocent the ſixt.

INnocent the ſixte borne in Lenonua called Steuen, doctour of both lawes being of an aduocate made biſhop of Claromont, and of the Cardinall of Hoſtia and chiefe penitenciary to the Pope, was made Pope him ſelfe. He was a man that in his Popedome was a cunning lawyer, but of hauty courage, wilfull minde, very rigorous, and one that frackly beſtowed benefices on ſuch as would pay for them.

After

[margin: 205 Carolus 4 us]

The sixt booke of the

After he was established, hee did wisely abrogate certaine reseruatiõs made by Pope Clement, because it made more for his cõmoditye in time to come so to do. And forthwith he decreed ý al Ecclesiasticall parsons, as many as had any benefices should go forthwith to their charge: for he sayd ý the flocke ought to be kept by their owne sheapeheard, and not by an hyrelinge. He like a couetous niggarde diminished his house keping, reducing & stinting the parsons of his family to a certin (but as Petrarcha sayth) not an honest nõber: Neither would he haue any to waite on him at home, but such as shoulde in al pointes feede his owne humour: he gaue straite charge to the Cardinals so to do, saying ý he & all other Ecclesiastical parsons ought to be an example of life to other. And for the more sparing he made cellars in his house for his auditour & clarkes of the kitchin to locke vp all thinges. For his table diet the wryters report of him that he was a great pincher, but for the maintenaunce of warres verye prodigall. He sente one Giles a Spaniarde Cardinal of Saba from his side into Italye, to persecute certaine robbers and theeues: and to assure the better to the Pope Ecclesiasticall iurisdiction. By Peter Thomas of Aquine a white fryer this Popes Legat, Bononia became subiecte to the Pope, which Peter did first plante there the doctrine of the Sorbonits: therefore the Pope bestowed on him ý bishopricks of Pacte, Mileto, Coranie, the archbishoprick of Crete, and at length the patriarckship of Constantinople. At the commaundement of this Innocent, Charles ý fourth was crowned Emperour by two Cardinals at Rome, but vpon this condition that he should staye no longer neither in Rome nor in Italy: he notwithstanding as soone as he returned home, warned ý archbishop of Mens to reforme the clergy in their apparel, shooes, hayre, and all the order of their life, vpon penaltye of forfeytinge all his benefices. Richard archbishop of Armachane in Irelande, did publishe before this Pope ix.

articles

Pageant of Popes. Fol.139.

articles againſt the begging fryers.

In the firſt yeare of his raigne this Pope commaunded that Iohn Rochdal a franciſcan fryer ſhould be burned, for ſpeaking certaine wordes againſt the clergye. The ſayde Iohn (ſayth Premonſtratenſis) did prophecye many things to come of Antechriſt and of the Popes, and therfore was ſuſpected of hereſye: for he begā to prophecye Anno 1354. in the time of Clement the ſixte, and manye of his propheces were found to come to paſſe. A certaine prieſt hauing had a bull of this Pope the ſpace of three yeares, came in the ende and did caſte it downe at the Popes feete ſayinge: Lo take your bull vnto you for it doth me no good, for the which cauſe the Pope commaūded him to be apprehended and whipped, and afterward committed to priſon.

This Pope made an holye daye for the ſpeare and hammers wherewith Chriſt was pearced and napled. He builded walles about Auenio, and foūded an houſe of Carthuſian monkes without the Citye. While he was preparing an army againſt the Turkes Anno 1362. he dyed for griefe vnderſtanding that the Romaines were at ciuill diſſentiō. There appeared ſo greate an Eclipſe of the Sunne before the death of this Pope as hath not bene ſeene. In his time alſo (ſayth Maſſeus) a certain flame brandiſhing in the ayre, after the going downe of the Sunne gaue a terrible light in the ſkie: afterward houge ſwarmes of Locuſts deſtroying and eating vp the fruites of the earth, did alſo ſeede vpon the very ſtalkes.

141. Vrban the fifte.

VRban the fift was alſo borne in Lemonia called before Grymold Griſon, ſonne of one VVilliam a Phiſition and an Engliſhman, in profeſſion hee was a Benedictine monke, and in the ende he being abſente in an Embaſſage was choſen Pope. Being therefore called to Auenio and ſaluted

The sixt booke of the

saluted Pope, he did forthwith addict his minde to maintaine the prerogatiue of the Church in couetousnes, ryot & pompe, with great diligence, vsinge herein the assistaunce of such as were proane to this purpose, especially one Giles a Spaniard whom he sent Legate in the behalfe thereof, who scoured Italye and oppressed the Vicountes, and other gouernours with great calamityes and slaughters, and compelled them al to submitte themselues for feare to the Church of Rome. Pope Vrban himselfe in the fourth yeare of his raigne cōming to Rome with his Cardinals, bestowed superstitious cost vpō idols & ruinous Churches. He couered the sculs of the Apostles (as he thought, which they had long sought for ere they could finde them, and yet missed of them also in the ende) in cofers of gould & siluer, valued at xxx. Thousand Florences, & set them in the place where they are yet seene. He repayred diuers houses of the Popes: he commaunded to preach the Crosse against the Turkes: he commaunded that the Nicene crede should be songe on S. Iohn Baptistes daye: he yelded soueraignity to the sea of Rome: he builded scholes for those that should studye Phisicke and the Decretals. Briget a woman of Sweaueland came to him to Rome, because of a vowe that she had made, and procured that there should be Religious parsons both men & women of the order of S. Briget. Afterward he returning into Fraunce, made one Iohn Hawcuth an Englishmā lieftenaunt of his army, in the steade of Giles that was dead, that he might still defende the Ecclesiastical iurisdiction vntil he should returne: for he purposed not to returne to Italye. But while he wente into Fraunce hopinge to returne to his court in Rome, Anno 1371. he dyed at Massilia, poysoned as it is thought. Sabellicus wryteth that he made great warre in Italye, yea cuē with the Princes y his auncetours had set vp against the Emperour, & he slue manye of them. In this Popes time (sayth Premonstratensis) the archbishop of Collen had a

wyfe:

Pageant of Popes. Fol.140.

wyfe. In his time also the order of the Iesuits & Scopetines orders first began, as Iohn Palionçdorus testifyeth in the third booke and second Chapter of his tripartite historye.

142. Gregorie the xi.

GRegorie the eleuenth borne in Lenomony called before Peter Belfortius, was Cardinall of newe S. Maryes and nephewe to Pope Clement, he succeded Vrban. This Gregorie (sayth Platina) was made Cardinall when hee was scante xvii. yeares old by his vncle Clement, and least he should seeme to haue more regard to his kindred then to the Church, he sent him to the best learned doctours in Italye, to be brought vp in learning, especiallye to one Baldus whoe then read the Popes decretals at Peruse, where he profited in all kinde of such learninge as Baldus coulde teache him: so much that the sayd Baldus for the assurance of his owne affayres being in daunger, vsed his auctoritye for his owne safetye. Gregorie being Pope sent a Cardinall into Italye to ouersee according to custome, the estate of the Church. But because (as Volaterain sayth) almost all the Cityes reuolted frō him (by the councell of Katherine a Nonne of Scene, which afterward became a saint, & of Baldus his scholemaster) he returned from Fraunce vnto Rome with xii. galleyes. Or (as Sabellicus saith) because that he reprouing a certaine bishop for being nonresident, was by the same bishop reproued againe, that he being the chiefe bishop did yet lye so farre and so long from the place of his Church. Anno 1376. he excommunicated out of the Church the Florentines, who were the auctours of the reuolting, and had taken to their vse al the Popes townes lying about them: and because they despised and defyed the terrour and vaine boults of his excommunication, he warred vpon them. Some other saye he returned into Italye for other causes. Masseus sayth, that one Briget a woman

S iii   returned

207

The sixt Booke of the

returned from Hierusalem to Rome, wrote to Pope Gregorie that it was the Lords pleasure that the Popes court should returne to Rome. Crantzius saith, it was because a certaine bishop did sharpelye rebuke him that he woulde leaue his Church and followe the Courte: Of whom the Pope receyued this aunsweare: And thou (quoth he) beinge Pope of Rome that ought to be an example to other, doest not returne to this bishopricke. And therefore he did againe translate his seate from Fraunce to Rome, by the perswasion of two women and one bishop, in the 70. yeare after the translation thereof. This Gregorie demaunded tenthes throughout the whole Empyre, and repayred the walles of the City and old buildings with great pompous cost. He added the eue to the holye daye of the byrth of the blessed virgin Mary. In ye time of this Pope, king Edwarde the third of Englande made many profitable lawes abridginge the Popes pilladge, vsurpation and ambition, within the Realme. Also certaine souldiours of this Pope Gregorie lyinge in a Citye called Cesenata, did not onelye take thinges as victuals and other necessaryes, refusinge to paye for it, but also did beate like slaues the Citizens, & vpon further sturre they murthered them pityfullye, sparing neyther man woman nor child though they were sucking babes, so that they filled all pittes in the Citye wyth dead karcasses, for in a fewe houres vpon one daye they slue in the Citye of all ages viii. Thousande, and then robbed & spoyled the towne, and so left it desolate & emptye. Theodoricus lib. 3. Cap. 2.

At the length Anno 1378. he dyed of extreame paine of the bladder. Euen at the houre of the Popes death the report is that ye Pallaice of Auenio was set on fyer, & coulde not be quenched till the greater part thereof were burnt. Afterwarde ensued the greatest sciesme and deuision that euer happened in the Popedome. Then (sayth Massæus) the clergye and people of Rome complayning to the Cardinals,

Pageant of Popes. Fol.141.

dinals, besought them to choose an Italian & not a French man Pope, that the Courte mighte not go into Fraunce againe. But when they began to make an election, sodenlye a controuersy began, for the Italians were but foure, and the French Cardinals were xiii. who mighte easelye haue preuayled but they durst not, for the Romaynes stoode readye in armour, and made a tumult. Therefore on Saturdaye being the ix. day of Aprill, they choose Vrban the sixt to be Pope, who was Crowned on Easter daye being the xviii. daye of the sayde moneth. Præmonstratensis sayth that in the time of this Vrban the sixte, began a newe and straung sect of bedlams both of men and womē, who used to skip and daunce against all modestye: who Anno 1375. came (sayth he) from Aquisgran into Hannonia and so into Fraunce, which might prognosticate y returne of Pope Gregorie and his Cardinals to Rome. This sect of Daūcers imagined with themselues that they daūced in riuers of bloud, but they y stoode by could perceiue no such thing. The people thought that these daūcers were euill baptized by priestes keepinge harlots, and therefore the people thoughte to haue risen against the clergye to slaye them, & to spoyle them of their goods, vnlesse God had withstoode it (sayth he) by certaine coniurations.

143. Vrban the vi.

Vrban the sixt being but a poore man and very obscure borne in Naples, called otherwyse Barthelmew and at length archbishop of Bare but neuer Cardinal, and absent (the Romaynes urging it very sore) was chosen Pope. He being chosen Pope, Iane Queene of Sicill bestowed great cost in trypumphing for ioye, and sente to him for presentes fourty thousand dukates in gould & siluer, besides wynes, victuals and other thinges, yelding also to him her kingdome and all that she had, to be at his commaundemente.

S iiii   Like-

The sixt Booke of the

Likewise her husband the noble Otto duke of Brunswick and Prince of Tarentum offered him the like curtesy. But (sayth Theodoricus of Nyem, lib. 1. cap. 7.) soue after Otto after dinner amonge many great estates and Cardinals drancke to the Pope, but Vrban was so proud that he suffered the noble Prince to kneele before him a great while, ere he would take the cup out of his hande, in so much that one of the Cardinals moued withall sayd vnto him: Most holy father, it is time for you to take the cuppe & drincke. Whereby he fulfilled the ould sayings:
Asperius misero nihil est qui surgit in altū. And againe: Corde stat inflato pauper honore dato. Claw a charle &c. But greater vnkindnes hee shewed in the ende both vnto this duke & Queene Iane his wyfe, for by his meanes Otto was taken and murthered, and Iane also committed to prison, and therein miserablye strangled to death by one duke Charles, who contrarye to his oath by procurement of this Vrban, violentlye wrested from them that had broughte him vp, $ kingdome of Sicill with their liues: for furtheraunce whereof Vrban sould the proprieties and lands of Churches and Monasteryes in Rome, beside great store of siluer and golden challecies, crosses, images and such like monuments turned into wyne, and giuen to Charles to the summe of fourescore Thousand Floreces to maintaine his warre against the foresaid Princes, in recompence whereof Charles should bestowe vpon a cowardlye wretch Francis Butillus nephewe to Vrban, the dukedomes of Capuan and Amalfitan, and manye noble Earledomes in the kingdome of Sicil.   Vrban being enstalled, warned $ clergye of their dutye, hee charged all the bishops with periurye, because they were not residētlying in the Court of Rome, and not in their bishoprickes, sayth Theodericus of Nyem, and seemed that he would purge his Court of idle parsōs. He warned the Cardinals diuers times to take heede of simonye, and to contente themselues with their porcions:

hee

be commaunded them to ryde wyth fewer horses, ẏ (quoth he) we maye euen from our hartes be a paterne to the people: and (quoth he) as touchinge that ye speake of returninge into Fraunce, ye knowe that I will continue still in Rome. Then viii. of them being Frenchmen wente first to Anagnia and afterwarde to Fundum becaufe they feared his feueritye, where they confpiring among themfelues & affirming that he was not true Pope, but violently thruſt in vp ẏ Romaynes, they chofe to themfelues another Pope the xx. day of September called Clement the feuenth, wherevpon arofe a fciefme which was more perillous and laſted longer then euer did anye, for it laſted almoſt xl. yeares. Theodoricus fayth lib.1.cap.11. that Clemēt being chofen, manye prelats, officials & courtiers, did on al fides flye to him frō Vrbā fo ẏ he was left alone almoſt, & as for thofe ẏ taryed w̄ him or reforted to him in hope of preferment, or about any fuetes, yet they mifdoubted the eſtate therof and murmured dailye, ſtill doubting what to do: which when Vrban fawe, he wept bitterlye repenting his roughe regimente the caufe of all, and to falue his fore, and to allure the fauoure of men for his owne ſtrength, hee made xxvi. newe Cardinals out of al fort of men, and gaue other offices and lyuinges franckly, by meanes wherof many begā to repayre to him from diuers places, hoping to fpeede wel in being partakers with him in this diuifion.

 Theodoricus in the 33. Chapter of his firſt booke, reporteth that Francis Butillus nephewe to this Pope Vrban, did rauiſhe a virgin being a Nunne in Naples keeping her perforce certaine dayes in his lodging: but what maruelie is it (fayth he) feinge the filthye will ſtill be filthye, for he was euer giuen to glotony, leachery, ſlouth and royat. And yet the Pope woulde not rebuke his nephewe for this villanye, but beinge told thereof and of his licencious life, he vfed to aunfweare: Tuſhe he is a yong man. And yet faith Theodoricus, Butillus was at this time fourty yeres old:

But

The sixt booke of the

But vpon this fact there was a great murmuring among the people, saying ỳ like pranke was neuer played before in Naples. And yet the Pope did not onely defende his nephewe being for it condempned to death by the kinge, but also with crackes & threates made the king glad to bestow a noble virgin of his owne bloud vpon the sayd Butillus, & threescore and tenne thousande Florences yearely, with the castle of Luceria.

This Pope Vrban (as Stella sayth) was a crafty man, & one that would remember an iniurye and seke to reuenge: Crantzius sayth he was a churlishe, cruell and vnmercifull man, who taking vpon him the Popedome, soughte not to make peace (as he should haue done) amonge Christians, but rather bent himselfe to reuēge the iniuries of his Cardinals and of Iane Queene of Sicill, and therefore to make the Florentines to take his part, he absolued them from ỳ excommunication of Pope Gregorie, and sent Iohn Hawcuth an Englishmā captaine of them against the Queene. Furthermore he being of nature giuen to wrāgling, strife, & cruelty, creating certaine new Cardinals at Nuceria, he cast vii. of ỳ old Cardinals into prison because they had cōspired with Clement the seuenth against him: and fiue of those vii. he layde vpon great stones, and in despite of Clement drowned them, which kinde of death also one Adam an Englishman being a Cardinal did hardly escape at the same time. And of those newe Cardinals being xxix. they were all Neapolitans and his cosens, sauing three. This Pope proclaymed warre against Charles of Hūgary king of Naples, because he woulde not make a nephewe of his Prince of Campania: he gouerned the Church with all tyrannye that might be, and to shewe his rigorous rage more openlye, thus wryteth his friende Platina of him: Vrban (sayth he) being deliuered from the terrour of Fraunce & gone to Naples, desireth the king to make his nephew king of Campania, which whē he could not obtaine, this fellow

vnder

vnder pretēce of a iust and honest man, being one whom no man neither loued nor liked, began forthwith to threat and crake the king, whereby he so offended the kinge that for a while he commited him to the charge of certaine parsons, and suffered him not to come abroade. But the Pope dissembling his malice for the time, departing with ye kings good will to Nuceria (because of the heate of the weather as he fayned) and fortifying the Citye sufficientlye, he doth both make newe Cardinals and imprysoneth seuen of the olde, because as he sayde they had conspired with the king and Pope Clement against him. Furthermore he sente out a processe against the king, and a citacion accordinge to the custome: the kinge aunsweared that he would shortlye come to Nuceria, and aunsweare his accusations both by word and by sword. So he came to Nuceria with a greate army and besieged the Citye, Ramond Balsian being moued with this discurtesye, beinge Prince of Tarent presuming of his power, and conueying Vrban wt all his Court to the next shoore, he put them into three Galleyes of Genewaies prouided for that purpose: wherby while the Pope is transported to Genua, he drowned fiue Cardinals fastened to rockes, of those seuen which he toke at Nuceria. Furthermore in the yere after the death of Charles, he passed to Ferentine (to see Naples as he sayde) but in deede of this minde, to depriue of their inheritaunce ye yonge Princes Ladislaus & Iohn being but a child, ye sonnes of Charles. This Vrban graunted to the sect of begging fryers, that they might chaunge theyr vowes to commit another vnhonest act, and challenge as it were to restore to righte vnlawfull goodes being in controuersy. He dyed in Rome Anno 1390. poysoned as some thincke, after he had misgouerned the Popedome x. yeares, and fewe or none were sorye of his death. The yeare before his death his Mule fel vnder him as he was rydinge, wherewithall he was sore hurt and brosed, so as he did neuer recouer it til his death:

he be-

The sixt booke of the

he being dead, his nephewe Frauncis was thrust from all his lyuing, and came to Rome poore and despised no man shewing him good countenance, according to ye old saying:

Cum moritur præsul, cognatio tota fit exul.

When as a prelate goes awaye,
then all the kindred do decaye.

And so this Francis with sorrowe and anguishe forsooke Rome at length and went to Sicill. This same yeare (sayth Funcius) this couetous miser Vrban brought vp the yeare of Iubelye, because he sawe it would proue gainefull to him and to the Romaynes. He also appointed annuities to be payed out of priestes landes, vnder pretence of waginge an armye against the Paganes: the Englishmen withstanding this constitution, calling a Parliamente did decree ye the Pope should haue no iurisdiction beyonde the limites of the Ocian Sea: but the bishops & prelats like traytours to their countrey, did take vpon them afterward to paye ye pention.

It would aske a great volume to touche euery vilanous practise of this Pope Vrban. Certaine comming to meete him on a time did first kisse the ground three times, & then his feete with al humility. He had giuen him by a certaine Ladye, a precious Miter and certaine garments valued at more then xx. Thousand Florences. He caused a Cardinal in one daye to depose, to racke, to tormente, to spoile & imprison, all the prelates of Sicilia, because they did not mauger their Prince assist him against Clement, and made in their steede 32. newe bishops and archbishops: and (sayth Theodoricus) there was not a clarke in al Naples so doltishe and beggerly, but that he was made eyther a bishop, archbishop, abbot, prior, or some prelate, if he woulde take it vppon him to take part with Vrban. He vsed the seruice of Charles king of Sicill on a time going before him as his vssher, and bearinge the Popes target following with his armye into a towne called Auersa. He put sixe Cardinals

in a

Pageant of Popes. Fol.144

in a dongion with their feete set in the stockes, and caused them to be myserably tormented and racked, onlye for suspition of falsehoode against him, and so kept them in prison where they pined through famine, thirst and cold, hauinge also wormes and lise breedinge in their bodyes: & yet they stoode stoutly in their innocencye. But no humble and importunate sute neither of them nor anye other, coulde euer moue ẏ stonye hart of Vrban to pitye their cases, but (saith Theodoricus) the more he was entreated the more wrathfull he was, so that his eyes would sparkle, his face burne and glow, his throte waxe dry for anger. And after sondry examinations he sent vnto them againe Theodoricus (the wryter of this historye) & other to examine them in a vaute of the castle where they laye, then (sayth Theodoricus) the Cardinall of Sanger was first broughte vp vnto vs, with a paire of iron shakles on his feete and a short mantel about him, because it was a colde and windy prison. Who when he came to the ende of the cellar and sawe aboue him ẏ roapes hanging wherewith he should be racked, and was by ẏ wayters striped out of his apparell, leauing him scarcelye his shirt on, and bound very hard to the racke, Fraunces ẏ Popes nephewe stoode by and laughed at this miserable sight without all measure: but I that loued this Cardinal of ould was sorelgreeued thereat, but I could not departe the place. But to be short, the said Cardinall was an aged man of a corpulent bodye, comlye and taule of stature, and being bounde he was thrise lifted from the grounde by the stronge pulling of those that racked him, so that he waxed verye feble, which when I behelde, when hee was let go to the grounde againe I said to him softly: O deare father do you not see how your bloud is sought for: I beseech you for Gods cause confesse something to deliuer your selues for this time from these tormentours? He aunswered, I cannot tell what I shal say. And when they would haue racked him againe, I bad them cease for he hath satisfyed

mee

The sixt booke of the

mee as I wil certifye the Pope in wrytinge, & so they losed him & caryed him out to take ayre: who comming to himselfe said vnto vs heauilye. Behould my brethren the time hath beene as ye know, that I liued in the pompe and royaltye of this world, but now I am become a moste myserable captife and despised wretch. And I woulde to God this were graunted to me as a singuler benefite, that I hauing nothinge might begge my breade from place to place: but out alas, this trouble & sorrow are iustly by Gods iudgemēt fallen vpon me, because euen in this kingdom of Sicil I was so cruel an executour of the Popes cōmaundemēt, in deposing without fauour the archbishops, bishops, abbots, and other of the clergye without respect of age or degree, hoping herein to haue pleased his minde. The next daye after this Pope Vrban called vnto him one Basilius to be chiefe tormentour of these Cardinals, which liked him verye well for hee was a malicious man and hated the clergye naturallye, and was a persecutour of God and his seruauntes, a notable pirate, and a plaguer of Christians whom he vsed to take captiue from his youth: at the first he lyued by theft and robbery, but when that fayled and he became a begger, he sought succour of Pope Vrban, who not for deuotion but to obtaine a priorship of an hospital in Tinacria made him a fryer. To this fellowe, Vrban gaue charge to torment on the next day, ye Cardinal of Venice, and to continue rackinge him vntill such time as Vrban himselfe might heare him crye for paine: So when Basilius and we came to the prison wher the Cardinal of Venice was, Basilius taking him out & bringing him to a certaine hall in the Castle did stripe of his apparell, and hauinge the roapes fastened aloft & hanging downe to the ground he tyed him hard to them. And although ye Cardinall were an ould man, broke and diseased, and weake of complexiō, yet he tormented him vppon the racke most cruellye from morninge till dinner time continuallye, but the sillye man

euer

Pageant of Popes. Fol.145

euer as he was haled vp cryed stil & saide: Christ hath suffered for vs, &c. In the meane time Pope Vrban walked in a garden belowe, and read on a booke so loude that wee mighte heare him, which he did to this ende that Basilius might the better loke to his charge to plong the Cardinal the more. But as for me (sayth Theodoricus) I could abide this wofull sight no longer, and therefore dissembling my selfe to be sicke I gat leaue to departe. And in like maner was the other Cardinals vsed afterward. Finally Vrbā remouing from Naples commaunded that these Cardinals and their fellow prisoner the bishop of Aquilo, should followe him, and ride next after him, assigninge to euerye one his garde to keepe them that they should not escape by the waye. But the bishop partly because he roade vpon a iade, partly because his bodye was yet after his racking so sore and feeble that he was not able to endure fast riding, but as the Pope galloped he came lagging after as fast as he might. And yet the Pope thinking that he lingred to haue stollen awaye, in a greate rage commaunded his villaines to kil him, and so they slew him mangling him with many woundes, and left his dead carkasse vnburied in the waye. Afterward at the sute of king Richard of England, Pope Vrban did partly release to the custody of a certaine priest one of the Cardinals called Adam Cardinal of Sicil: but he toke from him all that euer he had, and left him in case of a vagabounde till Boniface his successour restored him. But as for the other fiue he kept miserablye in prison in an abbey in a towne of Ianua, being next to þ Church where he laye: and if that he saw any man resort to that Church at extraordinary howers, he thought that he resorted thether to deliuer the Cardinals by stealth: and therefore he committed to prison & tormēted many of his owne Court onlye vpon suspition therof. And notwithstāding þ duke & citizēs of Ianua sued for those prisoners, yet he wold neuer shew them any mercy, but in the end caused them to be put

to

The sixt booke of the

to death, as some saye beheaded, other saye drowned, but how soeuer it were sure it is they perished. Furthermore Charles king of Sicil being at variaunce with Vrban, and hauing his nephew Fraūcis prisoner dyed at length. Then came Margaret the wyfe of the said Charles, humbly suing to Vrban to be gracious to her and to her children, and to graunt that her husbands body might be buryed, in which sute manye nobles of Florence and other Cityes ioyned with her, and yet his hard hart woulde nothing pittye her sute, nor graunt her so much as a graue for the king her husbād, thoughe she had freely released his nephewe to him, yet he added processe to processe, and heaped condemnation vpon condemnation against her and her poore children, because he did from his harte detest the name of the saide Charles. Thus reporteth Theodoricus word for word as he is alledged, whoe beinge Secretarye to Pope Vrban wrote that which he sawe with a sorrowfull hart. The cause whye that the Pope did dispatche those Cardinals was this: he was sodenlye forced to remoue from one place to another, and therefore thinking that those Cardinals if he shoulde carye them with him would hinder and comber him on the one side, & on the other side he was loath to leaue them behind least they should escape, and therfore flying from Nuceria to Ienua (as is sayd) it is thought that by the way he tyed them fast to the rockes, & so left them to be drowned. It is sayd that this yeare one Bertholdus Swart or otherwise Schuuartz an Alchymist and a monke, in the North parte of Germanye deuised first and contryued Gunnes to the spoyle of mankinde.

144. Clement the 7.

209 Clement the seuenth was a Frenchman, and by byrth Earle of Gebenny called in time past Robert, he being first a Cardinal was made Pope by the Cardinals. These
Cardi-

Pageant of Popes. Fol.146

Cardinals after the third month of the election of Vrban, perceyuinge howe he was giuen to tyrannye, and that he would not returne into Fraunce, they stale away & fledde from Rome to Fundus. But first they besoughte him to giue them lycence with his fauours to go to Anagnia, to chaunge the ayre for the Soimmer time, but they fearinge his melancholy mode and franticke fits, went away. These Cardinals were gotten together Iohn Preuestin, VVilliam of S. Steuens in Cœli hill, Bertrandus of S. Cicill, Robert aforesaide, Hugh of the 4. holye Crownes, Gui of the holye Crosse in Hierusalem, Iohn of S. Marcellus, Peter of S. Laurencis in Lucine, Gerard of S. Clements, Peter of S. Eustace, VVilliam of S. Angell, Peter of S. Maryes immaculate, and Peter of S. Maryes of Cosmidin. These sayth Platina did pilfer out the treasure of the Church at the death of the Pope, and did euerye thinge as liked them best. Who as sone as they fled to Fundus, rayled vpon Vrban as an vsurper of the Popedome, saying y he was creat perforce, and perforce receyued the Crowne of the Popeship, because that election was made for feare in a place of great daunger, in y which men ought to haue had libertye to do and speake their minds francke & free, and yet they were compelled by the people contrarywise, to chuse rather an Italian then a Frenchman. For these causes (they saide) the seate being voyde and Iane Queene of Sicill fauouring their purpose, they choose the foresaid Robert to be Pope, and called him Clement the seuenth. Because (sayth Theodoricus) they knew him to be ambitious, nedye and yet very prodigall, of a large cōscience but of noble birth, well befrended and of great power, hauing a strong troupe wayting vpon him: whereby (sayth he lib. 1.cap.10.) it may be iudged that this election proceded not of the holye ghost nor of good consciences. Hereuppon arose a greate discorde amonge Christian Churches, while some Princes fauoured Pope Vrban, some fauoured Pope

T. Clement,

The sixt Booke of the

Clement, and some there were that medled with neyther of them, and they were called neuters. Clement goinge to Auenio was worshipped of the Spaniards & Frenchmen, who did welcom him thether. He continued fiftene yeares making diuers lawes, whom beside the French king, the kinge of Aragon, of Castile & Nauar obeyed. In the meane time a councell was held at Paris to take vp the strife for the Popedome, which councell yelded to Clement as Tillius wryteth. In his time aboute the yeare 1387. arose a controuersy betweene the students of Paris and the Dominick fryers, concerning the conception of the virgin Mary. Pope Clement dyed Anno 1392. being buried at Auenio. These two Popes scattered about y worlde in diuers quarters their terrible and fearefull bulles, and spread abrode rayling bookes full of infamye, and defacing, backbytinge and excommunicating one another, calling each other so sharpe despite and bitter reproche, Antichriste, scismatick, heretick, tyrant, theefe, traytour, vniust, wicked sower of darnel in Gods Haruest, and the cursed sonne of Beliall. Iohn of Lignia doctour of both Lawes, set out a booke in the behalfe of Vrban, and the abbot of S. Vedast councellour to the French kinge, did publishe another for Clemēt against Vrban.

Amonge other broyles wrought betweene these 2. fyrebrands, it shal be sufficient to declare but some of the least, Theodoricus lib 1. cap. 14. sayth, that Clement with his Cardinals beinge in Campania, sente for their Captayne Bernard de Cazala with other men of warre oute of Gascony and Britany, who should passe ouer a certaine bridge vpon Tiber nighe Rome, but they that kept the bridge withstoode them, whereupon all the Citye was in an vproxe, & many ran out disordered to defend the bridge against Bernard and his Bryttaines who entred perforce, and in this conflict there were slaine as some thincke 8. hundred Romaynes, and the rest beaten backe into the Cittye, wherof
arose

arose great howling, crying, & lamenting through Rome. But ye Romaynes to reuenge themselues, fel vpon al such as mighte seeme in the Citye to fauour Pope Clement, as al those that were borne beyonde the Alpes, both Frenchmen and Spaniards that were weake and vnweaponed in the Citye: they spared neither man, womā nor childe, parson nor degree, some they murthered, some they chained in prison, the women they vsed vilanouslye without al shame, bishops and noble men they spoyled, robbed and long imprysoned with great misery: This hurly burly continued long. Yea I saw then (sayth Theodoricus) certaine matrones of Rome desirous to enflame the Romaine Citizēs against the courtiers & strangers, to iustle them ruffiantly in the streates, and without al honestye to spit and slauer in the faces of the courtiers both of men and women. But while the freinds of Pope Vrban did thus within the Citye molest the freindes of Clement, a certaine Frenchman being Captaine of Angel Castel, and keeping it to the vse of his countryman Clement and his Cardinals: did leuel a certaine engine out of the Castle against ye Citye, discharging and shooting arrowes & pellets violently into Rome amongē the Romaines and courtiers, and with this shotte he ouerthrew, shooke downe and fyred many houses. Thus was the Citye in a miserable broyle, and in these tumults were slaine diuers noble men. Iohn Vrsine, Rainolde his brother and one Honoratus, with Angelus lieutenant of Rome & diuers other estates, kept vp in armes in the quarell of Clement assaulting ye Citye round about: Rainold layde siege against it at S. Agnes gate a whole mouth, so ye the Romaynes were robbed of their cattell, and durst not peepe out of the Citye to followe their husbandrye during this storme. Whereupon Charles the Emperour and Lewis kinge of Hungary at the humble sute of Pope Vrban, sent to Clement their Embassadours, desiring him to yeld vp his Papacy for the ending of these sturres tending to ye

T ii   ruine

The sixt booke of the

ruine of the Church and Christian estate: but Pope Clement and his Cardinals in steede of reasonable answeares vsed the Legates vilanously, keeping some of them in pryson, some they racked cruelly, and by this meanes all christendome was deuided, some (as Almany, Bohemia, Thuscia, Lombardy, England, Polony, Denmarke, Sweueland, Norwaie, Prusia, Frizland, with diuers other countryes) toke part with Vrban: and likewise many countryes with Clement. Vrban made Charles king of Sicil, and Clement set vp Lewes of Andegana against him for it, to the spoyle of much bloud. Manye other notable histories are written of this Clement, which for tediousnesse are ouerpassed, onely I note that which Theodoricus sayth, that he being Cardinall vnder Gregorie the ri. was cause of the destruction and lametable spoyling of the Citye Cesanate, hauing charge of the souldiours that did it as is shewed in the said Gregorie. Also at the same time he sould the Citye Vercels vnto a couple of tyrants, to the great confusion of the same Citye in like maner, but those tyrants Galeatius and Barnabonis hauing ful possession thereof, robbed this Cardinal againe of all the treasure which they had payde him. But when he sate in the Papacye he was so prodigall in spendinge the Church goodes, that he graunted to euerye man especiallye noble men, large pentions, farmes & landes at an easye rent.

145. Boniface the ix.

BOniface the ix. borne in Naples, was first called Peter Thomacell being but a yonker scant rr. yeares old, but a toughe and sturdy fellow, he was made Pope by consent of those Cardinals y remayned in Rome. Theodoricus sayth that he could neyther write nor singe, and that when he was chosen he knewe not what belonged to the greate charge of the Papacye, and when supplications were offered him, he handled them so vntowardly as if he had neuer
beene

beene brought vp in the Court of Rome, neyther could he
vnderstand the contentes thereof. When any aduocates
during his gouernment moued any matter debated in his
consistorye, he neuer vnderstoode them, but woulde bolte
out an vndiscrete aunsweare to their demaundes. At the
first during the liues of certaine good Cardinals he durste
not openlye commit simonye, thoughe priuilye he vsed his
brokers therein: but they being dead after vii. yeares he v-
sed it openly. First he toke the first fruictes of all abbeyes
and great Churches voyde, and ere the lyuing were bestowed the money must be payed: pea often he was heard to
wishe, that the money being payed the party might not enioy it, that he might be payd new first fruictes againe by a
nother. This was the chiefest of those xxvi. Neapolitans,
whō beinge of his alleance Pope Vrban made Cardinals
at Nuceria: who (as Crantzius sayth) beinge confirmed &
established, did forthwith confirme those thinges which Vrban had decreed touching the Iubely to be kept euery xiii.
yeare, the feast of the visitation of the virgin Mary, and indulgences & pardons for the worshipping of Christes bodye. But by his couetousnes and simonye, because al benefices were sould for moneye, vsurye waxed so rancke in
Rome, that it was counted no sinne (sayth Theodoricus)
in his time: yea oftentimes vsurye was required openlye,
euen in the presence of the iudges and officials. And a-
gaine there was no sute made to the Pope for anye matter, but that brybes must be giuen for speakinge. The fifte
daye of Nouember in the first yeare of his raigne, hee, his
Secretaryes, and his chamberlaynes set benefices to sale
so impudently, offering and trying who would giue most,
so that al men laughed it to scorne. At which time he gaue
vnder seale any benefice where soeuer, were it in his disposition or no, his gift to take place vpō ye death of the incum-
bente: and this kinde of sale lasted longe in the Courte of
Rome, so that many poachers ran vp and downe ye countrye to espye where were any olde or sicke prelate, & there-

T iii   vpon

The sixt booke of the

vpon poasted to Rome to purchase a graunt of his lyuinge so that sometime the Pope sould one benefice to diuers parties, and vsed to set downe in the dating of it that the secōd third or the fourth graunt should stande aboue and before the rest: and therefore after diuers grauntes of one benefice yet some purchased one after al with this clause, to defeate the rest notwithstanding al former or after graunts, and for more assurance the last should be antedated. Thus the Pope played pollage so long till all men being weary of his mockery, his market decayed.

A thousande other practises were put in vre by him and his clergye as appeareth at large in Theodoricus, and yet because the Pope did it, is was no sinne, for so they sayd generallye. He sent abroad his collectours into diuers countryes with pardons, who thereby purloyned great treasures from the simple people, so that they brought oute of some one prouince an hundred thousand Florences: but the Pope calling these his officers to accompte, and findinge that some of them defrauded him, he put them in pryson, some he put to death, some murthered themselues, some were hewed in peeces by the people for their cruell exactions. When these and the former shiftes waxed stale, then the Pope and his complices deuised newe. They made newe grauntes of benefices which did disanull all the olde: but they were very deare, for they were sould for fifty dukates a peece, and they to whom the Pope graunted them, sould them with condicion that the sellar should haue porcion of the commoditye. And if one man had a benefice graunted him & the graunte were written and sealed, yet if another came in the deede doinge ere it were deliuered and woulde giue more, the former seale was broken, the wrytinge cancelled, and the graunte voyde, and so as often as the price was enhaunsed, the gift was chaunged: yea they that made the former offers were rayled on, and rebuked bitterly by Boniface, charging them that they went about to beguile

him in

him in bargayning, offering not so much as ye benefice was worth. At this time a contagious plague raigned in Rome wherof men dyed so fast, that (sayth Theodoricus) I haue seene one benefice sould to many men in one werke, euery one paying the price for it and dying immediatly, another came by and by and gaue money for it, and so he dying ye third did likewise. Then might a doult get a lyuinge better cheape then a learned man, for the Pope beinge ignorant loued those best that were likest to himselfe. Whē money wanted, yet rather then Boniface woulde leese his market, he was contente to take other stuffe, as hogges, horses, graine, wheat, neate, sheepe or any thing els. Thus were al the Popes courtiers become bargainers, brokers, vsurers and simonistes: and he that could deuise the most crafty shiftes, was counted wysest & most esteemed. Some hauing then a graunt to take for himselfe perhaps ii. iii. or iiii. of the benefices that he could espye next voyde, woulde by meanes of this commission cease vpon xx. and keepe the commoditye of them in his handes: they that vsed these shiftes were the Popes auditours, & by this meanes they disapointed other men that had the like grauntes, and thus they might do with pretence of law, because they had prerogatiues being chaplaines and officers vnto Pope Boniface. Wherevpon arose manye suetes and controuersyes in law, so that the clients being wōderfully encreased in nomber, the proctours and lawyers would not plead but haue vnreasonable fees. The Pope also for euery seale that hee graunted had his fee of al men except his Cardinals: thus was Rome on all sydes fleeced, filched and strayd. And yet in all this simony and briberye, euerye one that receiued a benefice had an oath ministred to him that he came by it without any vnlawfull conditions of bying or sellinge. Afterward the said Boniface decreed that euerye archbishop, bishop, abbot or such like, if within a yeare after the receyuing of his lyuing he had not fully satisfyed ye Popes trea-

T iiii   surye,

The sixt Booke of the

surpe, the lyuing to be voyde immediatly: and in this snare many prelates of all degrees was sodenly trapped, so that of archbishops, bishops and abbots they became my Lords quondam, & of rich men, beggers. Many fugitiue friers, hedge priestes, roages, rascals, verlets and pesaunts seing this, ranne thicke to the Popes court offering themselues to serue him as his slaues, on whõ he bestowed ÿ lyuinges whereof other were depriued: so that some ÿ to daye were ruffians, beggers & lackeyes, as to morrowe were become bishops, archbishops, abbots and priors: thus on all sides the miser Boniface made a miserable clergy for greedines of money. Beside this many monkes and fryers did purchase licence of him to dwel aloofe oute of their religious houses and cloisters: priestes boughte lycences to haue as many beneficees and dignities as they could get, to sel their olde and to buye newe, and to be nonresident at their pleasure. Neither (sayth Theodoricus) could any thing be demaunded so vniust and absurde, but for money it might be gotten. And as Boniface did, so his couetous mother and two of his brethren beinge in his court with him, obtained grauntes of him at their pleasure, and sould them for double the price. If any noble men came to ÿ court with fayre horses, then the mother and her sonnes woulde be sure to haue them or the most part of them: for no man durst deny them any thing that they craued. This Boniface had also a sister whom he gaue in mariage to the Earle of S. Flauiã, and made him Duke of Adria, geuinge him w his sister 17. Thousand Florences, but at length the said duke in a fraye slue her with a knife, for the which ÿ duke was afterwarde trayterouslye murthered. Manye tumults were made & procured by this Boniface in diuers places, and especially one bloudye sedition which lasted longe in Peruse. Also he entertayned very curteously a certaine abbot, who to gratifye him had murthered Beordus goueruour of Peruse in his bedde chamber, suffering him vpon especial good will

and

and amitye to come into him. In the ri. yere of this Boniface one Nicolas de Columna made a conspiracye to haue come in the nighte vpon the saide Pope, to haue depriued him of his temporall iurisdiction, but hee geuinge the attempt and cominge with his men in armour to the Popes gate, was yet disapointed and fled: but the next daye xxxi. of his seruauntes that by commaundemente wayted vpon him were apprehended, and though one worde of the Popes mouth mighe haue saued their liues, yet they were all hanged but one, who being but a striplin for wãt of an hangmã was promised pardon if he would hang the rest: who pausing thereat a while (because his owne father and brother were of the same companye) did yet at the last for sauinge of his owne life do the execution both on his father, brother and the rest, weeping tenderlye at this hard hap. And yet he also should afterwarde haue beene hanged, but at ye people moued with compassion, sued for his life.

This Boniface recepued to fauour maister Adam an Englishe Cardinal being skilfull in the Hebrew tongue. He banished vtterlye the Earle of Fundus, who at the first procured the discord. He raigned ouer the Romaynes not like a bishop, but like a saluage tyrant Nero or Caligula. He suspectinge diuers Romaynes of treason against him, did cause them to be put to death. He repayred and fortifyed ye Pallaice Vatican, the Capitol Angell Castel. There was neuer Pope that bare such rough sway ouer the Romaynes sayth Crantzius. He had no learning, but coueted to encrease the pompe of his estate, and therfore deuised a lawe whereby he purloyned the soueraintye of the world, that is, that it should not be lawfull for anye of the clergye to enter on a benefice which he shoulde obtaine, vnlesse he payed the first fruites to the Apostolicall excheaker or the Popes Chamber. He put downe the Banderesians a noble estate amonge the Romaynes: also he compelled the Romaynes by a cruell lawe, to fetch home their forreine Senatour

The sixt booke of the

natour Malatesta of Pisauria: He strengthened the Citye for his owne purpose with fortresses and bulwarkes: but making warres with the Vicountes he loste Bonome. he caused Ladislaus a yong gentleman sonne to Charles king of Naples, to be Crowned kinge in his fathers Realme by the Cardinall of Florence: whereupon Sigismunde kinge of Hungary thinkinge himselfe greatlye iniuried, greate warres ensued to the myserable slaughter of Thousandes, burning and spoyling of Cittyes, townes, monasteryes & castels in Hungarye: So great a thing it is to dispossesse a kinge. Boniface also canonized S. Brigit borne in Sweueland. He gaue to his cosens and kinred the aduauntage and commoditye of the Iubelye: He offended and sinned much in parcialitye, and because he subscribed & graunted certaine abhominable indulgences and pardōs, he ran into great infamye. He kept the Iubelye at Rome Anno 1400. where manye straungers were robbed, and greate Ladyes rauished by the pezantes of the Popes courte. Finallye Anno 1404. he dyed of the collicke and stone. The Summer before that Boniface dyed, there happened horrible tempestes, boisterous windes, hayle, thonder & lighteninges. And in the night a certaine house (new builded by Boniface) of square stone very costlye (wherein for the time he used to blesse the people) had ye roofe of it blowen downe by the violence of the storme, and the timber hurled to the earth. Also the strong pinacles of Angell castle were throwne to the groundz with much other mischiefe and ruine. Also another night appeared such terrible and vehemente lightning and thonder all night long, that all men beinge in a desperate feare, thought surely the Citye woulde haue beene ouerwhelmed withal. Another time also there was in Rome an earthquake, which though it did no hurt yet it amazed al men. Theodoricus lib. 2. cap. 33.

This Pope rooted out a superstitious sect called Albes, and burnt a priest of them, who came with a great traine of

that

that sect both men and women downe from the Alpes into Italy: for Boniface seing him come thus with his companye all in white (for y which cause they were called Albes) was afraid as some write, least his Popeship should be taken from him by the said priest. But some (sayth Platina) say that the man did purpose no harme, but that the Pope did imagine this to put away the rumour that went, how the priest was for spite and mallice taken and put to death.

146. Benedict the xiij.

BEnedict the xiij. was a Catalan borne and called Peter of the Moone: this man euen in the time of the sciesme duringe was chosen Pope to succede Clement by those Cardinals which continued at Auenio. This fellow while he was but Peter of y Moone & not Benedict Pope of Rome, did dispute against the auctoritye of the Pope and of his clergye, and said that it was not to be feared: and for this his true saying notwithstäding he became Pope, yet afterward he was and is still condemned by his successours for an hereticke. While he was but Cardinall being sente by Pope Clement Embassadour to Paris and other places, he vsed often to boast that if he might be chosen to succede Clement, he would spare no meanes to procure that this longe sciesme mighte cease. And therefore the Cardinals abused with his great protestations, did chose him in deede to succeede the other, but before the election they sware all and he among them, y whosoeuer shoulde be chosen Pope should be cötent at any time to resigne & giue it vp againe, if the Cardinals thinkinge it meete would require it. But afterward whë it came to tryal, he defying his oath would not yeld one iote, no though y Cardinals & diuers Princes did exhorte him to it, and chargde him with his oath: and councels conclude against him that he was no Pope. But certaine estates of Fraunce moued with his troublesome
obstinacy

211.

The sixt booke of the

obstinacy, did set vpon him by force of armes: toke him prisoner and kepte him so three yeares, and yet could not make him giue ouer, but that he would first dye ere he would deminishe his dignitye: so that they being wearye of him, deliuered him againe at the end of the three yeares.

By his lawes it appeareth that being Pope he woulde that euen the wronge sentence of condemnation vttered by him and his sonnes shoulde be feared. Hee aboue in his place (sayth Crantzius) till the time of the councell of Constance, and he swarued much in the auctorizinge of it: finally he began to be harbned being cast of in that coūcell. He continued in his obstinacye with his Cardinals, who also after his death endeuoured to continue and maintaine this strife by putting vp another to be Pope, but they were forbidden. Amonge other thinges this Pope gaue to the kinge of Fraunce (Charles the vi.) the tenthes of y Church, partly to bye the kinge to maintaine him in his quarel, partly that he might take part of this great lucre, and (sayth Theodoricus) he sawe it stoode him vpon. He at length followed Boniface his practise in bestowing benefices, geuing dispensatiōs, tolleratiōs, exemptiōs, totquots, pardōs and such like enormityes, according to the saying: If thou sawest a theefe run thou diddest run vvith him. This he did to allure men from the obedience of Boniface to himselfe, y better to maintaine his quarrel against him. Whē this Pope Benedict aboue & plated himselfe stronglye in his countrye, and auouched that he himselfe was y true vicar of Christe, he was shamefullye reproued by the auctoritye of the said general councell. And yet he sommoned and helde a Synode in Perpinian, and created manye Cardinals. At the length he dyinge at Pẽniscula Anno 1424. commaunded these his Cardinals to choose another in his steede forthwith: and they forthwith choose Giles Munyos canon of Barchynony, calling him Clement the eight, who out of hand at the motion of kinge Olphonsus

did

Pageant of Popes. Fol.152.

did both create newe Cardinals, and toke vppon him to do those thinges that appertayned to the Pope. But when Pope Martin the fift came in fauoure with kinge Olphōsus, this Giles at his commaundement yelded vppe all the righte and estate of the Popedome being appointed bishop of Maiory : and in like maner they whom hee had made Cardinals, did likewyse giue ouer their Cardinalship.

147. Innocent the seuenth.

Innocent the seuenth was borne at Sulmo & called Cosmarus of Peruse: he being Cardinal of the holy Crosse, while all Italye was in an vprore he was made Pope to succede Boniface 9. Whil̄e this Innocēt was but Cardinal (as Plat. sayth) he purposed to reproue hoastardlines & negligence of the former Popes, saying yͭ theyr sloath was the cause yͭ the scisme of xl. yeares in the Church of Rome and the destructiō of the common wealth was not redressed. But he hauing gotten the Popedome, and following the fashions of Boniface & Vrban in diuers things (which beinge but a Cardinall he had reproued) he did not onelye that which in other hee had so much condemned, but also would be highly offended if anye man should haue mentioned it vnto him. He gouerned all thinges so disorderly, yͭ when the Romaynes requyred to haue the Capitoll, theyr libertye, light brydge, and Adrian castel to be restorde vnto them, and were verye earnest that he should take awaye this daungerous deuision in yͤ Church, pacify the warres, and qualify the seditions, whereunto the French king promised his ayde, & Peter Moone denyed not to take peace: then the Pope sente the Romaynes to Lewis his nephewe (dwelling in the hospital called the holy ghostes hospital) as to an vangird for the purpose, who forthwith murthered xi. of the Citizens, which came to procure redresse for theyr countrye, which by the maliciousnes and negligence

of the

The sixt booke of the

of the Pope was broughte almost to confusion. The saide Lewis first stripped them naked, then he murthered them, and last of all threw them gasping for breath out at a windowe sayinge: We cannot cast out sedition by anye other meanes then this, Where their bodies lay mangled in the streates till it was night. By the which crueltye the Romaynes being much enraged seeking assistance of Ladislaus king of Apulia, they range a larum bell and put themselues in armour, to reuenge the villany vpon Lewis. But the Pope to shonne the furye of the people fledde in all post hast with his nephew the murtherer to Viterbium, in the extreame heate of the daye, so that he and some Cardinals that fled wyth him being sore heated were almost choaked and dead for wante of drincke, but xxx. of his companye perished out right. Also one of the pezantes killed the abbot of Peruse by the way hard beside the Pope, & another pezant killed one of the court for greedines of a pot of drincke before the Popes face: and all theyr bodies that dyed by ye waye were left vnburyed. Also after the Pope was come to Viterbium, many of his court dyed with drinkinge sodenlye cold wyne. Then the people for anger that they could not ease theyr stomackes vpon the woorkers of this treacherye, turned their rage vpon the courtiers, whose goodes for the most part was spoyled and taken away, but some courtiers by report were saued in Cardinals houses. Afterwarde they hauinge taken the Capitoll and wonne Right bridge, attempting in baine to assault Adriā castel. In this broyle Iohn Columna Earle of Troye, and other noble Captaynes of great bands, wyth Ladislaus his furtheraunce, ioyned wyth the Romaynes. And hereof arose a bloudy conflict ioyned wyth much villanye (sayth Theodoricus) betweene the Guelphes and Gibelines, these fightinge for the Citye, the other ioyned wyth the Vrsines for the Clergye lasted many dayes in the Citye w^t murther, rauishing of womē, robbing & spoyling w^tout cōtrolmēt.

Manye

Many Cardinals were vsed vnreuerently, taken & led to ye Capitoll and there beaten wt coodgels, some prelates had their garments torne of their backes and lay long in cruel prison, the Popes treasury was robbed and pilfred, many of his bulls and pardons with other such wrytinges were rente and torne. And (sayth Theodoricus) who can tell all the vile touches vsed in the Citye. The pictures of Pope Innocent were in al places daubed with durt and greater despites doone against him. But in the ende all thinges being appeased, because it was thought that Innocentius much misliked this murther done by his nephew as he dissembled it, the Pope returned to Rome and choose more Cardinals, among whom were Angel Corrarius a Venetian, Peter Philargus borne in Candy, and Otho Columna a noble Romaine. He hauing thus fortifyed his Popeship, created his bloudye nephewe Lewis Marques of Picene, and also appointed him afterward Prince of Firma. He commaunding the halfe of Ecclesiasticall liuinges both In Fraunce and England, toke the foyle in this matter for it was denyed him (sayth Gaguinus) after the which hee liued not longe but dyed Anno 1407. at Rome. Theoricus sheweth how ye whē these sturres were hot in Rome, on a nighte in Augusте such tempestes happened that two Nunnes standinge together, were slaine wyth a flashe of lightninge, and others houses, walles and towers were beaten downe. Also he reporteth ye this Innocentius refusing contrary to his oath at his election, to come to agreement with Peter Moone (the other Pope ye stoode against him) was straungelye touched by the hand of God ye same time: for hauing hyred his freindes to be a meanes that he shoulde neuer be more moued to giue vp his estate, he was sodeinly taken wyth a straunge Palsey in the face, all men saying it was Gods iudgement for his dissembling. But he was recouered of this ere he returned to Rome.

148. Gregorie

The sixt booke of the

148. Gregorie the xij.

GRegorie ý xij. a Venetian borne was first called Angel Corrarius, he being Patriarke of Constantinople, and S. Markes Cardinall was chosen to succeede Innocent. But hee was chosen at Rome vpon this condition, that if it should be needefull for ý behoofe of the Church he should depose himselfe of his Popeship, because that Benedict the xiii called Peter Moone, who at Auenio was chose to succeede Clement the vii. Gregorie beinge enstalled Pope, did confirme his promise by wrytinge before notaryes and witnesses, vpon condition that the other who also claymed the Popedome should do in like maner, and yelde vp his estate. But when Benedict woulde not but stoode stiffe to clayme his right, and fled from Auenio into Spayne, this Gregorie likewise woulde not giue place. But in the beginning they notwithstanding exhorting ech other by Legates, & offeringe on either side to yeld vp their titles, appointed to meete in Sauona to make peace. But by their conference vsed by Legates, they so mocked and disapointed one another (which caused many Christians to speake euill of them) they stirred a greater strife, and therefore a greate councell was helde at Pise Anno 1410. wherein these dalyers and deluders were both broughte before the Cardinals of either faction, who with one consente depriued them both of the Popedome. In this Sinode were 124. deuines, & almost 300. Lawyers which deposed them both, & choose forthwith one Alexander borne in Candy. This deede was allowed by al Nations, sauing the Spaniards, the Scots, & the Earle of Armenia, who whollye claue to Peter Moone: neuerthelesse Gregorie & Benedict desyping this councell, toke vpon them stil the estate as they did both before. But fearing least they should be apprehended, the one of them fled to Ariminus with Leonarde Aretine Se-

Pageant of Popes. Fol.154.

tine Secretarye, the other with his companions fled into Catalony. And thus at one time three Sunnes (for so the Pope calleth himselfe the Sunne of the world) did shine at one time in the Popedome, and yet none of them all shoane in heauen. Gregory after the degree of ye councell, was curteouslye entertayned by Charles Malatest Prince of Arminus. And while he stayed at Luca by the consent of ye Cardinals that hetherto forsaked him not, he created Gabriel Condelmerius his sisters sonne Cardinall. He drew by the eares one Nicolas of Luca a white fryer & doctour of diuinitye, oute of the pulpit, becaufe in his Sermon he moued and perswaded him to seeke for peace and vnitye to the profite of all Christendome: beside that he vsed him so violently in the Church, he afterward also sent him to prison to terrifye other that they should not talke of this matter. In the ende the fathers of the generall councell of Constance sent vnto him, that eyther he should come thether or send his messenger, and thereupon he sent Charles Malatest to be his proctour, who sesinge them thus to be minded to put him from the Popedome, he stept vp into ye Popes trone (being there for the purpose prepared) and comming downe fro n it againe, francklye gaue ouer the fourth day of Iulye Anno 1415. for the which free yelding the whole assemble made him Legate of Picene, which as soone as Gregory vnderstoode within a fewe dayes for anger, griefe and anguish of minde, he dyed sodenlye. But Peter Moone stoode stiffely in his dignitye, of whom Iohn Gerson doctour of diuinitye of Paris did (being present in the said Synode) speake of ye lunaticke Pope Peter Moone saying, ye Church shall neuer be at peace vntil the Moone be quite eclipsed. But he woulde not yeld neyther for entreating, perswasion, nor threatning of any man. Thomas VValden doth make larger discourse hereof in his Sermon preached before king Henry the fift of England.

Because that the doinges of these two Popes raigning

U   both

The sixt Booke of the

both at ons, that is Gregory the ix. & Peter of the Moone are so notorious that it were worthye to be knowen, but so longe that it were tedious here to be shewed, onelye this may suffice to signifye their treacheryes, which Theodoricus hath written as a preface to the rest of their storye compiled by him at large. I come now (sayth Theodoricus) to Gregory who succeded the former Pope Innocentius. A man should scante finde incke and paper sufficiente, and shoulde be tediouslye occuppyed to declare by what crafte, guile, deccite, iugling, caueling, hypocrysies & subtilties this Gregory was chosen by the Colledge of Cardinals, with whom he and Peter Moone afterwarde delayed to agree for the quietnesse of the vniuersall Churche: promisinge and not performing: and excused themselues for not agreeing, mocking and deluding with naughtye prauckes all Christendome: vsing shiftes, excuses, false forgeryes, & frumpinges on both partes by theyr messengers to & fro. But it is euidente that they haue their consciences seared, sayinge that they are plaine and simple men, when as they are in deede full fraughte with diuelishe delusions. And because it shoulde be a godlye deede, they haue saide and do say ye they would yeild to vnitye, which yet in their malicious hartes they neither do nor euer did purpose as by their deedes shall appeare, as I will reueale to the worlde for euer, not onelye in this booke, but also in my other worke called Nemus vnionis. Although alas there be manye kinges & princes, and many inferiour secular powers, Cityes, boroughes, townes, villages and castels, and the most part of Ecclesiastical prelates of al sortes, beside clarkes and Ecclesiasticall parsons both secular and regular in sondrye countryes, nations and landes walkinge & wandering in desertes of darcknes, and many of them not desiringe the common profite of the catholicke faythe, but beinge deuided into sondrye factions for theyr sondry affections, do yet cleaue to the said Gregory & Peter, vpholdinge

and

Pageant of Popes. Fol. 155.

and cherishing them most damnably in their obstinacye, scisme and heresye, and lifting them up as their idols, like the foolishe Egiptians &c. What ende therefore is like to come of this lamentable scisme which they foster which are Lords of this world, not to procure peace but greater discorde, and to be feared if God helpe not to the destructiō of lower powers, who being perilouslye bewitched & charmed with the vaine promises & sleightes of these two Popes & their adherents, do uphold them in the pride of their ranckour, mischiefe and errour, as if there were no God in heauen, but that the saluation of soules and bodyes did onelye depende upon these two priestes of Babilon: from whom more mischiefe hath sprongue and flowed ouer al the face of the earth, then euer proceeded from any that fought for the Papacye, from the beginning to this oure time. And out alas these biles and soares are so brast out in the eyes of al the world, that there is no shift to denye or couer the same: whereupon the Catholicke fayth is darkened with cloudes of ignorance, al religion hath suffered shipwracke: Christians being at iarre amonge themselues do deuoure one another: Gonnes and other instruments of mischiefe and murther are put in practise: feare of God, honestly and vertue haue departed farre from kinges and gouernours and from the people of all sortes, and vice hath stepte into their places: and finallye the whole & vniuersall Church is sicke frō the Crowne of ye heade to ye sole of the foote. &c. Much more to the like effecte complayneth Theodoricus, being then Secretarye to the said Gregory when these vprores were thus raysed by these prelates, whose particuler doinges as they are manye and diuers, so are they straūge, monstrous, horrible, and to be wondred at that anye man though he did but suspect that there were a God, would so beluue both the world & him, but ye the spirite of God hath saide ye they shoulde be blinded in their sinnes. And thus was all the worlde troubled with this Gregory on the one

U ii   side

The sixt Booke of the

ſide the Sunne of darcknes, and with Petrus Luna the mā of the Moone on the other ſide.

149. Alexander the fift.

ALexander the fift was borne in Crete, a franciſcan fryer in profeſſion, called Peter Philargus or of Candy. He ſucceded the foreſaid Gregorie in his Popeſhip, for the former prelates Gregorie and Benedict being depoſed in the coūcel of Pice as is ſaid, this Alexander was choſen Pope by general conſent of all that were there preſent. Which dignitye being beſtowed vpon him (ſayth Platina) he was worthelye called Alexander, becauſe he being before but a beggerly and begging fryer, might now be matched with the proudeſt Prince in Europe, for exceſſiue prodigalitye & hautye courage. Wherupon he vſed to ieaſt merelye oftentimes ſaying: I am a rich biſhop, a poore Cardinall, and a beggerly Pope. This Pope was of ſo ſtout a ſtomacke yͭ he caſt oute of his kingdome Ladiſlaus then moſt mightye king of Naples & Apulia, who did conuert to his vſe more conueniemtlye the lordſhips of the Church being euil gotten. To this wicked depoſition of the Prince agreed all yͤ clergye and prieſtes of the councell of Piſe. This beinge done, the Pope did moſt vnlawfullye beſtowe it on Lewes duke of Andegania. The councell of Pice being diſſolued this Pope went to Bononia, where Balthazar Coſſa Cardinall of S. Euſtace was preſident, being a moſte ſinnefull Sodomite & filthye baude. This man was confirmed Legate by Pope Alexander, becauſe that councell was ſommoned by his politicke deuiſe, and becauſe he was the man who mighte beſt encounter and deale againſt ſuch as durſt at any time go about to gouerne the Eccleſiaſticall eſtate. And this Pope (ſaith Platina) was more wild in maners, more ſaluage, more bould and more laymanlike then became his profeſſion. His life was counted almoſt a warrefare:

fare: he thought that souldiours and warrelicke prancks, and many other wanton toyes which are not to be named, became him well enoughe. Amonge other decrees this Pope made bulles for S. Frauncis markes ye they should be counted amonge the articles of Christen fayth, & made a solemne holy daye that they should be worshipped of all beleeuers, because he had beene a franciscan fryer. When this Pope began to be very sore sicke of a poysoned medicine which was mynistred to him by his Phisition Marcillius Parmensis, recepuing of Balthazar a great bribe to do it, (as Baptista Panætius sheweth in his sixe and fiftye Sermon) whereby Alexander perceiued yt his death drue nye, he exhorted the Cardinals that came to him to mutual concord, and to maintaine the honour of the clergye. And being now at the last gaspe, he said Anno 1411. in the viii. month of his Popedome: I protest by this death which I see to be at hand, all that was done at the councell of Pise was good and lawfull. After he had said this the company weeping and mourning, he breathed out very feebelye this sayinge of oure sauiour: I giue you my peace, I leaue my peace with you. Thus presumptuouslye durst he bring euen at deathes doare, take vpon him the power of Christ to giue ye peace of Christ (being peace of conscience though he did not so vnderstand it) which he could neuer do. And thus he gaue vp the ghost in his sinne neuer asking mercy of God for it.

After this Pope had thus at his departure bestowed his charitable blessing, there followed both dearth and pestilence, as if that God had turned his blessing into cursing.

150. Iohn the xxiiij.

IOhn the xxiiii. was borne in Naples, called Balthazar Cossa Cardinall of S. Eustace, a canonist, and yet most giuen to warlike featcs. He hauing caused Alexander to

U iii be

The sixt booke of the

be poysoned gat to be Pope. And some saye that by scuffling and manhoode he wanne the Popedome, and not by free election. For (sayth Stella) while he behaued himselfe in Bononia, more like a Prince then an Embassadour, and was liefetenaunt ouer a great armye, the elders meeting there to choose a new Pope, he threatned to trounce them terriblye, vnlesse they would choose him a Pope accordinge to his minde, and thereupon many were broughte forth to him to be approued, but he woulde allowe none of them. Therefore he was entreated to signifye and appointe whō he would haue to be Pope, hereupon giue mee (quoth hee) S. Peters roabe, and I will bestowe it on him that shalbe Pope, to the which they consented. He then taking it put it vpō him selfe, & hauīg it on his shoulders said thus (as it is vsed in pronouncinge him that is elected: In the name of God Amen, I Balthazar Cossa am Pope. This thing being done contrarye to all their expectacion they durst not yet reproue it, notwthstanding they much misliked it. And thus Pope Iohn beguiled the foolishe Cardinals, and bestowed liberallye the Popedome vppon his owne parson. He being crowned Pope did forthwith sende into Germanye to wil them to make Sigismond Emperour accordinge to the custome: he hauing obtained his purpose, held a coūcell at Rome to crowne Sigismond Emperour there.

In the first session or sitting of the said councell, the masse of the holye Ghoste being done as the Pope sat aloft in his throne, by and by an owle came in, which sitting vppon a beame of the Temple and fastning her eyes stedfastly vpō the Popes grim countenaunce, did with her irksome shriking and horrible noyse salute the Pope. The by standers were much amazed thereat, and some of them said in their whispering: Lo the holy ghost is come, to whō our Pope prayed so earnestlye to ayde him accordinge to his hope: Othersome lookinge one vpon another & vpon the Pope, fell to grinning & laughing. But Pope Iohn good man

was

Pageant of Popes. Fol.157

was in a sore perplexitye, for he blushed very red, he sweat, he freated, his greace melted within him, and he chafed inwardlye aboue measure, & at the length because he coulde not deuise how to remedy this his foule confusiō, he brake vp the councell and went awaye. Then followed another sitting, in the which he was in the like agonye againe, and that with more distresse. For the saucye owle without any sūmoning presumed to come into the coūcel place againe, and could not be desired awaye with hyssing, whopping, and hallowinge, neyther scarred nor terrifyed with coodgiels and bats, so that in that Sinode likewyse nothinge was done but chasing of the owle, and not ỹ. Hereupon manye sayd that such spirituall doues had long time beene the chiefe byrdes in the Church. This historye is written by one Nicolas Clemanges in an Epistle of his. Furthermore for the mutenyes & debate that was among the Italians, whereof he was author, Sigismond and his traine coulde not come safelye to Rome. He therefore beinge cited (as Massæus sayth) by all nations almost to appointe another place for the assemble, he choose Constance a Cittye in the prouince of Mens, & appointed the daye to be the Kalendes of Nouēber Anno 1414. Some in ỹ meane time perswaded him not to go thether, least perhaps he should be vnpoped ere he returned. Notwithstāding he went thether with ỹ most subtile aduocates & lawyers, to aunswere al obiectiōs ỹ might come. But in ỹ middest of his voyage he tombled headlong out of his chariot, which he toke to be a token of ill lucke to ensue. Whē this Pope Iohn came to Constāce, he began the general coūcel wt the consent of ỹ Emperour and other Christian Princes Anno 1414. The Emperour Sigismond came thether vpon Christmas eue, and as sone as after the first masse of the sayd night a deacon had song the Gospell beginning thus: There wente forth an edict from the Emperour Augustus &c. and they being set in councell in the presence of Sigismond, euerye man hauing

U iiii libertye

The sixt booke of the

liberty graūted to him to speake freelye, there were aboue fourtye haynous articles put vp and proued against Pope Iohn. As that he conspired the death of his predecessour Alexander, in hyringe his Phisition Marcilius to poyson him. &c. Therefore he was compelled by the voyce of the councell to giue vp his Popeship, because he was an heretick, a simonist, a lyer, an hypocrite, a poysoner, a dycer, an adulterer, a Sodomite, & of all kinde of trecherye shamefullye attainted. Therefore he chaunging his apparel, began to steale awaye the xxi. daye of Marche followinge to Scafuse a towne in Austria, and from thence to Friborow. But the councell prouided so that the xxix. daye of May in the v. yeare of his Popedome, he was vncased of al offices, sought out, founde, and committed to pryson in a stronge houlde in Germanye: where he was lockt vp three yeares and had none that assisted him, but onely the Germaynes, who to theyr great domage did not vnderstand neither the Latine nor the Italian tongue. It is also noted in the storye of Albanus, that this Pope Iohn was spoyled of al his riches at his deposinge, which amounted to 75. Thousand Floreces of goulde & siluer. In the meanetime (sayth Masseus the presidents of y Sinode published a decree, wherin they shewed that a general councel being lawfullye gathered together, is aboue the Pope, & that it hath power and auctoritye from Christ (who is y head of the Church.)

In this councell whereas manye thinges might haue beene done, both for the glorye of Christ and for the comon wealth, yet nothing was done but canons deuised against those that sought to reuiue the light of the Gospell, to suppresse both it and them. In this coūcell Iohn VVicliffe a famous, godlye and learned man was excommunicated and condemned for an heretick, because he by the Scripture in preachinge and writinge, detected the delusions of the Pope, and his monkes, fryers, nunnes, and such other, and manye yeares after his death, his boones were taken

out

out of his graue here in England (where he was buried) and were burnte. Also Iohn Husse and Ierom Prage hauing a safeconduct to come safe and go safe, were cited to this councell, & when they were come because they had inueighed against the Church of Rome (notwithstanding theyr warrant graunted and sealed with the Popes bull,) yet they were taken and cruelly burnt. Platina sayth they were burnt partly because they auouched that the clergye ought according to the example of Christ and of the Apostles liue poorelye. Such is the libertye which the Pope graunteth those that come to his councelles, such is the warrante that he giueth for safetye, and thus he keepeth his fayth. Amonge other Popelike pageants played by this Pope Iohn, he also broched and styrred most cruell & bloudye warre against Ladislaus, and helde a conspiracye at Rome to driue him out of his kingdome. He commaunded y they should say seruice w S. Iohn Baptistes heade set out in shew the whilest, the which he did for this pollicye, because he purposed to sell it to the Florentines.

While Martin the fift who did succeede him & supplied his roume was at Florence, this Pope Iohn being deliuered oute of pryson against all mens hope, to the greate marueile of the people he came thether to him, and kissing the feete of Pope Martin he did acknowledge him to be his Pope, to be Peters successour, and honoured him like a worldly God. Pope Martin being moued with this his greate humilitye, did make him Cardinall within a fewe dayes after and made him bishop of Tusculan, but within a fewe monthes after he ended his dolefull lyfe, throughe sorrowe and griefe of minde Anno 1419. where his Position Cosmus that did euer loue him hartelye, caused him to be buryed in S. Iohn Baptistes Church with great solemnitye, where this Epitaphe was made on him in Latine Uerse.

First Balthazer and then the name of Iohn I did obtaine,

But

The sixt booke of the

But being novve vnpoped I am Balthazer againe.
Of late I vvas the vvelthiest vvight vvithin the heauenly cope,
But in one houre all I lost deposed from being Pope.
VVhile I did sit on Peters chayre as soueraigne for a space,
Then manye men vvith lovvlye lookes vvere humbled to my face.
The greedy plague of couetousnes so bleard mine eyes vvith gould
That for to staunch my hungrye minde all holy thinges I sould.
Alas my loathed life hath stainde and tainted very sore,
The spouse of Christ that neither spot nor vvrinkle had before.
For this my filthy trechery Saint Peters councell pure,
VVould suffer mee in hauty trone no longer to endure.
Then let all Popes by mee bevvare that shall hereafter liue,
Do not vvith mee for cursed bribes your holy matters giue.

151. Martin the fift.

Martin the fift was borne in Rome & called Otho Columna Cardinall of S. George: he was made Pope by the decree of p̄ councell of Constance, which to establish him did depriue three other, that is Benedict, Gregorie & Iohn. He being broughte vp by his parentes in learninge from his youth, when he grewe to yeares attended vpon p̄ Popeship still at Peruse in such order as he mighte creepe forward toward it. He returning to Rome was made Remembrer vnto Vrban the sixt, which office he discharged with so great shew of humilitye and curteous nature, that Innocent the seuenth made him Cardinall. For in all controuersyes he woulde agree to neither parte, no not to the truer, but so keepe in a meane p̄ he pleased all, & offended none. For this cause he was so in fauour with the Emperour and Cardinals, that in the foresaide councell he was made Pope. At whose election the Emperour Sigismond was so ioyfull of it that he thanked them all for chusinge such a Pope, & humbling himselfe to him kissed his feete. The Pope again embrasing him like a brother did thanke him on the other side, because his diligence had at p̄ length
restore

Pageant of Popes. Fol.159.

restored ye peace to ye Church. After this salutaciō ye Pope moūted on his palfreye, his coronation being also ended in great triumph he passed pompously (from the place where he was crowned) through the Citye of Constance with his horse trapped in skarlet, and all his abbottes and bishops in roabes and miters rydinge after him, & his Cardinals wyth their horses trapped in white silke. But the Emperour on the one side of the Popes horse, and the prince Electour on ye other side wayted on foote vpon him throughe the Citye. And yet soone after he conueyed himselfe away, and as (Volateranus sayth) maugre ye Emperours head, he returned in all poast hast into Italy. He passed through Millen, Mantua, Ferraria, Rauenna, and other townes til he came to Florence: but mistrusting daunger he shonned Bononia. He abode at Florence two yeares lyuing in all fleshlye pleasures, pompe and idlenesse, and preached not the Gospell so much as once. Furthermore while he was before at Constance, when the Emperour & other Princes made often complaintes to him of naughty behauiour, and detestable maners of the clergye, he deferred the time to redresse it, saying ye it was a matter that required both leasure and good aduise. For (quoth he as Ierome sayth) Euerye prouince hath his fashions and customes, which cannot be altered without much hurlye burlye. And nowe because it was feared, that the generall councels auctority should be take to be aboue the Popes, he made this decree concerning councels, ye none shoulde be sommoned againe till fiue yeares were expired, and then from that time it should be continued for ten yeares, and so from ten yeares to ten yeares the generall councell should be kept. Therfore Pope Martin hauing spēt in his iourneing (as is said) two yeares, after he had beene much desired & longed for, he came to Rome and repayred ye Citye in outwarde buildinges and Popishe traditions. He demāded the Church inheritaunce w cruell warre. He established Lewis sonne
to Alō-

The sixt booke of the

to Alouicius in the kingdome of Naples, & deposed Alphōsus Arrogan: he appeased certaine sciesmes in ye Church: he caused the Germaynes to warre vpon the Bohemians, for heresye (as they call it). He hyred VValdenus an Englishe Cardinall, to write against those that defended the doctrine of Husse & VVickliffe. He made moe Cardinals, and codemned all those decrees which the Popes had made in the time of the sciesme. He had a nephewe (as they call theyr sonnes) called Prosperus Columna, and caused him to succede him in his Cardinalship of S. George. He published a certaine forme for bargeninge, byinge and selling. He heaped vp store of treasure: he entring into Rome and finding it all ruinous, did repayre not onely ye houses, streates and Churches, but the walles also with greate & sumptuous cost and gorgeous worke diuersly. Beside he bestowed much cost vpon Churches and cloysters: and repayred olde ruinous houses dedicated to the xii. Apostles. He held two Sinodes one at Sene, and another at Papia: & confirmed by his decree that the next councel after ten yeares should be held at Basill. Finallye he dyed of the falling sicknes at Rome Anno 1431, and was buryed in a brasen tombe in Lateran.

152. Eugenius the fourth.

217 EVgenius the fourth was a Venetian borne and a Cœlestinian canon, called before Gabriel Condelmerius: his fathers name was Angel. He being a Cardinal gatte the Popedome by this meanes (as Platina sayth) For whē Gregorie the xii a Venetian was made Pope, his nephew Antony Corrarius a canon of the order of Cœlestines goinge to Rome, toke this Gabriel with him being of ye same profession. Whom Gregorie lyking wel did first make his treasurer and afterward bishop of Sene, and made Antonye prelate to the Bononians. Afterward he mistrustinge
his

his estate, and departing from Rome to Luca minding to augmente the nomber of Cardinals, he made both his nephewes Cardinals. For first Pope Gregorie and afterwarde Pope Martin were much ruled by the councell of Gabriel, especially in embassages: whereby he succedinge them did trouble al the world. Certaine cauiling parsons were very busye about him to put into his head that Pope Martin his predecessour being a great hourder vp of treasure, had lefte greate aboundance thereof: whereby they brought him to this point, that he comaunded that his kinsmen, frendes, and vicechauncelour, shoulde be taken, and their goodes be confiscat. Hereupon the Romaines mindfull of their libertyes, raysed a maine crye, and put themselues in armour, and dryuing oute all the magistrates of Eugenius, and taking Frauncis Candelmerius his nephew prisoner, they choose newe officers whereof vii. were Citizens of Rome whom they called gouernours, who had power of life and death. In the meane time Eugenius amazed in this sturre deuised to runne awaye. And therefore disguising himselfe in his apparell and puttinge on a monkes weede, he entring into a fisher boote with one Arcenius a certaine monke beguiled his keepers, and was transported to Hostia. But the Romaynes vnderstanding therof did pursue him with arrowes and stoanes. But he gat from thence to Pisa, and from thence to Florence, hauinge his gallepes readye for the purpose: where he dwellinge for the space of certaine yeares, made xvi Cardinals. Afterwarde he wente to Bononia and there builded certaine sumptuous houses. He refused to come to the councell at Basil Anno.1432. because it was sayd that a councell was aboue the Pope, and againe because he being cited should haue bene called to aunsweare such faultes as were layed against him. And therefore he was deposed and condemned for an heretick, and Amadeus Duke of Sabaudia and an heretike was placed in his steede. In this councell

were

The sixt booke of the

were condemned they that kept concubines, and walkers in the Church in seruice time. Also the communion was allowed vnder both kindes in the xxx. session. They y were cosins to the Pope or Cardinals, were depryued from being Cardinals. The feast of our Ladyes conception (as they terme it) was then decreed. But Pope Eugenius to ouerthrowe this councell of Basill, did summon another at Ferrara, and afterward at Florence. There were at Florence the Embassadours of the Gretians, Aethiopians, Asians, Armenians, Indians, Danes, & other Legates oute of the East, who did there giue their consent to many thinges of the Popes religion, because they were (as Stella saith) al maintayned vpon the Popes charge. But the Legates being returned home especially the Danes, were not allowed of their countrye for that wherein they had yelded to the Pope as the chronicles of Polonia do testifye.

It is worthye here to be mentioned what a myserable destruction fell vpon Ladislaus kinge of Hungary. Pope Eugenius compelled this king being a pong ma, to breake his oath and not kepe the league which he had sworne vnto Amurithes the great Turke. But while this yonge Prince Ladislaus beinge xxii. yeares old, doth vnwarely seeke to obeye the Pope as his most holye father, hee was worthelye plagued by Amurithes. For while Amurithes bringing an houge host warred vpõ him, he hauing his armye slaine, at the length being beguiled by Eugenius was also slaine.

They saye that this Pope Eugenius was maruellouslye delighted in warres, and that he being moued with great grudge, did sturre vp Lewis the Dolphin of France sonne to Charles the vii. against the Basilians. Whereof greate mischiefe ensued. And afterward whẽ he came to Rome he bestowed many thinges on the Citye, as buildings and reparations, with diuers superstitious woorkes, to the enriching and pleasuring of monkes, fryers, and such like.

Hee

He first tormented cruellye Thomas Redonensis & VVilliam Estouteuill, and afterward did burne them most terriblye: for Thomas said that there were many abbominatious in Rome, and that the Church had neede of great reformation. Furthermore he sayd that the Popes curse for the quarel of Christe is not to be feared. This Eugenius canonized one Cyril that wrote many fantasticall visions under the name of Reuelations. Touching the foresaide Thomas, Illiricus sayth thus in his Catalog: Thomas Redonius a white fryer borne in Fraunce in the Dukedome of Britaine was a famous preacher flourishing (sayth Antonius) Anno 1430. He in his preaching tought through Fraunce & Italy that great abbominatiōs was vsed in Rome, that the Church wanted greate reformation, and that the prelates forsakinge their pompe and royal, oughte to liue more modestlye, according to the example of Christe and his Apostles: and that the Popes vniust curses are not to be feared. For these opinions Pope Eugenius caused him to be burned at Rome Anno 1436. This Thomas also thoughte reuerentlye of the mariage of the clergye, for he wrote that it was against the safetye of manye soules, if they were not suffered to marrye accordinge to the maner of the Greeke Church, who had not the gift of cōtinencye. Because at that time they were dishonest and blotted with vnlawful coniunction. Of this Thomas Mantuan saith thus: A certaine Frenchman called Thomas, whoas yet fostred in harte the zeale of old fayth, went into Italye accompanied with a fewe. For so it pleased God the same countreye which in all thinges excelleth other, should also enioye this parson being a mirror amonge men. But God prouided not onelye for Italye, but also for this holy man: for he gaue to Italye such au one whose life it mighte follow, and to the said man he gaue a crimsen crowne of martyrdome. For while he liued well and in godlye order, he was accused vnto the Pope of haynous treacherye by certaine

The sixt booke of the

taine spiteful fellowes, and after he had suffred prison, tormentes, vexation, at the length when they coulde finde nothinge in him worthye of death, they sifted him more narrowlye, and armed themselues stoutlye with iniquitye to fulfill that which by equitye they coulde not do. And so committed him to the cursed fyre. Of this man were manye Uerses and Epitaphes written to his greate prayse, bewayling of the tyrannye vsed toward his innocent body. Furthermore Eugenius ere he were Pope, did repayre S. Agnes Church at Ancon, and the gate of the Citye, and in his Popedome he Crowned Sigismond Emperour at Rome. He also after Boniface confirmed the annuities of all benefices. At length he dyed at Rome Anno 1446. and was buryed at S. Peters. He caryed the Miter of S. Syluester (being brought from Auenion to Rome) out of Vatican to Lateran, with great worship and a procession. He punished certaine priestes that had pilfred certaine precious stones oute of Peters and Paules head. One Lewis Cardinall of Aquilegia was the first of his order that began first to maintaine houndes and horses, in steede of the poore.

153. Fœlix the fift.

Fœlix the fifte borne in Fraunce was an heremite called Amadeus before his Popeship. He being first Duke of Sauoy, hauinge a wyfe and two children (Pope Eugenius being deposed) was aduaunced to the seate by the voyces of xxvi. Electours. And notwithstandinge he were chosen & by the auctoritye of Basil Synode confirmed in the Papall chayre, yet he being hindred by the faction of the said Eugenius, could neuer set foote in ye Romaine seate, which they call Peters chayre. A scisme rose hereupon that lasted x. yeares, and many tumultes sprange in the kingdomes of Christendome, because some would obeye Eugenius, some
Fœlix

Fœlix and other some would be counted neuters. And in this sciesme it made much controuersye, because some held opinion that the Pope was vnder the iurisdiction of the general coũcell, and other some maintayned the contrarye. And of this arose another waightye and bitter controuersye whether the Pope were head of ẏ Church or no, which continueth to this day. This Fœlix being an aged man ere he came to be Pope liued to see the day, that the sonnes of his sonnes matched in mariage with kings doughters. And in the end geuing ouer all worldly charge, he purposed to go into a wildernes to lead an heremites life with 6. knightes. But as sone as he vnderstoode that he was chosen Pope by the auctoritye of the general coũcell, he shaued himselfe both crowne and chinne and came thether wyth a trayne of noble men, and being consecrate Pope toke the function vppon him, and did all thinges that belonged to the Pope to do, to giue orders, minister Sacramẽts, excõmunicate &c. and played the Pope x. yeares. He was so bountifull to the poore, that being demaunded whether he kept any houndes and to shew them: he aunswered that he would shew them another day. But when they that asked this question were with him the next day, he shewed them a great company of poore & needye people that sate downe together at dinner: saying, these are my houndes which I feede dailye, with the which I hope to hunte for the glorye of heauen.

It liked this mã at ẏ length for vnitye sake Anno 1447. to vnpope himselfe, and giue place to Nicolas the fift: whõ he therefore made Legate of all Germanye and Fraunce, and also Cardinall of Sabin, but he dyed sone after.

154. Nicolas the fift.

Nicolas the fifte was a Genewaie borne of a base stocke, his father was a Chirurgeon called Barthelmew Sarzan:

The sixt Booke of the

zan: and so this Nicolas was first called Thomas Sarzan. In this one yeare he gatte to be bishop of Bononia, Cardinall, & Pope of Rome. This Nicolas being made Pope after the death of Eugenius, did hange vpon the walles of Angell Castell, Steuen Porcarius a Romaine knight, wt other conspiratours raysing a tumult for the libertye of ye Citye. He celebrated ye Iubilie for lucre sake Anno 1450.

At the time of this Iubelie while they chaunced once in the crucifixe to returne from Vatican to the Citye, it is very certaine to be true that ye preace of people followinge was so great, that the Mule of one Peter Bardus a Cardinall could not passe by, because of those that came to & fro: so that the people also were so thronged that there was no passage, but in the ende they fell vpon the Mule first one & then another, til the beast was euen perforce borne downe with the crowde, and ere it was ceased two hundred parsons were troden to death and smothered vppon Adrian bridge: & manye fallinge beside the bridge were drowned, which were about 136. men. The Pope whose pompous superstitious & idolatrous Iubelie had caused this miserye to fall vpon the fonde people, did in this maner redresse ye case: He was sorye (sayth Platina) for the death of them ye were slaine, and therfore he remoued certaine cotages that made the waye to be straite and narrowe entringe to the bridge. For the enryching of his cofers he spent all that whole yeare in this kinde of solemnitye, & he himselfe with his troupe of Cardinals did vewe the stages. He prouided both by curse and wayters, that rooges and vagaboundes comminge to the Citye, shoulde not misuse straungers and robbe them of their money. In this Popes time ye Turke wanne Constantinople, to the great griefe of all Europe. This Pope crowned Frederick the third Emperour, and his wife Leonor He builded a sumptuous librarie in Vatican. And reuiued with great dilligēce learning and knowledge, which was then almost drowned with grossenes &

barba-

barbarous sophistrye. He appointed stipendes for learned men. But amonge these his vertuous doinges and good affection towardes learning, he had his vices withall and those notorious, namely he was greatly giuen to dronkennes, and so muche delighted therein, that he soughte for all kinde of wynes from euery place. He bestowed great cost vpon buildinges both of y͏̄ towne walles, Churches, Pallaces & Castels. Concerning his building (Platina saith) he began to fortifye with stronge walles the gates and towers of the Citye, the Capitoll and Angell Castell. He builded sumptuouslye & magnificentlye both in the towne and at Vatican, as in the towne the Popes house: also hee repayred the house of S. Steuen in Celius hill. He raysed euen from the ground S. Theodors Church. He couered w lead an olde Church in Rome called Panthion He transported the Popes house in Vatican, & brought it to a statelye fourme. He began to laye the walles of Vatican wyth greater foundation. He restored Right brydge, and builded a greate and large house beside Viterby bathes. He ayded diuers with money, that builded in the Cittye. And at his commaundement almost all the streates in the Citye were strowed. There are yet remayninge certaine Cllessels of gould and of siluer, crosses beset with Pearles & precious stones, certaine priestes roabes gorgeouslye decked w golden ouches and pearles: also certaine coueringes & hanginges wouen of gould and siluer, beside a certaine pontificall Miter, which remaine as monumentes of his plentiful pompe and magnificencye &c. Finallye he being troubled with an agewe and the goute, dyed Anno 1455.

155. Calixtus the third.

CAlixtus the third a Spaniarde borne in Valentia called first Alphonsus Borgia, his father was called Iohn and his mother Frauncis; Pope Nicolas being dead, this

Alphon-

The sixt Booke of the

Alphonsus being an old impotent man was chosen in his steede. This Pope as wryters do testifye of him was very cunning in the Popes canon lawe, but whollye ignoraunt in the Scripture as it appeareth by his deedes. He was first Secretarye to Alphonsus king of Aragon, and made bishop of Valentia by Pope Martin the fift, and Cardinal by Eugenius the fourth. As sone as he was Pope he forthwith prouided and addicted himselfe (not to preache to nations) but to followe warres against the Turke, proclayming it oute of hande as he had vowed before. And to further this purpose he sent out a rable of fryers with bulles and pardons, to encourage the Christian nations against the Turke. Among these Iohannes Capistranus and Robartus Licius were of moste renowne, being both minorite fryers and notorious hypocrites: who to drawe the more fishe to their net, and to the greater filling of their purses, vsed many shameful shiftes deluding men with dissembled and counterfaite holines, Letanies, penaunce, fasting, false merites, shryuings, reliques, images, crosses, songes, canticles, notes, ringing of belles, & singing cakes. The Pope also for his part was busye to sturre vp all Princes by his letters to take the quarell in hand, as a matter very needefull and godlye. Also he commaunded the priestes euerye daye at noone to ringe the sacringe bell, and at night with an Aue Maria: that (saith Stella) they might by this holye prayer, helpe them that foughte against the Turke. Certaine sillye countrymen seing this folly in ye Pope laughed thereat, whereupon ye Pope caused them to be hanged for it. He decreed that no man should appeale from the Pope to a generall councell. He suffered his nephewes and bastards to liue licenciouslye. He poured out (sayth Valerius) his letters of pardon in pure fashion, whe, by selling them then for fiue ducates which now are sould for trysles, he left to his successour in treasure, an hundred millions & fiftene thousande ducates. At the length he dyed for age Anno 1458.

1458. and was buryed in Peters Pallaice, or the rounde Church.

156. Pius the second.

Pius the second borne in Hetruria called first AEneas Picothomineus, hauing his brest boyling long with ambition, did at length obtaine the Papacye. He of a poore bope became so worthy a man, as all wryters do testifye of him that amonge the learned Popes he was the best learned, and most diligente wryter. In the councell of Basil he was the Popes scribe, and did with his Epistles and orations stande against y auctoritye of Eugenius. Afterward he was made Poet Lawreat of the Emperour Frederick the third, and being called to attende in his Court, his first promotion was that he was made countellour and Secretarye. Afterward he being sente Embassadour to diuers Princes, was first made bishop of Tergest by Pope Nicolas, then of Scene, and finally Cardinall by Pope Calixtus. In the end he attayning to the Papacye did as his elders, he began to proclaime y warres agaist y Turke, but he dyed ere he could proceede in his purpose. He sought still to enlarge the dominion of the Church, for y which (sayth Stella) it appeared that he feared neither kinge, nor prince, nor duke. If anye man offended him he would sore molest him with warre and tares, till he made him satiffaction. And therefore he was an heauye enemye to king Lewis the xi. of Fraunce, because he went about to abridge y licentious libertye of the clergye in his Realme. He warred vppon Borsius duke of Mutina, because he did fauour Sigismond Malatesta, and the estate of France against Frederick: for he set Ferdinandus bastarde of king Alphonsus in y kingdome of Naples violentlye with auctoritye and men of armies, agaist Iohn of Angewe sonne of kinge Renatus. He cursed Sigismond duke of Austria euen to the pitte of hell,

221

X iii becaufe

The sixt booke of the

because he bridled the polling of Cardinal Cusan: furthermore he did euen as an angry Viper (sayth VVolphanius VVissemburgius) spit out the poyson of his curse vpō his Embassadour George Haimburg a worthye lawyer, and did so persecute him with his thoūdringe letters, ỹ he was faine to flye into Bohemia, and liue there. He chased Deitherus Archebishop of Maguntia like a madde man out of his diocesse, and planted another in his steede: wherevpon great discorde arose betweene Frederick the Palatine and Duke of VVittenburg, with other in Germanye, by meanes wherof ensued great slaughter and bloudshed, and the City of Mentz being before a free Citye lost his freedome then. The cause of the Popes displeasure against Deitherus was, first because that Deitherus woulde not consente that the Pope shoulde charge his countrye with certaine great taxes & tallenges: secondly because ỹ he would not be bounde vnto the Pope, that he beinge Prince Electour should not as the Pope required withoute his lycence, call the other Electours together: Thirdly because he would not suffer the Popes Legate to call together the clergye within the diocesse of Mentz as the Legate listed: but as he being bishop thoughte best. For these causes the Pope disquieted both him and Germany. Also he remoued the Archbishop of Beneuent for making newe orders against his will. He commaunded George kinge of Bohemia to aunsweare vpon an appointed day touching his fayth, vpō perill of leesing his kingdome, because he fauoured the opiniōs of Husse. He deposed many bishops for his owne lucre. He subdued many townes of Campania, and encreased marueilouslye the reuenues of the Church. He was verye beneficiall to his frendes & kindred. He caused an head to be translated from Peloponesus, which was saide to be S. Andrewes head, beside hewroughte diuers other Popishe pranckes. He powred out riches vpon diuers vaine, sumptuous and prodigall buildinges. He made Corsian

the

Pageant of Popes. Fol.165.

the towne wher he was borne to be a Citye, calling it after his owne name Pientia, buildinge a statelye Churche of wrought stone in it. In the ende he dyed of an agew at Ancona, goinge thether aboute his warres. He was muche troubled with diseases while he liued, as with the coughe, the stone, and the goute. Volateranus sayth that ambitiou did ouerwhelme manye vertues in him: for he was euer greedye of promocion, and therefore he toke great paynes and sought the fauour of Princes.

This Epitaphe was founde written of him in an olde booke.

> Frigida membra Pij retinet lapis iste loquacis,
>   Qui pacem moriens attulit Italiæ.
> Summe Deus, quantum mortalibus alme dedisti,
>   Fulmine cum tetigit hoc caput æqua manus?
> Vendiderat precio gentes, & crimina multa
>   Virtutis specie gesserat ille Pius.
> Impius hic fuerat, quamuis sub nomine pulchro,
>   Crediderit falsis posse iuuare fidem.
> Nunc fidi comites, scelerataq; turba clientum,
>   Ingemuere Pium: nam scelus orbis erat.
>   CONCLVSIO.
> Impius hic situs est, crudelis, raptor iniquus,
>   Aeneas, fatuę quem genuere Senę.

Platina and Sabellicus do testifye, that among other his prouerbiall sentences he lefte this in writinge: There is a great cause why the clergie shoulde be depriued of mariage, but greater cause why they should be suffered to marrye. He hath the same sayinge also in his seconde booke of Coūsaile: Perhaps (sayth he) it should not be worse if most priestes were wedded: because that in maryed priesthoode manye shoulde be saued, that in vnwedded priesthoode are damned. This Pius the second (saith Cœlius secundus) did breake vp diuers nooueryes, cōmaunding them to come out of their cloister and to burne no longer in cōcupiscēce,

X iiii   and

The sixt booke of the

and not to play the trompets secretelye vnder pretence of Religion. Iohn Maria Polutianus sayth ỹ in these dayes the Minorites and Bullistes in Italye fell out bitterlye, arguing whether of them should visite, keepe and rule the nunnes.

157. Paule the second.

PAule the second was borne in Venice called first Peter Barbus, nephewe to Eugenius the fourth: he beinge Cardinall of S. Marke succeded Pope Pius. He before his Papacye purposed to fall to the trade of marchandize, but when hee heard that his vnckle Gabriel was created Pope, he began to applye his minde to his booke: and so arose from one degree to another, till in the end he gat the Papacye. He was a man of a goodlye parsonage, but of a hautye minde: he was verye couetous and bestowed benefices for rewardes. Touchinge his pontificall pompe, ye neede not doubte (sayth Platina) that he furnished it in such sort as he excelled all his predecessours, especiallye in his royall kingdome. Touching his Miter he bestowed infinite treasure thereon, procuringe to haue broughte to him fro euery place of great price, Diamants, Saphyrs, Carbuncles, Chrysolits, Jasperstones, Pearles and all other kinde of precious stones. He being thus royallye attyred like Aaron with Jewels, shewed himselfe abrode in such a maiestye, as neuer did anye earthlye creature. Then his desire was to be gazed on & to be worshipped: and for this cause he stayed straungers often in the Citye, shewinge his haudkerchiffe in the streate, that the greater companye might behold him. He commaunded also that none shoulde presume to weare a scarlet hat but the Cardinals, on whom bee bestowed much cloth of the same colour in the first yeare of his Popeship, to make them trappinges for their horses and Mules, sayth Platina. He precurs both

222

both by worde & by sworde to aduaunce the maiestye of his
seate, did nothing all his life time but moue warre in Italye sodenlye when he spyed his aduautage. Amonge diuers
others Cityes hee assaulted Arminium, and caused both
Suburbes and Citye to be myserablye shaken, rente and
torne, with force of gunneshotte and other engins. He abhorred euen from his harte the decrees and deedes of his
predecessour Pius. He restored the regular Canons whom
Calixtus had expulsed out of Lateran abbey: and bestowed
greate buildinges at S. Markes & at Vatican. He condemned all those to be heretickes that should make any mention of vniuersityes, for he was a very doult and of grosse capacitye, and therfore he loued neither learning nor vertue.
He being whollye addicted to ambition, ryotousnes and
pleasure, spent the whole daye eyther in feasting (as Volateranus sayth) or in takinge vp his money, or els in searching oute and beuing of olde coynes, images or Iewels.
His greatest care was that the Citye shoulde neuer lacke
victuals. Finallye after he had created tenne Cardinals
whereof Fraucis Ruerius was one, and assured himselfe
to liue longe, Anno 1470. he dyed of an Apoplexi. sodenly
by him selfe alone, after he had supped meerelye. After his
death his cosins the Cardinals bestowed on him a wōderfull riche and costlye tombe.

From this time forward the estate of the Papacye begā
to impaire and decay. Stanislaus Ruthenus reporteth this
one notable thinge of this Pope Paule in these wordes:

VVhen Pope Paule had seene certaine latine Verses
written against him and his daughter, it is reported that
he wept, and cryed out against the hardnes of the lawe of
single life amonge his frends. Because that he who ought
to be not onlye the head of the Church but also of chast
life, shoulde see his doughter liue in the face and countenaunce of the Citye, with great shame and disdaine: who
although she were verye beutifull, yet it greued his harte

that

The sixt booke of the

that it should be said he begat her in whoredome, because he knewe that there was a law of God, whereby she mighte haue beene borne in wedlocke, vnlesse this lawe of single life had disanulled it. They saye therefore that he toke councell how he mighte restore againe the mariage of the clergie: but beinge preuented by death he coulde not attaine to his purpose.

158. Sixtus the fourth.

Sixtus the fourth was borne at Sauona in Liguria called Frauncis Ruerius before, and generall minister of the Franciscans, succeded Pope Paule. He being at a time of solemnitye caryed in an horselitter to Lateran, there arose a sodein tumult, so that the Pope was in great daunger of loosing his life being so pelted with stones, so that the dryuers did almost forsake him in the Litter. This Pope vsed to graunte one benefice to diuers and sondry parsons. He loued his frendes so well, that to gratifye them he did manye things against all law and equitye. He promoted his companion Peter Ruerius both of his owne order and countrye, whom with his brother Hierome he broughte vp for purpose to be a Cardinall, a man otherwise borne to wast riches: for within the space of two yeres after (then which time he liued not longer) he spent of himselfe alone by his ryotous lyuing, two hundreth thousand Crownes, beside this he endebted himselfe three score Thousand, and spent in siluer three hundred poundes. He dyed beinge wasted through his incontinent life, when he was but xxbiii. yeares old Anno 1474. His death was most hinderaunce to handieraft men, for he euer filled their shoppes with store of knackes. Iohn Textor in his officine sayth thus: Peter a priest and Cardinal in the time of Sixtus the fourth, wasted about vanityes & luxuriousnes, three hundred Thousand Crownes within the space of two yeares. Againe Iohn

Riuius

Riueus in his booke De erroribus pontificiorum sayth, y̆ Fulgosus reporteth of the increbible prodigalitye of the saide partye. It were to longe to rehearse all his woordes for breuityes sake these fewe may suffice, which I thinke is the leaſt to be spoken of: namely that he ware goulden roabes at home in his house, that he had his couerlets of gould for his beds, his Chamber ſtooles and pottes of ſiluer: Alſo he prouided for his concubine Tyreſia, ſhoes couered wyth Pearles. By this a man maye geſſe the reſt of his vnmeaſurable pompe and prodigalitye.

But Hierome brother to the saide Peter, beinge made chiefe of Liuius court and Cornelius court, after him did rule and order the matters of the Church: being a man of more ſeuere nature and leſſe laſciuious, ſauinge one waye not to be named. After theſe Sixtus aduaunced the childrē of his brethernne and ſiſterne, amonge whom he made one Iulian Cardinall and his brother Iohn Preſidēt of the Citye, and Prince of Sora & Senogallia. He loued (ſayth Platina his kindred aboue meaſure, beſtowing and lauiſſhing on them that which belōged both to man and God againſt all iuſtice. And by the iudgement of manye he plonged all Italye with bloudye bryoples, & that without cauſe. Therefore ſayt' Volateranus, when he was driuen to neceſſityehauing waſted his wealth vpon theſe tumults, he was the firſt that began to practiſe this ſhifte: He deuiſed to picke oute certaine Colledges. Againe Agrippa ſayth of him thus: amonge the bawdes of late yeares that ſet vppe and builded ſtewes, Pope Sixtus y̆ fourth was moſt famous, who builded a notable ſtewes at Rome and (as he ſayth in his declamatiō to the Louanians he ſheweth at large) not onlye for harlots, but otherwiſe horrible to be thought vpon. He following y̆ example of Heliogabalus, did maintayne his traine of harlots, and beſtowed them on his frendes and ſeruauntes. Beſide he had his fee comming into his treaſure of that moneye, which the harlots earned by

their

The sixt booke of the

their misdemeanour, to the enryching of his cofers: for ẏ strompets of Rome do yet paye theyr Iuly tribute (as it is termed) euery weeke to the Pope, which in yearely reuenues hath oftentimes amounted to xx. Thousand ducates, and now by report ariseth to fourtye Thousande. And so ẏ treasurers of the Church are bound to make accompte as well of harlots tribute, as of the Church landes.

VVesselus Groningensis (called the light of the world) in the discourse of the Popes indulgences wryteth of this Pope Sixtus, that at ẏ sute of the foresaid Peter then Cardinall of S. Sixtus, and Patriarke of Constantinople, and of his brother Hierome, he graunted the whole familye of the Cardinall of S. Lucia (who in his former yonge yeares had in like maner yelded himselfe to the detestable lust of Pope Paule the second) to file theyr bodyes lawfullye, in most vnlawfull, vnnaturall and vnspeakable maner for 3. hot monthes June July and August, which he graunted with this clause: Fiat vt petitur, Doe accordinge to your requeste. O horrible and monstrons men, more saluage then brute beastes, weare it not but that malice of Antichrist and the deuill (sparing no blasphemye to slaunder ẏ Church of Christe) dryueth me to detecte their loathsome treacherye and nakednesse, I would rather helpe to burye these villanyes in silence then to vtter these their filthines, which I cãnot but with blushing remember. Loath were I to plucke of the shéete of theyr shame, & to reueale their ribaldrye, but that vnder such roabes lurketh hiddẽ so manye foule soares enfecting Christian soules, and deceauing their simplicitye with an outward visard of innocencye. And yet while I forbeare euen for honesty & ciuilitye sake, to discouer their filthye commedyes and Iewishe pranckes at large, as they themselues are not ashamed to doe, sportinge thereat with ballades, songes and sonets, and other vnhoneste wayes. Mantuan and other haue spoken and vttered thereof enoughe, & to much, wryting of this Pope

Sixtus.

Sixtus and his nephew, & of Alphonsus. But as touching Sixtus (sayth Volateran) he being disposed to exercise himselfe in warrefare, wherunto he was of nature more enclined then to religiō, moued quarrels of warre as he might right or wronge. He inuaded without any cause Vitelius Tiphernates, the Florentines, the Venetians, the Columnians, Ferdinand king of Sicilia, the Duke of Calabria and other nations and Princes. It was his chiefe delighte to haue Christian Princes at commaundemēt, whom at his pleasure he did both set vp and put downe: He set his confederates the Heluetians with fyre and swoorde vpon the Lombardes whom he had cursed, and gaue the Heluetians a pardon and an ensigne, to encourage them to the slaughter of the Lombardes. He aduaūced his cosins & bastardes (to the shame of the Church) to all that he mighte: for he made two of his nephewes Leonarde & Iohn to be Presidentes of the Citye by course one after another, beside other dignities diuers and many ȳ he bestowed on sondrye of his kindred, & among other one Raphael his sisters sonne was made Cardinal. But one Laurence Medices honge vp the saide Raphael and Saluatus Pisanus and diuers other, because they had murthered his brother. He was verye beneficiall to the begging sect of religious roages, graūting them reuenues in this life, and heauen in the life to come. He is counted as it were a newe builder of Rome. He bestowed cost of pauinge the streates & repayring the wayes, appointing skauingers to loke to ȳ streates: beside diuers other lesse necessary & more vaine and superstitious deedes about Churches, Chappels, and Pallaces. In the xv. yeare he celebrated the Iubelie for the encrease of his lucre and gaynes, and to pleasure his frendes. He diuised many polling & bribing offices of scribes, abriogers, sollicitours, waighters, and notaryes of the eschcaker, to enrich hys cofers, which offices are to be bought of ȳ Pope. He made diuers newe holy dayes, and diuers Saintes, and manye

decrees

The sixt booke of the

decrees to enriche the clergye. He excommunicated and cursed to hell Laurence Medices of Florence, for hanging his nephew Raphael. In the ende he being sicke of þ goute dyed throughe rancour and malice, the soner because the Duke of Ferraria had takē peace with the Venetians against his will, Anno 1484. And therefore diuers men made these Epitaphes of him.

Of his death.

Non potuit Sęuum vis vlla extinguere Sixtum:
Audito tandem domine pacis, obit.

No force was forceable enoughe to make Pope Sixtus dye,
But when the name of peace was heard it kild him by and by.

Of the peace that ensued his death.

Dic vnde Alecto pax ista refulsit, & vnde
Tam subito reticent pręlia? Sixtus obit.

Say hag Alecto whence haue we this peace? and how are fled
The bloudye brawles so sodenlye? Pope Sixtus nowe is dead.

Againe another wrote this.

Mortuus est Sixtus, gaudet nunc Roma: trahatur,
Vt dignum est, vnco mortuus in Tiberim.

Pope Sixt is dead and Rome is glad: therefore as it is meete,
To Tiber draw his carkasse with an hooke fast to his feete.

Another.

Sixtus obit, gaudent omnes: ne funere sicco
Transeat, amissa plangite glande sues.

Pope Sixt is dead, all men are glad: but least that noone bewayls
While he is buryed: weepe ye hogs and howle your acornes fayle.

Another.

Extulit auratas sed postquam maxima glandes
Ecclesia, innumeris patefacta est ianua porcis.

When mighty mother Church gan once her goulden acorns yeld,
It was set oape to howgy heardes of swyne that haue it fild.

Another.

Sixte iaces tandem, fidei contemptor & æqui:

Paci

Pageant of Popes.   Fol.169.

Pacis vt hostis eras, pace peremptus obis.
O Sixt thou were a foe to peace, and peace hath slee now slaine,
That diddest long in life both fayth and equitye disdaine.

Sixte iaces tandem: lætatur Roma, tuo quæ
   Passa sub imperio est funera, bella, famem.
Now dead is Sixt: and Rome is glad who walle as he did raigne,
Oft burials and westing warre with famine did sustaine.

Sixte iaces tandem, nostri discordia secli:
   Sæuisti in superos, nunc Acheronta moue.
Nowe Sixt is dead that nopde this age with discord and with euill,
Thou raged hast against the heauens, now wrangle with the deuill.

Sixte iaces tandem fraudisq; doliq; minister:
   Et sola tantum proditione potens.
Now Sixt is dead that did contriue such falsehoode craft & guile:
And onlye bare so great a sway by treason all this while.

Sixte iaces tandem, pressa est quo sospite virtus,
   Leges, sacra, pium, relligioq;, fides,
Now Sixt is dead: who while as he did liue did keepe in awe
Religion, fayth, zeale, godlines, all honestye and lawe.

Sixte iaces tandem, deflent tua busta cinædi,
   Scortaq;, lenones, alea, vina, Venus.
Now Sixt is dead, vpon whose graue there both lament & howle,
Baudd, stropets, bankruts, ribaulds, stewes,& etc y drōken nowle

Sixte iaces tandem, summorum imfamia, fexq;
   Pontificum, tandem perfide Sixte iaces.
Now Sixt is dead: the shame of those that hye in honour be
The scoom of Popes: most faithlesse wretch now dead at legth is he.

Sixte iaces tandem, vos hunc lacerate Quirites,
   Dentur & impastis membra scelesta feris.
Now Sixt is dead: his carkasse then ye Romaynes rent & teare,
And giue the gubs to carraine crowes, & to the saluage beare.

Quid pia profuerint Funóto solemnia Sixto?
   Tradita sunt celeri vota precesq; noto.
What doth it boote to pray for soule of Sixtus being dead,
Your prayers are but blastes of winde that in the ayre are fled.

                                            Riserat

The sixt booke of the

Riserat vt viuens coelestia numina Sixtus,
 Sic moriens nullos credidit esse Deos.
As Sixtus in his life did scorne the God celestiall,
So at his day of death he thought there was no God at all.

Sixte iaces tandem, superis inuisus & imis:
 Inclusus grauido ventre necandus eras.
Thou Sixt at length art dead whom heauen doth loath & also hell,
If murdred thou in mothers wombe, had bene, it had bin well.

Stupra, famem, strages, vsuras, furta, rapinas,
 Et quodcunq; nefas, te duce Roma tulit.
Thou being Captaine wretched Rome, no mischiefe could escape,
As robbing, murther, vsurp, theft, famin, whordome, rape.

Magna licet tardę soluenda est gratia mortis:
 Omne scelus tecum, Sixte cruente, iacet.
Much are we bound to death though long it were ere shee thee sped,
For now with thee O cruell Sixt all villany is dead.

By these Verses which were made vpon Pope Sixtus after his death, it maye appeare what opinion men had of his holinesse in his life. But to proceede, Leander & Tritemius say that about the yeare of our Lorde 1470. Alanus de rupe a Dominican, after he had seene certaine dueliske visions and illusions, contriued his worke called Rosariū out of our Ladyes Psalter, and preached it in steede of the Gospell: which Iames Sprenger did aduaunce with counterfaited myracles, and at the length Pope Sixtus did confirme it to be holye and autenticall with his bulles and indulgences. Whereupon a certaine booke was published, in the begiuning wherof it is written that vpon a time the blessed Virgin came into the Cell of the said Alan it being shut, and made him a ring of her owne haire, and betrouthed her selfe to ye monke, that she kissed him, giuing him leaue to handle and milke her breastes: and finally to be as pleasaunt and familiar with him as a woman would be to her husband. And these grosse monkishe myracles are yet

defended

defended by the Popishe priesthoode. Of this Alan came the order of religious lotterers called after his name.

159. Innocentius the eight,

Innocentius ye eight was a Genewaie borne, his fathers name was Aron, and his name before was Iohn Baptist Cibo: he beinge Cardinall of S. Cicilia was chosen Pope after the death of Sixtus. He was sometime a poore boye but of excellent beautye: and brought up among those that waighted upon Alphonsus king of Sicill, wher he learned perfitly courtly fashions. Afterward he cōming to Rome, continued a long season in the companye of Philip Cardinall of Bononia. In time he was made prelate of Sauon then of Melphit, afterwarde Secretarye by Sixtus and so came to be Cardinall, and last of all Pope. He was tall of stature, fayre of complexion and of a comly parsonage: but of a grosse and dull wit, voyde of learninge, and so heauye headed that sometime euen when he sate busye about publick affayres, he would take a nap and fall a sleepe. He was welbeloued of Sixtus for his comlye behauiour and curtesye, wherein he excelled all other. But verelye he fawned vppon all men with flatteringe face, but was freind to no man in deede: and being of nature addicted to couetousnes, yet he would shift it and colour it with myrth and pleasant icastes. Euen at his entrye almost to his Papacye, he conspired with the Princes of Sicill againſt their king Ferdinand, sending for Robart Seuerinates to be Captaine of the enterprise: So well doth the Pope requite his bringinge up in the king of Sicils house. He said that a man oughte to make warre for the dignitye of the Church, for the defence of subiectes, and for procurementes of peace to ensue, contrarye to the Apostle sayinge: Do not euill that good may come thereof. But at length he seing himselfe disapointed toke peace perforce, and yet with these conditions:

P that

The sixt Booke of the

that a tribute shoulde be payed out vnto him, and that the rebels should haue no harme. But yet ye wyse Prince king Ferdinand kept neither of the conditiōs: though the Pope sente thether his stoute champion Peter Vincent to challenge them, and his Secretarye with him. Also he deposed George Boebracius kinge of Bohemia from his kingdome, for fauouring Iohn Husse, & bestowed it vpon Mathias: but because the Emperour Fredericke woulde not plant this Mathias therein, great warre ensued thereof to the subuersion almost of the said Emperour. After this, Innocentius being wearyed with warres, gaue him selfe to pretensed peace: and applyed him selfe whollye to ease and idlenesse, which breedeth al wickednesse. He following the example of Sixtus, did erect a Colledge of secretaryes, for his greater gaine, encreasing the nomber of them. He beutifyed the Papacye with a newe Pallaice. He did openlye lauishe out ritches and treasures vpon his bastards, giuing them honours without all shame: for he bestowed vpon one Fraūcis his bastard certaine townes adioyning to the Citye, & gaue a great dowrye to his bastard daughter Theodorina, maryed to an exceeding wealthye Genewaie. He made his base begotten children his chamberlaynes, & his companions Cardinals. He sould pardons for ye quick and the dead. He bestowed great treasures superstitiously on diuers Churches in Italy, and on religious houses. He graūted leue by his bul to those of Norway, to say masse w^toute wyne. He diuising a new trade to fishe for money, because ye neither ye aduantages of his pardōs, nor of his Iubelie, nor the taxe against the Turke coulde suffice him, he found out the title that was set vp ouer ye Crosse of Christe by Pilate, written in three tongues. Iesus Nazarenus rex Iudeorum, which was hidden within a wall: also he found out the iron head of the speare wherewithal the side of our Sauiour was wounded, and ere a man mighte see or kisse these Iewels he must paye well for it. But after long sicknes this

Pageant of Popes. Fol.170.

nesse this Pope dyed Anno 1492. Of whom this Epitaph was made.

Quid quæris testes, sit mas aut foemina, Cibo?
Respice natorum, pignora certa, gregem.
Octo recens pueros genuit, totidemq́ puellas:
Hunc merito poterit dicere Roma patrem.
Spurcities, gula, auaritia, atque ignauia deses,
Hoc, Octaué iacent, quo tegeris tumulo.

About the yeare of our Lord 1464: Baptist Mantuan being then xviii. yeres old wrote his ix. Eglog calling it Post religionis ingressum, entreating of the corrupt maners of the court of Rome: & his tenth Eglog of the controuersye of ye fryers Obseruants and not Obseruants. Also he wrote a Diolog in prayse of the blessed life. In his ix. Eglog he painteth out ye treacheryes of Rome, saying that all kinde of naughtye parsons are had in honour and are promoted at Rome: and that none are there aduaunced but such villaines as deserue rather to be imprisoned and driuen out. His sayinges are partlye thus:

Quó magis appropias, tanto magis omnia sordent.
    ¶ And after he addeth.
Fama est Ægyptum coluisse animalia quędam,
Et pro numinibus multas habuisse ferarum.
Ista superstitio minor est quám nostra: ferarum
Hic aras habet omne genus, contraria certe
Naturę res atque Deo, qui dicitur olim
Prępoluisse hominem cunctis animātibus vnum, &c.

160. Alexander the sixt.

ALexander the sixt was a Spaniard borne in Valentia, called first Rodericus Borgia, succeeded Innocentius: his deedes were so opprobrious and wicked, as hath beene sildome heard. He was a very ryotous tyrant & in league with the deuil to obtaine the Papacye. He being long vice-

P ii,   chaun-

The sixt Booke of the

chauncelour in his Cardinalship, did search and boult out all the estate and trade of the Court of Rome, and all the councelles and secretes of all the Princes and encorporations of Italye. And therefore being Pope by the helpe of of his bastarde Valentinus (whom of a Cardinall he made captaine calling him Cæsarius) he did almost destroy them all: and rooted out and banished the most mightye and honourable houses of Rome, so that afterward he stoode not in awe of anye of them. In the which vickeringe (sayth Valerius) the garrison of Frenchmen and Heluctians being murthered both man and woman, this proud Captaine Cęsarius beinge by meanes of his wyfe duke of Valentia, purposing to get a hcotpe of money, gaue to certaine Cardinals a pocion of Aconita wherof his father also dräncke, so that he fell a sleepe with the rest, and then ye sonne with the stroke of a weapon quenched the vndeserued honour of both. This Alexäder held ye Iubelie at Rome Anno 1500. whither infinite multitudes of people resorted: but for those that either would not or could not come, ye Pope by his bull imparted to them the blessing and benefite of ye Iubelie if they woulde giue moneye for it. He spared no shamefull shifte to make money withall: and therefore he did found yet another newe colledge for clarkes of briefes (for so were they called that write the abridgements of all matters) & these were in nomber foure score, of the which euery one payd for his place vii. hudred crownes. He cited al Princes by auctoritye of his bull to come to the Iubelie, and appointed standings in euery countrye in the streates, whither the people should resorte to send their money thether. By his Legate Iohn Borgia he crowned Alphonsus king of Naples, and (sayth Platina) made him sweare to be true to Rome in paying his yearely tribute faithfullye. He bestowed infinite riches in repayringe and garnishing Churches, Castels, towers, hye wayes and houses in Rome. Volateranus sayth that he murthered manye vertues

tues by his notorious vices which are not to be named, onlye (sayth he) I will touche those that were knowen in the eyes of the people. If he were at anye time at leasure, he had no regarde what kinde of recreation he vsed withoute respecte of his estate. He flitted often to Adrian castell because he might the better come out openlye to beholde such shewes and delightes, as maskers, mommers, dauncers, harlots and strompets, and other worse kinde of people vsing these brauerpes vpon hollydayes and other times: he delighted much to see the lasciuious comedyes of Plautus and other like enterludes played. At the mariage of one of his doughters he procured extraordinarily to haue it solemnized with running at the tilt and hunting. Fensers & roisters were neuer so suffered in Rome, neither the Citizens so bridled as in his time. Beside, the Citye was much encombred with vagaboundes so that men coulde neither walke safe in the Citye by night, nor without the Citye by daye. Now was Rome become a slaughterhouse, which hath somtime beene a refuge and defence for men. All these (sayth Volateran) he suffered for his bastards sake, to whō he graunted all thinges at pleasure &c. But as ye haue heard before he dyed in ye ende of the same poyson which he caused his sonne to prouide for other: farther of his doīges and of his sonnes warres by him procured & maintayned, Volateran wryteth at large.

Platina sayth howe that when Charles the eight king of Fraunce should passe throughe Italye to Naples with an army to challenge it as his enheritaunce, this Pope Alexander fearing the puissāce of that noble king, did for feare of him make a league with Alphonsus king of Naples against the French kinge, & planted a garison of souldiours in Rome least the king should inuade it. For it is ingrafted in the Italians that they enuieng the prosperitye of the Frenchmē, do alwayes detest euen ye very name of Fraūce: so that they swearing and vowing freindship with them,

Y iii. are

The sixt booke of the

are not nothing abashed in despite of God and iustice, to breake their leagues. And yet notwithstandinge this the Popes power, yet kinge Charles preuayled in his purpose maugre their hartes and came to Rome, where for feare least he should by violence breake awaye from himselfe to their greater damage, the Pope comaunded that he should be curteouslye let in, and that none of the Romaine souldiours vpon paine of death should make any sturre, and so did Charles likewyse commaunde his armye. And yet the cowardlye Pope wyth a bande of men fled bastardlye into Angel castell: but after he perceyued that quietnesse was kept in the Citye, he maketh a league with Charles, sending home to Alphonsus his souldiours againe. But after this when Charles had beene in Apulia and conquered it, he prepared to returne home into France: but the Pope forgetting or neglecting his league & oath, thoughte to cut him short of his purpose and to take the aduauntage of Charles while he trustinge to the league, shoulde not mistrust anye such falsehoode. And therefore the Pope making another league with the Venetians, Maximilian the Emperour, Ferdinand king of Aragon, and Lewis Sfortia, prouidinge an armye laye in wait for Charles his comming at Fornonium not farre from Parma, euen in the waye where he should passe. But notwtstanding this ambush were fourtye Thousande men, and Charles had with him but vii Thousand trayned souldiers, wearyed with traueling and want of necessaryes, yet the bickering continued sharpe & doubtful a long time with great slaughter of the Popes armye, and in the ende Charles with little losse of his part gat the victorye. Thus reporteth Platina or rather the author that continueth the historye of Platina where he ended it, who wrote but to the time of Paule the seconde, thoughe yet he beareth the name of the whole worke for those that follow are added by other. In the time of this Pope an Angell that was placed aloft in Angel castell, was throwne downe by the

violente

Pageant of Popes.

violente force of thonder and lightninges, which as some thincke mighte well prognosticate the fall of the Popes estate. Iohn Tisseranus a Minorite founded at Paris an order of harlots, as if Christian religiō were to be edifyed by such orders.

¶ Verses made vpon Pope Alexanders death.

Fortasse nescis cuius hic tumulus siet,
Adsta viator, ni piget. &c.

Perhaps whose tombe this is (my freinde) ye do not know,
Then pause a while if that ye haue no haste to go.
Though Alexanders name vpon the stone be grauen,
Tis not that great : but he y late was prelate shorne and shauen.
Who thirsting after bloud deuourde so many a noble towne,
Who tost & turnde the ruthfull states of kingdomes vpsidedowne.
Who to enrich his sonnes so manye nobles slew,
And wast the world with fire and sword & sporting to him drew.
Defying lawes of earth and heauen and God himselfe ere while,
So that the sinful father did the daughters bed defile.
And could not from the bandes of wicked wedlock once refraine,
And yet this pestilent prelate did in Rome tenne yeares remaine.
Now freind remember Nero or els Caligula his vice,
Or Heliogabali, enoughe: the rest ye may surmise:
For shame I dare not vtter all: away my freind with this.

¶ Another Epitaph vpon Pope Alexander.

The Spaniard lyeth heare that did all honestye defye,
To speake it briefely : in this tombe all villany doth lye.

¶ Another.

Least Alexaaders noble name my freind should the beguile,
Away: forbeare both treachery doth lurke and mischiefe vile.

¶ Another.

Though Alexander after death did vomit matter blacke,
Yet maruel not: he drancke the same and could not cause it packe.

Diuers other like ill fauoured verses accordig to his il fauoured maners were made of him, which for modesty sake are

The sixt booke of the

are partlye to be suppressed, because it is not to be doubted but that chast eares would be ashamed to heare those thinges, which Pope Alexander was not ashamed to do. But amonge other Iohn Functius reporteth of him out of Volateran, that the Cardinals which chose him did first finde him vnthackfull: for he plagued them all with diuers myserpes, thrusting some into prison and punishing some with imprysonmente. He warred vpon the Vrsins and conqueringe them layed them in irons and fetters. His greatest care was (as Innocentius did) to bestow great honours on his bastards. He made one of his yongest sonnes Prince of Sicilia, and another called Cæsareus a Cardinall, and his eldest sonne a duke in Spaine, who win a while after was murthered in the night & tumbled into Tiber. His other sonne the Cardinall after the death of his brother, renounced priestcraft & ranne into Fraunce with a mightye masse of gould, where he maryed a kinsewoman of kinge Lewis, hauing with her the towne of Valentia: then by the ayde of the kinge beinge at perpetuall league with him, he purloyned to himselfe great dominion in Italye, being therein much furthered by the Pope his father. The daughter of this Pope Alexander called Lucretia, with whom the monstrous father had vsed carnall companye, was maryed to 3. Princes one after another. First to Iohn Sfortia duke of Pisauria, then she being deuorced was matched to Alosius of Aragon bastard of king Alphonsus: he beinge slaine she was wedded to Alphōsus duke of Ferraria. What her honestye, religion, and modestye was in the Court of Rome duringe her fathers estate, it maye be gathered sufficientlye by these two Uerses made vppon her death, by Iohn Iouianus Pontanus.

Hic iacet in tumulo Lucretia nomine, sed re
    Thais: Alexandri filia, sponsa, nurus.
Here lyes Lucretia chast by name, but Thais lewd by lyfe,
Who was to Alexander Pope both doughter and his wyfe.

The

¶ The Verses of Actius Sannazarius vpon the
yeare of Iubelie kept by Pope Alexander.
Pollicitus cœlum Romanus, & astra sacerdos,
  Per scelera & sedes, ad Styga pandit iter.
The Romaine priest that promised both heauen & starres to sell,
By treacherye and murtheringes hath made a gap to hell.

¶ The Verses of the same auctour againe Lucretia the daughter of Pope Alexander the 6. reprouing her horrible incest vvith her father.
Ergo te semper cupiet, Lucretia Sextus:
  O fatum diri numinis: hic pater est?

Ierom Marius in his booke Eusebius Captiuus speaking of this Pope Alexander hath these wordes: What should I disclose ye detestable treachery of Alexander the 6. wherof the like hath not bin heard He making a league w the de-uils of hell, bequeathed him selfe bodye & soule vnto them if by their helpe he mighte attaine to the Papacye: which when the deuils had perfourmed, Pope Alexander began so to refourme his life, that he neuer went about anye busi-nes, but that he did first take councell of the deuill.

Other prankes of this Pope Alexander were partlye written in these Verses compendiouslye.
Vendit Alexander cruces, altaria, Christum:
  Emerat ille prius vendere iure potest.
De vitio in vitium, de flamma transit in ignem,
  Roma sub Hispano deperit imperio.
Sextus Tarquinius, Sextus Nero, Sextus & iste:
  Semper sub Sextis perdita Roma fuit.
Pope Alexander selleth Christe with aares & crosses store,
And reason good ye he should sell the thinges he bought before. &c.

In the time of this Pope the pall of the bishop of Mentz was enhaunsed, to be payde for it for euer heareafter vnto the Popes Chamber xxv. Thousand Florences. Among other enormities wherewith this Alexander swarmed, he poysoned Gemen brother to Baiazetes the great Turke & prisoner

The sixt booke of the

prisoner at Rome, receyuing for the same deede wherwith he was hyred by Baiazetes two hundred Thousand Crownes. Furthermore to maintaine his tyrannye he ioyned league with the Turke against the French kinge and craued his assistaunce, vsing both the kingdome of Naples & Rome it selfe for his owne royal sake: as the fortresses to the Empyre of Ottomannus. Beside he comaunded the tongue of Antonius Mancinellus and both his hands to be cut of, because he in a learned and eloquente oration reproued his licentious and loathsome demeanour. But as he liued wickedlye so he dyed myserablye, for he preparinge a feast for diuers Senatours and Cardinals, purposing to poyson them with the same bane, that he poysoned Cemen: but by the prouidence of God one of the wayters ignorantly gaue the Pope the same bottell wherein the poyson was, wherof he drinking dyed with the reste. Finallye in one thinge this Alexander matched the wickednes of his predicessours in graunting leaue to a Spaniard Petrus Mendoza Cardinall of Valentia, to vse his bastard sonne Marquesse Zanatensis otherwyse then becommeth vowed chastitye: but hereof enough. And beside this Mendoza was well knowen greatly to dishonour the spowsall bed of his soueraigne king Ferdinand.

Anno 1499. one Ierom Sauonarola a dominican monke with other his fellowes were burned at Florence, for defending the communion vnder both kindes, condemninge the Popes pardons, and for reprouing the loose life & negligence of the clergye generallye. They denyed also the Popes supremarye: sayng that the keyes were giuen to the whole Church, and not to Peter. Againe the Pope followed Christe neither in life nor doctrine, because he attributed more to his owne pardons & traditiōs then to the merits of Christ: & the his cursinges & excōmunicatiōs are not to be feared. He prophecied also of certaine thinges to come as of the destruction of Florence and of Rome, and the re-

storing

Pageant of Popes. Fol.175.

ſtoring of the true Church at length: for the which Picus Mirandula calleth him an holye Prophete, and defendeth him in his wryting againſt the Pope. Alſo one Marſilius his neighbour, and Cominœus in his French hiſtorye, do attribute to him the ſpirite of propheſynge: and diuers other learned men do defend that he dyed an innocent.

161. Pius the thirde.

PIus the thirde borne in Hetruria and nephewe to Pius ye ſeconde, called firſt Franciſcus Picolhomeneus after great debate amonge the Cardinals ſucceded Alexander.

Valentine Borgia after ye death of his father purloyning his treaſure did beſet ye Vatican with xii. Thouſand ſouldiours, it beinge the place where the Pope was elected, thinking by this drift to make the Cardinals ſtoupe to his purpoſe: but they to auoyde this daunger did forthwith conueye themſelues into the Temple of Minerua, where they were forthwith encloſed by him. Hereuppon a rumour ran through ye Citye that the elders were apprehended, that all the Citye was moleſted with ſlaughter and ſpoyling, ſo that all men were amazed. This being hearde doores were ſhut vp, men toke them to their weapōs, the ſtreat paſſages were ſtopt with timberlogs & irō chaynes: and thus was all in an hurlye burlye and a great vprore, as if the hoaſt of Hanniball had bin battringe the gates of Rome. But Valentine becauſe he ſawe that he had attempted an harde matter, being requeſted by ye Cardinals to giue ouer his wilfull purpoſe, did promiſe to ceaſe by & by and to obey them. Then when this Pius was choſen, Valentine abating his courage, did thanke the Cardinals becauſe they had choſen him Pope whom he moſt deſired. He being Pope did forthwith rayſe an armye to driue out thoſe Frenchmen that dwelt in Italye, taking it in diſpite that their king had ſubdued Apulia and a great part of Italye: but the Pope hoped for a daye to gall the French-

men

The sixt booke of the

men to enclose them in a trap, and in the end to hunt them vtterlye out. But while he purposed these thinges he dyed of an vlcer in his legge, the xvii. daye after his creation Anno 1503. the same yeare also that Alexander also dyed, the xv. of the Calendes of Nouember.

And here endeth the sixt booke of these prelates, contayning in it 41. Popes from Innocentius the 4. to this Pius the 3. whose corrupt liues as is partly shewed thoughe not so largelye as mighte be, do argue of what spirite they were and howe farre from Christian conuersation. But if their fantasticall and superstitious decrees were ioyned hereunto, wherewithall they loaded the Church and cloaked the Gospell, their doctrine would appeare to men of any iudgement, as vnsauoxye as their trade of life: but it would be ouer tedious, and pertayneth not so much to our purpose.

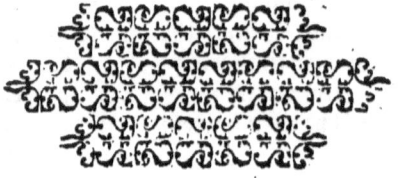

THE

Fol. 176.

THE SEVENTH
Booke contayninge the fift parte of
the third sort of Romaine Popes, in whom appeareth the wayninge of Antichrist and imparing of his
vsurped estate, wexing still weaker and weaker till the
ende of the worlde, accordinge to the Prophecye
of S. Paule in the seconde Chapter of the seconde Epistle to the Thessalonians: that
Antichriste must be reueled before
that Christe come.

It appeareth by these former Popes how ye Prophecies (in the Reuelatiō of Iohn of Antichrist, that he should be an Abadon, which being an Hebrewe word signifyeth a Destroyer or Conquerour) haue bin aboū-dantlye and in perfit measure fulfilled & verifyed in them. In the rest that followeth may appeare the diminishing of that seat, for so much as many people in their times haue & do from daye to daye renounce the Popes auctoritye. Ma-ny parsons first began in Germanye openlye to detect him as Luther, Zuinglius, Oecolampadius, Melancthon with diuers other till in the ende the whole counntryes forsooke him, so that (God be thancked) at this daye a great parte of the worlde doth acknowledge him to be Antichriste, and despyeth his doctrine: as Englande, Scotland, Denmarke, Sweden, the dukes of Saxonie, the duke of Brunswick, the Palsgraue of Rhene, the duke of VVittingberges, ye Lant-graue of Hessia, ye Marquesse of Brandenburg, the Prince of Russia: and all other Earles and noble men with their dominions and great Cityes through the whole countrey of Germanye, beside the great commō wealthes of Helue-tia, Rhetia, Vallis, Tellina, with many hūdred Thousands
more

The seuenth booke of the

more of a states in Flaunders, Italye, Spayne, & Fraunce, and in the kingdome of Polonia. Thus especiallye from the yeare of our Sauiours incarnation 1503: vnder Pope Iulye the seconde, the credite of the Romaine Sea began to cracke and dayly ryueth more and more, and shall by Gods grace so continue till it be cleane rente in peeces and torne awaye. Whereof God hath giuen certaine signes & tokens, plainlye prognosticatinge the greate fall of this proude Babilon, which with these reuoltinge of regions from him being compared, may comfort those that reioyce in the aduauncing of the Gospell and in the ruine of Antichriste: although it is not to be wished that any man should ground any doctrine or point of religion barely vpon these prognostications. The obseruations that the Papacye shall melt awaye, decresing more and more till the daye of Iudgement are these. First the forenamed Prophecye of S. Paule in the 2. Chapter of the seconde Epistle to the Thessalonians, that Antichriste must be reuealed before Christe come: with diuers other Prophecyes of the holye Scripture in the Reuelation and other places. Other proofes hereof maye be those straunge thinges that haue come to passe of latter times in the Church of Rome: as þ Pope Iohn the 24. was wonderfullye vexed by an owle in open consistorye, as is before in his life declared: againe that going to Constance he fell oute of his chariot by the waye. Afterwarde he was in the same councell of Constance reprochfullye deposed, and it was there declared that a councell ought to be aboue the Pope, and the Pope to be subiect to the controlment of the councel, which thing gaue a great pushe to the ouerthrow of his supremacye: & surelye from his time and the time of Paule the second, the Popes maiestye began to shrincke more & more. Againe in the time of Alexander the sixt by a tempest of thonder & lightninge the Angell set on the toppe of Angell castell in Rome the Popes chiefe place was beaten downe into the

riuer

riuer Tiber. Furthermore it appeareth that it was not so much the fonde furye of Iulye the second, as fatall prouidence, ẏ Pope Iulye the second when he could not preuaile by Papal auctoritie, did hurle away into Tiber S. Peters keyes (as they tearme them) the counterfaite euidence of his supremacye: for as he cast the keyes away, so other reiected his supremacie euer since. Furthermore in ẏ time of Pope Leo it came to passe that he created in one day 31. Cardinals, and the same daye while Leo and his Cardinals were in S. Peters Church, there fell such mightye stormes of windes, thūder & lightnings vpon the Church, that it shooke downe a little idoll made for the picture of Christe in the lappe of the virgin Marye. Also it stroke ẏ keyes oute of the hande of S. Peters Image in the faint Church. These and manye other such matters as haue come to passe, are to be so construed as they may best serue to the glorye of God and signification of his will, which is that Antichriste shall be destroyed with the breath of his mouth; that is the power of his holye word, and not by the might and arme of man. Ioyning therefore the successe that Christe hath giuen to his Gospel, with the shaking of Antichriste his kingdome foreshewed by the spirit of God, it shall not be amisse to take these signes as witnesses that God sheweth hereby that he is mindefull of his promisse made to his elect, that the dayes are at hand when Babilō must fall, and our Sauiour Iesus Christe come againe in glorye to the subuerting of him. The Lorde hasten it for his mercy sake, and make vs readye to receiue it with ioye. Amen, Amen.

162. Iulius the second.

IVlius the secōd was a Geneware borne (who as Erasmus wripting vpon the prouerbe A remo ad Tribunal sayth) was in his youth a whirrye slaue, and yet at length preased vp to

The seuenth booke of the

vp to the Papacye. And yet (sayth he) not contenting himselfe with that estate as he founde it, did enlarge his dominion and would haue made it larger but that death preuented his purpose. Vicelius sayth that he was rather giuen to warres then to serue Christ. Iohn Functius in his Commentaryes wryteth thus of him: Pope Iulius being borne of a base stocke rysing by degrees throughe good lucke and craftye witte attayned to the byest. He being a fellowe of a subtill and compassinge heade, and most giuen of nature to play the warriour, did like Nimrod enlarge his porcion by the dint of the sworde: so that by his procuremente within seuen yeares were slaine and destroyed to the nomber of two hundred thousand Christians. He besieged Rauenna cruellye, and in the ende preuayling made it subiecte to his Empire. And with the like violence he wrested Seruia, Imola, Fauentia, Foroliuium, Bononia and other Citpes from the Princes with great bloudshed. Sleidā sayth that whē this Iulius was Pope, he toke an oath that he would haue a councell within two yeares. But when he troubled and disquieted all Italye with warres beinge enemye one while to the Venetiās, another while to ye king of Fraūce, nowe to the Duke of Ferraria, now to the Bononians: certaine Cardinals ix. in nomber steppinge asyde and assembling at Milken, do summon a cōsicell to be held at Pisana. The chiefe of these were Bernardin Crucetius, VVilliam of Præneste, & Fraūcis Cossetinus, w whom were the proctours of the Emperour Maximilian and of Lewis the xii. king of Fraunce about the same purpose. This councell was called the yeare 1511. the xir. day of Maye, to beginne in September next following. The cause hereof is sayde to be, because the Pope had broken his oath and forsworne himselfe: for notwthstādīng he had raigned so many yeares, yet contrarye to his oath they could get no hope of hauing a cōsicell. And furthermore for yt they had heynous crimes to charge him withall, they purposed to depriue him of his dignitye

Pageant of Popes. Fol.178.

dignitye, which he had gotte by bribery. But Iulius chargeth all men vpon paine of great punishmēt, that no man should obey them, & summoned another coūcel to be held ȳ yeare following in Aprill in Lateran at Rome, whereunto xxi. Cardinals subscribed. For this from time to time hath bin the practise of the Pope when any councel hath bin assembled against his doinges, then to assemble another Synode against the other in some place meete for his purpose.

There was at this time a famous Lawyer at Papia called Philippus Decius, who published a booke defendinge the doinge of the Cardinals against the Pope. Diuers other wrote against him some in prose & some in verse, as Hulricus Huttenus in certaine Epigrams to this effect in Englishe translated verse for verse.

This Iulie, vvho by long diſcent did ſit in Peters ſeate,
Through nevv cōceite doth vvorke theſe broyles, vvith many a monſtrous feate.
He neither prayeth for his flocke, nor lyuing yet in peace,
He ſeeketh not as Peter did their knovvledge to encreaſe.
But kindleth vvarres, and iets in armes, and doth delight in goare,
Yea Peter backe he puts, and needes vvill ſet S. Paule before.
S. Paule yet ſmites not vvith his ſvvord: but therevvithall vvas ſlaine,
But Iulie doth his handes vvith bloud of many Chriſtans ſtaine.

¶ The deſcription of Pope Iulie by
the ſayde Auctour.

VVhy goeth Iulius in ſteele, and in his coate of plate?
VVith griſelye beard and ouglye lookes vpon his bullſhye pate.
VVhoſe frounced forhead hideth deepe his loathly ſteaming eyes,
Frō vvhence vvith helhoudes threatning loke the ſparkling fier flyes.
This terrour vnto VVeſterne men by ſea and eke by land,
VVith bitter bovves and bloudie billes and ſhaking ſvvord in hand.
That vnto all the kings on earth hath vvrought ſuch vvarlick harmes,
And is a ſcourge toth vvorld vvhich he hath rayſed vp in armes.
The author of ſuch maglinges made ſuch ſlaughter and ſuch ſpoyle,
That did both Prince and people all in daunger put of foyle.
VVho both vvith hand and head doth put all vilanye in vre,

Z.　　　　　　　　　A crea-

The seuenth Booke of the

A creature borne the ruine of mankinde for to procure,
VVhose vvorke is death: vvhose leasure is fulfilling filthye lust,
And plucking peace from eueiye man hath broached vvarre vniust.
VVhat is there in him vvhye that anye man dare giue his dome,
VVhye such a caytiffe maye deserue the naire of Pope of Rome.

The French kinge vnderstandinge that the Pope with the helpe of the Venetians, wente aboute to disinhe those whom he set in garrison, did summon a councell at Turney in September, where he propounded these questions to be discussed: Whether it were lawful for the Pope to warre vpon anye Prince without any cause: Whether a Prince defendinge his owne in that case may set vpon the Pope, & withdraw himselfe from obeing him: And answeare was made that the Pope ought not to do so, and that a Prince might do accordinge to the questiō: & that vniust thondring boultes of excommunication are not to be feared. Here-vpon the king sent his Embassadour to Pope Iulius to declare the determination of the councell, and to desire him eyther to be cōtent with peace, or els to call a general councell to bulte oute these matters the better. But the Pope would graunte to neither request, but did excommunicate Lewis, and gaue his kingdome for a praye to those ỹ would make hauock of it. Of this Iulius it is written in a certaine Commentarye of the maisters of Paris againste the Lutherians, that he did most villanouslye commit ỹ which is not to be spoken of, with two noble yonge gentlemē who were put to a certaine Cardinall called Robart Nauetensis to be broughte vp, by Ladye An Queene of Fraunce. The like thing is reported of him by another writer, wher vpon Conradus Gabriel wrote these two Verses.

 Venit in Italiam spectabilis indole rara,
  Germanus: redijt de puero mulier.

It were not tollerable to set out all the treachery wher-with this monstrous Pope defiled himselfe. In his time
                among

Pageant of Popes. Fol. 179.

amonge the religious men began diuers grosse and diuerent opinions touching the incarnation of Christe, & the conceptiō of the blessed virgin mouing many vnnecessarye, vnprofitable, and vnhonest questions, and medling impudentlye with matters belonging to midwiues and not to scholedoctours, and therefore rather to be suppressed then heare reuealed: onelye this maye suffice to the wiser sort, to consider what sectes were amonge those holye siers and what diuinitye they studied. One of these busye brayned sophisters was called Ptolomeus Lucensis a mounke, who preached his filthye fantasyes touchinge ye maner of Christes conception, in a Church at Mantua.

This Pope Iulius being a lustye warriour, and going forth on a time with his armye out of the Citye, did hurle Peters keyes into Tiber with these wordes: Because that Peters keye is able to do no more, let the sworde of Paule helpe to do it. By which deede sayth Bibliander, Pope Iulius hath resigned all his power vnto the riuer Tiber, if the Pope haue receiued any power of Peter in that Christ said vnto him, Behould I wil giue to thee the keyes of the kingdome of heauen. For he that casteth awaye the keyes being ye testimonye of auctoritye, doth depriue & spoile himselfe and his successours of S. Peters inheritaunce. Of this made be mancke of Iulie hurling his keyes into Tiber, diuers men wrote verses, as Melancthon, Bruschius & one Ducherius, the Englishe whereof doth followe.

While Iulius to mischiefe frāde did bloudy warre prepare,
He marched foorth, in armed Hoaste his weapons for to beare,
A sword hong by his side which our coragious holy syre,
And Peters keyes into the deepe of Tiber ſlud he flyng.
With blustring thus if Peters keys inwarre cannot preuaile,
Then with the Sword of Paule we wyll our enemies assaile.

Huldericus Huttenus made this Epigrame of Pope Iulius perdons.

By craft Pope which he soddainly may change dost intrude.

Z ii.   Thou

The seuenth Booke of the

Thou sellest heauen, and yet no part therof by right is thine,
Sell me the thing thou hast: great shame yvill els therof proceede,
VVhen thou dost sell the thinge vvhich thou thy selfe dost vvant and
O saluage soyle, vvhy bidst thou not an hundred giants fel, (nede.
To helpe Iuly to beate out Ioue, that he the heauens may sell?
For till an other God get heauen, and thunder from the skies,
Friend Iuly Ile not byee of you such vvoightie marchandise.

But after he had made many great slaughters, he died
Anno, 1513.

163. Leo the tenth.

Leo the tenth was a Florentine borne, of the noble house of Medices, and called ere he were Pope Iohn Medices. He being Deacon and Cardinal of saint Maries, contrarie to all hope was chosen to succede Iulius. He beinge diligently from his youth trained vp in learninge vnder learned schoolemaisters, and especially one Angelus Politianus, did afterward greatly fauour learned men. When he was but xxxi. yeres olde he was made cardinall by Innocentius the. viii. and at the yeres of. xxxviii. he obtained the papacie. This Leo was of his owne nature a gentill and quiet person: but oftentimes ruled by those that were crabbed and contencious men, whom he suffered to do in many matters according to their insolent will: He addicting him selfe to nicenesse, and takinge ease did pamper his flesh in diuerse vanities and carnal pleasures: At banquetting he delighted greatly in wine and musike: but had no care of preaching the Gospell, nay was rather a cruell persecutour of those that began then, as Luther and other to reueale the light thereof: for on a time when cardinall Bembus did moue a question out of the Gospell, the Pope gaue him a very contemptuouse aunswere saying: All ages can testifie enough howe profitable that fable of Christe hath ben to vs and our companie. Sithens faith he sente letters and bulles of pardons into all nations for suche as wolde woulde giue money for them, the effectes of his pardons were diuerse, some especially to sell licence to eate butter, chese, egges, milke, and fleshe vpon forbidden daies, and for this purpose he sent diuers treasurers into al coūtreis, and namelye one Samson a monke of Millaine into Germany, who by these pardons gathered out of sundrie places such hewge sommes of money that the worlde wondered at it, for he offered in one day to geue for the Papacie aboue an hundred and twentie thousand duckates. Martin Luther being singulerly wel studied in the scriptures, and cōtinuing at Wittemberge in Germanye (where these pardons polled maynely) began to enforme and teache the people, howe muche they were abbused, to giue suche greate sommes of money for suche trifles as were nothing profitable, and wished thē to be better aduised in bestowing theyr money, wherevpon he purchased the Popes bitter curse againſt him and his adherents, to the no littell disturbance of the whole estate of Germanye: for because by the preaching of Luther, and his bookes painting out the treacherie of the court of Rome, the princes of Germanye, as the Duke of Saxony, the Lantgraue and other wold not yelde so muche as in time past the Pope had commaunded by vsurpation. The Emperour and they in the ende fell together by the eares, by the Popes procurement, as at large is set forth in Sleidan, and can not so aptly in this place be reported. Other enormities which in the Popes pardons moued Luther were these: The people were perswaded that if they bought these pardons they nede not to seke any further for saluation, and that no sinne coulde be so horryble, but that by these indulgences it shuld be forgeuen, and that the sowles that lye tormented in Purgatorie shoulde flie into heauen forthwith, as sone as the money receyued for these pardons at the charge of their friendes shoulde be put into the Popes cofers. But to returne to Pope Leo: he made xxxi. cardinals in one day, wherby he gat greate bribes

The seuenth booke of the

bribes and muche treasure, but the same day appeared manye horrible sightes and great tempestes arose, with vehement windes, thonders and lightninges, vehementlye rushinge vpon the Churche where the Pope and his Cardinals were with such force, þ it shooke downe an idol made for the picture of Christ like a child in the lappe of the virgin Marye: also it stroke S. Peters keyes out of his hand. These thinges were enterpreted to prognosticate the decay of the Popes kingdome, and thereupon many wrote bitter verses.

Anno 1521. the same yeare that in Christmas hollydayes Solyman the Turke wan the Rodes, as the Pope wente out of his closet to morrowe masse, a great roofe of Marble stone fell downe sodeinlye behinde his backe, and slewe manye of his guarde. This Leo did enriche aboue measure his bastardes and cosins, aduauncing them to dignityes both spirituall and temporall with robbing an vndoinge other. For he made Iulianus his sisters sonne duke of Mutinensis, and Laurētianus duke of Vrbin, marpinge the one to the sister of Charles duke of Sauoye, & the other to the duchesse of Polande: for he deposed the duke of Vrbin to the entente to aduaunce the one of these in his place: which also he attempted against the duke of Ferraria, but was disappointed. He made one of his nephewes called Iulius a Cardinal. In the yeare of our Lord 1571. and the first day of December, as sone as this Leo in deede a Lion, heard it reported to him that the Frenchmen were by his meanes slaine, taken and driuen out of Italye, he reioysed and laughed at this newes so vehementlye, that therwithall he fell downe dead at his table, being a man that in his life time thought that there was neither heauen nor hell, & countinge the Scripture sa is aforesaid to be but a fable. One Actius Sannazarius wrote these verses of him.

 Sacra sub extrema, si forte requiritis, hora
  Cur Leo non poterat sumere? Vendiderat.
            Pasquil

Pageant of Popes. Fol. 181.

¶ Pasquil against Leo.

Pastor vt ambiguo Proteus dignoscitur ore,
Et dubius liquidis sæpe vagatur aquis:
Sic Leo nulla fides tibi, nec constantia rebus,
Factaq; promissis sunt odiosa tuis.
Nec bona, nec mala sunt dubio credenda Leoni,
Est etiam in verum vix adhibenda fides.
Quum ventrem imprudens auido natura Leoni
Fecisset, rimas prębuit huic geminas.
Non excrementis fuerat satis vna: sed harum
Altera nunc clausa est, nec minus illa vorat.
Gaude Roma, breui hac solueris peste: satiscet
Aluus, tàm magni ponderis impatiens.
Differat à Decimo quàm Iulius ipse Leone,
Discere ab amborum nomine Roma potest.
Iulius est hominis, bruti Leo, Iulius egit,
Quæ suasit ratio : quod libet, iste facit.

In the time of this Leo doctour Benbrick an Englishman Archbishop of Yorke and Cardinall, lyeng Embassadour in the seruice of K. Henry ỹ eighte, was poysoned by report at Rome and dyed there.

164. Hadrian the sixt.

HAdrian the sixt was borne in Holland of a base stocke: he was first scholemaister to Charles the Emperour, & afterwarde made a Cardinall & by this meanes obtayned the Papacye, and still kepte the name that he receiued in Baptisme being called Hadriā. He promised Princes by his letters that he would do his endeuour wherby the Citye of Rome (being the mother & welspringe of mischiefe) should be first resourmed with al seueritye: But this was but an hypocriticall dissemblinge. For he being once placed in his dignitye, did euen as the rest trouble and sharplye molest those that any way debased his pardōs or reproued his

Z iiii.

The seuenth booke of the

ned his ambitiō as Luther, Ecolampadius and other did: but in the fourth yeare of his pontificalitye he dyed Anno 1523. the tenth daye of September.

165. Clement the eight.

CLement the viii. borne in Florence nephewe (at ye least) to Pope Leo the tenth, and called before Iulius, succeeded this former Hadrian, And that by force of acmes as Valerius sayth. But as he gat the place by violence, so had he it as troublesome as euer anye before him. For while this Pope putting himselfe valiantlye in armour did skirmishe amonge the Emperours souldiours and those that fought for the gouernmēt of Italye, his Citye Rome was taken, sacked and spoyled, and made a bootye to Germaines and Spaniardes: and the Pope himselfe also was apprehended, mocked and scoffed, and reprochfully vsed. And from thenceforth the greater Churches in Germanye detesting ye Papacye as the bloudie kingdome of Antichrist, haue euer defyed and despised his souerainitye. But this subtile man being afterward by his pollicye ayded with ye helpe of diuers Princes and people, did purpose to persecute the Lutheranes wyth fier and sworde. But in September Anno 1534. he was poysoned by such a strange practise as was neuer heard of: for both he and certaine Cardinals with other his freinds, were poysoned with the smell and smoake of a Taper, which was poysoned for that purpose by a straunge confection.

¶ Of this Clement thus wryteth Vulteius touching a fault vvherof he vvas mistrusted.

De Clemente, quod est cōscriptum carmine, crimen,
Id verum, aut falsum protinus esse scio.
Si verum est, verè iam possum dicere, mundi
Vina breuis vitium claudit, & omne scelus.

Si fal-

Pageant of Popes. Fol.182.

Si falsum est, verè iam possum scribere, mundi
Dux, pax, lux, paruo contegitur tumulo.
Et falsum esse reor. Quis enim committere summum
Pontificem Romę talia monstra putet?

John Tillius sayth in his Chronicle, that this Pope beinge taken pryfoner by the Emperours armye, (as shal be at large declared) was redeemed for fourtye. Thoufande Floreces. Also of this Clement it is reported in a certaine Commentarye vpon the articles of the maisters of Paris, that he was one that practifed poysoninges, a murderer, a baude, an vncleane liuer, and that in such fort as for offending of chast eares is not to be named. Also he is charged there with Simonye, adulterye, rauishing of women, periurye, coniuring, and to be a Church robber fraught with al kinde of villanye, and therfore a certaine Poet wrote thus of him.

Clementi nomen dedit inclementia fati,
Bellorum hic fomes, effectorum Lætitia malorum.

Valerius Anselmus wryting of this Clemēt sayth thus, Clemēt being of a dissembling wit, in the last yeare of his Papacye repayred to the French king at Massilia: where they two agreed so together, that the king toke Kathrine nice vnto this Pope Clement at his motion, with a great dowrye of Ecclesiasticall dignityes, and maryed her vnto his second sonne Henry Duke of Orleans. This the Pope wrought to arme him selfe the stroger agaīst the Lutheranes, whose bloud he hunted after. But in September he and other of his Cardinals and familiaritye were preuented by the straunge poyson of a charmed Taper. &c.

Clement in making this mariage would first haue had the saide Katherine bestowed on the Frenche kinges eldest sonne if it could haue bin. But it came to the same effecte in the ende, for soone after the eldest sonne dyed, and then her husband Henry duke of Orleans was nexte heire and kinge of Fraunce: and by this meanes the Popes nyece according

The seuenth booke of the

cording to ye desire of her uncle became Queene of Fraūce, being the same woman that yet lyueth in Fraunce in these bloudye dayes being mother to Charles that now is king.

For this her aduauncement she hath shewed her selfe verye thanckfull vnto Italye and vnto the Court of Rome, both in plantinge Italians in diuers greate offices in the Realme of Fraunce, and also fortifyinge the Popes auctoritye to the vttermost of her power, with greater beneuolence to her owne countrye Italye, then is thoughte profitable to the countrye of Fraunce.

Iohannes Baptista Folengius in his Cōmentarye vpon the 105. Psalme hath these woordes: For it is reported that in our dayes Pope Clement the seuenth dyed of that most lothsome and filthye disease called morbus pedicularis, yt is to be eaten wyth lyce: & some say that he was poysoned. He was a mortall creature and therefore subiect to infinite miseryes and diseases as other men are. &c. Clement being dead, this Epitaphe was made on him, whereby it appeareth how the worlde iudged of his life.

Clementem eripuit nobis clementia fati,
Humanum toto gaudeat orbe genus.
Hic est qui fuerat iam dedecus vrbis & orbis,
Et fuit ætatis magna ruina suæ.
Hic est, si nescis, qui iam tibi, Roma, parauit
Excidium, pestem, funera, bella, famem.
Hic est, per quem tot prostrant & in vrbe puellę,
Per quem pulsus honos, virgineumq; decus.
Hic est, qui molles euexit ad astra cinædos,
Formosum à tergo munere iuuet Hylam.
Hic est, qui fuerat viuens infamia mundi,
Imperij labes spurcitiesq; sui.
Contemptor diuûm, scelerum vir, publicus hostis,
Perfidus, ingratus, raptor iniquus, atrox.
Exosus vitam, & morbo tenuatus amaro,

Stabat

Stabat Pæonia non reuocandus ope:
Mortem implorabat, nec mortem fata sinebant,
Gaudebant longa sed cruciare mora.
Hic vidit mortis centum tormenta futuræ,
Pœna tamen mortis non fuit æquâ suæ.
Ex ista tandem migrauit luce tyrannus,
Quo nullus toto peior in orbe fuit.

¶ Pasquil to Rome.

Roma vale, vide, satis est vidisse: reuertar,
Quum leno, aut meretrix, scurra, cinædus ero.

Under this Clement Nicolas Machiauel Secretarye of Florence and a famous Historiographer did flourishe, who in the first booke of his historye of Florence sayth: that for the most part the mischiefes that happe amonge the Christians, proceede of the ambition of the Popes. And that before the time of Theodoricus kinge of Lombardes, that is till about the yeare of our Lorde 500 they were euer subiecte to kinges in ciuill matters. But (sayth he) they encroached by little and little the ciuil iurisdiction, and finallye do vsurpe Lordship euen aboue the verye Emperours. They haue growen to this height (as he sheweth) by three meanes, by excommunicating, by geuing pardōs, & by þe sword. Furthermore in his discourses vpon the fift decade of Liue Cap. xii. he sheweth, þ contempte of Religion is cause of the ouerthrow of al common wealthes, & namelye that the occasion both of discorde and euill successe in Christendome, is because that Religion is contemned, whereof there can be no greater coniecture (saith he) then that those people which are nearest to the Church of Rome, þ heade of our Religion, haue least Religion. And he that by experience would know the truth of this matter, (if he were of sufficient power and auctoritye to transporte the Court of Rome into Zwitzerland, where onelye at this daye the people do liue both according to Religion & warlicke sort of antiquitye) he should perceiue that þ detestable demea-

nour

The seuenth booke of the

nour of the Popes Courte, would cause moꝛe disoꝛder in y͞e countrey then any chaunce els that mighte happen at anye time, &c.

166. Paule the thirde.

Paule the third, boꝛne in Rome, was first called Alexander Farnesius: He beinge a Cardinall and bisshop of Hostia, and a man almost spent in yeeres, was chosen to succede Clement, and yet he raigned fiftene yeeres. Valerius wꝛiting of him saith: This holy man did his endeuour accoꝛdinge to the custome of his auncestours to aduaunce his childꝛen and to suppꝛesse Luther and his adherentes. He was very cunning in astrologie, southsaying, and coniuring, by meanes whereof, being a young man he did manye strange feates. He caused his owne sister to yelde her selfe concubine vnto Pope Alexander the sixte, that hee might therby obtaine the red hatte. But in his Papacie, beinge an aged man, he deuised a newe pꝛofession of religious men. He purposing to reforme the estate of the church of Rome, sommoned a generall councell at Mantua, but to no purpose: and likewise in the later Tridentine councell he consto no purpose.

Valerius Anselmus, Paulus Vergerius, Iohn Sleidan, and other late writers do report these thinges that follow of him: It were to long to speake all that might be saide of this miserable man touching his hainous factes, as manslaughter, theft, poysonings, treasons, tyꝛannies, incest, foꝛnication, and such other. But yet it shall not be amisse to disclose a few of his pꝛactises. This Paule was an Astrologian, a Magitian, a wyzard: He made one Dionysius Seruita a pꝛactiser of Geomancy, that is a kinde of coniuringe with earth clay and sande, oꝛ suche matter, also he alwaies vsed as his familiar companions Ganricus a Poꝛtugall, Cetius, and Marcellus being coniurers, and say-

ters

Pageant of Popes. Fol.184.

sers of euyl spirites in the bodies of dead men: He acquainted him selfe with these, because he wold haue them to cast the natiuities and destenies of him and his children, by constellations. By playing the bawde he first gat to be made cardinal. He deliuered his sister Iulia Farnesia vnto Rodoricus Borgia a Spaniard, otherwise Pope Alexander the sixt, wherby he might obtaine of him to be made cardinall and byshop of Hostia, and so gat money to pay his debtes. By such meanes haue many fished for the fattest benefyces in the court of Rome, by seruing the Popes fleshely appetite, and saith (Cornelius Agrippa) there is no way redyer to get preferment there then this is. Furthermore this vnnaturall and wicked Pope Paule coulde not withholde his mischeuous hande from his owne kinred, no not from the wombe that first gaue him breath and life: for he poysoned both his nephew and his owne natural mother, that he might therby enioye the whole inheritaunce of the Fernelians. Beside this he liued carnally with another sister that he had: and because he perceyued that she loued other better then him (which in the ende the harlot shewed openlye) his iealousye was such, that to reuenge the despite as he counted it, he so watched his oportunitye, that in ȳ ende he poysoned her for it.

He beinge Legate vnder Pope Iulius the seconde in the prouince of Ancona, did villainouslye beguile a noble yong gentlewoman of the same Citye. For he shifted his apparell & counterfayted himselfe to be a noble man of the Legates companye, resorting to her as a woer, and craftelye vnder colour of mariage laye with her. But in the ende when the poore gentlewoman had vnderstandinge of him what he was in deede, and saw how she was deluded, being made not a lawfull wyfe but a priestes cōcubine (accordinge to the Popes lawe) she was so greeuouslye wounded with griefe hereof, that she was almost mad and rauished of her wittes. But she conceyued by him and was deliuered of a sonne

The seuenth booke of the

sonne called Peter Aloysius, who afterward shewed himselfe to be the liuelye image of such an adulterous father. At another time this Paule hauing a nyce called Laura Fernesia, committed incest with her also: but her husband Nicolaus Querceus toke him in the deede doing, & in a greate rage so wounded him, that the skar thereof remayned till his death. Againe he had a daughter called Constantia, with whom he was so entāgled and bewitched, ȳ (O most sinnefull man) to enioye her the more freelye as his concubine, he poysoned her husband Bosius Sfortia. Such is the double corruptiō of their single life: such villanye ensueth of their vowed chastitye. Thus doth God giue them ouer to their owne lustes that presume vpon themselues, & thus doth he detect the man of sinne, suffering him to come to ȳ fulnes of iniquitye: who neuerthelesse is so blinded in his owne fantasyes, that wallowing in this wickednes, he thinketh yet himselfe to be perfite holye, and the generall Vicar of Christe vpon earth. Yea & for so much as he is able to forgiue vnto other (as he thincks) greater sinnes, if greater maye be then these are, why maye he not dispense wyth himselfe in the like: Or rather why should it be counted sinne in him. For so sayth one Enuodius, to speake but of one among many such sayinges: The Pope togetherwith the power of teaching, hath receiued free libertye to do ill without controlment. And such is their affiance in the holines of their chaires, that the presumption thereof hath caused them thus to decree: Distict. 40. Non Vos in Glossa Papa de homicidio, vel adulterio accusari non potest vnde sacrilegū nō licet esse disputare de facto suo Nam facta Papæ excusantur vt homicidia Samsonis, furta Hebræorum, adulteria Iacob. The Pope cannot be accused of adulterye or manslaughter: Therefore it was as muche as Churchrobbing to dispute of his doing. For the Popes deedes are excused, as the murthers of Samson, the theft of the Hebrewes, the adulterye of Iacob. And againe it followeth

Pageant of Popes.   Fol.185.

wyth in the same place: In Papa si desint bona acquisita p meritum: sufficient quæ a loci prædicessore præstantur. If ý Pope lacke good deedes gotten by his owne merites: the good deedes which his predicessour (S. Peter) did, do serue his turne. This being considered it is lesse to be marueyled at, that the Pope should thus embrewe his handes with the bloud both of his freindes, kindred and parentes, and defyle his body most shamefullye with his owne sister, nyce and daughter. But to returne to the historye.
After that this Paule gatte the Popedome he created two Cardinals, whereof the one was Alexander sonne to his bastard sonne Peter Aloysius, and the other was Ascanius sonne to his bastard daughter Constantia. By his tyrannye he oppressed the Perusians: and in a madnesse he draue Ascanius Columna out of his kingdome. He clopned into his owne handes by vyle treacherye a towne called Camery, dryuinge out and dispossessing the Queene thereof being a godlye, wyse and vertuous Ladye. By his crafte he so inueigled ý Colledge of Cardinals, that he brought to passe by their consente to chaunge Camery for Parma & Placentia two noble Cityes, and to make his sonne Peter Aloysius Lorde and Prince thereof. But the iust vengeance of God did afterward plague this their pollitick packing, for this aduauncement of Aloysius fell oute to his destruction in the ende.

Oftentime this Paule consulted wyth his Cardinals how he might hinder the nationall councel holden in Germanye, and hee commaunded his Legates to enflame the mindes of other Princes against the king of England, and he purposed to giue his kingdome awaye from him, and to make it a praye and bootye to those that woulde make hauocke of it. Anno 1542 he summoned a generall councell to be holden at Trent, against the Gospel, the preachers & fautors thereof: But because he coulde not there haue all things accordinge to his owne minde, he remoued it to Bononia,

The seuenth booke of the

nonia, pretending that it was done onely for choyse of better ayre, which was but a shifte, when as his purpose was by this meanes to defeate many of geuing theyr voyces in the Sinode. He oppressed wyth all force the professours of the Gospell, some wyth sword, some wyth fyer, some wyth poyson were destroyed. He spared not so much as his Cardinals if they did once but sauour of that sect, wherof Cardinall Fulgosius & Cantarenus felt the proofe: And but ÿ it pleased God otherwyse to prouide, his owne brother Paulus Vergerius bishoppe of Iustinople had not escaped his rigour. He sent out his marcials as cruel persecutours on all sides, who tormented ÿ Gospellers with fyre & sword, burning and drowning, banishing and imprysoning, confiscating their goods, & pyning their carkases euen to death. The chiefe of these tormentours were Alexander Farnesius Cardinall, & Octauius his brother duke of Parma, who were the sonnes of the forsaid Peter Aloysius the sonne of this Pope. These two wyth great blustring and threatnings, came out of Italye & entred into Germanye Anno 1546. vauntinge and boasting verye arrogantlye, that they would shed so much bloude of the Dutche Lutherans, that their horses should be able to swim in the streame thereof.

In the meane time the wicked Pope at home was more pleasaunt with his daughter Constantia then the vse is: & beside this (like a sinnefull wretche) he prouoked to incest and most detestable whoredome another beinge his nyce, a yonge gentlewoman in time past commended as well for womanlye modestye as beautye.

He had a booke kept of 45. Thousande harlots, who for the libertye of their stewes did paye vnto him a monthlye tribute: These dames (sayth Eusebius Captiuus) are had in great honour wyth the Pope, these kisse his feete, these haue familiar communicatiõ wyth him, these are his companions both by daye and by night.

In the time of this Pope Anno 1534. the Franciscan
monkes

monkes played a cruel and bloudye pageant at Orleans in Fraunce, in despite of a dead woman beinge the Maiors wyfe of the Citye, who in her life desired that she might be buryed without any funerall pompe. The woman beinge dead the monkes in whose Church shee was buryed receyued of her husband vi crownes, and because the gifte was not greater they grudged much at it. And therfore they set a certaine nouice aloft in the roofe of the Church who shoulde in the nighte time counterfaite to be the womans spirite, and shoulde crye out and say that she was damned perpetuallye for Luthers doctrine. At the length the matter came before the kinges councel at Paris, where in presence of the Chauncellour Antonius Pratensis, these two Coleman & Steuen Atrebatensis being found gultye & conuicted of this villanye, were condemned to be put to open shame. One Vulteius Remensis wrote these Uerses against this illusion.

   Cum clamat laruas, furiosa caterua Icōnum,
    Infestare suam nocte dieq́; domum:
   Res vera est, falsi, laruati deniq́; fratres,
    Quos vestis sanctos prodigiosa facit,
   Sunt lemures, laruę, furię, vulposq́; lupiq́;,
    Qui infestant vitijs seq́; suamq́; domum.

One Pontacus a Popeling in his Chronicle set out ꝑ last yeare, being the yere of our Lord 1573. printed at Louany by an Englishe fugitiue called Iohn Fowler, reporteth in the 153. leafe thereof that this Pope Paule the third, did openlye excommunicate & curse the most renowmed Prince K. Henry the eyghte, & donauit regnum primum occupaturo, gaue his kingdome to him p̄ woulde first inuade it.

Nowe folloeth it to speake of Peter Aloysius duke of Parma & Placentia, and bastarde sonne to Pope Paule the thirde, who because he was proud, cruell and a most lasciuious tyraunte was murthered by his owne nobles Anno 1548. the tenth day of August. When this wretched villayne

The seuenth Booke of the

kinge (as both Vergerius & Sleidā report out of certaine Italian histories) beinge lieuetenaunte generall of the Romishe armye arriued at Pane, and founde there Cosmus Cherius bishop of the same Citye, beinge aboue thirtye yeares old, a man of great wysedome, learning, and of godlye lyfe, he committed vppon him such an horrible villanye, that I thincke since Sodom & Gomorra were by the hande of God for the same sinne destroyed wyth showers of fier and brimstone raynninge from heauen, the like hath not beene hearde of. For euen by force and violence hee caused his vassals and pezauntes, to holde the bishoppe while he (mauger his harte) in the meane time without all shame committed that deede; which shame wil suffer no ciuill pen to put in wryting. This treacherye & infamous filthines strake such a griefe in the harte of the good bishop, and was such a corsey to the innocent man, that for sorrowe & shame together he dyed within three dayes after. And (as some thincke) the same Aloysius perceyuing how greuouslye he toke it, gaue him poyson to dispatche him out of the waye, least he should haue made complaint thereof to the Emperour. For so vnaduisedlye in greate anguishe of minde he had threatned Aloysius. Beside this Aloysius beinge priuye to the incest of his father, presumed to committe the same deede oftē with his sister Constāria. And thus, while his father was Pope hauing power (as he thought) of heauen and hell, he presumed that he might do any thing lawfullye & without feare, and thereupon bye licentious luste did oft defile him selfe with eyther kinde. He committed manye robberyes and murthers, spoylinge of Churches, and thondring out his blasphemyes against the maiestye of God. And notwithstanding all this the Pope made of his sonne as his deare darlinge, and whollye endeuored himselfe to aduaunce him to honour, and when any made complaint of his wicked conuersation, the Pope would litle or nothing be moued therewith, but would saye after a smyling maner: that, he learned not this of his father. O-

ther

Pageant of Popes. Fol. 187.

ther correction of his sonne he vsed none, no not for that notorious crime vpon the bodye of Cosmus.

O what a miserable estate is this, that he who counteth himselfe to be the vicar of God (that is felous ouer ye least sinnes, and a seuere reuenger of iniquitye vppon his owne elected people) should thus against ye maiestye of that God as it were in defiance of his iustice, wincke at such an horrible treacherye and suffer it to be vnpunished, which Paganes and heathē sed onely by the light of reason haue loathed. Yea euen ye brutishe beast taught of nature cōmitteth not, and as I maye plainlye say, if the deuil himselfe hath any remorse to be touched wyth the hydiousnes of sinne, I am sure he would detest & abhorre such an acte most of all. If anye man be so vaine to repose his Religion vpon man, and to measure the truth of doctrine by the conuersation of the person, (As many missed by Popishe traditions refuse the sinceritye of the Gospell for the corruption of them ye professeth): If those kinde of parsons loke vpon this one Pope (a mightye piller of their Religion) I hope they would roote out that affiaūce in his doctrine which is planted in their breastes, or els be taught to measure the power and truth of the Gospell, not by the frailtye and weaknes of man. But if this waywarde reason be so beaten into their braynes that it cannot be digged oute, but that they will still affirme the doctrine is not true, and saye: I wyll not accept of it because the professours thereof are wicked men, Then let them beholde this Pope Paule a mightye patrone of their vndoubted Religion, and they shalbe compelled by their reason to say and speake with their tongue as the foole sayd in his hart: Surelye there is no God, no Iesus Christe, no holye Ghost, no Gospell, no heauen nor hell, I wil no beleeue anye such thinge, because that euē the Pope himselfe the great professour hereof is become a sincke of sinne, and a puddle of all filthines, to commit in his owne parsō adulterye and incest, and to foster those

Aa ii.   euils

The seuenth Booke of the

euils in his sonne, and suffer him to be as it were Prince of Sodom. &c. Thus (I say) if a man wil iudge Religiō by meanes he shall be so farre from attayning to the knowledge of God & from faythfull seruinge of him, y^t he shall rather despye vtterlye his glorious maiestye, & thincke that there is no God at all. But thus we see y^t as no people haue attayned so much to the true vnderstanding of God, as they to whom it hath pleased ye mercye of the father to reueale him selfe by his sonne Iesus Christe: so againe no people haue at anye time swarued farther from his holye wil and pleasure, and bin more fowlye polluted & stayned with all kinde of abhominable wickednes. But to returne to the historye of Peter Aloysius.

This outragious villanye against the sayd bishop together with other matters of iniurye, extorcion & crueltye, but this chiefelye, emboldned diuers parsons of all estates to grudge his doings. And amonge other he being on a time at his owne Citye Placentia, sone after this former facte Anno 1547. he did ceasse into his owne handes al the goods of sondrye parsons, and amonge them one Ierome Palauicinus, and when as he to auoyde the danger of displeasure fled to Crema a towne subiect to Venice, Peter Aloysius apprehended the wyfe and children of the sayd Ierom, and imprisoned them all. This being a matter wherof greater trouble might ensue, the Cardinall of Trent bearinge good will to the Fernesians, wrote his letters to Aloysius in ye behalfe of Ierom, but Aloysius gaue him a lighte aunswere. Afterward Octauius sonne to ye sayd Peter, came from ye Emperours campe to Trent purposing to returne home: The Cardinall of Trent came vnto him, and toulde him the whole matter touchinge Ierom, and desired him to be a meanes to his father for him. Hee made him promise to do it: and afterwarde sente woorde to the Cardinall that Ierom shoulde be receiued into fauour if he him selfe woulde come and craue his owne pardon in humble maner, manner. But because it was feared that promise beinge broken, he shoulde be put to some greuous punishmente, therfore the Cardinall with a trayne of men went to Crema, and called for Ierom. He mistrusting treason, would not appeare tyll he had good proofe that the Cardinal was come in deede. After they had longe talked in counsell together, and the Cardinal had at large promised his helpe, they toke their iourney together: The Cardinall sent one of his men before to geue knowledge to Aloysius that hee and Ierom were comminge, by whom Aloysius returned this message contrary to that whiche his sonne Octauius had shewed before, that if they came he coulde not restore Ierom. And although that bothe diuers Legates, besides other wise and graue men, did bothe intreate and vse perswasions to appease his wrath, yet he persisted obstinately in his purpose: And now certaine of the nobilitie that had hated him for his former prankes, conspired to murther him. They hauing entertayned for their purpose certaine ruffians for their sauegarde, watched a conueniente tyme for theyr purpose, and being garded with this their traine, they diuidinge them selues into diuers companies, came now and then out into the streates, euery man pretending that it was done for priuate quarrels towching him selfe: and therfore euery man demaunded of those whom he had hyred to attende on him, whether they woulde faythfully take parte with him to reuenge his iniurie, whiche he had susteined at the handes of Duke Aloysius: the seruing men made aunswere againe that they would do their endeuour not onely to reuenge an iniurie on hym, but further, if it were to kill him.

About this time, Pope Paule ye thi\[rd\] wrote to his sonne Peter Aloysius, willinge him to take heede to him selfe, and to beware of the tenth day of September, for he saide that the starres did threaten great mischiefe towarde him: for this Pope by constant reporte was skilful, not onely in

The seuenth booke of the

Astrologie, but also in Necromancie: vpon the sighte of these letters Aloysius was very sad and pensiue for feare. And when the same tenth day came, he passed out of his castell, being borne in a horselitter, and accompanied with a great trayne, to biewe the fortifiyng of the citie, which he had appoynted to be doone: The conspiratours were also there in a redinesse, but because they coulde not then obteine their purpose, therfore they made no sturre at al, but when he shoulde returne home, they gaue attendaunce on him, and as it were for duetie towarde him, they went before him. xxxvi. in al, and when he with his horselitter was entred into the castell, forthwith they drewe vp the bridge after them (for it was a drawe bridge) so that none other coulde follow them in: where, euen presently they set vpon hym with their swordes, and after they had rated him and vpbrayded him bitterly with his tyranny, they slew him in his litter, and a certaine priesti, beside the groome of his stable, and fiue Germaines. This beinge doone, they ran vp and downe in the castell, and made spoyle of al thinges, where among other things they founde an heuge masse of money, which he had laide in store to mainteine the charge of fortifiyng the citie. In the meane time the people of the citie ran thither, demaunding what the matter should be, because they harde such cryinge, weeping, and howlinge, within the castell. The murderers spake out to them againe, saying. we haue slaine the tyrant and recouered the libertie of our citie. But because that matter could hardly be credited vpon the warrant of the people, promissinge to saue them harmelesse, ẏ murderers tyed the deade body of Peter Aloysius to an iron chaine, and so hong him out ouer the castel wall, in sight of all the people, and after they had there let him hang a while, they threwe him downe into a dike. As sone as he was downe, the people ranne thither, drew him out, stamped on him and spurned him with their feete, and thrust their daggars into his bodie, so desirous

they

they were to worke their mallice on his hatefull carkasse. This being done, the people forthwith submitted them selues to the obedience of the Emperour, to whom they vttered the shameful demeanour of Aloysius and causes of his death, as hath ben saide. Thus he whom the Pope his father fostred in his villanie was plagued, both with losse of life in his own person, and alienation of his dominion from his children. So alwaies the iustice of god awaketh when the iustice of man sleepeth.

167.   Iulius the third.

IVlius the thirde an Aretinian borne, before his papacie was called Iohn Mary of the mounte. After the Cardinals had iarred many a day about the election, in the ende this man was chosen the seuenth daye of February, in the yere of our lord 1550. This Iulius because he was a melancholy fellowe, and one that hated from his hart the doctrine of Luther, was admitted into the colledge of Cardinalles, by the former Pope Paule the third, and was president for the Pope in the counsell of Trent, againste the Lutheranes. As sone as he had the Popedome he renewed the Iubelye to make moneye for himselfe. And therefore there repayred apace to Rome minstrils, pipers, harpers, fidlers, players, iesters, iuglers, ruffians, bawdes, harlots and Sodomites, with all kinde of rascall people. The Papistes conceyued a great hope that this Iulius woulde reforme Religion & clergye accordyng to their desire. But his delight was to feede like a glotton: Peacocks, porke and bacon and all kinde of swines flesh were his ordinarye fare that he most desired, He promoted none so soone to ecclesiasticall dignityes as yonge and wanton Ganymedes, especiallye one of that sorte called Innocentius in whom was no good qualitye. Beside that with his detestable doinges did staine, the Popes Pallaice, he was as wicked in

Aa iiii   his

The seuenth booke of the

his wordes: for in his talke he was so vnciuill and such a ruffianlye ribauld and blasphemer, as amonge all the varlets in Italye was not a worse.

Pantaleon, Vergerius, Sleidan and other late wryters do report this of him that followeth: Anno 1550. the seuenth daye of Februarye Iohn Marie of the mounte after great wrangling among the Cardinals was chosen Pope and called Iulius the third. And because this newe Pope might bestowe his Cardinals hat by custome one whom it pleased him: he made one Innocentius a boye whom hee fansied carnallye aboue measure while he was Legate at Bononia. Against which deede al the Cardinals much repined and cryed out on it, yet the Pope did it and furthermore made him his companion in his house. But to rifle this matter farther modestye will not suffer, it is better to ouerpasse both the rumours and talke of the people touching it: and those abhominable speaches wherewith the Pope himselfe was neither afraide nor ashamed to least of his owne villanye, & to displaye it openlye. Neyther could any honest eares endure to heare the contentes of certaine leud amorous letters fraught with all kinde of ribauldrye and wantonnes, which one Camillus Oliuus companiō to the Cardinal of Mantua, wrote to one Hāniball Cotiuus: there loathsome letters being in their vulgar tongue writen in most dishonest and amarous verse, were intercepted the same day that the Pope was chosen, the Cardinals being together in the consistorye: These rimes were copied out and seene of diuers both in Italye & Germanye, who reported of them that they neuer saw such detestable, vilanous and abhominable wrytinges. By this the Reader maye iudge with what spirite this Romishe clergye is endued in whom lyeth the electiō of Christ his vicar (as they saye.) But so farre they are from beinge (as they boast) exempted from sinne, that these treacheryes are common amonge them, and by theyr owne shamelesse tongues and pennes

pennes detected to all the worlde, which gaue occasion to
one Velteius to write this Epigram of Rome.

    Roma quid est? Quod te docuit præposterus ordo,
      Quid docuit? Iungas versa elementa, scies.
    Roma amor est. Amor est? qualis? Præposterus. Vnde
    Roma mares. Noli dicere plura, scio.   (hoc?

Touching the making of that boy Innocentius Cardinal, Vergerius sayth thus: Pope Iulius purposed to make a certaine lad called Innocentius Cardinal. This boye was not onelye of very base parentage, & endued wyth no good qualitye, but also was one of vile life and euill behauiour. Therefore when the Pope propounded the matter to the Cardinals and euery one stroue against it, one of the Cardinals more boulde then the rest saide to the Pope: Sir I praye you what do you see in this yonker, that you woulde thus honour him with the scarlet roabe? To whom the Pope said againe: And I pray you what did you se in me, þ you should thus aduaunce mee to this pontifical dignitye? And therefore as this is the game of Fortune þ she should aduaunce whom it pleaseth her, so ye haue promoted mee vnworthelye: and so let vs I pray you promote this boye and create him Cardinall.

Because that Paulus Vergerius, Bernardus Ochinus, & Hieronimus Marius did inueigh against the monstrous blasphemyes & horrible treacheryes of this Pope Iulius: therefore he suborned Ierom Mutius to defende and maintaine these things in publicke bookes. And auctorised him by his bulles not onelye to apprehende these reprehenders of the Popes treacherye and Sodomitrye, but also that he should by his wrytinges defame & slaunder with all kinde of bitter and dispitefull reproch, the Cittyes and Princes of Germanye. Thus may euerye man see how the bishop of Rome doth not onelye fall into this filthie sinne, but also defende them and vpholde them as well and lawfullye doin euen in open wrytinge.

                                                    Further-

The seuenth booke of the

Furthermore the said Vergerius in a certaine wrytinge amonge other thinges sayth this: Where as the name of Pope Iulye the third is foulye tainted with this former offence, and in such sort that he refrayned not from his Cardinals &c. I haue hytherto forborne to detecte his doinge touching this notorious enormitye. But seing euery man doth constantlye report that he doth ordinarilye vtter those same kinde of blasphemyes that vile bauds and other such leude parsons are wonte to vse in contempte of God: men ought rather to condemne such an ouglye monster and not Chrystians &c.

In the time of this Pope Iohannes Casa a Florentine Archbishop of Beneuentum, Deane of the Chamber Apostolicall, and in all the Dominions of Venice the Popes Legate with full power and auctoritye did flourishe. This Iohannes Casa wrote in the commendatiō of that most vnnaturall and abhominable filthines of Peter Aloysius, setting forth with most loathsome wordes, flourishing Retoricke and wicked eloquence in Italian rime, that matter which is not to be named among men: yet he hath so prapsed and commended it as no man withoute sinne maye reporte. This cursed worke and detestable booke was in printed at Venice by Troianus Nauus. In his recordes of malefactours made in the time of his Legacye, he reckneth none but such as professed the Gospell. Whereupon Vergerius sayth vnto him: Art thou not ashamed thou abhominable Archbishop? Darest thou shewe thy face abroade and burne holy bookes? Euen thou that hast written those rimes, euen thou that hast aduaunced the ouglye sinne of Sodom as an heauenlye deede &c.

Such was the tyrannicall rigour of this Iohannes Casa against the professours of the Gospell, that one Franciscus Spiera a lawyer for feare of his crueltye did reuolt from the Gospell & subscribe to the Pope, but vpon the same deede he fell into desperation and so continued a most myserable

man

man to his death tormented in conscience.

 Paulus Vergerius did also hardlye escape the rigorous hand of this Iohn Casa. But to be short it were a tedious thinge to declare at large all the demeanour of this Pope Iulye the thirde in the time of his Iubelie, and in the Tridentine councell in establishing the idoll of Lauret: and in his quarell & braule with the bishop of Armin comptrollour of his house for one peacocke,& other such like trifles. For he delighted much in the eating of peacocks and swynes flesshe: but when his Phisitian had giuen him warning that he should forbeare swines flesshe, because it was hurtfull for ye goute his disease, yet Iulius would not forbeare. The Phisition therefore gaue councell to the Popes Steward to take order that ye Pope should haue no such meate serued at the table. Whereuppon the Pope wantinge his dish asked, What is become of our bacon? The Steward aunswered that the Phisition willed him that hee should not set it on. The Pope forthwith violently brast into these wordes sayinge : Fetche me my meate hether Aldi spetto di Dio as he might say in English, In spite of Gods hart. This blasphemous outrage is a common phrase amonge ruffians and varlets of Italye in their rage, and as common with Pope Iulius as to other, beside other lasciuious and vnciuill speach. On a time he had at his table a peacocke which was vntouched, and therefore he commaunded that it should be kept for him til Supper : for I wil (quoth he) haue certaine of my freindes with me at supper in my garden. When supper time came the Pope was serued with hot peacocks, but his cold peacocke came not in accordinge to his commaundemēt : And therefore he began accordinge to his custome to blaster out his blasphemyes raginge and raylinge. One of the Cardinals that sat at the table sayd: I beseeche your holines not to be so highlye offended for so small a matter : No? (quoth Iulius) If God were so offended for one apple that he threw our first parentes out of Pa-

The seuenth booke of the

of Paradise: why shoulde not I that am his Vicar be angrye for my peacocke, seing a peacocke is of greater valew then an apple.

This Iulius caused this sentence to be printed on his coyne: Gens & regnum peribit quod mihi non inseruit. That nacion and kingdome shall perishe which doth not serue me.

When he shoulde create one Peter Betauus Cardinall, certaine of the Cardinals stoode against it, vrginge especiallye that the sayd bishop was infected with Luthers heresye: What then quoth the Pope, were it not better for vs by putting on him the Cardinals hat to purge him of that vncleanes, and by that bonde to knit him vnto vs, rather then to suffer him by escaping from vs to ioyne wyth oure ennemyes in Germanye as Vergerius hath done. After fiue yeares raigne this Pope Iulius died Anno 1555. the xxiii. daye of May. Vpon whom these verses were made.

Quò ventum est superi? quò vis progessa Diones?
    Quò gula? quò luxus? quò genus omne mali?
Ambrosiæ fœtent epulæ, marcotica sordent
    Vina, nisi Iliacus porrigat illa puer.
Cætera mens horret meminisse: ea discat ab vno
    Crimine, me quisquis legerit, atq; gemat.

Among diuers other Epitaphs this was written of him and sent from place to place as followeth.

Iohannes Maria A Monte. &c. Iohn Maria of the mount, by haphazard obteining the papacie in the time that the Cardinalles were at a great braule, which he durst neuer presume to hope for? In 6. yeres he did shed more Christian bloud then any other Antechrist hath done at any tyme.

    Fex sacrificulorum, grex Episcoporum, armentum Cardinalium gratitudinis ergo monimentũ eternum posuit.

Ciuill eares perhap will be offended that a man shoulde

Pageant of Popes. Fol.192.

here set down the sluttishe behauiour vsed in three pointes by this Pope Iuly, euen at open table, otherwise then any person of meane modestie would do in priuate chamber: As Beza sheweth in this Epigrã made of this Pope Iuly.

> Ebrius ad mensam quum Iulius ille federet,
> Impia quem potuit Roma nec ipsa pati:
> Tres pariter fertur pelues habuisse paratas:
> Vt triplici triplex vase leuaret onus
> Vna alui pondus, vomitum altera peluis habebat
> Tertia uesicæ concipiebat onus.
> I nunc, pontifices Germania dira negato
> Omnia clausa suo iura tenere sinu.

Theod. Beza in poemat.fol. 172.

And yet this Pope was he whose auctoritie and supremacie was with all humilitie and deuoute reuerence restored here in England in the yere of our Lorde 1554. by queene Mary. From this man Cardinal Poole, who before was outlawed and banished for high treason against king Henry the viij, came into England, and brought with him this Popes blessinge, pardon, and absolution. For the whiche Cardinal Poole was made Primat of England and Archbyshop of Canterbury. Thus the Popes blessing and pardon was receiued by the estate of Englande. And Pontacus in his cronicle published Anno. 1572. printed in Louany by Iohn Fowler an Englishman, that blotteth much paper to publishe grosse vntruthes, for the defamynge of his countrey by him forsaken, is not ashamed Folio 179. to reporte, but boastingly writeth it, that kinge Phillip and Queene Mary, with the whole Parliament house did humbly kneele vpon theyr knees to receiue the Cardinals blessinge and absolution from the Popes holynesse. But it is well known, and the knowledge therof dearely bought by Englande, how that noble Queene being otherwise of great wisedome, and godly minde, yet ouermuche deceyued by ignorance in scripture, and putting too great a confidence in the Popes autoritie, the antiquitie of her religion and

The seuenth booke of the

on and the professours therof, did euen of simple zeale yeld the disposition and orderinge of her affayres ouermuch to the crafty clergie, who with fyre and faggot followed in England the rygorous example of Iuly practized in Italy, against those that dissented from the Popes doctrine. But this is both at large set forth in the actes and monumentes of the Church, and further is not pertinent to this purpose, and therefore not here to be mentioned at large: Onely this is that whiche I note, to what kinde of person of lyfe and conuersation England in these later dayes submitted it selfe as to his generall Pastour, and the vicar of Christ. Of what maner of man we receyued blessinge and absolution so deuoutly, whom we did so highly commend, honour, and reuerence, aboue our natural prince with heauenly title of our moste holy father the Pope. To whom and to whose seruile yoke our prynce dyd yelde her selfe to be at his commaundement, whose curse we feared, whose loue and fauour, we sought to purchase with infinite treasure, whose displeasure caused bothe prynce and people to quake as it were at bel fyer. If the person that thus blessed vs be considered, I doubte not but we shall firste be ashamed of him, secondely ashamed of our selues, that we haue thus fallen downe and worshipped the beast, and fynally hereafter detest him and his successours.

The selfe same thinge is declared in Graftons Cronicle Folio. 1346. Where he at large sheweth howe Cardynall Poole was receiued by kinge Phillip, Queene Mary, and the Parleament, and how he perswaded them to be reconciled to this holy father the Pope, and how vpon their submission he gaue them absolution in these wordes folowing.

The Popes absolution set by the Cardinall.

¶ Our Lorde Iesu Christ whiche with his moste precious bloudde hath redeemed and washed vs from all our sinnes and iniquities, that he might purchase to him selfe a glorious spouse, without spot or wrinckle, and whom the father hath appointed head ouer all his Church: he by his

mercie

Pageant of Popes. Fol. 193.

mercie abſolue you, and we by the Apoſtolike auctoritye gyuen vnto vs by the moſt holy Lorde Pope Iulius the thirde, his vicegerent on earthe, do abſolue and delyuer you and euery of you, with the whole Realme and dominions therof, from all hereſie and ſchiſme, and from all and euery iudgements, cenſures, and peines for that cauſe incurred. And we alſo do reſtore you agayne to the vnitie of our mother the holye Churche, as in our letters of Commiſſion ſhall more plainely appeare. &c. *The Pope and the Cardinals fellowes in cōmiſſiō with Chriſt for remiſſion of ſinnes.*

This beinge done, the kynge and the Queene and all the reſt went to the Chappell, and chaunted Te deum for ioye of this ſweete bleſſyng of ſo holy a Pope. It maye be that thoſe burgeſes and the reſt of the Parleamēt houſe, at the time of this abſolution, thought better of his perſon when they receyued his bleſſing: but I wyſhe thoſe that are yet remayning of them, and reade this his lothſome life, now to conſider what a ſtinking idoll they honoured ignorantly at that time, and what a villains bleſſing they receyued ſo deuontly. Conſider alſo what benefittes euery way followed this bleſſynge: for ſone after there fell ſo great extremitie of raine (as thoughe the heauen had bewept our iniquitie) that the aboundance therof rayſed great and perylous fluddes, doinge muche harme in diuers places: The Thames ſwelled ſo high, that for the ſpace of fower or fiue dayes boates and barges rowed all ouer ſaincte Georges fielde, and ſo at Weſtminſter a boate mighte haue rowed from one ende of the Hall to the other. Alſo that yere and the yere following there raigned hot burning feuers, and diuers other ſtraunge and newe diſſeaſes ſo contagiouſly, that many people periſhed in all partes of Englande, eſpecially of the moſt auncient and graue men, for in London betwene the xx. of October and the laſt of December ther dyed ſeuen Aldermen: Alſo the yere followinge there enſewed a great dearth and famin throughout all England: And agayne the yere after that, Newenam bridge, Rye banke

The seuenth booke of the

banke, Callice, Hamines, and Guynes were taken by the Frenchmen, and the Englishmen dryuen cleane out of that parte of Fraunce, to their perpetual damage, which they had so long enioyed before: Ad vnto this also, that where as Queene Mary prouided a sufficient power to be transported for the rescewe hereof, whiche mighte haue saued it, there arose such terrible tempestes of windes and weather continuing foure or fiue dayes, vntill such time as the Frenchmen had wrought their purpose, and the Englishmen in the meane time by meanes of the terrible tempest were kept of mauger their hartes: and such shippes as did aduenture the passage were so shaken and torne with violence of weather, as they were enforced to returne with great daunger, with losse of all their tackle and furniture. Finallye euerye thinge wente so to wracke, that (as it was thought) the noble Prince Queene Mary seing her Realme so to go to wrecke, concepued such an inwarde sorrowe of minde that by reason thereof aboute September she fell into an hot burninge feuer, which sicknes also was common that yeare throughe all the Realme, and consumed a marueylous nomber (as Grafton noteth) both noble men, bishops, Iudges, knightes, gentlemen and farmours, and in the ende the Queene dyed thereof and also ye Cardinal in one day, the 17. day of Nouember Anno 1558. And this was the successe of the Popes blessing, therefore God send them plentye of the tree ye like the fruite therof.

168. Marcellus the second.

Marcellus the seconde borne in Hetruria was first called Marcellus Ceruinus: he was Cardinall of the crosse of Hierusalem, when with ye consent of all the Cardinals he was made Pope. He being created the ix. daye of Aprill, would not chaunge his Christian name but would be called Marcellus the seconde, and the next daye he receiued all

ned all the Papall ornamentes in Lateran Pallaice.

Charles the Emperour and his brother Ferdinand on a time thoughte it meete to prepare an armye againſt the the Turke, and wrote to the Pope to moue him therein: This Marcellus aunſwered by his letter, that the armye ſhould rather be addreſſed againſt the Lutherans, for theſe men he ſaide were worſe then all Turkes. But this he did before he came to the Popedome. But in his Papacye he was an hotte defender of the Romiſhe ſuperſtition, and a ſtronge enemye to the Lutheranes: but he beinge one that was long troubled with the iaundies, his diſeaſe toke him ſo ſore that he dyed thereof the xxiii. daye after his electiō, being the third daye of Maye.

¶ Theodoricus Greſmundus of the royat of Rome wryteth theſe Uerſes followinge.

Roma caput ſcelerum, niuei iactura pudoris,
   Exitium fidei, luxuriæq; parens.
Sola Venus diſpenſat opes, diſpenſat honores,
   Sola facit ſerua quicquid in vrbe libet.
Extollit, magnosq; facit ſapientia turpes:
   Sit procul, in tenero cui ſedet ore decor.
Tartara ſunt molli potius adeunda iuuentæ:
   Si non eſt alius, ſit tibi barba comes.

Marcellus Ceruinus was borne at Mount Publican in the field of Florence, who when he had well ſtudied humanitye, began to be a ſcholemaiſter. Afterward when Pope Paule the third had created Alexander Farneſius (his nephewe by his baſtard ſonne Peter Aloyſius) Cardinall being but a boye, he made this Marcellus Ceruinꝰ his ſcholemaiſter. But ſone after Alexander the Cardinal leauing his learninge and forſaking his booke, addicted himſelfe wholly to other affayres, wherein both he and Pope Paule the third vſed the ſeruice of Marcellus as of their Secretarye. When the biſhopricke of Nicaſter fell voyde he was

Bb   created

The seuenth booke of the

Vergerius when he shoulde departe out of the sinode came to Ceruinus, and demaunded of him for what articles especiallye he would haue him cast out from the companye of ye other bishops? Ceruinus aunsweared him saying: because I haue hard that thou deniest that the Legendes of S. Gregory and S. Christopher are true. So it is (quoth Vergerius) I haue denyed them & do still denye them to be true, emboldning my selfe herein by ye auctoritye of Pope Paule the thirde: for when he commaunded both these Legendes to be taken out of the Breuiary, he sheweth in that preface that he commaunded that onelye such Legendes should be razed as were not true. Ceruinus being thus entangled, made aunswere that they were not to be counted good mē which would agree with ye Lutheranes in any one point, & therfore auaunt out of our councell. Such was the rancour of this Ceruinus against the Gospell, and yet he was one voyde of all knowledge in diuinitye, but peuishe in retayning superstitiō. But otherwyse he was a man of good discretion, of verye honest life, and of great wysedome, and therfore he was had in great estimation and reuerence, so ye if he might haue raigned Pope, it was to be hoped that he would haue reformed many thinges in ye Court of Rome, & especially that he would haue eschewed all ropotousnes. And so it came to passe for Pope Iulye ye third being dead Ceruinus was chosen Pope. But wheras he was long before sicke of the pelowe iaundise, then the disease began to woorke so sore vpon him that he died the twentye daye after the election. The report was that he was poysoned but there was no such thing. A litle before he would haue bin crowned but with moderate coste. Cardinall Farnesius wyth his freinds in election gaue his voyce to this man although he had long before had a brawle with him, because he hoped that no man would more diligently aduasice him as Paule the thirde did determine. But especiallye he hoped that he would maintaine ye house of Farnesia that they

shoulde

shoulde not be depriued of the dukedome of Parma and Placentia: For Cardinal Farnesius debated it wyth Iulye the thirde, to make promise thereof before he would assist him to obtaine the Papacye. Some said that many Cardinals did therfore chose Ceruinus Pope, because they saw him so decayed by sicknes, that there was no hope of longe life in him: For that is their practise of old.

169. Paule the fourth.

PAule the fourth borne in Neaples, called first Iohn Peter Carapha, the same yeere Anno. 1555. was chosen Pope the xxiii. daye of Maye with one agremente of the Cardinalles, and exalted with all ceremonies. This man founded a new sect of Religious men in Venice, called by an holy name Iesuites, of the name of Iesus, but this he did before he was Pope: but after this deede he beinge made Cardinall, applied his minde to other matters, namely to scrapinge richesse together. Before his Papacie he publyshed a booke concerninge reformation of the Churche, but in his raigne he regarded it not. All his mynde was on warres, delightyng rather in battell then in peace, and so he played rather Saule the persecutour, then Paule the preacher of the Gospell.

Cælius Secundus and Vergerius do thus report of him: Paule the fourthe, a Neapolitan, called Iohn Peter Carapha, was chosen in May to succede Marcellus, by the consent of the Cardinalles, desirous therein to gratifie Henry kinge of Fraunce. This Pope saith Cælius dyd found a sect of priestes at Venice called Iesuites, but afterwarde hauinge obteyned his purpose, which by this meanes he aymed at, he gaue them ouer. For he so cast his net, that forsaking a byshoprike he fished for a Cardinalship, & caught it: Thereupon when he shoulde departe from Venice, the Iesuites demaunded of him whither he went: to whom he aunsweared

The seuenth Booke of the

aunswered sayinge. Whither I go ye cannot come, meaninge thereby that he wente to the Pompe and dignitie of Rome, as to an other heauen, and that he shoulde leaue them in wretchednes and beggerye: Thus it pleased hym to dally & sport him selfe with the phrase of the holy ghost. Many thinges are reported of him, as that he was a stoute Champion for Purgatory, and that he knewe the secretes of some mindes, and that he dyd many wonders. Vergerius sayth, he dedicated a booke of reforminge the Churche to Paule the thirde, and yet hee made no reformation in his owne time: But saith hee, who so euer readeth that booke shall see that he confirmeth al those poyntes almost, whiche we reproue in the papistes: that is to say, that the Churche is so decayed amonge them, as it is rather the Churche of Sathan then of Christ. For he saithe that the Popes do for their owne luste store them selues with maysters hauing itching eares, that the name of Christ is blasphemed amonge the Gentiles, throughe Cardinalles and Bishops, that the power of the keyes is wiped away with money, that lewde persons are made priestes, that Simonie is vsed as it were in open fayres, that the prelates doe swell with Ambicion and Couetousnes, that horrible villanies are practised in monasteries, y Rome swarmeth to shamelesse harlots and strupets, beside many lyke matters onely towching theyr detestable maners: but of their manifold superstitions, of theyr butcherly slaughters and cruell tyranny raging at that time in Italy, England, France, Spayne, and other countries, he speaketh not a woorde. And yet saith Vergerius (who made faithful searche therof) win lesse then thirty yeares theyr inquisition of heresye, hath deuoured and destroyed by diuers kinde of torments an hundred and fiftie thousande Christians. This acompt Vergerius made aboue twenty yeares ago: And since that time (sauynge onely (God be thanked for it) in England) in al the former countries this bloudy persecution for Re-

ligion

Pageant of Popes. Fol.197.

ligion hath not onely continued, but mightely encreased. Italy dayly tasteth the bytter gall of it, as occasion serueth, Spaine findeth that the heate therof burneth more feruent ly in the middest of winter, then the scorching Sonne in the middest of sommer at noone daye, the flame of the one turneth and tanneth theyr skynnes to black: the coales of the other burneth theyr bodies to graye ashes. And as towching Fraunce, al Europe knoweth that as yet the worme in the grounde hath scant taputed the karkases of thousandes, whiche within these fewe dayes haue ben martyred. Thus we see howe that prowde Prynce of Babilon hath made all Christendome as it were his burning furnace, to destroye those that wyll not fal downe to worshyp his golden image: and yet howe that this littell Ilande walketh as it were in the myddest of this vniuersall flame, and not so muche as our garmentes are once cinged therewith. And yet it is well knowne howe carefull and busie the byshoppe of Rome with his accomplices hath bene to sturre coales amonge vs, and to enkendle that fier in Englande, the smoke whereof were sufficient to destroy vs: who knoweth not howe that if his hotte thunderboltes of excommunication could any thing harme vs, we had therewith ben beaten to pouder longe since. If the rancke breath of his blacke curses might haue preuayled, we had bin blowne to hell, bequeathed aliue both bodye and soule to the deuil & dampnation longe since. If holye leagues (as they terme them) and conspyring vowes of sondrye estates by his procurement, could haue bin stronger against vs then ye hand of God with vs: how many are we that should haue tasted miserye, but how fewe should haue bin left to bewaile it at this day? When forren inuasions haue bin to weake, hath not that Romaine prelate sought to procure treason amōg vs heare at home, to delude the simple with bulles & pardons, enticing them to renounce their alleageaunce, to reuolt from their naturall Prince, to rayse rebelliōs against

Bb iiii. their

The seuenth Booke of the

their owne countrey? Hath not his bulls roared at Paules Church gate dischardginge subiectes of their dutye? And howe they haue wroughte in huggur mugger to steale awaye the hartes of Englishe subiectes, manye poore widowes and wretched orphanes at this daye in the North part of England with heauye harts can testifye, who haue lost their parentes and husbandes throughe detestable rebellion and sedition, the roote whereof is the Romishe religion. But because that these tumultes, treasons and broyles wroughte since the raigne of oure most Gracious Queene againſt her maieſtye and royall eſtate, haue bin practiſed not in the time of this Pope Paule the fourth, but by thoſe that haue ſucceded him, as Pius the fourth & Pius the fift: the gentle Reader is to be deſired not to looke for the perfite diſcourſe hereof as yet, neyther the hiſtorye of their liues, treachery and hurlye burlyes ſturred in Chriſtendome, for ſo much as yet they are not to be ſufficiently gathered by thoſe Chronicles that haue bin latelye ſet forth or augmented. As for Onuphrius who hath writtē their liues added to the hiſtorye of Platina, becauſe he is one hyred by the Pope to put his pen in vre for the cracked credit of their eſtate at this daye, there is iuſt cauſe to thincke his wryting to be parciall, as one that turneth the beſt ſide of his Popes face outward, and that which is blemiſhed eyther he hideth it, or payneteth it with a fayre colouere to couer the foule blots thereof. And therefore ſeing maiſter Bales trauaile doth ſtaye heare in Paule the fourth, this maye ſuffice till it ſhall pleaſe God to giue occaſion of proceeding in the liues of thoſe that haue ſuccecded during the raigne of the Queenes maieſtye. In the meanetime good Chriſtian Reader, cōſider thoſe treacheryes which by thy owne experience thou maieſt knowe ſince her highnes came to the Crowne, of the Popes dealinge againſt her Maieſtye and her Realme, weigh whereunto they tende by the example of theſe former hiſtoryes ſet forth in this woorke, & then I doubt

doubt not but euerye one shall fynde that he hath iust cause to saye: Blessed be Almightye God that hath thus preserued vs from the mouth of the Lion, and from the wolfe in a Lambes skin.

I doubte not but they that haue ben false harted againste our most gracious Queene, wyll consider theyr own folly, theyr owne iniquitie & madnes, in enuyinge the good estate of so noble, merciful, godly, & most lawful a prince: whom it hath pleased Iehoua to make oure Debora & a most blessed and worthy instrument, to the aduauncing of his glory, the comfort of his Churche, the preseruation of the happy and quiet estate of all trewe Englishe hartes, the whiche greate treasures of Gods mercye so plentifullye powred vpon vs the Lord geue vs grace to vse them more thankfully then heretofore, to glorifie his name with greatter zeale, to loue honour and serue, with all humilitie in Iesus Christ, our most noble soueraigne, to pray for the most blessed continuaunce of her maiesties raygne ouer vs, to graunt vs as trewe subiects to hate her enemies, as those that wyshe our confusion, especially the Pope of Rome, and all suche, euen to the deathe, as in his behalfe or for any iote of his accursed superstition would forbeare but to wysh well vnto her maiestie. The Lord gyue vs the harts to beware, renounce, and abhorre, the secrete societie and friendshippe of all those that seeke to trouble her quiet gouernement, as the ennemies of goddes glory. That neyther one affection nor other, cause vs to winke at theyr sedicious wordes, nor to iudge fauourably of the corrupt doinges and sayinges of suche hollowe hartes; whiche twoo thynges haue muche emboldned leude attempts, but that hauinge suche proofe of their practyses we may henceforth become euen iealous in the behalfe of Religion and of our most gracious Prince, and be ready euery man lawefully in his vocation, to beate downe blasphemie againste God,

and

and to suppresse the broode of sedition in the shell before it be hatched readye to flye. That England may neuer hereafter become a neast and filthye cage of those foule byrdes that are bred in the bosome of Rome. Amen. Amen.

FINIS.

Laus Deo.

Diuers cases wherin the Pope doth sell Dispensation contrarye to Gods Lawe
and his owne Canons, and the price of the dispensation accordinge to the rate in his Courtes.

¶ Dispensations for dronkards.

If a dronkard wil haue a congregation in his owne house, he must paye for his licence xxx. Turons or poundes of Towrs, vii. ducates and vi. Carlines.

If he will haue licence to erecte a newe publicke Synagog, three score Turons, xv. ducates.

For licence to heale with assistaunce, a dronkard payes vi. Turons

¶ Dispensations for such as haue bin or are to be promoted being vnder age.

If a boye of sixe yeares old wil take that step to priesthoode called Prima Tonsura, the first clep: he must pay. ix. Turons, two ducates: ix. Carlines.

If one at sixtene yeares or as sone as he coms to be xvi. wylbe Subdeacon his fee is. xii. Turons, iii. Ducates: viii. Carlines: It xvii. peres. vi. Turons: ii. Ducates: It xviii. yeares to be Deacon. xii. Turons: It. xix. yeres. vi. Turons:

To be Priest at xxii. yeres. xii. Turons: ii Ducates: x. Carlines. It. xxiiii. vi. Turons:

¶ For

Of dispensations.

⁋ For licence to take Orders.

He that taketh the first clyppe and the foure lesser orders, not of his ordinarie, payeth, iiii Turons: one Ducate: ix. Carlines.

To take all holy Orders, or but ii. or onely one of any body, the fee is xii. Turons: ii. Ducates : x. Carlines.

To take orders without the time, eyther one or more, or al. x. Turons: ii. Ducates.

If any come to receiue Benediction to the vse of an Abbot. xxiiii. Turons: vi. Ducates. To the vse of a Byshop. xxiiii. Turons.

⁋ Dispensations for those that want some of their lymmes, to take Orders.

If any wantinge some member be admitted to Clarkeship in any of the lesser orders, he payes vi. Turons: ii. Ducates.

If any such be admitted to orders, or to executiue function, he payes xvi. Turons : iiii. Ducates.

If any that lacketh fingers be admitted to a single benefice, his fee is. xii. Turons : iii. Ducates : vi Carlines.

If any be blinde of the right eye, xvi. Turons : xii. Ducates.

If any be blynde of the lefte eye, so as he maye holde the booke in the middest of the altare, and the blemishe be not great : xxx. Turons vii. Ducates : vi. Carlines.

He that hauinge but one stone or none well be priest, payeth. vi. Turons : ii. Ducates.

He that hath gelded hym selfe. xii. Turong : iii. Ducates: vi. Carl.

⁋ Dispensations for wilfull murthers.

He that is a wylfull murtherer maye haue a Dispensation to enioye one benefice : but if that suffice him not then for the seconde : if that serue not, then for the thirde, and together with the absolution, he payes. xii. Turons: iii. Ducates: vi. Carlines.

And that he may enioye the priuileges of the clergie. xviii. Turons: iiii. Ducates: ix. Carlines.

And if he require iii, benefices. xviii. Turons: iiii. ducates: ix. Carlines.

A Byshop or Abbot, or the head of any Order, or one of S. Johns knightes paies to be absolued from wilful murther fifty Turons: xii. Ducates : vi. Carlines.

That a wylfull murtherer maye be secretly admitted into holy Orders, and to mynister at the altar by dispensation, or to any eccleſi-

asticall

Of dispensations.

asticall ioynges in the court of conscience onely paying .xxxvi. Tu-rons: ix. Ducates.

If one man be gyltye of many murthers at one frape and one tyme, he payes, xxxvi. Turons. ix. Ducates: But for. ii. murthers in diuers frayes, he paieth fyfty Turons, xii. Ducats, vi. Carlines.

He ÿ killeth his father, mother, brother or sister, payeth for his pardon for any one of them iiii. Turons i. Ducate 8. Carlines. And so he that killeth his wyfe, and if he aske lycence to marrye another, he payes viii. Turons, ii. Ducates ix. Carlines. And for all they that assist a man in murthering his wyfe, the pardon is dearer by ii. Turones for euery such.

For murthering of priestes.

If a laye man kill a priest, vi. Turons, ii. Ducates.

If he kill a single clearke or a priest in holye orders that is forbidden to execute his office, vi. Turons, ii. Ducates.

If one man kill many priestes at one time and in one fraye, he fines but vi. Turons. If diuers at diuers times, for the first ÿ whole fine and for euery one of the rest halfe.

That he who hath bin a priestkiller maye obtaine ecclesiasticall liuinges, the dispensation is ii. Turons, ii. Ducates.

For killing a laye man.

For one laye man onelye. iii. Turons, i. Ducate, iiii. Carlines.

If one kill diuers in one conflict, he fines but for one.

For murthering of children.

If the father, mother or kinseman, murther a childe, iiii. Turons, i. Ducate, viii. Carlines. If a straunger do it, iiii. Turons. i. Ducate, iiii. Carlines. If the husband and wyfe both do it, vi. Turons, ii. Ducates.

If a woman take a pocion to kill the fruite in her wombe. Or if the father giue it to the mother, the price of their indulgēce is iiii. Turons, i. Ducate, viii. Carlines. If a straunger offer it, iiii. Turons, i. Ducate, v. Carlines.

For charminge and vvitchcraft.

A woman witch or enchantresse after shee hath renounced her sorceryes payeth, vi. Turons, ii. Ducates.

For heretickes.

For absolution from heresye before a man haue renousced it by oath,

Of dispensations.

to as he may be receyued againe to enioye all priuiledges as before in ample maner, the price is xxxvi. Turons, ix. Ducates.

For sacriledge, theft, fyring houses, rapes, periurye and such like.

Absolution with restoring of the parson in ample forme in euery one of these cases, is xxxvi. Turons, ix. Ducates.

For frailtye of the flesh.

Absolution for fleshlye frailtye in any Venerius acte committed by one of the clergye though with a nonne within and without the abbey walles, or with women of their kindred or affinitye, or their ghostlye doughters &c. with dispensation for retayning his orders is (if he aske absolutiõ together with them) xxxvi. Tur. iii. Ducat. But if with them he sue also for absolution of sinne against nature, and sinning with brute beasts in former sort, the price is fourescore and ten Turons, xii. Ducates, vi. Carlines. But if he sue for absolution onelye of sinne against nature &c. as aboue the price is xxxvi. Turons, ix. Ducates.

The price of a pardon for a nonne which hath lyen with diuers men within or without the abbeye walles, and to be restored to her former estate in the nonnery, or to be Ladye Abbesse, is xxxvi. Turõs, ix. Ducates.

Absolution for him that keepeth a concubine with dispensation for orders and spirituall liuing, xxi. Turons, v. Ducates, vi. Car.

For a laye man offending in anye carnall lust in the court of conscience, the dispensation is vi. Turons, ii. Ducates.

For incest, iiii. Turons, for adulterye and incest both, vi. Turons,

¶ Of diuers transgressions.

For burying an excommunicated in Churche soyle. vi. Turons: two Ducates.

For hym that hath concealed the carkas of a dead priest, whereby to obtayne his benefice. vi. Turons, two Ducates.

For a prieste that sayth masse ignorantly in an interdicted place, vi. Turons, twoo Ducates.

For a priest that blesseth man and wyfe at the second mariage, which were blessed in the firste. vi. Turons and two Ducates.

The absolution for a marchaunt that transporteth Irrellery to Infidelles and returneth without gaynes, xii. Turons. iii. Ducates, vi. Carlines

Of dispensations.

vi. Carlines.
If he returne with gaines the fee is all one, and he muste agree with the Datary to the Pope.

¶ Were it not gentel Reader that bothe I my felfe am euen tired alreadie with settinge forth to shewe this the Popes paltry ware, and that besyde I thinke this may suffice both to fyll the eyes of the gredie chapman, and to geue knowledge what the reste is lyke to be, I mighte yet open the pedlers packe muche wyder, and bringe oute stranger stuffe, fonder topes and knackes then these are, yea what pedler is he thoughe his boochet be neuer so byg that is able to shewe so greate store and so many sortes of fyne feates as is the riche pedler of Rome, There are in the same packe, from whence I culled these about. 400. sondrye cases, wherein he geueth free dispensation for the loue of an olde friend of his the good lady moneye. for what can man deuise betwene heauen and hel, yea heauen and hell both, but he hath it to sell: If any of his friendes be offended that I should thus boldly take vppon me to rifle his shop, and to publishe his secretes, or wil saye y I charge him with some kinde of baggage & riffe raffe, that is none of his, If I maye knowe so muche of their myndes, that this my doinge doth not pleafe them If it myghte pleafe god to geue me tyme, I wyl to content them open other of his boxes, and shewe such workemanshippe of hym and his vnderlynges, that I hope any man, that loueth his owne honeftie, wyl for euer be ashamed to buye & sel w suche a shamefull makeshifte, suche a cofonynge broker, or to fighte vnder the banner of suche a bloddy Prelate. In the meane tyme the wyfe maye be warned by this howe they meddle with any of his coūterfayte marchaundise, though it hath neuer so farre a florishe.

FINIS.

¶ IMPRINTED AT
London in Fleeteftreate neare
vnto S. Dunstones Church by
Thomas Marshe.

Anno. 1574.

www.ingramcontent.com/pod-product-compliance
Lightning Source LLC
Chambersburg PA
CBHW051728300426
44115CB00007B/515